# NATIONALISM AND GLOBALISATION

This book addresses a seemingly paradoxical situation. On the one hand, nationalism from Scotland to the Ukraine remains a resilient political dynamic, fostering secessionist movements below the level of the state. On the other, the competence and capacity of states, and indeed the coherence of nationalism as an ideology, are increasingly challenged by patterns of globalisation in commerce, cultural communication and constitutional authority beyond the state. It is the aim of this book to shed light on the relationship between these two processes, addressing why the political currency of nationalism remains strong even when the salience of its objective—independent and autonomous statehood—becomes ever more attenuated.

The book takes an interdisciplinary approach both within law and beyond, with contributions from international law, constitutional law, constitutional theory, history, political science and sociology. The challenge for our time is considerable. Global networks grow ever more sophisticated while territorial borders, such as those in Eastern and Central Europe, become seemingly more unstable. It is hoped that this book, by bringing together areas of scholarship which have not communicated with one another as much as they might, will help develop an ongoing dialogue across disciplines with which better to understand these challenging, and potentially destabilising, developments.

# Nationalism and Globalisation

Edited by
Stephen Tierney

·HART·
PUBLISHING
OXFORD AND PORTLAND, OREGON
2015

Published in the United Kingdom by Hart Publishing Ltd
16C Worcester Place, Oxford, OX1 2JW
Telephone: +44 (0)1865 517530
Fax: +44 (0)1865 510710
E-mail: mail@hartpub.co.uk
Website: http://www.hartpub.co.uk

Published in North America (US and Canada) by
Hart Publishing
c/o International Specialized Book Services
920 NE 58th Avenue, Suite 300
Portland, OR 97213-3786
USA
Tel: +1 503 287 3093 or toll-free: (1) 800 944 6190
Fax: +1 503 280 8832
E-mail: orders@isbs.com
Website: http://www.isbs.com

Hart Publishing is an imprint of Bloomsbury Publishing plc.

British Library Cataloguing in Publication Data
Data Available

ISBN: 978-1-84946-674-5

Typeset by Compuscript Ltd, Shannon
Printed and bound in Great Britain by
CPI Group (UK) Ltd, Croydon CR0 4YY

# TABLE OF CONTENTS

New Legal Orders: The Challenges of European Integration
and International Human Rights

# LIST OF CONTRIBUTORS

**Richard Bellamy** is Professor of Political Science at University College London and Director of the Max Weber Programme at the European University Institute.

**John Breuilly** is Professor of Nationalism and Ethnicity at the London School of Economics.

**Michael Keating** is Professor of Politics at the University of Aberdeen, part-time Professor at the University of Edinburgh and Director of the ESRC Scottish Centre on Constitutional Change.

**Cormac Mac Amhlaigh** is a Lecturer in Public Law at the University of Edinburgh.

**Zoran Oklopcic** is Associate Professor at Carleton University.

**Dejan Stjepanović** is IRC Post-Doctoral Fellow at University College Dublin.

**Stephen Tierney** is Professor of Constitutional Theory at the University of Edinburgh.

**Neil Walker** is Regius Professor of Public Law and the Law of Nature and Nations at the University of Edinburgh.

**Asanga Welikala** is a Lecturer in Public Law at the University of Edinburgh and Associate Director of the Edinburgh Centre for Constitutional Law.

**Steven Wheatley** is Professor of International Law at the University of Lancaster.

# 1

## Nationalism and Globalisation: New Settings, New Challenges

STEPHEN TIERNEY

## I. Introduction

The nation-state is in flux. It is beset by seemingly contradictory challenges from within and beyond its borders. On the one hand, the very fact of statehood and the meaning of nationalism, the ideological building block which has sustained the state since the nineteenth century, have each been brought into focus by a series of dramatic centrifugal trends. The territorial re-ordering of Central and Eastern Europe since the early-1990s; the emergence of new states such as Eritrea, East Timor, Kosovo and South Sudan; the intensification of already fraught nationalist conflict, particularly in Africa and Asia but also now on the borders of Russia and Ukraine; and the continued resilience and ambitious constitutional plans of sub-state nations in Canada, Latin America and Western Europe, characterised by the dramatic referendum on independence in Scotland in 2014, together render nationalism, which many assumed had ceased to have purchase in a homogenising world, one of the most perplexing and yet urgent concerns both for states and for international relations today.

At the same time, and in a seemingly paradoxical way, the competence and capacity of states, and hence the vitality of nationalism as an ideology, have been challenged by another development in seemingly stark contrast to these fissiparous moves. While nationalist movements challenge the state from below, patterns of commerce, cultural communication and constitutional authority are moving increasingly to sites beyond the state. This process has varied from sector to sector: in the economic sphere through the expansion of the 'free' or relatively open markets through which trade is able to transcend national borders, backed by international institutions which have evolved significantly since the Bretton Woods era; in cultural terms through the technological revolution in communications, supported by the open market in goods and services; and in new political and legal sites of power as patterns of authority and institutional apparatus emerge or strengthen to support the different ways in which economic and popular vectors of interaction continue to transcend state borders. In all of this Europe must be treated as a special case since the processes of economic and constitutional integration proceed within the European Union at a pace unrivalled by any other territorial sphere, but this does not detract from the fact that these wider trends are in many ways truly global in nature.

It is the aim of this book to shed light on the relationship between these two processes, addressing why the political currency of nationalism remains strong even when the salience of its objective—independent and autonomous statehood—becomes ever more attenuated in the face of homogenising and centralising currents beyond the state.

***********

This book emerges from a symposium organised by the Edinburgh Centre for Constitutional Law at the University of Edinburgh in May 2012 entitled, 'Nationalism and Globalisation: New Settings, New Challenges'. The symposium resulted in two very fruitful days of deliberation, which also involved a keynote address by Michael Ignatieff. Building upon these discussions, the book brings together a multi-disciplinary group of scholars to address the interface between the broadening and deepening of political demands founded in nationalism and multiculturalism on the one hand, and the evolving dynamics of transnational constitutionalism on the other.

Most of the contributors to the book are legal scholars and legal theorists. Within the discipline of law, those who approach the interface between nationalism and globalisation tend to belong to three schools: those addressing the status of states and the changing normative environment within which they operate through the prism of international law (see contributions by Oklopcic (chapter nine), Walker (chapter eight) and Wheatley (chapter seven)); those applying constitutional theory in attempting to understand the changing nature of sovereignty and the pluralisation of legal authority beyond the state, often in the context of the European Union or European human rights law (see contributions by Mac Amlaigh (chapter eleven)) and Bellamy (chapter ten)); and those who have combined constitutional theory with nationalism studies in an attempt to analyse the constitutional implication of constitutional claims made by sub-state national societies for constitutional change within plurinational states (see contributions by Tierney (chapter four) and Welikala (chapter six)).

One aim of the book is to encourage a conversation among these different spheres of work across the legal academy, because even within a common overarching discipline there has been a tendency to work in silos, which has prevented a full exchange of different and important insights. Building upon the deliberations of the symposium, therefore, the book provides an opportunity to re-think how our understanding of the nation and the state as legal concepts has changed within the doctrines and practices of international law; how these changes affect the ways in which we understand fundamental constitutional doctrines and traditional approaches to constitutional design, such as federalism; and how new challenges by increasingly sophisticated political actors at sub-state level confront the traditional underpinnings of both international law and constitutional law theory with radically new claims which, in particular, challenge the unitary conception of sovereignty which has undergirded traditional patterns of authority within the Westphalian model.

But it is also the case that a study confined within the legal academy can provide only a partial account of these issues. In my own work on sub-state nationalism I have discovered that legal scholars have much to learn from other disciplines. In attempting to approach the nationalism-globalisation nexus in a more holistic fashion, the book therefore also seeks an engagement between law and the social sciences—history, sociology, political science and political theory which offer the contextual story without which much of our theorising as lawyers can make little sense. To that end the book also brings together leading scholars from each of these core areas of enquiry.

Historians of nationalism are of course key to any attempt to situate the nation and the state as the central institutional planks of political modernity within current debates about how this role is changing. The book would have been incomplete without a reflection on the contribution offered by this school, and in particular the central role played by the LSE in this field (see the contribution by Breuilly (chapter two)). The sociology of nationalism is an area of scholarship which developed at the LSE, taking on particular significance since the 1960s, as sociology has helped describe and explain not only the survival of national identity but, more surprisingly, its consolidation, particularly at the sub-state level within democratic, liberal states. This work was the first to provide a more sophisticated explanation of this development, and to help us move away from stereotypes of nationalism, focused as these were in particular (and for no obvious reason) upon the sub-state variant, as inherently outmoded and backward-looking.

Again building upon these insights concerning social attachments, lawyers working in this area also have much to learn from political scientists (see contributions by Keating (chapter three) and Stjepanović (chapter five)). Scholars who have addressed the political dynamics of the new nationalism have found, in a similar way to the discoveries of political sociologists, that political actors adopting the nationalist mantle are often fully attuned to the globalising patterns which increasingly transform the canvas upon which political authority plays out.

There is much, therefore, that legal scholarship can learn from other disciplines: the historical origins and development of nationalism; the evolution of the nation-state as a functional resource; the continuing salience in sociological terms of national identity; and the political dynamics, strengths, weaknesses and agendas of nationalist political movements and parties. On this basis the book seeks to combine the various different voices from the legal academy with the related disciplines from the humanities and social sciences, including political theory (see Bellamy (chapter ten)), in order more comprehensively to illuminate the interface between studies of nationalism and globalisation today.

It is of course one thing to note what legal scholars can learn from other disciplines, but what are the particular insights which legal study brings to the table in a study of the current challenges facing nations and nationalism? Law and legality are central to nationalist political strategies because in these we see the crystallisation of political claims as constitutional claims. The normative arguments advanced by sub-state nationalists tend to be rooted in a sense that the hegemonic state has marginalised the position of sub-state nations. According to this narrative, this dominance has been further entrenched through patterns of constitutional authority which offer purported legal legitimacy to what is essentially a power imbalance. It is no surprise therefore that so much of the focus of nationalist disputes within states centres upon the nature of the constitution and arguments for its reform. Constitutionalism is also central to globalising projects since legal regulation has been fundamental to building structures that facilitate the economic and communicative patterns of global interaction. Again lawyers and legal theorists are in the vanguard of studies of globalisation because it has opened up a struggle not just for political power but also for the legal authority that will help consolidate this power.

The main methodological focus of the book, from the perspective of legal scholarship, is upon constitutional theory (notwithstanding the other valuable contributions from international law). There have in recent times been attempts to define what it is that is discrete about the nature of constitutional theory[1] and it is in exploring this further that we see how constitutional theory, as a particular area of enquiry, can help us draw connections between nationalism and globalisation. The discipline of constitutional theory is concerned with analysing and evaluating a particular area of social activity: the framing, founding, practice and changing of constitutions, operational through internationally comparable institutions and rules. This area of study combines empirical observation with a theoretical turn which brings to bear upon any set of constitutional arrangements a critical eye informed by the fundamental purposes which constitutions, and more broadly constitutionalism, is supposed to serve. In this context it can be said that constitutional law scholars engage with the connection between nationalism and globalisation as this interface plays out in the practice of constitutional politics. Constitutional theory does not offer a study in abstract first principles of (moral) normative theory, but rather meets politics in practice, in particular on the ground where politics transforms into constitutional practice.

A key part of the work of constitutional scholars is to respond to claims. Nationalism, particularly sub-state nationalism, manifests itself as a set of political claims, but as I say, these claims tend to have constitutional ambitions and these ambitions sooner or later have institutional implications. Whether it is a demand for a constitutional amendment, for a referendum, for statehood or for

---

[1] M Loughlin, 'Constitutional Theory: a 25th Anniversary Essay' (2005) 25 *Oxford Journal of Legal Studies* 183.

international recognition, the circle inevitably comes back to law as facilitator of political claims. In this way legal scholarship has much to learn from historians, sociologists and political scientists who together frame where these claims come from and how they are to be understood in wider societal context.

Building upon this, law can then help to explain the terrain within which these claims are turned into legal and constitutional practice. For example, when a group claims a right to self-determination, we know that the political rhetoric this produces also operates within a system of international law that has sought to circumscribe tightly the meaning of this right and the subjects to whom it applies. When a group claims constitutional rights, such as the right to stage a referendum, again we should be able to illuminate the constitutional terrain upon which this claim is made and its consistency with existing constitutional law and practice. Comparative law can also be informative as we look to a range of constitutional orders where similar issues have arisen in the past. In short, legal scholarship in being responsive to political claims must build upon the insights of others, but in doing so it also offers a crucial piece of the jigsaw in demonstrating whether, and if so how, political claims can be meaningfully institutionalised within the current, and changing, normative environment of state constitutional law and supra-state constitutional orders. It is to help build such a holistic picture in the current trans-formations of nationalism and the nation-state that this book aspires.

## II. Structure of the Book

The book also aims to offer legal scholars insights into some of the deeper under-currents which will help us understand the 'why questions' (why is the nation-state under challenge from below? why are global normative orders emerging?) as well as the 'how questions' (how can or should each of these processes be met by institutional ordering?), while at the same time offering legal insights to other disciplines and thereby informing these of the capacity which the fluctuating legal environment leaves open for nations and nationalist movements in their interac-tion with forces of institutional, political and economic globalisation. The book is laid out in two parts, each of these composed of two sections. Part One seeks to map the terrain of nationalism and globalisation, assessing the persistent salience of nationalist movements in social development and considering their impact upon the constitutional state.

It opens with two essays which approach the global context within which con-stitutional and nationalism theories play out today. John Breuilly has spent his career studying the historical trajectory of nationalism as a political project. In his chapter he offers a broad account of how nationalism has been theorised in recent times, setting out the key debates in the development of nationalism studies and then drawing out key comparisons between theories of nationalism and contem-porary thinking about globalisation. His focus is largely upon the role of actors, and in particular of lawyers, in seminal historical periods of nation-building and globalisation. With lawyers as his case study he draws links and identifies common trajectories across time with regard to the role law has played in nation-building and in parallel processes of international and global interaction, in particular in the globalisation of the very concept of the nation-state. This leads him to conclude that there is an important contrast between the age of nation-building in the nineteenth century and our own time: in the earlier era nation-building and global interactions operated in tandem—emerging nation-states supported by a nascent international state system. But this he concludes is no longer the case. What is new and unsettling about our age is that while, in Breuilly's view, we are heading back to a world of hegemons comparable to the imperial age, the state system itself is now unsettled; instead of the stability of the state system we now find 'an unstable combination of ethnonationalist and supra-state challenges to the nation-state order' which provides a new context within which such hegemonic power struggles will play out. Powerful states still exist but they do so in a system where the very salience of the state as the locus of political power is being challenged from above and below.

Michael Keating's approach, based upon empirical social science, draws similar conclusions to those of Breuilly, although his case study and methodology are very different. He centres upon the distinction between the terms 'nation' and 'state', recognising that the term nation is in definitional terms 'slippery and often subjective'. His approach also echoes Breuilly's in arguing that the nation is neither an entirely objective nor an entirely subjective category, but rather is 'an intersubjective set of understandings and meanings, which emerges from social and political interaction in specific circumstances'. One of the challenges of our time is to recognise that national sovereignty and territorial integrity are still salient political subjects but that both are also being transformed by the regional and global environments within which they operate. Territory as a physical space for social, economic and political processes remains central to political claims, but these are no longer restricted by an exclusively state-centred focus. It is in this context that Keating addresses the evolving constitutional trajectories of sub-state nations in states such as the UK, Belgium, Canada and Spain, challenging some of the myths which often accompany the new nationalism. In addressing the new and unsettled environment which Breuilly identifies, he calls for an 'unbundling of territory', rejecting the view of territory 'as closed space belonging to one integrated national-institutional community or another'. What is needed in fact is a 'constitutional pluralism in which competing claims to sovereignty can be managed, as long as the working of government is not made impossible'.

In the second section of Part One, essays by Stjepanović, Tierney and Welikala in some sense take up this challenge, deploying the idea of constitutional pluralism and using this in exploring the interaction of constitutional globalisation on the one hand and the ways in which the nature of the constitutional state, particularly the plurinational state, is changing to meet this challenge.

Tierney addresses how the rise of sub-state nationalism in the Western world since the 1960s challenges from below the modern model of the state. The focus of much of the attention given to globalisation by constitutional theorists has been upon constitutional reordering above the level of the state. But Tierney, like Keating, is also drawn by the radical and innovative challenges not only to particular constitutions but also to the very idea of constitutionalism presented by sub-state nationalist constitutional projects. Nationalist movements present adaptable political strategies which rather than being at odds with a globalising world in which the state is itself arguably losing traction, in fact present ways in which to fashion new constitutional orders which might offer a more suitable fit for a globalising era than do certain increasingly outmoded versions of the purportedly sovereign modern state. That said, Tierney is sceptical of the idea that the state itself is in fact in terminal decline. Territory, as Keating points out, remains a vital political resource. This is also backed up by an international legal system which remains highly supportive of the prerogatives of states. If sub-state nationalist movements focus upon secession rather than a radical internal constitutional reordering of the polity, this in some cases owes as much to the resistance of international law to give meaningful international recognition to non-state territories as it does to the resistance of states to radical constitutional change.

Dejan Stjepanović studies the constitutional changes which have been applied to the troubled Balkan region in the past two decades. It is in the collapsing Yugoslavia that so many of the problems of national struggle are to be found, but it is also here that some of the most imaginative responses to these issues have emerged since the mid-1990s. In his chapter Stjepanović examines some less well-trodden territorial developments in the post-Yugoslav space and in doing so identifies innovative interactions between globalisation, theories of nationalism and what we might call a 'new regionalism'. In particular, echoing Keating's work, he uses the political and constitutional history of the historic regions of Dalmatia and Istria (Croatia) and Vojvodina (Serbia) to argue that there is not, a clear, categorical distinction between nationalism and regionalism in theory or, in these areas at least, in practice. As ideologies and political projects nationalism and regionalism have a lot in common. Taking the regions of Croatia and Serbia that are the focus of his chapter, he argues that these contradict the 'teleology of total exit' thesis, which suggests that granting autonomy to ethnic regions is always a slippery slope to secession. Instead, he traces the development of regional dynamics in these regions, signifying how territory has been used far more instrumentally as a concept and as a resource (again per Keating) than might have been expected by traditional understandings of nationalist dynamics. He argues that these examples show how, in a globalising environment, territory is not 'bounded and exclusive' but is instead a 'political and social construct', within which sub-state territories will seek to interact with state and supra-state legal orders in instrumental ways. The consequence is that we see a fluid crossover from sub-state nationalism to plurinational regionalism, which for Stjepanović offers an alternative form of government compatible with a 'globalised integrationist setting'. This seems to be an

8    *Stephen Tierney*

example in practice of Breuilly's notion that in a world of powerful states, more assertive and better equipped regions, and more powerful international organisations and constitutional orders, serve to unsettle any simplistic idea that we have merely returned to a world of imperial hegemons, or that nationalism has lost its resilience as an adaptable focus for identity and loyalty within territorial polities whether at state or sub-state levels.

Asanga Welikala in his chapter reminds us that much of the focus upon resilient sub-state nationalism and instrumentalist 'nationalist-regionalism' has been upon Europe. The work of Keating, Tierney and Stjepanović has centred largely upon a liberal, democratic and constitutionally integrating environment within which sub-state nationalism and regionalism play out in largely consensual and democratic ways (Croatia and Serbia can now largely be identified by such a description notwithstanding the highly fraught environment in the former Yugoslavia until very recently).

In light of this Welikala instead addresses the very different case of South Asia. His focus is a comparison of India and Sri Lanka, examining the very different ways in which they have responded to competing nationality claims by groups within their borders. This chapter brings out how much of the existing empirical and theoretical work on national pluralism has focused upon Western states and how the challenges for such a conception of the state, and for promoting plurinationalism as a normative project, is all the more difficult in younger post-colonial states. For Welikala, India and Sri Lanka are useful comparators given that their historical processes of state-formation and constitutional development bear, for him, striking similarities. And yet notably India has been generally more accommodating of pluralism than its neighbour, particularly in the context of the Tamil minority nation. Welikala addresses how the Westphalian model has been adopted in the South Asian context, in part in reaction to colonialism, and how the legal power of the juridical state has facilitated a strongly monistic approach to the 'state nation', consolidating its dominant position, a phenomenon particularly apparent in Sri Lanka. His analysis of South Asia suggests not only a resilient but a retrenching state, which in some cases is openly disavowing the very idea of societal pluralism in favour of a strong central state power. Welikala also highlights how the ideologies underpinning these moves often do not have parallels in Western state dynamics. These unsettling conclusions call upon us to reconsider our assumptions concerning the breadth of legal 'globalisation' (which becomes more a series of supra-state regionalisms) but also of the underpinning values at stake in these processes, which again vary greatly from one locale to another. Given the current focus in Western constitutionalism on the weakening state within a globalising context, Welikala's chapter is a salutary reminder that much of this account is 'an historically contingent' and geographically specific experience, 'which does not hold true in other regions of the world, at least for now'.

Having mapped out how processes of globalisation and sub-state nationalism have interacted and continue to interact in varied ways across space and time, the book then turns in Part Two to consider ongoing changes in the context of global constitutionalism, and how both international law and supranational constitutional orders are attempting to manage the aspirations of sub-state nationalists for recognition of national pluralism within states on the one hand, and the trajectory towards global constitutionalism beyond the state on the other. The focus of Part Two therefore is the international settings within which contemporary nationalism interacts with globalising dynamics. It is appropriate to begin with three chapters which seek to re-think the well-trodden terrain of international law and how it approaches the issue of national pluralism.

One issue about which much has been written is international law's treatment of the issue of secession. Steven Wheatley re-opens this issue by taking a radically different approach founded in 'systems theory'. He asks whether a model of democratic secession might be acquiring normative valence in international law, based upon the growing body of rules and practices that seek to ensure the legitimacy of political authority. He utilises the third wave of systems theory thinking known as 'complexity' to define the nature of states, looking at the detailed and complicated network of relationships between law and politics in creating the 'fact' of statehood. The picture he paints is of the state existing within patterns of communication involving multiple actors. This inevitably raises the issue of global interactions. The condition of the state is no longer, if it ever was, defined by the simple fact of internal sovereignty; sovereignty is itself conditioned by the ever more elaborate system of international authority and the increased political acceptance of this authority.

From here Wheatley adapts what he takes to be the developing norm of 'legitimate' political authority—in other words, a notion that statehood is no longer treated as a simple fact of control of territory, but one which is conditioned by the recognition of other states, and this recognition depends in part now upon the democratic credentials of the territory in question. From this premise Wheatley argues in support of the right of democratic secession in the event of three conditions prevailing: the rejection of the sovereign authority of the territorial state by certain subjects; the acceptance of the authority of emergent systems of law and politics of the new political entity; and the recognition of the political entity as possessing legitimate political authority. He utilises Raz's idea of practical authority to reach this conclusion.

There is a certain paradox here when we consider the interaction of nationalism and globalisation. The ever more extensive breadth and depth of international law as a regulatory system is creating firmer norms in relation to the internal governmental systems of existing states, which in turn can delegitimise sovereignty claims of those states over territories where the state's authority is considered to be illegitimate. Again then it seems we are seeing the 'unsettling' of the state system identified by Breuilly. Sub-state nationalism where it can call upon democratic legitimacy can gain succour from a strengthening international legal regime which increasingly reviews the democratic credentials of states. It seems that states are finding it more difficult to use the simple principle of territorial integrity to resist democratic claims to secession and that states which repress such aspirations can find their own sovereignty claims to the territory undermined in the eyes of the international community.

Neil Walker also addresses the issue of secession. In much of his work he has analysed the emergence of constitutional orders beyond the state. He brings these insights to bear in reflecting upon the way in which the European Union responds to sub-state nationalist claims, an issue brought into focus in 2014 by the Scottish independence referendum. This raised the question of whether an independent Scotland would be admitted to the EU, the process by which this would be done and upon what terms. Although the referendum ended in a vote against independence, Walker uses this case to reflect upon how the EU could have been called upon to act as regulator of its own terms of entry and in doing so, intervene in major issues of secession, the nature of statehood, and international processes of state recognition—in other words, as a mediator between the level of the state and international law of the path to statehood itself.

The dominant response of EU institutions and actors to secessionist movements within Member States he calls 'conservative neutrality', whereby the EU power structure seeks to avoid 'taking sides either in individual cases or in terms of general policy towards internal enlargement' but also emphasises the importance of 'the existing framework of rules and practice as a template of disinterested process'. In many ways, argues Walker, the EU itself lacks a certain self-confidence since it does not have a strong historical narrative or a set of evidently pre-eminent (in relation to Member States) central institutions that would support a clear position on the nature and limits of its own internal composition. He argues further that the inchoate position of international law in relation to self-determination claims offers little assistance to international organisations faced with membership issues, and the tendency to fall back on the constitutional position of the host state in question is all too inviting. And so, for Walker, the EU finds itself unable either openly to welcome new national claims or to take a dogmatic stance in defence of the territorial integrity of its Member States. In the end, all the EU can do, Walker contends, is seek 'to manage and defuse' the problems of secession 'by reframing rather than direction', and in doing so offering an international example in pragmatism over dogmatism. Again this echoes Wheatley's conclusion that globalising processes of normative ordering, and the increased emphasis on democratic legitimacy as an international and European regional principle, is an ally of the sub-state nation seeking recognition for its democratic political claims, and increasingly a thorn in the side of the nation-state which seeks to foreclose the state claims of sub-state *demoi*.

Zoran Oklopcic takes a broader approach to the right of self-determination, looking at this as a normative (moral) claim and addressing how this has been discussed by political theorists in recent decades. At the same time he uses international law practice as a mirror with which to contextualise his account. Oklopcic argues that the international law principle of self-determination remains both *elusive* and *allusive*, a point also made by both Wheatley and Walker. The past 20 years has seen many normative theories attempt both to make sense of self-determination as a moral claim and to offer prescriptions for how it ought to apply. In his chapter Oklopcic does not seek to offer another theoretical account of external self-determination. He begins instead by mapping the state of the theoretical debate and in doing so addresses the political factors that lie behind much of the recent theorising. In particular, he looks at three recent 'pluralist' contributions to the field: what he calls *bounded, constitutional* and *radical* pluralism. In different ways, he argues, each of these has abandoned the idea of external self-determination as a justification for new statehood, seeking political solutions to national claims within the state, or relegating these to levels alongside or below a range of ideological and identity-based difference. As Oklopcic puts it, in these recent interventions there is 'a conscious privileging of other forms of political emancipation that depart from the conventional view of external self-determination as an ultimate vehicle for a nation's self-government'. The new pluralists focus upon other forms of hegemony but the result is, according to Oklopcic, a 'toothless account of territorial self-determination'. It seems that these accounts are at odds with the political reality of increasingly assertive sub-state national claims identified by Keating, Tierney and others, and of an international normative environment the commitment of which to principles of democracy and self-government cannot in fact resist claims to radical constitutional re-ordering or even independent statehood when these are made in democratic ways which can only be resisted by ignoring or repressing the wishes of sub-state *demoi*.

But nonetheless Oklopcic does hit upon a potentially important tension between the aid given to sub-state nationalism by the internationalising principle of democracy on the one hand, and a cosmopolitanism which remains deeply sceptical of nationalism—at least in its sub-state variant—on the other. As he points out, this raises a series of new questions for those interested in self-determination. The globalising environment for nationalism has, as Breuilly and Keating observed, changed the nature of the game of statehood as an impregnable fortress for existing states which sub-state territories can't hope to join. But Oklopcic also considers how the new pluralism represents a new form of hegemony in international affairs which raises questions such as: 'will heightened concern for national pluralism in international law provide a springboard for great power interference?' This echoes Breuilly's reference to the return to a hegemonic question, and based upon Wheatley's argument that international law is taking an ever greater interest in the legitimacy of political authority, it does indeed raise the question whether significant powers will use the repression of sub-state nationalism as an argument for heightened levels of intervention in the affairs of states. Finally, he asks: 'do the registers of national, social and geopolitical emancipation have to be pitted against each other?' He notes that normative political theory so far hasn't shown an interest in interrogating the relationship between these three registers but this relationship is an 'irritant' which should be addressed.

In the final section, two chapters consider the challenges posed by European integration and international human rights for contemporary nationalism, and by contrast, the challenges to these integrative and homogenising processes by the rise of vernacular national movements. Richard Bellamy's work on political theory in the past two decades has addressed the interface between constitutional theory and normative values, particularly the value of democracy, underpinning state legitimacy. He brings this broader work to bear on the construction of normative orders beyond the state, addressing issues of justice and legitimacy in Europe as a 'union of peoples'. In his chapter Bellamy also develops themes taken up by Keating and Tierney. His focus is the European Union but in this context he also turns to the apparent contradictions within contemporary European politics between increased integration on the one hand and heightened demands for vernacular self-government on the other, coupled with mounting disaffection towards the EU across Europe. He notes also how the latter trend faces pejorative stereotypes as 'anachronistic and regressive'. Bellamy however questions the cosmopolitan view that national identity and state sovereignty are outmoded. He observes that self-government and cosmopolitanism are not necessarily at odds. The former aspiration takes place in the context of mutual inter-dependence. The European Union he considers to sit awkwardly between the trend towards globalisation and cosmopolitan justice, on the one hand, and the continued communitarian demands for forms of national self-determination on the other.

Bellamy goes on to discuss both cosmopolitanism and communitarianism, concluding that cosmopolitanism cannot overcome or replace the communitarian impulse. He also introduces the distinction between justice and legitimacy, arguing that the legitimacy of particular cosmopolitan conceptions of justice 'can only be determined by political communities with sufficient intrinsic qualities to be able to support a democratic regime', and that the 'the most normatively desirable and empirically feasible way of conceiving the EU polity is in what can be called cosmopolitan communitarian terms'. In this way the EU's approach to globalisation and the sustenance of democratic political communities become mutually supportive. In light of the financial crisis a federal EU polity is ever more unlikely. And as such Bellamy argues for the alternative of 'a Union of self-governing, democratic nation states'.

Mac Amlaigh also confronts the tension between national democracies and the specific values generated within these on the one hand, and the homogenising and universalising dynamics of the global plane, and like Bellamy he also argues that international cosmopolitanism can co-exist with nationalism, including its sub-state variant. His focus is upon international human rights law. He begins by outlining recent tensions between the Scottish government and the UK Supreme Court over the human rights compatibility of certain measures of the devolved Scottish institutions. He then explores the scope within international human rights theory for diversity in standards within states. MacAmlaigh defends the room for diversity relying upon a theory of legal pluralism. He concludes that there are valid normative arguments for national minorities having some say in how universal human rights norms are 'domesticated' within their particular cultural and historical contexts distinct from the dominant culture of the metropole. In this context, the tools of pluralism which are being deployed more and more in human rights law, offer a particularly useful way of thinking about how this might be achieved.

The challenge for our time is considerable. Global networks grow ever more sophisticated while territorial borders, such as those in Eastern and Central Europe, grow seemingly more unstable. From the brief summaries above it should be evident how a careful reading of the chapters contained in this book will bring out many cross-cutting themes and insights from one discipline which help answer questions and alleviate difficulties in others. It is hoped that this book, by bringing together areas of scholarship which are only now beginning to communicate more fully with one another in these important areas, will help develop an ongoing dialogue across disciplines with which to understand better the continuing relevance of nations and nationalism as global phenomena.

# Part 1

# Nationalism and Globalisation: Mapping the Terrain

# Nationalism in Global Context

# 2

## The Globalisation of Nationalism and the Law

JOHN BREUILLY

## I. Introductory Remarks

This book has at least two key concerns. The first is the empirical one of analysing the challenges posed by globalisation and separatist or autonomist movements to state sovereignty. This analysis focuses on legal aspects, especially in the field of constitutional law. The second concern is a normative one: how can one construct forms of government, in particular as embodied constitutional and other legal arrangements, which address these challenges in such a way as to help preserve values of liberty and democracy?

My contribution as an historian with little expertise in normative theory, contemporary politics and constitutional law does not directly address these concerns. Furthermore I do not intend to 'theorise nationalism' in the sense of proposing a 'theory of nationalism' as I do not think this is a feasible enterprise.

Instead my focus is on the narrower, though still large, issue of the global spread of nationalism as political ideology and movement in the modern period. Do notions like 'export/import' capture such processes adequately? Can we discern historical patterns or tendencies in the diffusion of nationalism? More specifically, why have lawyers and law apparently played such a central role in this diffusion?

I begin by outlining a framework for writing a global history of nationalism. Then I suggest where law and lawyers fit into that framework. I will relate these arguments to two historical cases: Britain's first and second empires as one 'declines' and the other 'rises'. Then I will look at how legal understandings of national self-determination and state sovereignty came to be so central to the diffusion of the nation-state model following imperial collapse after both world wars. I will conclude with some remarks on the diffusion of nationalism and the role played by law and lawyers and whether we can expect this to continue.

## II. Framework for a Global History of Nationalism

The standard approach to the relationship between nationalism and globalisation in political science literature is to treat the first as preceding the second. The standard questions raised concern the future of nationalism and the nation-state when key economic, political, military and even cultural decisions are taken by institutions beyond the control of the state and where sub-national movements challenge established notions of the sovereign nation-state.

However, globalisation not only preceded but shaped nationalism and nation-state formation which continually changed as one element of a global process. I focus on the political dimension of this process, relating nationalism to patterns of global politics, by which is meant the distribution of coercive power across the world, and how this has changed from the late-eighteenth century to the present.[1]

There is not space to consider debates on globalisation and nationalism.[2] They are difficult to connect because they take such different forms. Nationalism debates have focused on origins and agents. One view is that modern nationalism arises on the foundation of a much longer history of community which shaped national identity and that consequently the prospects for nationalism to change or disappear are limited by the strength of this sense of identity.[3] Framed against this is the argument that nationalism is a constructed, even invented, identity which only arises under modern conditions and is liable to rapid change, or even disappearance, if those conditions disappear. There are many intermediate positions (eg constructed but not modern, modern but not constructed) and each theorist highlights different elements. Thus there are modernists who stress industrialism,[4] or print capitalism,[5] or new kinds of warfare.[6] There are non- or anti-modernists who highlight the rise of written vernaculars,[7] core polities,[8] communal symbols transmitted from one generation to another,[9] or group difference based on kinship.[10]

---

[1] J Breuilly, 'Nationalism as Global History' in D Halikiopoulou and S Vasilopoulou (eds), *Nationalism and Globalisation: Conflicting or Complementary?* (Basingstoke, Palgrave Macmillan, 2011).

[2] AD Smith, *Theories of Nationalism* (London, Duckworth, 1971); U Ozkirimli, *Theories of Nationalism* (London, Palgrave Macmillan, 2010); J Osterhammel, 'Nationalism and Globalisation' in J Breuilly (ed), *The Oxford Handbook of the History of Nationalism* (Oxford, Oxford University Press, 2013).

[3] AD Smith, *The Ethnic Origins of Nations* (Oxford, Blackwell, 1986).

[4] E Gellner, *Nations and Nationalism* (Oxford, Blackwell, 1983).

[5] B Anderson, *Imagined Communities: Reflections on the Origins and Spread of Nationalism* (London, Verso, 1991).

[6] C Tilly, *Coercion, Capital and European States AD 990-1990* (Oxford, Blackwell, 1990).

[7] A Hastings, *The Construction of Nationhood: Ethnicity, Religion and Nationalism* (Cambridge, Cambridge University Press, 1997).

[8] S Reynolds, *Kingdoms and Communities in Western Europe, 900–1300* (Oxford, Clarendon Press, 1997); A Roshwald, *The Endurance of Nationalism: Ancient Roots and Modern Dilemmas* (Cambridge, Cambridge University Press, 2006).

[9] Smith, *Ethnic Origins of Nationalism* (n 3).

[10] PVD Berghe, 'Race and Ethnicity: a Sociobiological Perspective' (1978) 1(4) *Ethnic and Racial Studies* 1.

The political science debate on globalisation devotes little attention to origins as it is regarded as very recent and linked to obvious features like the internet, collapse of Soviet power, triumph of neo-liberalism and new forms of rapid and mass transportation. There is little discussion of agency, due I think to a tacit assumption that globalisation is beyond the control of any one agent, whether institution, elite or class. Globalisation literature is much stronger at identifying and describing key impersonal processes (global movements of capital, commodities, information, technology and labour) and their impact on a prior set of conditions (nation-state, national culture, national economy). On that basis it can sketch pictures of a post-national/ist world. Globalisation is always eroding, rarely constructing, even if some writers hint at the latter with notions of cosmopolitanism, global capitalism or models of global governance.[11]

To connect the two literatures I narrow the definition of globalisation and highlight the role of particular agents who can be linked to nationalism. First, I treat globalisation in terms of power relationships, focusing on coercive (political and military) as distinct from economic and ideological power.[12] Global politics arises when holders of coercive power engage in regular, frequent and significant conflict across the world. Although there are precursors to this in the European 'discovery' of the Americas in 1492, its first intense manifestation is Anglo-French conflict from the mid-eighteenth century. Not accidentally, it is in the zones of this conflict that one observes the emergence of nationalism as an ideology which informs and justifies the objectives of political movements seeking political power.

Second, I conceptualise these global conflicts in a triadic form, involving hegemons, challengers and peripheries. By hegemons I mean those power units— usually but not always territorial states—which dominate global politics in a particular era. By challengers I mean those power units, again usually but not always territorial states, which credibly seek to share or even replace hegemonic power. By peripheries I mean regions which are subject to the power, whether directly or indirectly, of hegemons and challengers.[13]

Third, I propose a periodisation of modern world history based on epochal changes in the pattern of hegemonic domination. I label these: Anglo-French conflict, British hegemony, global imperialist rivalry, world war, Cold War and US hegemony.

Fourth, I suggest that nationalism diffuses globally by three means. *Transformation* involves fundamental changes such as industrialism and print capitalism. These are often seen by modernist theorists as providing the conditions

---

[11] JA Scholte, *Globalization: A Critical Introduction* (New York, Palgrave Macmillan, 2005); J Osterhammel and N Petersssen, *Globalisation: a Short History* (Princeton, Princeton University Press, 2005); D Held and A McGrew, *Globalization/Anti-Globalization: Beyond the Great Divide* (Cambridge, Polity, 2007).

[12] M Mann, *The Sources of Social Power: Volume 1 A History of Power from the Beginning to AD 1760* (Cambridge, Cambridge University Press, 1986); G Poggi, *Forms of Power* (Cambridge, Polity, 2001).

[13] This leaves a fourth portion of the world which are external to such conflicts. I follow Immanuel Wallerstein's 'world systems' schema here.

for nationalism. Such transformation is often seen to be most important within hegemons. *Learning* is where elites investigate the principles on which current hegemonic power is based and then seek to use the lessons learnt to emulate the hegemon. This is usually seen to be of particular importance amongst challengers. *Imitation*, especially associated with peripheries, involves elites seeking to reproduce some of the effects of power displayed by hegemons or challengers in the hope or belief that this will enhance their own power.

I suggest that there is an overall directionality to diffusion, moving from hegemon to challenger to periphery.

This is a model. Coercive power, most dramatically in the shape of military power but also as routinised administration, is conditioned by technology, economic and ideological power and much else. The triadic distinction is often hard to operate, as when global hegemons such as Britain and France encounter regional hegemons like Russia. The concepts of transformation, learning and imitation are ideal types; diffusion processes in reality are always mixed. Directionality is only a general trend; one can find feedback loops, as when colonial politics influence metropolitan practices. The justification for the model is not that it mirrors a complex world history (nothing can) but provides a framework which helps us understand central features of that history.

## III.  The Role of Law and Lawyers

There are various ways in which law and lawyers play important roles in the global diffusion of nationalism.

First, they are one component of a cluster of occupations, both traditional and new, which constitute the core of what one might call an intelligentsia.[14] Many historians have seen nationalism—understood as elite doctrine and politics—as initiated and driven by such an intelligentsia. Kedourie, seeking to explain colonial nationalism, focused on these 'marginal men', trapped between the society of their origin and the imperial institutions in which they were educated and worked.[15] Learning the values proclaimed by imperial power but experiencing discrimination from its representatives, these intellectuals used nationalism to combine emulation and resistance. One case often cited is that of educated, high caste Hindus within the British Raj, a relatively privileged and expanding group. Those who joined the Indian Civil Service found the top positions denied to them within what was proclaimed to be a meritocratic institution. Those trained as

---

[14] B Giesen, *Intellectuals and the Nation: Collective Identity in a German Axial Age* (Cambridge, Cambridge University Press, 1998); R Suny and M Kennedy (eds), *Intellectuals and the Articulation of the Nation* (Ann Arbor, University of Michigan Press, 1999).

[15] E Kedourie, *Nationalism* (London, Hutchinson University Library, 1961); E Kedourie, 'Introduction' in E Kedourie (ed), *Nationalism in Africa and Asia* (London, Weidenfeld and Nicolson, 1971).

lawyers, within the Civil Service and in private practice, formed the largest occupational group within the ranks of these indigenous, Western-educated elites.[16] As reforms expanded the size of this group in administrative and judicial positions and began establishing lower-level legislative bodies, often chosen by election, so such people became increasingly prominent in public life and acquired political as well as professional skills.

The early Indian National Congress, founded in 1888, largely consisted of such people. The two most prominent nationalists within Congress—Gandhi and Jawaharlal Nehru (whose father Molital was a distinguished lawyer)—trained in law at the Inns of Court (Inner Temple) and Cambridge University respectively. The 'founder of Pakistan', Muhammad Ali Jinnah, studied law at the Inns of Court (Lincoln's Inn). Bhimrao Ramji Ambedkar, a leader of the Untouchables (Dalits) and principal author of the Constitution of independent India, studied law (as well as economics) at Columbia University and the London School of Economics.[17]

In one respect lawyers played no necessarily different or more prominent a role in elaborating nationalist doctrines and leading nationalist movements than did members of other professions subject either to Western transformation (medicine, the arts) or introduced from the West (newspaper editors and journalists, school and university teachers, scientists and technicians). Generally these people (almost exclusively men) were oriented to the colonial state or the market-place rather than being dependent upon patrons from within the traditional upper class of colonial society.

However, in a second sense law and lawyers play a distinctive role in the spread of nationalism. This is to do with the very processes of transformation, learning and imitation which diffused nationalism.

In eighteenth-century Western Europe and British North America, the commercialisation and globalisation of economic relationships increased the need to regulate and enforce property rights and contractual obligations, both amongst modern property owners as well as in contention with government and non-capitalist groups. Increasing numbers of lawyers were needed to handle such matters. For the most part such lawyers were part of the existing order rather than in the vanguard of those challenging it.[18]

Nevertheless, conflicts between different notions of property or different groups of the propertied, including over involvement in state affairs, stimulated some lawyers to envisage alternatives to the existing order. In the absence of routinised mass elections, political parties and a class of professional politicians, lawyers were at the heart of such challenges. In mid-eighteenth-century France the notion of

---

[16] A pioneering study was that of A Seal, *The Emergence of Indian Nationalism: Competition and Collaboration in the Later Nineteenth Century* (Cambridge, Cambridge University Press, 1971).

[17] A bust of Ambedkar is located in the foyer of Clement House on the Aldwych, part of the London School of Economics.

[18] Gramsci makes a useful distinction between 'organic' intellectuals who are a functioning part of an established order, usually serving specific class or elite interests, and 'subaltern' intellectuals who articulate and often lead resistance to such an order.

'national liberties' was elaborated by lawyers in *parlements* which resisted royal encroachments upon such liberties. Yet those self-same encroachments were constructed and justified by royal lawyers who argued that the crown embodied the 'national' interest by attacking selfish, sectional privilege. Lawyers articulated peasant objections to seigneurial privilege through a critique of 'feudal' law. Most of the *cahiers de doleance* drawn up for the consideration of the Estates-General which Louis XVI summoned in 1789, and which elaborated criticisms of 'feudalism' and 'absolutism', were drafted by lawyers, even if they genuinely expressed the views of peasants and other commoners. These disputes and how they were publicised by petitions and polemical publications helped form a 'public sphere', a forum defined by lawyers who in turn played a leading role within it.

Lawyers were less prominent in the rise of a national opposition in British politics, maybe because this was a less closed system which provided space for people to acquire political prominence in other ways, especially in Parliament and the press. Yet, a century earlier it had been lawyers like Sir Edmund Coke who formulated an idea of historic ('national') rights vested in Parliament which could be used to make claims against the crown. Leading parliamentarians and writers in late-eighteenth-century Britain were trained in the law and used their skills in political disputes, for example Edmund Burke and the impeachment of Warren Hastings.

So in the two countries in which nationalist politics first emerged, in settler societies which took the legal practices concerning property and rulership of those countries elsewhere, and in colonies such as the British Raj which produced a numerous Westernised elite, lawyers played a leading role in formulating and organising political claims in the name of the nation.

These general arguments can be filled out with particular examples.

## IV. Global Politics and Nationalism in the 'Age of Revolution'

The British empires established in North America and South Asia were very different. North America[19] was an empire of settlement. There was no serious consideration of the rights and customs of indigenous populations; consideration which later gave rise to arguments about national peculiarities preceding imperial rule and to which nationalists could appeal. Instead British Protestant settlers brought their own legal practices from the mother country, even if property law had to work differently in an initially unmapped, large and expanding territory.

---

[19] I confine my comments to British North America, that is the colonies which acquired independence as the United States of America. The region that subsequently became Canada is very different, principally because of the role played by Catholic settlers from France.

At the heart of that work was quasi-legal reasoning about *tertia nullius* which was deployed to establish both property and political rights in the new lands. Interestingly, George Washington—apart from extensive farming interests and military activity—spent much of his early career as a surveyor, mapping and making claims on unsettled land.

None of this activity directly led to nationalism. Lawyers and related professions such as surveyors and town planners acted as 'organic intellectuals'. As in Britain and France it was only when more significant political disputes developed, in particular about representation and taxation, that it was considered necessary to characterise as national the society on whose behalf political demands were being made. Initially these demands formed within the given institutional context that was both more and less than national. It was more than national because demands were framed as those of British subjects entitled to the same rights and liberties as other such subjects. Thus the radical and liberal critiques taking place in Britain itself were also deployed in the colonies.[20] It was less than national because the institutions which crystallised these demands were the 13 distinct colonies.

This radicalism, whether in the movement for extension of the franchise in Britain or for the sweeping away of absolute monarchy in France, began to shift from basing demands on specific, historical rights to appealing to universal, natural rights. Strictly speaking, this took one from the domain of lawyers to that of philosophers, but lawyers were often best placed to flesh out the detail of natural rights theory in a quasi-legal form. Such lawyers turned especially to John Locke to provide them with a congenial natural rights position, one which began by asking how a new civil society such as that of North America had been established and how one could justify that establishment, using the language of contracts, rights and obligations.

Finally, a violent breach with existing political arrangements, such as took place in north America in the late-1770s and early-1780s, and in France in 1789, opened up space for turning arguments about natural rights and political sovereignty into the work of devising a constitution for a new kind of state, one in which sovereignty lay with its citizens, now called the 'nation'. Those engaged in this project no longer confined their attention to a provincial *parlement* or an individual colony but generalised it to the 'national' territory. Once again lawyers were central in this, writing the Federalist Papers, drafting the US Constitution as well as successive French Constitutions. Every major step in this process required detailed legislation on rights and obligations both private (property, religion, etc) and public (forms and powers of a national parliament, the administrative and judicial structures of the state). The modern territorial state was being constructed. Its concerns with representation and legislation, with establishing individual liberty but also

---

[20] Opponents of the existing order like Thomas Paine, could move easily between North America, France and Britain. Most of the critical literature on British, including colonial, politics was published in mainland Britain.

providing a legal framework for the exercise of collective will in the form of state action, always had lawyers at its heart.

In principle one could analyse the way nationalism diffused from Europe, especially Spain, to Ibero-America in similar fashion. One notable theorist of nationalism, Benedict Anderson, has seen the origins of nationalism in this particular conflict, one which again goes back to global competition between Britain and France.[21]

However, space does not permit this and I turn now to India. As Britain was losing one empire in North America she was gaining another in India.[22] This was not an empire of settlement but of administration and trade. Its key embodiment for the first century or so was not a colonial state or a settler class but a trading company, the East India Company.

As in continental Europe and the Americas we encounter French conflict with Britain and the involvement of local rulers as junior figures or proxies in that conflict. Yet we do not see in this period a diffusion of nationalism from Europe to India; there are no Indian Jeffersons or Bolivars at this time. Why the difference and, following that, what role might law and lawyers play or not play?[23]

One might object that the question is a false one as any collective actions—such as those of 1857—seeking to throw off British rule merit the name nationalism, even if they did not use European enlightenment language or demand a territorial state based on the sovereignty of the nation.[24] The argument has an especial plausibility when the collective resistance has a novel character, transcending the forms of solidarity displayed at the time of the first imperial incursions.[25]

---

[21] Anderson, *Imagined Communities* (n 5).

[22] PJ Marshall, *The Making and Unmaking of Empires: Britain, India, and America c.1750–1783* (Oxford, Oxford University Press, 2005).

[23] There are historians of colonial India who would dispute this sweeping claim. See P Chatterjee, *The Black Hole of Empire: History of a Global Practice of Power* (Princeton, Princeton University Press, 2012), who argues first for a very similar kind of radical politics based on British models developing in the late-18th and early-19th century, such radicals active above all as journalists. The first came from Britain but there were also indigenous figures. Chatterjee further argues that the ruler of Mysore, Tippu Tipp, was in many respects a modernising figure who adopted Western methods in military, agricultural and administrative fields. But the radicals had little weight in relation both to British rule and native rulers and Tippu Tipp was wholly exceptional and defeated and executed by the British. The key difference is that the British and Spanish creole opponents of imperial rule—including lawyers—were drawn from the dominant interest in the Americas but their equivalents in India were not.

[24] Arguments over what to call this event reveal something of the problem. The 'Indian Mutiny' was a British term at the time but is now rejected as patronising and also too narrow given that violent rejection of British rule soon extended beyond Hindu soldiers in the Company army. There is, however, no clear consensus on an alternative such as 'first national revolution'. See Chatterjee, *The Black Hole of Empire* (n 23).

[25] CA Bayly, *The Birth of the Modern World 1780–1914* (Oxford, Blackwell, 2004). In his world history of modernity he proposes a notion of 'old patriotism' and supports this with reference to detailed research by himself and other historians of India. Historians of East-central Africa have made a similar argument for collective resistance to German and British rule such as the Maji-Maji rebellion in Tanganyika in 1905–07. For an overview of the treatment of 'patriotism and nationalism' in colonial sub-Saharan Africa, see J Lonsdale, 'Anti-colonial Nationalism and Patriotism in Sub-Saharan Africa' in Breuilly (ed), *Handbook* (n 2) as well as his earlier piece, J Lonsdale, 'Some Origins of Nationalism in East Africa (1968) 9(1) *Journal of African History* 9.

However, the danger of taking this stance is that nationalism becomes an impossibly vague term, referring to any extensive (if non-traditional) collective resistance to colonial rule. The problem for these early resistances to imperial rule (as opposed to the initial incursions which were led by established forms of authority) was that of formulating a political alternative beyond the impossible vision of restoring an imagined pre-imperial rule.[26] One can take this argument further: the very incommensurability of the political languages deployed by the conflicting parties blocked meaningful political interaction, something which extends beyond violent conflict. To make that possible one requires political dialogue and that could only happen with the diffusion of a common set of political concepts.[27] At the time of these resistance movements the obstacles to the diffusion of such shared concepts were insuperable. There was a clash between very different conceptions of property, community and sovereignty. This was emphatically not the case in North America, at least between white settlers and the imperial government.[28] So the very framing of a political dispute in nationalist terms required the diffusion of a certain kind of language about rights and identity which was distinctively modern. Furthermore, this language was often a legal one, drawing upon legal concepts and dominated by trained lawyers.

That a very different situation obtained on the Indian subcontinent in the mid-nineteenth century was recognised at the time. One way in which this played itself out was as disagreement between what one might call 'nativists' and 'modernisers'. This began as an argument amongst British administrators but soon came to be adapted by elite Indian figures. The first position, initially represented by scholarly Orientalists, insisted that Indian society was unique and worthy of respect, and that there should be as little intervention by the British as possible. The second, most clearly expressed by the historian and East India Company employee Thomas Babington Macaulay, argued that India had stagnated—it was at a stage Europe had been centuries earlier—and that Britain had a responsibility to reverse that by transferring to India British values and practices. He recognised that could only begin at elite level focused on the coastal cities but there he outlined a programme of establishing 'Englishness', for example through appropriate elite education.

---

[26] 1857 is such an example. Certainly novel and extensive forms of action were exhibited by both the British and their opponents as detailed in C Bayly, *Empire and Information Intelligence Gathering and Social Communication in India, 1780–1870* (Cambridge, Cambridge University Press, 1996) and W Dalrymple, *The Last Mughal : the Fall of a Dynasty, Delhi, 1857* (London, Bloomsbury, 2006). But it is also clear that beyond the restoration of Mughal rule there was no positive goal.

[27] I draw especially on the ideas of Reinhart Koselleck who pioneered the study of historical concepts ('Geschichtliche Grundbegriffe'). For him concepts were more than ideas but rather essential ways of 'grasping', that is, acting in the world. (*Begreifen* is the verb drawn from *Begriff* (concept).) For there to be a conceptual conflict there must exist a common conceptual field on which that conflict takes place. This insight has been put to work for Indian and Sri Lankan history by Madura Rasaratnam in an LSE PhD soon to be published in book form.

[28] It would be interesting to consider the ways in which native American groups framed demands in relation both the British imperial and settler local rule but there is not time to do so.

Following the rising of 1857 many British observers deemed this policy not merely to have failed but to have played a key part in provoking the rising because of its ignorance of and contempt for deeply held indigenous values, including especially but not only religious beliefs and practices.[29] Sir Henry Maine, a lawyer and legal historian, for a time the legal member of the Viceroys's council, developed a sophisticated version of the traditional/modern distinction and, though recognising that British rule would inevitably introduce irreversible change, sought to ensure this was done gradually. As part of this programme of gradualism and respect, Indian laws and customs should be recorded, even codified, and, so far as possible, upheld.[30]

The reason why, however, change was irreversible was because the British Raj was what Maine called a legislating as opposed to a taxing empire. The contrast can be illustrated with reference to land revenue. A taxing empire like the Ottoman Empire imposed tribute with little idea of what could be afforded and how it was to be raised.[31] No questions were asked about indigenous law, no attempt made to integrate the various communities or subjects or to standardise laws across the empire. A legislating empire works very differently. Thus, in regard to land revenue, Company officials already in late-eighteenth-century Bengal began by defining property and identifying its owners. This generated disputes between those who wanted to make the landowner and those the direct cultivator the bearer of property rights and consequently fiscal obligations. Maine criticised both positions for treating land as an absolute, individual possession and not as goods shared by a collective such as family or village community. Whatever choice was made, the official used these legal notions to establish the distribution and value of property, as European absolutist monarchies had been doing for some time. In this way conceptual oppositions such as that of private and public, community and individual, were taken up by elites and sometimes even non-elites in the colonial society. These would in turn become key concepts underpinning nationalist arguments. Lawyers were at the forefront of this process. As imperial government expanded territorially and in its range of interventions, so an ever larger proportion of those lawyers were drawn from indigenous society.

Not surprisingly therefore, such lawyers figure at the heart of the new nationalist movements, its demands and its programmes. 'Private' rights and obligations of individuals or communities were being elaborated and enforced in land and tax and other laws. This pressed those trained in law to think through the forms of a 'public' sphere which would complement this private sphere. It turns out that

---

[29] The 'mutiny' was said to have been triggered by the requirement that Indian Hindu soldiers handle cartridges which had been covered with pork grease.

[30] K Mantena, *Alibis of Empire: Social Theories and Ideologies of Late Imperialism* (Princeton, Princeton University Press, 2009).

[31] R Harris, *Dubrovnik: a History* (London, Saqi Books, 2006). Ch 5 details a typical case of the kind of negotiations that took place, here between the city-state of Dubrovnik and the Ottoman Sultanate in Constantinople, once an arbitrary tribute was imposed. The process was diplomatic, involving different power units within a hierarchy rather than one involving citizens and 'their' state.

Kedourie's 'marginal men' are not at the margin at all but rather on the front line of arguments, intellectual and political, concerning different conceptions of community, sovereignty, territory and representation. Here we observe a complex process of imperial transformation and indigenous learning resulting in a nationalist critique and movement. However, that would only go on to take the shape of practical independence demands after the weakness of British rule had been exposed through two world wars.

We can extend such arguments to account for the centrality of lawyers in many nineteenth-century nationalist movements, especially those making radical or liberal demands. For example, the German National Assembly which met in Frankfurt-am-Main in 1848–49 was dominated by lawyers.[32] It was sarcastically dubbed the 'Professors' Parliament' but the largest group of university professors were from law faculties and they were joined by many others trained in law and either working in government or private practices. English usage tends to connote 'professors' and 'intellectuals' as unfitted for the practical, hurly-burly world of politics and further implies that this might be one reason for the failure of the parliament.[33] Yet in authoritarian polities with few professions outside the traditional ones of law, medicine and religion, and especially where state bureaucracies—as in the German lands—emphasised legal education as the key qualification for holding office, these 'lawyers' were bound to be at the heart of any opposition. Only the landed nobility were as central to the exercise of power and generally speaking members of that class were conservative.[34] Furthermore, as in France after 1789 and British North America after 1776, when it appeared the main task was to define the form the new polity should take, drafting constitutions and legal codes became central tasks and were naturally dominated by lawyers. The same points apply to the emergence of reformist Ottomanism from the 1830s, the drafting of the Meiji Constitution in Japan in the 1880s, the negotiations between the Raj and Congress in India from the late-1920s and many other cases. Only when nationalism primarily took the form of violent resistance rather than relatively non-violent negotiations, did lawyers cease to be central to the work and hence the language of nationalism.

Up to 1914 the diffusion of nationalism took place in a world dominated by imperial blocs and rivalries. It was partial both in its spread and its ambitions. Law

---

[32] F Eyck, *The Frankfurt Parliament 1848–49* (London, Macmillan, 1968); H Best, *Die Männer von Bildung und Besitz. Struktur und Handeln Parlamentarischer Führungsgruppen in Deutschland und Frankreich 1848–49* (Düsseldorf, Droste Verlag, 1990).

[33] This was a central argument in LB Namier, *1848: the Revolution of the Intellectuals* (London, Oxford University Press/The British Academy, 1946), mirrored in the very title to his book and contrasting with the way he approvingly wrote the history of the English Parliament, dominated by practical men who represented concrete interests (land, trade, etc).

[34] One must qualify this point. Great (as opposed to medium or petty) noble landowners were often at the forefront of liberal reforming movements, partly because these could curb the power of a monarchy detached from its aristocratic milieu and partly because they could afford the transition costs of moving from seigneurial privilege to the cash-nexus as the means of commanding labour on their estates.

and lawyers played a central role in some cases but for quite specific reasons to do with the transformations wrought by the growth of capitalism and new forms of imperial rule. After the First World War, nationalism was able to diffuse more widely and in a more standardised form, one in which once again law and lawyers played an important part.

## V. Nation-State as Legal Template: Nationalism after World War

The relationship between law and the diffusion of nationalism took on a new form after 1918. In January 1918, US President Woodrow Wilson—an academic who had studied history and philosophy at university but also law for one year in graduate school—set out his 'Fourteen Points' as providing the basis for US war aims and the principles for a post-war order. At the heart of these points were the ideas of national self-determination[35] and rule of law both at state and international levels. The Allied victory and the application of the principle of national self-determination in the Versailles Settlement, applied to the territories of the former Habsburg and Ottoman empires, along with the establishment of the League of Nations, placed legal concepts at the heart of the envisioned new order. The notion of international law as something over and above the agreements made between sovereign states spawned a virtually new profession. Above all, the settlement provided a 'template' for nationalists across the world. In French Indochina, China, Egypt, Korea, Ireland and many other places, Wilson's principles were used to frame national demands and to appeal to the USA for support.[36] Admittedly there was always a tension between the legal presumptions of dealing with 'sovereign individuals', whether persons or states, and the idea that nation-states be regarded primarily as the property of cultural (ethnic, linguistic, religious) collectives, as well as between the rule of international law and the inviolable sovereignty of the state. One should note that such tensions did not inform the other great stimulus to nationalist movements at this time, namely the support proclaimed by the newly formed Soviet Union for 'national liberation' movements. Here lawyers and legal concepts emphatically do not figure in the forefront of the original revolution or the subsequent nationalist movements supported by the USSR. Indeed one can make a distinction between bourgeois, reformist nationalism in which 'organic intellectuals', including lawyers, were prominent and socialist, and

[35] The phrase does not actually occur in the 14 Points speech but is used in later speeches. Wilson later stopped using the phrase, tending to favour less incendiary formulations such as 'with the consent of the governed'.
[36] E Manela, *The Wilsonian Moment: Self-Determination and the International Origins of Anti-Colonial Nationalism* (Oxford, Oxford University Press, 2007).

revolutionary nationalism in which 'subaltern intellectuals' drawn from a variety of backgrounds took the lead. The USA provided the template for the first form, the USSR for the second form.

Nationalism may have diffused widely but it failed to translate itself into a global order of nation-states in the decades following 1918. Indeed, as the USA and the USSR retreated into 'isolation' and 'socialism in one country', the key global conflicts were between the satiated imperial powers of Western Europe and the imperialist ambitions of Germany, Italy and Japan. Only after the latter were comprehensively defeated and the former exhausted and weakened by that 'triumph' could once more the US and Soviet templates of the nation-state resume their global diffusion.

The end of the Second World War was a victory for a legal, 'civic' nationalist discourse across the European overseas empires. Decolonisation[37] would focus on the rights of 'peoples', not 'nations' as the latter implied some pre-political definition of a collective of the kind which had just been discredited with the defeat of the Axis powers. 'The people' were entitled to freedom as citizens and people had rights as human beings. The theoretically insoluble problem of which comes first—the collective which should form the citizenry of the new sovereign state or the individuals who make up that citizenry and are the bearers of human rights—was short-circuited by treating the administrative units of imperial control (the 'colonial state') as 'states in waiting'. The intention was to undermine from the outset any notion that national sovereignty was a right attributed to pre-political collectives with all the implied problems such as ethnic cleansing, secessionism and irredentism. Instead the entire focus was on the internal arrangements of the new states—arrangements framed in terms of public (above all constitutional) powers and their relationship to a sphere regulated by private law. Once again, lawyers were bound to be at the forefront of such nationalist negotiations even if other groups frequently held more political power.

The establishment of the United Nations provided the key forum in which a particular template of the sovereign nation-state could be projected globally. As the 'nation-state order' was expanded and stabilised under the bi-polar global domination of the USA and the USSR, so concepts of territoriality, sovereignty, legitimacy, public/private distinctions and the claims of individual human rights against that of state sovereignty—concepts framed in essentially legal ways—came to dominate political discourse. That dominance enabled John Meyer and others to argue that if an entirely unknown society was discovered tomorrow, one could safely predict that the international community, with lawyers in the lead, would proclaim the formation of a new nation-state as the key objective for this society and would set in hand the appropriate means for achieving this. Furthermore, this

---

[37] The term itself is revealing, suggesting a deliberate, programmed transfer of control rather than some combination of imperial collapse and colonial assertion.

way of imagining the world as divided into nations and nation states diffused to even (perhaps especially) the most marginal of societies.[38]

# VI. Concluding Points

I have suggested a framework by which one can understand how nationalism spread across the world in the last 250 years or so. I have also outlined the roles played by lawyers and law in this diffusion process, both in terms of the characteristics of lawyers as a modern profession and the centrality of legal discourse to modern nationalism. Finally, I have argued that the concept of the self-determining nation-state as the legitimate unit of public power, first after 1918 applied to the defeated dynastic empires, and then after 1945 extended to overseas European empires, established a template that could be and actually was globalised. This template was suffused with the language of rights, obligations, constitutional enactments and international conventions which were framed in legal terms.

Perhaps we can discern this trajectory for the diffusion of nationalism and the global expansion of the nation-state order because it appears to be coming to an end. The occasion for this was the collapse of the Soviet Union. Ironically this 'ending' was accompanied by the last great burst of nation-state formation which combined the ethnonational claims of the post-1918 wave with the 'state-in-waiting' principles of post-1945 European decolonisation. The non-Russian republics of the USSR were named after the 'titular' nationalities that it was presumed dominated them numerically and politically. The constituent republics of former Yugoslavia all had national names (Serbia, Croatia, Slovenia, etc) with the signal exception of Bosnia-Herzogovina which, not coincidentally, became the most contested site of nationalist conflict and remains divided into 'national' units to this day. These constituent republics (or what Roeder calls 'segment states')[39] were given the same function in the succession to the USSR and Yugoslavia as that played by the 'colonial state' in European overseas empire. Where ethnicity and segment-state status were in conflict (Kosovo, Chechnya) it was initially the sub-state principle which prevailed.

Yet at the same time that collapse removed the stabilising effect of the Cold War and gave rise to euphoria about the victory of the USA and the 'free world', a euphoria variously expressed in the rapid 'privatisation' of the Russian economy, the expansion of NATO and the EU into Central and Eastern Europe, and

---

[38] L Malkki, 'Citizens of Humanity: Internationalism and the Imagined Community of Nations' (1994) 3(1) *Diaspora: A Journal of Transnational Studies* 41; JW Meyer, 'World Society and the Nation State' (1997) 103(1) *The American Journal of Sociology* 144.

[39] PG Roeder, *Where Nation-States Come From: Institutional Changes in the Age of Nationalism* (Princeton and Oxford, Princeton University Press, 2007).

interventions in Afghanistan and Iraq in pursuit of a global 'war against terror'. We can now see more clearly than in the early-1990s that stable US hegemony was actually part of the bi-polar Cold War world order. The forces which enabled that hegemony in part were articulated through the notion of a 'free world' of sovereign nation-states. The 'freezing' effects of the Cold War had sustained as sovereign states entities which had little real power or legitimacy. The thaw which followed the collapse of the USSR did not expand the possibilities for nation-state sovereignty but actually, as we can now see, diminished them.

The legal fiction that the world consists of sovereign nation-states continues to be upheld. Yet one can now see this less as a description of how political power has been and is organised globally but instead as the legal expression of a particular kind of hegemonic coercive power which took increasingly legal and institutional forms after 1918 and then 1945 and stabilised during the Cold War. Regions of European decolonisation in Africa and the Middle East became increasingly fragile, unable to defend state boundaries or enforce rule of law internally, surviving mainly because it suited the hegemons that they did so.[40] Yet that form of hegemonic power is itself increasingly being questioned. Russia, against some expectations, did not challenge the nation-state territorial order established on its borders immediately following the Soviet collapse. (Indeed, one could argue that Boris Yeltsin's government actually 'imposed' independence on many of the non-Russian republics.) However, that challenge has come subsequently. At first it took informal forms such as economic pressure and covert support for 'de facto' states as in South Ossetia and Transdniestria. Now it has become open territorial revision with the annexation of the Crimea. Admittedly the formal territorial argument is still employed as is the ethnic argument for national self-determination, for example in the claim that Crimea is 'essentially' Russian and should never have been 'given away' by Khruschev.

Arguably China is engaged in similar challenges to the legal state order in the South China Seas, and has already made territorial revisions in the case of Tibet. We seem to be moving back to a world of hegemons (Russia, China, USA) in which informal power and regional zones of conflict increasingly challenge the legal order of sovereign states. Part of that challenge includes questioning the 'nation-ness' of many existing states. The Crimea is Russian, not Ukrainian. Syria and Iraq should be the core of a revived Caliphate rather than territorial nation-states, let alone some pan-Arab state. There is an unstable combination of ethnonationalist and supra-state challenges to the nation-state order.

I have deliberately avoided the term 'globalisation' to frame this notion of an undermining of the nation-state order. That is not because I think the processes most closely linked to globalisation—huge multinational capitalist com-

---

[40] A sustained argument to this effect is made for Sub-Saharan Africa by P Englebert, *Africa: Unity, Sovereignty, and Sorrow* (Boulder, Colorado, Lynn Riener, 2009).

panies, the capacity to communicate almost instantaneously across the world, the speeding up of flows of money, goods and people—are unimportant. They are important but their earlier historical forms (railways, telegraph, the gold standard, mass migrations) have long been vitally important. However, in one particular historical epoch these forces articulated with, not against, the diffusion of the nation-state template as the legitimate form for public, coercive power. This legal form is now unravelling. Whether that will continue to be the case as the fictive nature of this legal form becomes increasingly clear remains to be seen.

# 3

## Nationalism After the State

MICHAEL KEATING

## I. State and Nation

The concept of the nation-state is fundamental to both political science and law but it is notoriously difficult to define. In some national traditions, the compound word is redundant, as state and nation are almost synonyms. For many scholars of international relations, the nation-state is defined by reference to sovereignty, as the fundamental building block of global order. In political theory, nation and state are usually distinguished, so that a nation-state is one in which nation and state are co-terminous, as opposed to complex states containing more than one nation, or situations where a nation covers more than one state. The doctrine of national self-determination is then a normative principle according to which nations should be allowed a state of their own. As the nation is the 'people' or *demos* underpinning democracy, this provides a principle of popular self-determination in conditions of freedom. Yet, as Ivor Jennings famously pointed out, before the people can self-determine, someone has to define who the people are.[1]

This encounters two principal difficulties. First, the definition of a nation or people is notoriously slippery and often subjective. While political theorists often take the nation for granted,[2] sociologists are practically unanimous in seeing it as socially constructed and usually contested.[3] Second, even if we could define the nation scientifically, how can we draw normative implications from this? These difficulties were often brushed aside in the heyday of the nation-state, when the legitimacy of existing states was largely taken for granted. It was those who advocated changing boundaries or setting up new states who had to make their case and it was always easy to dismiss this as somehow 'artificial' or as violating legal

---

[1] I Jennings, *The Approach to Self-Government* (Cambridge, Cambridge University Press, 1956).

[2] See W Kymlicka, *Multicultural Citizenship* (Oxford, Oxford University Press, 1995); W Kymlicka, *Multicultural Odysseys. Navigating the New International Politics of Diversity* (Oxford, Oxford University Press, 2007).

[3] M Keating, *Rescaling the European State: The Making of Territory and the Rise of the Meso* (Oxford, Oxford University Press, 2013).

norms and impossible to operationalise universally. Hence, doctrines of self-determination tended to be defined rather narrowly, to be applied in exceptional circumstances.[4] In the twenty-first century, however, the established states are both losing their functional capacity to meet citizen demands and the mystique which invested them with an element of unquestioned authority, while they are faced with the claims of competing normative orders, at global, continental or sub-state level. They are thus forced to justify their authority, as we see in Europe with debates about the need for, and meaning of, national identity, and with rival Europhile and Eurosceptic political projects. As both nation and state are in question, their relationship becomes ever more problematic.

In this context, we must see national self-determination not so much as a universal right but as a twofold claim. The first is the ontological claim, that the nation and people in question exists and is conscious of existing. The second is a normative claim, that the people in question are the subject of self-determination. This means that they have a right to negotiate their own constitutional status. The object of self-determination, which has traditionally been seen as an independent state, is another matter. We know that in the modern, interdependent world sovereign statehood is merely one form that self-determination might take. It is useful to keep these elements analytically separate, although they are connected, since nationalist movements will play on them all simultaneously. So in the past regionalist political movements have often moved on to define their territory as a nation precisely to put it in the same normative category as the nation-state and thus advance self-determination claims. At the end of the nineteenth century, Catalan leaders moved from the language of regionalism to that of the nation,[5] while northern Italian regionalists in the 1990s sought to invent the nation of Padania, even endowing it with a suitable past.[6]

The turn towards social constructivism in studies of nationalism, which presents the phenomenon in this way, might seem to make the accommodation of nationalist claims even more difficult. If it means that nations are purely subjective and can be invented at will, this seems to provide a rather flimsy basis for building an agreed legal order. The constructivist approach, however, is more than this. The nation is not an objective reality, which can be defined and measured scientifically and distinguished from other social phenomena, but nor is it purely subjective. It is, rather, an inter-subjective set of understandings and meanings, which emerges from social and political interaction in specific circumstances. Nation-building and mobilisation is not costless and it is not obvious that, given the choice, people would always choose to define themselves and their interest by nationality rather than in other ways. The objection that a more liberal

---

[4] A Buchanan, *Justice, Legitimacy, and Self-Determination: Moral Foundations for International Law* (Oxford, Oxford University Press, 2004).

[5] E Prat de la Riba, *La nacionalitat catalana*, republished 1998 (Madrid, Biblioteca Nueva, 1898).

[6] G Oneto, *L'invenzione della Padania. La rinascita della communità più antica d'europa* (Bergamo, Foedus, 1997).

approach to self-determination would thus encourage 'vanity secessions'[7] seems overblown. Indeed, the constructvist approach may even be helpful in sorting out self-determination issues, since it allows them to be deconstructed and repackaged in ways that allow accommodation outside the old model of one nation-one state. That model was based on two elements: national sovereignty and territorial integrity. Both of these are in question. They are still with us, but are being substantially transformed.

## II. Sovereignty

Sovereignty, for legal scholars, is a normative principle referring to the ultimate source of legitimate authority. State sovereignty thus implies that national governments and parliaments can in practice govern, through law and regulation. Political scientists often add a practical element, that they have the capacity to make their policies effective. It has been argued widely that states are losing this capacity, as they are subject to global market forces, and are inserted into complex webs of interdependence in transnational organisations, including the European Union, NATO and the World Trade Organization. Sovereignty risks becoming an empty principle if states lack the capacity to enforce their will. Legal purists may respond that this does not affect the normative element of sovereignty and that states can always withdraw from international organisations and even from the global economy, however costly that might be. Some scholars, however, have gone beyond this to argue that the principle of sovereignty itself has been transformed so that we are a world of 'post-sovereignty'.[8] This is not to say that sovereignty has disappeared but that it has been transformed. There are multiple sources of sovereign authority, of which the state is but one.

The expression 'post-sovereignty' suggests something new but in many places sovereignty has long been contested. The modern state struggled to establish its normative supremacy against other forms of authority, be they ecclesiastical, traditional or territorial. The Peace of Westphalia, often held up as the basis for nation statehood, was nothing of the sort but concerned the territorial alignment of secular rule and religion.[9] It was the French Revolution that brought the idea that popular sovereignty must be based on a unitary *demos* and therefore national. Only in the late-nineteenth century did states penetrate deeply into society,

---

[7] RS Beiner, 'National Self-Determination: Some Cautionary Remarks Concerning the Practice of Rights' in M Moore (ed), *National Self-Determination and Secession* (Oxford, Oxford University Press, 1998).

[8] N MacCormick, *Questioning Sovereignty. Law, State and Nation in the European Commonwealth* (Oxford, Oxford University Press, 1999).

[9] A Osiander, *The States System of Europe, 1640–1990. Peacemaking and the Conditions of International Stability* (Oxford, Clarendon, 1994); A Osiander, 'Sovereignty, International Relations and the Westphalian Myth' (2001) 55 *International Organization* 251.

requiring states to have a functional capacity commensurate with their claims to authority. Even then, there survived, in various parts of Europe, distinct ways of thinking about sovereignty, some of which have been revived in modern times and adapted to the new conditions.

Under conditions of post-sovereignty, claims to sovereignty cannot be resolved by reducing them to a single source. Rather, there are competing foundations, invoked by different parties, which can be accommodated only within a constitutional pluralism.

# III. Territory

The nation-state has also been defined as a closed territorial system. Sovereignty claims have, in the modern era, focused on territory, with limited scope for extra-territorial jurisdiction. On the functional plane, the closing of national borders turned economic, social and political systems inwards, facilitating national social compromises.[10] Again, this was never complete, as national integration met opposition at the periphery and states had to make compromises with territorial forces. In the 1990s, faced with the challenges of global economic change, some scholars in political science and international relations started to write about the end of territory.[11] Others, latching onto the enhanced importance of regions in economic development, wrote of the end of the nation-state, which meant much the same thing.[12] In fact, territory was not being destroyed but reconstituted as social, economic and political systems rescaled to multiple levels.[13]

Territory, too, is now being reconceptualised in a more complex, constructivist way.[14] In this new thinking, coming from social geography, territory is more than a mere topographical concept. It is also a sociological concept as physical space is a context for social, economic and political processes, which give it its meaning. Attention is focused on space as the basis for relationships, networks and extra-territorial connections.[15] Territories are never self-contained but are open and constantly reconfiguring. There is no single spatial 'fix' for all social, economic

[10] S Rokkan, 'State Formation, Nation-Building and Mass Politics in Europe' in P Flora, S Kuhnle and D Urwin (eds), *The Theory of Stein Rokkan* (Oxford, Oxford University Press 1999); S Bartolini, *Restructuring Europe. Centre Formation, System Building, and Political Structuring between the Nation State and the European Union* (Oxford, Oxford University Press, 2005).

[11] B Badie, *La fin des territoires. Essai sur le désordre international et sur l'utilité sociale du respect* (Paris, Fayard, 1995).

[12] K Ohmae, *The End of the Nation State. The Rise of Regional Economies* (New York, Free Press, 1995).

[13] Keating, *Rescaling the European State* (n 3).

[14] ibid.

[15] J Allen and A Cochrane, 'Beyond the Territorial Fix: Regional Assemblages, Politics and Power' (2007) 41(9) *Regional Studies* 1161.

and political purposes, but a multiplicity of possible territorial configurations for different purposes. These are not given by technical or functional imperatives but are often contested as the definition of territory does have implications for the distribution of power and resources.

The nation, sovereignty and territory can thus be deconstructed and demystified. All are contested and escape precise scientific definition. At first sight, this seems to make the existing conundrum about self-determination even more difficult, pushing us into a kind of post-modernist morass, in which there are no solid ontological foundations to anything, so that anything goes. Yet, it might also help us accommodate nationality claims in new and complex ways, escaping the impossible problems of aligning nation, state and territory that have bedevilled European history.

## IV. The New Nationalisms

It is in this context that the 'new' nationalisms have developed in Western countries, including Canada, the United Kingdom, Spain and Belgium. These are states whose capacity for economic and social regulation is constrained by rescaling and the loss of the old mechanisms for territorial management, including regional policy and fiscal transfers. They are embedded in transnational economic regimes such as the North American Free Trade Area (NAFTA) and the European Union (EU), which collectivise public goods such as market access and regulation, so lowering the threshold for becoming an independent state. Thinking in economic development in recent years has emphasised the importance of territory; this is the 'new regionalism' paradigm.[16] As states have lost their capacity to manage the balance of their territorial economies, regions have started to compete against each other for investment, markets and technical advantage, or at least are presented as doing so. The idea of regional competition and competitiveness has then been taken up by states and by the European Commission as the basis for spatial development policy. Political movements in wealthy regions argue that they are being taxed excessively to pay for their poorer compatriots, hampering their own competitive position.

In the past, nationalism had often been presented as a result of backwardness, retarded modernisation or discrimination; this was a 'revolt of the poor'. Now it is more likely to found among wealthy regions as a 'revolt of the rich'. Some observers have concluded that its basis is therefore purely functional or economic. Alesina and Spoloare reduce the nation (which they identify with the state) to

---

[16] M Keating, *The New Regionalism in Western Europe. Territorial Restructuring and Political Change* (Cheltenham, Edward Elgar, 1998).

an economic machine.[17] In the past, nations/states needed to be big to sustain large internal markets and exploit economies of scale. Now, international free trade guarantees the markets so that states can be small. They even argue that, historically, new states have been formed in times of free trade. This is simply untrue. In fact, most small states are the result of decolonisation or, in Europe, the fall of empires, including the Habsburg, Ottoman and Russian empires after the First World War and the Soviet Union in the late-twentieth century and had nothing whatever to do with free trade. The aftermath of the First World War led to protectionism and some of the new states, like Ireland, consciously adopted protectionist policies during the 1930s. Economic considerations hardly featured in early-twentieth-century debates about independence, which were driven by nation-building and identity politics, and nationalists tended to be economic protectionists.[18] Like Ohmae, Alesina and Spoloare fall into functional reductionism in arguing that because something may have economic consequences, that is why it happened. This ignores the critical role of politics and political choice.

Another of Alesina and Spoloare's arguments is that smaller states will better serve their citizens by giving them policies that they like. This is a superficially appealing argument but, in this version, is actually quite incoherent and leads to some alarming conclusions. They start from a body of social science thought known as public goods theory. It is assumed that people know what policies they prefer and that the task of government is to realise these preferences. Small states are more desirable because, with a smaller population, their citizens are more likely to have the same preferences for public policies. In fact, this does not follow since there is no particular reason to think that a population of five million people is more likely to agree among themselves than one of fifty million. Some of the smallest states and regions are deeply divided.

Alesina and Spoloare, however, prop up their argument about people in small places sharing preferences by assuming that small regions and countries will be more ethnically homogeneous. So the argument is not just about small states but about small, ethnic states. As they put it, 'in today's world of free trade, relatively small ethnic regions can "afford" to stay small and homogeneous'.[19] Now this is entering a minefield. Sociologists these days are practically unanimous in thinking that ethnicity is not something inherent in individuals but, like nationality, is socially constructed. Individuals have multiple identities, which they use for different purposes—class, gender, nationality or age for example—and share these differently with different other people. In so far as ethnicity can be measured, it is inevitably seen as a compound of other characteristics including language, religion, subjective feelings and inter-subjective meanings, which are always contested and always changing.

---

[17] A Alesina and E Spoloare, *The Size of Nations* (Cambridge, MA, MIT Press, 2003).

[18] D Bohle and B Greskovits, *Capitalist Diversity on Europe's Periphery* (Ithaca, Cornell University Press, 2013).

[19] Alesina and Spoloare, *The Size of Nations* (n 17) 14.

It is widely accepted within liberal political thought that ethnicity provides a poor basis for founding states. As it is defined so arbitrarily and is so difficult to measure, there can never be agreement on the boundaries of groups and, even to the extent that it can, they are never neatly concentrated in one place so allowing us to draw territorial boundaries around them. Making ethnicity the basis for statehood just encourages losing groups within the new state to create or reaffirm their own ethnic credentials, so producing an infinite regress.

Indeed, much of the opposition to non-state nationalisms in the modern world is based on the view that these are 'ethnic' while the nationalisms of the large states are 'civic'. This appears to be the thrust of Joseph Weiler's attack on Catalan nationalism,[20] if he does not use those exact terms. It is that employed by Ralph Dahrendorf,[21] a German Liberal (who became a member of the British House of Lords) and who argued that community should never be based on the local nation; the bigger state-nation was another matter. This is another instance of giving unthinking normative legitimacy to existing states while denying it to their challengers. The ethnic exclusiveness or civic inclusiveness of a particular nationalist movement, in fact, has nothing to do with whether the nation happens to have its own state. Indeed, at the time Dahrendorf wrote his 1995 commentary, Germany had an ethnically exclusive citizenship law, while Catalonia was making great efforts to integrate incomers into the national community. Weiler did not even bother to explore the basis for Spanish nationalism (which actually has both a civic-republican and a reactionary-religious-exclusive tradition) while condemning the Catalan version.

It is for this reason that nationalists in Scotland and liberal nationalists elsewhere have insisted that theirs is a civic project for the realisation of an inclusive nation. This is built, not on ethnic homogeneity, but on a shared political identity. This opens up an argument for the nation based on entirely different premises. It is not a place for conformity and for agreement on anything but a deliberative space in which political differences can be debated and resolved through majorities or through compromise. A nation does not have a single, economically determined, interest but contains the whole spectrum of social classes and economic sectors. It is a place where opposition thrives and where political minorities can become majorities.

This does not mean, as is sometimes assumed, that a civic nationalism is not a nationalism at all. All nationalisms seek to define the boundaries of the political community in a particular way. So the British nationalist (we might say UK nationalist if there was such an adjective) would define the political community in one way and the Scottish nationalist in another, but both could insist that theirs is a civic project, which includes everybody within the boundary whatever

[20] J Weiler, 'Editorial' (2013) 24(4) *European Journal of International Law* 909.
[21] R Dahrendorf, 'Preserving Prosperity' (1995) 13(29) *New Statesmen and Society* 36.

their origins. A similar argument can be made about Spain and Catalonia, while Basque nationalism in recent decades has moved beyond the exclusive ethnic particularism of its founder, Sabino Arana. Drawing the boundaries may indeed have consequences for public policies, not because people on either side are essentially different but because the outcomes of political deliberation and social compromise may diverge both in the short term and over longer periods as institutions take on their own dynamics. Shared identities may develop not on the basis of ethnic exclusiveness but because of shared historical experiences. These are never hegemonic and co-exist with other identities and interests that shape policy preferences. They may underpin the legitimacy of institutions so that losers will accept the outcome, but on condition that losers have the opportunity to become winners in a future round.

Non-state nationalisms in the Western world have thus come to take on the same characteristics as their state counterparts; they may be more open and inclusive, or ethnically exclusive. They are about defining the boundaries of political community, an inescapable task in a democratic order, at least until world government is achievable. They seek new mechanisms for managing economic change in conditions of free trade and transnational order. They provide a basis for social solidarity and sharing. Criticisms from state nationalists that this makes them selfish and anti-solidaristic are unconvincing given the fact that welfare nationalism at the level of the nation-state makes exactly the same assumptions about the relative entitlements of insiders and outsiders. Understood in this sense, nations do not have to be based on different or conflicting values. Indeed, in societies such as Spain and the United Kingdom, there is a continuing convergence about basic social and political norms, even as political behaviour is territorialising and diverging. Stéphane Dion,[22] in the context of the Quebec debate, labelled this 'de Tocqueville's paradox'.

It might seem at first sight that this would make the accommodation of nationalism easier and, in some ways, it does. On the other hand, minority nationalist movements are now claiming the same normative space as the state itself, which creates problems of its own. There is a contest for the definition of the relevant communities for politics, collective action and social solidarity, which does not yield simple solutions. Another irony is that, if it is the failure of the traditional nation-state to deliver on its economic and social promises that has provoked the rise of new nationalisms, it is hardly plausible that the answer should be to re-create the nation-state model at a smaller spatial scale.

---

[22] S Dion, 'Le nationalisme dans la convergence culturelle. Le Québec contemporain et le paradoxe de Tocqueville' in R Hudon and R Pelletier (eds), *L'engagement intellectuel. Mélanges en l'honneur de Léon Dion* (Sainte-Foy, Presses de l'Université Laval, 1991).

# V. The Object of Self-Determination

Nationalist movements in Western states are, by and large, aware of the limitations of statehood and of traditional ideas of sovereignty and have tailored their plans accordingly. Mainstream Catalan nationalism has not traditionally been secessionist but, for over a hundred years, pursued a policy of home rule for Catalonia while seeking a bigger place within Spain. In the form of Convergència i Unió (Convergence and Union) it has been a strong supporter of European integration, which weakens the state framework while potentially providing an economic and political space for self-governing nations and regions. The other main Catalan nationalist party, Esquerra Republicana de Catalunya (Catalan Republican Left) has favoured independence since the 1990s but expressed this as a gradual process, linked to the idea of a Europe of the Peoples, in which the old states would gradually fade away. Basque nationalism was historically more separatist. The founder of the Partido Nacionalista Vasco (Basque Nationalist Party), Sabino Arana, was an uncompromising separatist, at least until the last part of his short life. The party did, however, embrace European integration as early as the 1930s and since then has divided between those seeking full statehood and advocates of advanced autonomy. In 2004, Basque First Minister Juan José Ibarretxe produced a plan for a 'freely-associated state', resembling earlier Quebec designs for 'sovereignty-association', keeping a link with Spain.[23] The Scottish National Party (SNP) has long supported independence but many of its supporters would settle for less. Since the 1980s, it has placed its project within a European framework with the slogan 'independence in Europe'. Plaid Cymru/Party of Wales, has not historically been separatist but is rooted in communitarian and anti-statist politics. Flemish nationalism in its various forms has sought, successively, federalism and confederation, with a minority seeking full statehood. The Parti Québécois has fought two referendums (in 1980 and 1995) on a platform of 'sovereignty' accompanied by continued links to the rest of Canada.

It used often to be assumed that these parties were disguising their real aims of independence within apparently moderate formulas since nationalists must be after a state of their own. Yet, historically, nationalists have by no means always been separatists. There is now abundant evidence that, in the early-twentieth century, nationalists in the European empires as well as Ireland really did seek home rule within a broader, overarching order. They were well aware of the dangers of statehood and its exposure to aggression, and of the presence of minorities on their territories.[24] Nations emerging in the shadow of aggressive neighbours

---

[23] M Keating and Z Bray, 'Renegotiating Sovereignty; Basque Nationalism and the Rise and Fall of the Ibarretxe Plan' (2006) 5(4) *Ethnopolitics* 347.
[24] M Keating, *Plurinational Democracy. Stateless Nations in a Post-Sovereignty Era* (Oxford, Oxford University Press, 2001); Keating (n 3).

had little to gain from absolute sovereignty and everything to gain from overarching international order in which the larger nations would be constrained. It is not surprising, then, that it is these places where alternative traditions of authority have survived and can be used to underpin post-sovereigntist projects. Catalans draw on the memory of pre-1714 Catalonia, as a self-governing entity within a federal Crown of Aragon, which was then linked into another confederal entity, the Spanish Crown. Basque nationalists, putting the radical separatist tradition of Arana to one side, picked up the theme of the *fueros*, traditional privileges of the Basque provinces which kings of Castile and then of Spain had to respect. Before the nineteenth century, these provided for a radically asymmetric constitution, in which the Basque provinces enjoyed free trade with the rest of the world but there were customs barriers with Spain, while the Basques collected their own taxes, passing on a share to Madrid for common services. Scotland, while united with England into the United Kingdom of Great Britain in 1707, maintained its own legal system and (defying the Westphalian principle) its own established Church. It was argued by many Scottish lawyers that, since the old Scottish Parliament had never asserted absolute sovereignty, it could not have passed this onto the new Parliament of Great Britain, so the issue of sovereignty in Scotland was unresolved.[25] In Quebec, scholars tended to emphasise the 'two founding peoples' doctrine under which Canada was presented as a compact between the Francophones (later defined as Quebeckers) and the Anglo-Canadians (or rest of Canada). This contrasted with the dominant view outside Quebec, that Canada consisted of a single people, with whom sovereignty resided, but with different languages spoken across the country.

Many modernist scholars are sceptical of these traditions as having any normative relevance, asking how historical stories, even supposing that they are true, can affect rights.[26] Herrero de Miñón,[27] however, has presented a sophisticated argument as to why we should take historic rights seriously. They are not, he argues, just rights to *have* a particular status, but also rights to *be* a self-determining unit. In other words, these arguments address both the ontological and the normative claims we referred to at the beginning of this chapter. We could add that these are in practice the very arguments on which states themselves depend when forced to defend their own sovereignty claims. Such arguments do not yield definitive answers in the scientific sense but they do move the argument onto the ground of constitutionalism as tradition, practice and accommodation.

---

[25] MacCormick, *Questioning Sovereignty* (n 8); N MacCormick, 'Is There a Scottish Path to Constitutional Independence?' (2000) 53 *Parliamentary Affairs* 721.

[26] W Norman, 'The Ethics of Secession as the Regulation of Secessionist Politics' in M Moore (ed), *National Self-Determination and Secession* (Oxford, Oxford University Press, 1998).

[27] M Herrero de Miñon, *Derechos Históricos y Constitución* (Madrid, Tecno, 1998).

# VI.  The Elusive Third Way

Nationalists have devoted a lot of effort into finding a 'third way' between union with their host state and setting up a state of their own.[28] They have foundered on two obstacles, in the state and in the international order. State governments have widely conceded devolution of competences to their constituent nationalities but have not accepted that they are the subjects of self-determination and thus able to negotiate an accommodation. Often the objections appear purely symbolic. So English Canada for long was unable to accept that Quebec should use the term 'nation' about itself and even the term 'distinct society' used in the Meech Lake Accord of 1988 was too much for many, explaining its ultimate failure. The revised Catalan Statute of Autonomy negotiated in 2006 was undermined in the Spanish Constitutional Court because it had suggested (albeit in the preamble) that Catalonia was a nation. Of course, these arguments are not purely semantic since behind the use of words lie claims to sovereignty and self-determination. In the case of the United Kingdom, symbolic language is less important and nobody quibbles about the use of the term 'nation' in regard to Scotland and Wales. UK governments have even accepted that Scotland and Northern Ireland could leave the state if they so choose by referendum, but have not accepted that Scotland could negotiate a 'third way'. Margaret Thatcher in 1993 explicitly said that Scotland could secede but could not have devolution. The British political class later accepted devolution but insisted that the sovereignty and power of the central parliament remain unaffected. More recently, under the 2012 Edinburgh Agreement between the UK and Scottish governments, the UK conceded a vote on independence but explicitly ruled out a second question on a more moderate form of self-government.

The second obstacle is that there is no place in the international institutional architecture for entities that are more than regions or federated units but less than states. During the 1990s, there was a lot of excitement about the idea of Europe of the Regions. This was an elusive concept that tended to confuse quite different things. One was an effort by the European Commission to manage spatial development and put in place policies to balance the centripetal tendencies of the single market. The main instruments were limitations on state aids to industry, which were confined to poor regions, and development funding provided by the Commission itself under the Structural Funds. A second element was the effort by regional governments to overcome their own marginalisation by getting access to EU policy-making. In the Treaty on European Union (Maastricht Treaty) they gained a right, where national law permitted, to participate as part of their national delegation in the Council of Ministers; and a consultative Committee

---

[28]  M Keating, 'Rethinking Sovereignty. Independence-lite, Devolution-max and National Accommodation' (2012) 16 *Revista d'Estudis Autonòmics i Federals* 9.

of the Regions. A third element was the aspiration to a three-level federalism, in which states, regions and the EU would all have a defined place. Finally, some idealists envisaged a Europe of the Peoples, in which states would give way to smaller communities. These elements did not comprise a coherent project and momentum stalled after Maastricht. The Committee of the Regions grouped a heterogeneous collection of federated units, regions, stateless nations and munici-palities without a common constitutional agenda. At the time of the Convention on the Future of Europe, a group of Regions with Legislative Powers emerged but made little impact in practice. During the 2000s, opportunities for non-sovereign governments to operate in European space failed to expand as policy-making become more intergovernmental.

Having failed to establish a third way, nationalist movements shifted back from post-sovereignty to independence. Plaid Cymru declared itself for full national status in Europe. The Parti Québécois abandoned sovereignty-association after the failure of the 1980 referendum. Flemish parties that had pursued federalism lost ground during the 2000s to the New Flemish Alliance, which has independ-ence as a clear, if long term, goal. After the revised Catalan statute of autonomy was partly eviscerated by the Spanish Constitutional Court, Convergència (if not Unió) made a turn to independence, demanding a referendum on the same terms as Scotland. These moves are significant but, when it comes to defining the terms of the proposed new settlement, nationalists drift back towards post-sovereigntist formulations. So Plaid Cyrmu still seeks a Europe of the Peoples. Faced with their second referendum, in 1995, the Parti Québécois agreed on a formula of sovereignty with partnership, almost indistinguishable from sovereignty associa-tion. The need for agreement with two more moderate pro-sovereignty parties (the Bloc Québécois and the Action démocratique du Québec) led to a particu-larly convoluted question. The narrow failure of the second referendum led to more debate but no definitive policy for the future. Convergència in Catalonia similarly came out with a complex and ambivalent question in two parts: asking first whether Catalonia should be a 'state'; and then whether that state should be independent. Even Esquerra Republicana de Catalunya in 2003, when it produced proposals for what an independent Catalonia would look like, had earlier opted for keeping many ties with Spain. The Scottish National Party had traditionally been in favour of full independence but its proposals in advance of the referendum of 2014 amounted to what has been described as 'independence-lite', proposing to keep the Pound Sterling in a monetary union with the United Kingdom and sharing the scientific research councils and a range of regulatory authorities.[29] Meanwhile, the Flemish parties continue in semantic games about the meaning of federalism, confederalism and independence.

---

[29] Scottish government, *Scotland's Future: Your Guide to an Independent Scotland* (Edinburgh, Scottish government, 2013).

# VII. Finding Common Ground

It does seem ironical that, in a world in which sovereignty has lost much of its meaning, political debate is so often still obsessed with the idea. There is a search for a definitive outcome in which agreement can be found on the foundations of authority, if only we dig deep enough. There are no doubt states in which this is the case, and nationhood and sovereignty are unquestioned. The states we are concerned with, however, are plurinational in the sense that there are not only multiple nationality claims, but nationality itself is interpreted differently in different places. So for people in Spain outside the historic nationalities (Catalonia, the Basque Country and Galicia), Spain is both a state and a nation. For many people within those nationalities, Spain is a state but not a nation. Others can feel an attachment to nations at both levels. The United Kingdom is in one sense simpler, since there are four nationalities, but many people in England have traditionally confused it with the United Kingdom. People in Scotland and Wales mostly have two national identities, although some do feel only British or only Scottish or Welsh. Canadians outside Quebec will insist that there is a single nation, while people in Quebec will mostly insist on two national identities, although some insist on being only Québécois. These asymmetrical identities do not lend themselves to simple constitutional formulas. There is, in the cases we have mentioned, no clear majority for independent statehood nor for the idea that they are mere regions with no more rights than other component territories of the state.

So there are differences as to the implications of nationality and about sovereignty. Traditional nationalists may insist that each nation should have its own state, but these are fluid concepts, not easily identifiable. In practice, nationalists have been more flexible. Nationalists, whether at the state or sub-state level, may insist that their preferred level is the very foundation of sovereignty but this, as we have seen, only leads to semantic arguments and to debates with no conclusion.

It is more fruitful to marry the normative debate on self-determination to a constructivist approach to the social and political actors and issues, seeing the debate as a series of ontological and normative claims, which have greater or lesser plausibility. There is no one fundamental principle against which these claims can be measured. Rather, the tests to be applied are cumulative and include the existence of a defined territory, a historic evolution, shared identity and will to be self-governing. To these, we might nowadays add respect for internal minorities. In some instances, there is little debate and the issue of self-determination is not problematic. This is the case in many established cases and in some secessions like that of Norway from Sweden in the early-twentieth century. In others, claims are made which do not correspond to the sociological reality or any plausible historical account, such as the notion that Padania (the imaginary homeland of Italy's Northern League) is a historic nation. In between are cases that seem to meet some criteria and not others. In these cases, compromises can be made.

# VIII.  Unbundling Territory

Self-determination claims are almost invariably based upon a territory, which in some cases is clearly defined but more often is disputed. Traditional thinking presents this as an insoluble conundrum, given the physical nature of territory. Partition of territories has proved an unstable solution, since the dividing lines are always arbitrary and disputed. Moving populations to fit the territory is now seen as ethically unacceptable. Modern understandings of territory, however, allow it to be seen in more complex ways, allowing it to be shared and to take different borders according to the task in question.

The territorial element of self-determination claims itself has a number of components, including sovereignty, ownership, settlement and access.[30] Places may also have a symbolic importance. In some cases it may be possible to align these meanings of territory, as in the ideal-type nation-state. In some cases, there is a core territory but dispute about how far it extends. So Basque self-government demands have been realised within the autonomous community under the Spanish Constitution but there is a broader concept of Euskal Herria, which includes Navarre and three provinces in France. The autonomous community of Catalonia comprises a historically institutionalised unit but the concept of the Països Catalans, based on linguistic and cultural criteria, is much wider. Brussels is territorially surrounded by Flanders and claimed by Flemish nationalists, but is predominantly French-speaking. As one moves further east into Europe, the drawing of lines becomes increasingly fraught.

There are communities that share a territory but are politically divided. Sometimes these include national minorities, that is groups which have a political affinity with the majority in a neighbouring state. In Northern Ireland, the community is divided on allegiance to two neighbouring states. Euskal Herria reaches across two states. Central and Eastern Europe contains many apparently stranded national minorities. Such situations are intractable within the traditional view of territory as closed space belonging to one integrated national-institutional community or another. Shifting the boundaries only creates more minorities. More fundamentally, it does not address the complexities of identities in these cases, where people rarely identify simply and uniquely with their kin-state. The national minorities of Central and Eastern Europe have varying degrees of allegiance to their putative kin-states and their mobilisation is often the consequence of political entrepreneurship.[31]

---

[30] A Buchanan and M Moore (eds), *The Making and Unmaking of Boundaries* (Cambridge, Cambridge University Press, 2003).

[31] R Brubaker, *Nationalism Reframed: Nationhood and the National Question in the New Europe* (Cambridge, Cambridge University Press, 1996).

One response might be non-territorial forms of accommodation but this is not enough. Demands do not merely concern the right to practise a culture or speak a language but extend to the boundaries of political community and broader political identities. Yet a more open conception of territory can allow us to unpack its various dimensions and allow different territorial expressions to each. An elaborate version of this is the Northern Ireland settlement, which allows people to choose their own imagined community, be it Northern Ireland, the island of Ireland or the United Kingdom. In the Basque Country, territorial autonomy has been achieved in three provinces but there is a provision allowing the autonomous community to merge with Navarre, in contrast to the general prohibition on autonomous communities merging or federating. There are complex ways in which the imagined community can be extended into France, taking into account that Basqueness itself is felt very differently in the various component territories.[32] The point about these various arrangements is that they are not territorial in the traditional sense, establishing bounded spaces, but neither are they non-territorial. Rather they employ territory in complex ways to allow institution-building, functional capacity and identity all to be accommodated. This is not to say that they always work well. Belgium, with its complex constitutional arrangements, is riddled with veto points and the electoral and party systems tend to entrench community divisions. It is not clear how the Northern Ireland settlement will develop including, as it does, two opposed visions about the *telos*. The Dayton arrangement for Bosnia and Herzegovina incorporates consociational elements which give vetoes to rent-seeking elites. Yet, properly designed, they allow for evolving relationships among territory, function and identity, rather than fixing them for all time.

Sharing of territory is also possible through cross-border cooperation and extending certain citizenship rights across borders. The success of such arrangements does not depend on eliminating borders or de-territorialising politics and institutions. On the contrary, it requires the mutual acceptance of the state border as a condition for transcending it through free movement, cultural cooperation and economic exchange. Where extending citizenship rights across the border is seen as a nationalist move, it is seen as a threat to the neighbouring state. This was the fate of Hungarian status laws, seen as part of a move by Hungarian nationalists to 'reverse Trianon'. In the Northern Ireland settlement, on the other hand, people enjoy reciprocal rights and cooperation with the understanding that the border can be changed only with the consent of the majority according to a specified procedure.

---

[32] M Keating and Z Bray, 'European Integration and the Basque Country in France and Spain' in TJ Mabry, J McGarry, M Moore and B O'Leary (eds), *Divided Nations and European Integration* (Philadelphia, University of Pennsylvania Press, 2013).

# IX.  Constitutional Pluralism

This also implies a constitutional pluralism in which competing claims to sovereignty can be managed, as long as the working of government is not made impossible. Instead, there is a suspension of disbelief and agreement to disagree. So one could argue that it really does not matter if Catalonia wants to call itself a nation but the rest of Spain does not agree. To take another contentious issue, the Basques have argued that their historic, foral rights are pre-constitutional, while the rest of Spain insists that they were extinguished and only brought in again by the 1978 Constitution, to which they are subordinate. The failure to resolve this doctrinal dispute has not caused many practical problems, although it has been used by Basque nationalists to withhold consent from the Constitution, while not boycotting its institutions. The Westminster Parliament insists that it has absolute sovereignty over the whole of the United Kingdom and that the Scottish Parliament is its creature, a view widely disputed within Scotland. We have in fact lived with a disputed interpretations of the Acts of Union for over three hundred years. Quebeckers hold to the 'two founding nations' theory and saw the 'distinct society' clause in the Meech Lake Accord as recognition of this, while many people in the rest of Canada saw it as a violation of civic equality. It is difficult so see how the latter could have been materially disadvantaged by it.

Another helpful move is to take these debates away from ontological debates about nations and history and on to the terrain of democracy, seeking shared values in the democratic principle. This was the gist of the judgment of the Supreme Court of Canada in the Quebec secession case of 1998.[33] While agreeing that the Constitution did not give Quebec a right to secede unilaterally, the Court declared that if any province decided in a referendum that it wanted to do so, then Canada was bound to negotiate in good faith. It subjected this to the provisions that there be a clear question and a clear majority, influenced by the ambiguous question and narrow majority in the referendum of 1995, although one might argue that there are no clear questions in this field. A similar approach was taken by the government of the United Kingdom in 2012, when it recognised the political reality that the Scottish National Party had won a majority in the Scottish elections with a pledge to hold a referendum. Without conceding that the Scottish Parliament had the right to stage such a referendum, it passed enabling legislation at Westminster allowing it to do so within a specific time period. As the Scottish government had argued that it did have the power to hold a referendum on the principle of independence, the issue of constitutionality was not resolved so much as side-stepped. What neither of these moves did, however, was recognise that Quebec or Scotland could negotiate a 'third way' between independence and union.

---

[33] *Quebec Secession Reference* [1998] 2 SCR 217.

In Spain, there has been less progress. Successive Spanish governments and parliaments and the Spanish Constitutional Court have insisted that referendums on independence in Catalonia and the Basque Country would be unconstitutional whatever the electoral mandate in those territories. This is derived from the doctrine that all authority stems from the Constitution of 1978 and an unwillingness even to consider amending it. The result is a confrontation that, at the time of writing, does not seem to have a solution.

A degree of constitutional pluralism can thus be a stabilising force in disputed nationality claims, especially where the claims are not for statehood in the classic sense but for new forms of divided authority; but it is not a panacea. This assumes, of course, that there is security, which constitutional subtlety on its own cannot supply, and that actors are prepared to compromise. It is a form of liberal democratic politics rather than the answer to polarisation and violence, which themselves have multiple social and political causes. Nor does constitutional pluralism resolve the distributive questions that are, at least partially, driving the territorial nationalisms of Europe. These require other, complementary approaches and are addressed elsewhere as part of the debate about rescaling and state transformation.[34]

---

[34] Keating (n 3).

Re-Thinking the Constitutional State

Controlling the Constitutional State

# 4

# Sub-State Nations and Strong States: The Accommodation Impasse?

STEPHEN TIERNEY

## I. Introduction

The emergence of sub-state nationalism since the 1960s continues to puzzle despite the close attention it has received from historians, political scientists and sociologists for nearly 50 years. A basic conundrum remains: why should nationalist sentiment have strengthened below the level of the state not only within Western European states but also and increasingly in Africa and Asia, when the currency of nationalism itself was so tainted in the first half of the twentieth century and when the principal economic and political dynamics of the post-war period have been the pooling of national sovereignty, most prominently within new international organisations and economic communities?

The continuing political impetus of the 1960s wave of nationalist parties in the UK, Belgium and Spain may seem even more incongruous today as the integrative trajectory of the EU continues to broaden and deepen.[1] The nationalist movements which emerged half a century ago did so against the backdrop of a still resilient system of European 'nation'-states. The European Communities were the result of a modest treaty system of six states to which the UK and Spain had not even subscribed. The European Union after the Lisbon Treaty, and now embracing 28 Member States, is of course far more state-like in institutional organisation and policy competence, which acts increasingly to restrict the Westphalian prerogatives of its constituent members. And the EU is of course only part of the story. The European Convention of Human Rights, under the auspices of the Council of Europe, has extended its influence with a vastly expanding caseload, no opt-out of judicial oversight for new member states, a more assertive homogenisation strategy effected in part by tightly delimiting the operation of the margin

[1] J Weiler, 'Catalonian Independence and the European Union' (2012) 23 *European Journal International Law* 909.

of appreciation doctrine,[2] and an increasingly expansive interpretation of the Convention's articles, not least in relation to extra-territorial jurisdiction.[3] To consolidate these developments the EU and Council of Europe regimes now cooperate to an unprecedented degree, with human rights in particular opening up an area of shared jurisdiction. And beyond Europe we see other international institutions broaden and deepen the range of their competences, creating a matrix[4] of supranational authority, which some see as proto-constitutional,[5] which further contracts the once exclusive space of state jurisdiction.

Together these developments scarcely seem to offer a propitious environment within which sub-state nationalist movements can formulate new state-like ambitions. And it is unsurprising that most constitutional scholars interested in such matters, rather than focusing upon constitutional aspirations below the state, have become preoccupied with the trend towards, or at least the idea of, 'global constitutionalism'.[6] And this is merely the institutional setting for the more pronounced dimension of globalisation which is the spread of the private sphere as provider of formerly public goods and the internationalisation of this service-provision through transnational corporations and joint ventures with the protection and promotion of powerful states.[7]

But despite this apparent diminution in state-centred political power and jurisdictional authority, sub-state nationalism as a political force in Belgium, Spain and the UK, as well as in Quebec, far from dissipating, is in many ways stronger than ever. The result is something of a paradox: a deeply unsettled international environment in which we see the weakening of the state's capacity to govern and where the supranational drive to move competences increasingly beyond the level of the state must, it seems, affect sub-state territories no less than existing states. But instead of accepting the declining salience of territory as a political currency, sub-state nationalists continue to demand statehood or at least 'state-like' autonomy, often praying in aid as a reason for these sub-state constitutional aspirations the very globalising forces which seem to undermine the state as a constitutional enterprise. How can these seemingly contradictory phenomena be reconciled?

---

[2] K Dzehtsiarou, 'European Consensus and the Evolutive Interpretation of the European Convention on Human Rights' (2011) 12 *German Law Journal* 1730; J Kratochvíl, 'The Inflation of the Margin of Appreciation by the European Court of Human Rights' (2011) 29 *Netherlands Quarterly of Human Rights* 324. See Mac Amlaigh's chapter in this book.

[3] *Al-Skeini and others v United Kingdom* (2011) 53 EHRR 18; *Al-Jedda v United Kingdom* (2011) 53 EHRR 23.

[4] N Walker, J Shaw and S Tierney (eds), *Europe's Constitutional Mosaic* (Oxford, Hart Publishing, 2011).

[5] D Sarooshi, *International Organizations and their Exercise of Sovereign Powers* (New York, Oxford University Press, 2005).

[6] J Dunoff and J Trachtman (eds), *Ruling the World?: Constitutionalism, International Law and Global Governance* (Cambridge, Cambridge University Press, 2009).

[7] See J Tully, 'On Law, Democracy and Imperialism' in E Christodoulidis and S Tierney (eds), *Public Law and Politics: The Scope and Limits of Constitutionalism* (Aldershot, Ashgate 2008).

One clue, it would seem, lies in the nuance of this last point—'state-like' autonomy. In this respect we need to reconsider the very term 'nationalist' when applied to sub-state political movements. First, 'nationalist' is not a synonym for 'separatist' but instead needs to be extended to those political actors who assert the existence of a sub-state 'nation' but seek improved constitutional accommodation for the sub-state national territory within the state. We see this in the Quebec Liberal Party and the Scottish Labour Party etc. Even the Scottish Conservative Party, a firmly unionist organisation, accepted the legitimacy of the independence referendum in 2014 and is now a firm supporter of devolution, arguing for further powers for the Scottish Parliament.[8]

Secondly, even those parties which are 'independentist' in outlook often present very nuanced aspirations. When the detail of political manifestos are examined what we frequently find are agendas which, defying the stereotypes often associated with these groups, cannot in any meaningful way be described as separatist. In fact, they often propose versions of autonomy which challenge the state to share areas of sovereignty, and to work towards what are in some ways confederal arrangements. A recent example is the Scottish government's proposal for 'independence' which also suggested that currency and social unions ought to remain in place between Scotland and the UK.[9] This point is often missed by those who dismiss these movements in a pejorative way as outmoded and revanchist, failing to analyse their political goals in any detail. In fact, it is often more accurate to locate the aims of 'independentist' or 'sovereignist' parties at the interstices between the remaining prerogatives available to states to develop their own domestic policies on the one hand, and on the other, the opportunities for territories—including sub-state territories—to operate at the international level, seeking to exert leverage through an engaged approach to the new sites of interdependence between the national and international levels.[10]

In this chapter I seek to cast light on the continuing political relevance of sub-state nationalism in two ways. In section II, I demonstrate just how the constitutional aspirations of these movements are often the subject of simplistic misrepresentation. I begin by suggesting more broadly that the nation itself and its historical trajectory have often been misconstrued, which is a key backdrop to the ongoing misunderstanding of its sub-state variant. I argue that these sub-state movements are not outliers in relation to the deeper and wider trends of globalisation but are in many ways in tune with these globalising dynamics. This can be seen in understandings of constitutional doctrine, in particular sovereignty. I use examples from contemporary nationalism to make this case, and to show that often it is the mindset of the central state that is more beholden to outmoded

---

[8] Smith Commission, *Report of the Smith Commission for Further Devolution of Powers to the Scottish Parliament* (Smith Commission Agreement) (27 November 2014).

[9] Scottish government, 'Your Scotland—Your Referendum—A Consultation Document' (Edinburgh, Scottish government White Paper, 2012).

[10] M Keating, *Nations against the State—The New Politics of Nationalism in Quebec, Catalonia and Scotland* 2nd edn (London, Palgrave, 2001).

visions of the unitary nature of sovereignty, and that takes a more outmoded stance vis-a-vis its international environment.

Secondly, in section III, I further suggest that the notion of a post-state age is something of an overstatement. Although international institutions are growing in range and authority, this is still a partial development, felt more in Europe than elsewhere. In other ways, particularly in the developing world, we are seeing a hardening of the state and a growing assertiveness that comes with economic development.[11] This is facilitated by a system of international law which, although in some ways playing host to new or more expansive international institutions, has nonetheless been built by states through a body of rules and models of institutional design and of rule-making which remain highly state-centric, ensuring that such roles that do remain the preserve of sovereign territories belong exclusively to states which are inclined to exercise these in a monistic manner, excluding any meaningful role for sub-state territories.

As a final point of introduction I would like to make a plea for enhanced interdisciplinarity. In order better to understand these dynamics it is important to bring more closely together scholarship on global constitutionalism and that relating to sub-state national constitutionalism. Within each we can identify comparable lines of empirical enquiry and normative concern. In empirical terms each is addressing, albeit from different perspectives, the realignment of traditional conceptions of state sovereignty. Scholars of global constitutionalism examine how the state's sovereign capacity and competence is diminishing,[12] while those addressing sub-state nationalism engage with how these territories are trying to re-imagine the very idea of state sovereignty as something that can be pooled or even pluralised across the same political space.[13] And both are also alive to similar normative concerns, particularly the democratic challenge of maintaining an unbroken chain of representation and accountability between citizens on the one hand and, on the other, whichever polity or decision-making body is making policy that affects citizens' lives in an era where political accountability does not necessarily follow the movement of political and constitutional competences away from the state.

Combining different fields of study, embracing also political science and the sociology of nationalism, will also help us explore the extent to which the dual dynamics of the current international order—the globalising trends which diminish the role of the state, and the institutional underpinnings of international law which still leave the state, albeit a weakened one, as the only game in town for either resisting or managing this transference of power—have created a path dependency for the seemingly schizophrenic constitutional aspirations of sub-state national societies: in reality seeking reformed constitutional unions, but in practice having to advance an agenda of independent statehood. It is no surprise

---

[11]  See Asanga Welikala's chapter in this book.

[12]  Dunoff and Trachtman, *Ruling the World* (n 6).

[13]  S Tierney, 'Reframing Sovereignty: Sub-State National Societies and Contemporary Challenges to the Nation-State' (2005) 54 *International and Comparative Law Quarterly* 161.

that observers will be confused by this. But sub-state nationalists have to manage their aspirations within an environment where both domestic constitutional structures and the international order of states are not receptive to radical constitutional re-thinking. In reality, the more complex forms of union and shared sovereignty which they often seek do not fit well with either of the binary options on offer: traditional models of limited decentralisation on the one hand or full statehood on the other. Given the resilience of the state-centric nature of the international order and, in some parts of the world, the hardening of the state as its power is challenged by international developments, national independence can become the only realistic model for significant change.

## II. Misconceiving Nationalism: The Functionalist Account of the Nation and the Globalising Environment

In order to explain better how contemporary sub-state nationalism is often misunderstood it is necessary to see these misconceptions as part of a broader stereotyping and oversimplification of national identity as a social phenomenon and nationalism as a political project. There is a tendency among observers of sub-state nationalism today to fall back upon those teleological accounts which have traditionally situated nationalism and national identity on a pathological trajectory from nineteenth-century utility to twenty-first-century redundancy.

This account has some resonance, particularly in Europe, where the role and capacity of the nation-state is certainly changing, but as many scholars of nationalism have shown, it is over-stated and in need of considerable qualification.[14] It is certainly the case that the instrumentalism of the nation was a key element in the triumph of nationalism as a major political ideology in the nineteenth century. The changing technological landscape of Europe which offered economies of scale, coupled with the imperial opportunities open to the emergent continental powers, encouraged the creation of larger states; the nation became the adhesive binding the new state together.

And it is precisely this functionalism of the state that is currently being called into question in Europe. In the developing normative environment beyond the state, the role of the state itself as comprehensive dispensary of what we might call 'the outputs of citizenship' is diminishing. The EU's jurisdictional reach into many areas of economic and social welfare has seen it take on, or at least share with Member States, many of the traditional roles of states. And so, from an instrumentalist conception of the nation and of its institutional embodiment in the state, it

---

[14] See John Breuilly's chapter in this book.

must inevitably be asked: is the nation-state, once the exclusive depository for the identity and loyalty of the citizen, also destined to wither as the state ceases to offer the portmanteau of services it once did?

But, as I say, within nationalist theory we find that the instrumentalist account has in fact been qualified in important ways over the past four decades or so. What the work of scholars from what we might call the LSE school[15] has proven is that the nation itself is a more complex repository for personal identity and social attachment than a simple functionalist account would allow, and that in historical terms its origins in some cases clearly preceded nineteenth-century industrialisation. The nation-state did not in most cases invent the nation out of nothing, it built upon pre-existing forms of collective identity and in some cases already well-established national, or if preferred, proto-national, collective attachments; nations were to be forged but the process was in some cases more one of welding than smelting.

Here the work of Anthony Smith is particularly illuminating. Smith accepts that the material conditions of modernity played a dramatic role in the shaping of contemporary national identities but also suggests that central to a fuller understanding of national identity is an appreciation of the resilience of older attachments which have endured in the process of identity formation within ethnic groups (or 'ethnies' as he would have it), something missed in the instrumentalist accounts of, among others, Ernest Gellner which 'fail to account for the historical depth and spatial reach of the ties that underpin modern nations because they have no theory of ethnicity and its relationship to modern nationalism'.[16] And in the 'post-modern' age when the nation-state is itself facing increasing pressure, the functionalist account seems in many ways less, rather than more, instructive.

Nor has national identity been subordinated to other attachments. Coming into being in the modern period, nationalism found itself challenged by the other great ideological movements of the age, liberalism and socialism. But nationalism as the underpinning ideology of the state has not been supplanted by these cosmopolitan creeds. Nor are national identities transferable by virtue of such political commitments. One may look admiringly at the Scandinavian economic model but it does not make the citizen feel more Swedish and less English.

And in this light, the levels of identity and loyalty which came with nation-building cannot be seen in retrospect as a simple utilitarian barter. The nation-state encouraged the acquisition of patriotic loyalty and totems and symbols came to encapsulate this. This endeavour was remarkably successful as people came to identify with the nation in deep and inter-generational ways. The upshot is that

---

[15] J Breuilly, *Nationalism and the State* 2nd edn (Manchester, Manchester University Press, 1993); J Hutchinson, *Modern Nationalism* (London, Fontana Press, 1994); AD Smith, *Nationalism and Modernism: a Critical Survey of Recent Theories of Nations and Nationalism* (London/New York, Routledge, 1998).

[16] Smith, *Nationalism and Modernism* (n 15) 46. See the debate between Smith and Gellner in *Nations and Nationalism* (1996) vol 2, issue 3.

these attachments are not necessarily lightly tossed aside by citizens even as the functional utility of the state, in Europe at least, diminishes.

And nation-building also took place below the state. The emergence and resilience of sub-state nations has helped fuel further deconstructions of the functionalist story of the development of national identity in the modern era. A number of sub-state national societies, far from disappearing in the face of statal nation-building, embarked upon processes of nation-building similar to those occurring at host state level throughout the nineteenth and twentieth centuries. The examples already discussed from Canada, Spain and the UK are the most clear, where distinctive societies such as Quebec, Catalonia, the Basque Country, Scotland, Ireland and Wales survived and modernised, in certain cases by fostering a linguistic culture (mainly Quebec, Catalonia, the Basque Country and Wales), but also by developing modern institutions of civic society and, where possible, distinct governmental and legal institutions. These sub-state processes of nation-building, and indeed the resilience of sub-state national identities in general, were largely ignored in the broader construction of the modern nation-state and its constitutional apparatus.[17] Indeed one lacuna in Smith's own work is that he does not take seriously the notion of plural processes of nation-building within the state.[18] But history has shown that the cultural and societal homogeneity which was sought for in the construction of states composed of more than one emerging nation—and which would make sense by the functionalist account—could not always be achieved since such homogeneity did not exist in fact, and efforts to create it were successfully resisted by resilient sub-state national societies.

Quietly, rival processes of sub-state civic nation-building evolved within these territories, processes which would later result in the strong nationalist movements which emerged towards the end of the twentieth century. And so the background to today's relationship between globalisation and nationalism is one in which multiple processes of modern nation-building took place within certain states, creating polities within which different internal territories engage with a globalising normative order in different ways.

Although it is now clear that multiple processes of nation-building took place in some states in the nineteenth century or earlier, notably in Spain and the UK, it has still become common to treat these processes as expressions of some form of pre-modern or indigenous identity that modernism had somehow passed by—the nations that time forgot. By this image the resilience of sub-state nationalism is hard to explain. Why are outdated models of nationalism emerging into the light in a post-national age? But this characterisation is a long way from the social reality of the sub-state nationalist politics which remains politically pertinent today in, for example, Scotland and Catalonia. Here very modern and in some ways

---

[17] Quebec's 19th-century constitutional history is a partial exception to this generality, as is Catalonia's emerging status under the first Spanish Republic in 1873.

[18] See A Welikala, 'Beyond the Liberal Paradigm: The Constitutional Accommodation of National Pluralism in Sri Lanka' (PhD thesis, University of Edinburgh, 2014).

post-modern political movements have consolidated and grown over the past five decades.

Despite the very modern approaches we find in the political goals of national-ist movements in, for example, Scotland, Catalonia and Quebec, the term nation remains a central feature of this political development. These movements have advanced a self-conscious and categorical distinction between their own territories on the one hand and regions on the other, and between their own constitutional agenda and that of regionalism. For regionalism itself and the push to decentralise ran in parallel to the rise of sub-state nationalism, but sub-state nationalists are at pains to distinguish themselves from regional variants, asserting in particular state-like ambitions rather than aspirations for regional autonomy.

The reality therefore of multiple nation-building projects taking place within the one state has required scholars to disaggregate the nation and the state which came to be elided in many of the oversimplified instrumentalist accounts. The work of different strands of scholarship in recent decades has been illuminating here. This work not only challenges the instrumental account in empirical terms, it also refutes some of the negative caricatures of the nation and national identity as undemocratic, dangerous and unfit for purpose in an age of state transforma-tion, which have tended to flow from this account.

We saw the first challenge to this stereotype in the work of sociologists who have since the 1960s demonstrated the resilience of national identity at the sub-state level even within Western, democratic polities where much of the debate on dimin-ishing nationalism has focused. This research also found that national identities within sub-state nations were, in a similar way to state nationalist variants, based increasingly upon civic rather than ethnic markers of belonging.[19] These sub-state forms of nationalism continue to prove very resilient, as nationalist movements in, for example, Scotland and Catalonia, continue to show, even though an age of global communications seems to draw the world closer together in cultural terms.[20] Another feature of nationalism today is that people can also hold multiple identities—Scottish and British for example.

Secondly, research by political scientists generally supports these findings. What we find is that the political aims of these nationalist movements are, contrary to many negative stereotypes, not atavistic or romantic but in fact are well in tune with contemporary democratic attitudes to social policy, civic conceptions of citi-zenship and universal human rights standards.[21] In Europe, these movements are also well acclimatised to the shifting of power beyond the state; in fact, nationalists

---

[19] D McCrone, *Understanding Scotland: The Sociology of a Nation* 2nd edn (London, Routledge, 2001).

[20] S Dion, 'Le nationalisme dans la convergence culturelle: le Québec contemporain et le paradoxe de Tocqueville' in R Hudon and R Pelletier (eds), *L'engagement intellectuel: Mélange en l'honneur de Léon Dion* (Québec, Presses de l'Université Laval, 1991).

[21] Keating, *Nations against the State* (n 10); AG Gagnon and J Tully (eds), *Multinational Democracies* (Cambridge, Cambridge University Press, 2001).

in Scotland, Catalonia and Quebec have developed political strategies—such as the SNP's 'Independence in Europe' approach—that are as or more pro-integration than the states to which they belong.[22] In other words, the new nationalism was found to fit consistently within the 'progressive' trend of modern politics, further undermining any link between these movements and the forms of state national-ism of the early-twentieth century which tarnished the name of nationalism in general.

Another related development has been in political theory, most notably liberal political theory, where a new school of 'liberal nationalist' thinkers has called into question the idea that nationalism and liberalism are inherently incompatible. A leader in the field is Will Kymlicka. He has argued that sub-state nationalism can be wholly consistent with liberalism and that in fact liberal states have a duty to accommodate these political and constitutional aspirations if it is to be true to its own values of liberty and equality.[23] Individual people advance their own life goals through the societal culture to which they belong, and only if the societal culture is accommodated will their individual rights of equality and liberty be secured.[24]

Inevitably it will be asked why these dynamics continue to develop even within Europe at a time of further integration at state level. Various reasons have been advanced such as end of empire, the collapse of communism, the end of the welfare-state consensus etc. But as Michael Keating has suggested, none of these reasons are sufficient in themselves.[25] Instead it seems we need to look closely at the detailed political conditions, both those which affect sub-state nations and regions in general and those specific to each state, in order to understand why nationalist movements, as political parties, have been successful in gaining popular support. I have noted that independence claims may be partly path-dependent. A core con-cern of citizens, which extends beyond the rhetoric of political parties, is that their national society is able to set its own societal priorities. In a sense of course many nationalists are trying to join the club from which they had been excluded, namely the community of states, but there was and remains no hard and fast line between the constitutional aspirations for autonomy and for statehood. We see this par-ticularly in the attitudes of citizens who are often more interested in territorial autonomy in relation to certain sectoral concerns than with the constitutional apparatus. This has certainly been the case in Scotland where nationalists lost the

[22] M Keating, *Plurinational Democracy: Stateless Nations in a Post-Sovereignty Era* (Oxford, Oxford University Press, 2001).

[23] W Kymlicka, *Multicultural Citizenship: A Liberal Theory of Minority Rights* (Oxford, Oxford University Press, 1995); M Moore, 'Normative Justifications for Liberal Nationalism: Justice, Democracy and National Identity' (2001) 7 *Nations and Nationalism* 1; F Requejo (ed), *Democracy and National Pluralism* (London, Routledge, 2001).

[24] W Kymlicka, *Politics in the Vernacular* (Oxford, Oxford University Press, 2001); S Tierney, 'The Search for a New Normativity: Thomas Franck, Post-Modern Neo-Tribalism and the Law of Self-Determination' (2002) 13 *European Journal of International Law* 941.

[25] Keating, *Plurinational Democracy* (n 22).

independence referendum in September 2014 but where opinion polls show that a majority of people are in favour of further, and in many ways radical, levels of devolution.[26]

When nationalism is broken down in this way—reflecting a form of functionalism rather than a binary choice between one of two national selves—it appears less obviously incongruous in the context of globalising trends. In fact, globalisation can itself be seen in a parallel, functionalist sense. The extension of competences to the EU, for example, has taken place incrementally, and most often for functional purposes, either to support the free market, facilitate enlargement or to face international competition.

When viewed through a functionalist lens it seems that sub-state nationalism has emerged not so much in direct tension with broader global trends, but at least in part because of them. In fact, sub-state nationalist movements are developing highly imaginative strategies and progressive political agendas in the face of these globalising forces; and these strategies and agendas require a re-thinking of traditional constitutional doctrines given the ways in which these sub-state movements envisage radical reconfigurations in the state polity(ies). It is notable that when sub-state nationalists do make radical claims for divided sovereignty, for power over policy sectors such as tax, immigration and foreign policy, or for access to international relations, the generally negative reaction of states can serve to show that it is often they who are least well acclimatised to a reorganisation of constitutional competences, on functional bases, both above and below the level of the state.

Certainly the lesson of the past 10 years seems to be that sub-state nations are finding that their claims to shared sovereignty within the state fall upon deaf ears. In countries such as Spain the state increasingly asserts a hard line between devolved arrangements and independence, and that is only in the Western world; the experience elsewhere is even more pronounced.[27]

## III. The Wounded State: The Backlash Against Pluralism

In this light some of the claims concerning the demise of the state are clearly exaggerated. As David McCrone reminds us: 'It is too facile to claim that, in a globalised world, the age of the state is dead',[28] although he qualifies this by also observing that it is also now much harder to sustain the argument that the state is all-powerful. Perhaps the main reason for the state's resilience is its control of

---

[26] J Curtice, 'So Where Does Scotland Stand on More Devolution?' (ScotCen Social Research, 2013).
[27] See Welikala's chapter in this book.
[28] D McCrone, 'Neo-Nationalism in Stateless Nations' (2001) 37 *Scottish Affairs* 3, 11.

territory and the continuing normative authority which comes with territorial jurisdiction. International law, essentially a state system, remains a powerful force in their defence. There is also a strong functional dimension to territorial control; territory remains a key focus for the link within liberal democracies between political representation and political accountability.[29]

Europe can distort our sense of the state's enduring strengths, but even here we should qualify the notion that the impact of European integration is a simple linear story leading to the slow death of the state. As we consider the implications of an integrating EU for sub-state nations and regions within states, at least three factors are relevant. I will consider first, the statal origins of the European Communities, a provenance which continues to exert an influence on its future trajectory; ongoing processes of integration which although arguably supplanting this state-based foundation, have also in recent times come into considerable tension with the statist mentality of its members; and thirdly, the approach the EU has taken to regions which, to say the least, has not provided fertile ground for territorial polities below the level of the state to develop any serious role within European institutions.

In terms of origins, the relationship between the institutions of the European Union and its Member States may be changing, but it is still exclusively a binary relationship. This is embedded in the mentality that remains one of interaction between the institutions and the states. States retain considerable constitutional competences; it might not seem that way to states, but it is starkly clear to regions within them. These at times may seem fictional, but at moments of crisis or even disquiet it is clear that they can be called upon to upset the centralising trajectory of the Brussels institutions. And one potential problem for the EU is that it is not the only polity that is changing; states themselves are increasingly challenged by citizens to improve the democratic legitimacy of decision-making and the transparency and behaviour of elected representatives. And this disquiet with the state of democracy within states has also led to demands for a greater popular role in decision-making. This has had two knock-on consequences for the EU. The first is that the contrast with the deeply undemocratic nature of the Union becomes ever more clear. Secondly, it has opened the door to state prerogatives—particularly that of treaty ratification—to the people, who when offered the opportunity are increasingly prepared to stand up to their own elites as we have seen in referendums, most dramatically in the French and Dutch referendums on the draft Constitutional Treaty.[30]

The spread of the referendum as a mechanism of constitutional amendment across a number of Member States may yet be something of a time-bomb for the Union. We see this already with the UK which edges closer to a referendum on the

---

[29] AG Gagnon, 'Quebec: The Emergence of a Region-State?' (2001) 37 *Scottish Affairs* 14, 24.

[30] M Qvortrup, 'The Three Referendums on the European Constitution Treaty 2005' (2006) 77 *Political Quarterly* 89.

very subject of membership. The soundings from Brussels on this are increasingly bullish, suggesting no attempt to alter British terms of membership as a sweetener. But for all the bluster, the secession of the UK would be a blow to the prestige of the Union, would see the exit of one of the largest and richest members, and may well unsettle other states. The alternative, a re-working of the UK's commitments, might well be equally unsettling in different ways. This comes on top of other problems. The Euro crisis seems to have hardened the resolve of integrationists to centralise further its institutional structure and areas of competence, for example over fiscal policy through the Fiscal Compact. But this has led to further disquiet among Member States which are feeling the full effect of austerity measures. As states are further squeezed, there is evidence, for example from Greece, that political movements will mobilise to protect the remaining powers of the state.

A second issue is that recent processes of integration, while accruing more powers to the centre, have also met considerable resistance as we saw in the French and Dutch processes. In many ways this was an internal rebellion against not only EU elites but also domestic elites who were attempting to push through treaty changes.[31] But these events do remind us that treaty ratification remains a process requiring Member State unanimity, and with the referendum now out of the box as a mechanism which many citizens expect as part of the ratification process, we may begin to see a stronger national assertiveness emerge.

A third factor, from the perspective below the state, is that regionalism has been a non-event within the EU, and there seems no prospect of it being taken more seriously as the Union faces more pressing problems today. The state may be weakening within the EU but it is still the only other game in town. Attempts at regionalisation, such as the Committee of the Regions, have not significantly altered the status of regions and nor have we seen any meaningful devolution of competences to regions. Any sub-state territory with strong constitutional ambitions, looking beyond the traditional conceptions of sovereignty both within and beyond the state, comes up against the reality that only states have any serious representation within the EU, only states can join the EU, the process to new membership is not easy, and any new state looking to join requires the approval of all existing states including the one they are leaving.

Beyond the EU, general international law clearly remains a state-based system. One interesting example is that of the treaty-making process, since if we are to draw an analogy in international law to the type of competences sub-state nations seek within the state then law-making would be an obvious area. A sub-state nation, in forming aspirations short of statehood which include an international presence through what is sometimes called paradiplomacy, may seek some role in international treaty-making. This may be facilitated by the state, permitting the territory to act on the state's behalf in negotiations with other states, or to transact with

---

[31] P Taggart, 'Questions of Europe—The Domestic Politics of the 2005 French and Dutch Referendums and their Challenge for the Study of European Integration' (2006) 44 *Journal of Common Market Studies* 7.

other sub-state territories which themselves have the domestic competence to do so, or underwriting as it were any treaties made by the territory with other states. But when it comes to processes of international treaty-making, the structure of international law simply does not offer a role for such territories. Only states make treaties and only states are represented in the institutions where international laws are made. We see this in the general failure of NGOs (non-governmental organisations) to make much headway into the process of international law-making. NGOs are often the focus of attention by those who consider there to be a pluralisation of actors in international affairs because for some they have been relatively successful in influencing the international law-making process. In fact, such a role varies greatly from one process to another, tends to take place only in technical areas or human rights areas where powerful and some might say hegemonic Western NGOs are able to exercise their relative wealth and power, and even in these cases is often marginal, and always indirect.[32] Most obviously, such bodies do not, and cannot, have voting rights, since treaty-making remains a state-based activity.

And in general we see within states themselves a clear reluctance to try to broaden out international agency to sub-state territories. As sub-state nationalists attempt to negotiate greater prerogatives within states, or seek novel forms of 'union state' arrangement, it is increasingly clear that some areas are off-limits either for devolution or for more complicated arrangements of shared sovereignty. In this category we can include defence, foreign relations and at least certain aspects of macro-economic policy. This is no surprise to students of federalism, where these issues are the core preserve of the centre in all or almost all federal states today.

A case study is the recent proposal for independence for Scotland. On 18 September 2014, 55 per cent of Scots voted no to the proposition: 'Should Scotland be an Independent Country?'. During the campaign attention focused upon major substantive issues of contention such as currency relations between an independent Scotland and the United Kingdom, and the ease or difficulty with which an independent Scotland would achieve membership of the European Union. We saw in the course of the campaign that there were a number of lines in the sand for the British state concerning how much more it is prepared to devolve, and more pertinently share, authority over such issues. In fact the dynamic became one whereby the SNP proposed a model of independence that fell short of a traditional idea of full statehood—in its proposals of currency union and social union—while the UK government emphasised that a vote for independence would be for a very traditional model of the Westphalian system. It does indeed seem that for states there is a limit to how much they are prepared to cede power, and that for sub-state nations to gain radical powers may lead them to conclude that statehood is the only alternative.

---

[32] A Boyle and C Chinkin, *The Making of International Law* (Oxford, Oxford University Press, 2007).

This echoes the Quebec referendum of 1995 of course where Quebec offered sovereignty and partnership and the federal state said, no you can have one or the other but not both. The ironic situation that emerged in the Scottish case, as it did in Canada twenty years ago, was that the Yes side were in effect asking for a partnership with the rest of the UK, putting forward a model of independence which did not look like Westphalian statehood, but in response the UK state replied that in fact such an option was not on the table. If Scotland voted for independence then in could not expect close relations with the remainder of the United Kingdom unless it was in the UK's interests to agree to this.

And it is certainly the case that international law encourages, and some might say, causes states to take such an approach. When it comes to external affairs the culture of international law and relations does not lend itself to territorial pluralism within the state. We see this for example in the Vienna Convention on the Law of Treaties which for example does not accept internal law, including federalism, as an excuse for a state's failure to comply with its international obligations.[33] Membership of the EU and other international bodies is only possible with statehood. Another reason is the idea of a tipping point. The collapse of the USSR and Socialist Federeal Republic of Yugoslavia led for complicated reasons to a situation where only those territories already recognised as full republics within these federal states could apply for recognition as new states. The logic of this for states worried about centripetal tendencies is not to recognise sub-state particularity through a federal model since it could offer a slippery slope to separatism.

Another example is the attitude taken by senior figures in the European Union in relation to the Scottish independence referendum in September 2014. Former President of the European Commission, Jose Manuel Barroso, said it would be 'extremely difficult, if not impossible' for an independent Scotland to join the European Union.[34] This view was heavily criticised by observers,[35] and was neither substantiated nor elaborated upon by Mr Barroso. It should also be noted that Jean-Claude Juncker, elected on 15 July 2014 to succeed Mr Barroso as the new President of the Commission (his appointment as President took effect from 1 November 2014), was reportedly 'sympathetic' to an independent Scotland joining the EU.[36] Although Mr Juncker took the general view that there should be no further enlargement until 2019, clarification from EU officials indicated that this 'ban' on further enlargement did not apply to an application for membership by a newly independent Scotland which would be treated as a 'special and separate case'

---

[33] Vienna Convention on the Law of Treaties, (adopted 23 May 1969, entered into force on 27 January 1980). 1155 UNTS 331, Art 27: 'A party may not invoke the provisions of its internal law as justification for its failure to perform a treaty'.

[34] BBC News, 'Scottish Independence: Barroso says joining EU would be difficult' *BBC News Online* (16 February 2014).

[35] N Walker, 'Hijacking the Debate' (*Scottish Constitutional Futures Forum Blog*, 18 February 2014); S Douglas-Scott, 'Why the EU should welcome an independent Scotland' (*Scottish Constitutional Futures Forum Blog*, 11 August 2014).

[36] S MacNab, 'Juncker bans any new EU member for 5 years' *The Scotsman* (15 July 2014).

as it already meets 'core-EU requirements'.[37] But it is notable that senior figures, including leading commentators, certainly do not encourage the idea of 'enlargement from within'.[38]

What remains is a situation in which sub-state nations have been asking imaginative questions for a decade or more, but where increasingly it looks as though they are almost boxed into looking for statehood. This can be caused either by the unwillingness of the state to meet aspirations for more power as in Spain, or in part by the failure of international institutions to offer any level of personality to territories other than states. We see this also in the Catalan aspiration for a *via media* in the form of plurinational constitution-building *within* the state, which has been frustrated as much by Brussels as Madrid. An exception is the United Kingdom where the closeness of the referendum race led to a commitment by the UK government to further devolution for Scotland. Immediately before the vote, on 16 September, the main unionist parties (Conservative, Labour and Liberal Democrat) issued 'the Vow',[39] undertaking that in the event of a majority No vote they would produce agreed proposals on additional powers for the Scottish Parliament, setting out a short timeframe within which these powers would be agreed. On 19 September, the day after the referendum, Prime Minister David Cameron announced that Lord Smith of Kelvin had agreed to oversee the process to take forward this commitment to further devolution for the Scottish Parliament.[40] On 27 November, the Smith Commission published its report detailing Heads of Agreement on further devolution of powers to the Scottish Parliament and promising a range of new powers in policy areas such as taxation, welfare, employability and transport.[41] These proposals have now been published in the Scotland Bill[42] and look set to be passed into law by 2016.

And maybe this is the reality which is often missed both by the sub-state nationalist scholars and the global constitutionalists. The squeeze on statehood both from above and below has its limits. Either because the state remains strong in unexpected ways, or because it feels threatened and, leaving the UK aside as exceptional, will not allow its shrinking power to be diminished further. Here it is useful to return to the European context. It is one of the paradoxes of European integration that the regions have been given no meaningful role in the new space that has opened up. This is particularly paradoxical since many of these are vehemently pro-European in their outlook and aspiration.

---

[37] ibid. See also A Whitaker, 'Independence: Juncker "sympathetic" to Scotland EU bid' *The Scotsman* (20 July 2014).

[38] Weiler, 'Catalonian Independence and the European Union' (n 1).

[39] D Clegg, 'David Cameron, Ed Miliband and Nick Clegg sign joint historic promise which guarantees more devolved powers for Scotland and protection of NHS if we vote No' *Daily Record* (15 September 2014).

[40] UK government, 'Scottish Independence Referendum: Statement by the Prime Minister' *Press Release* (19 September 2014).

[41] Smith Commission Agreement (n 8).

[42] Scotland Bill 2015–16.

For example, it is curious that one debate concerning the referendum on independence in Scotland in 2014 focused upon whether and if so how Scotland would need to apply for membership of the EU. Sub-state nationalism becomes a phenomenon which is either misunderstood or not tolerated or both; it may well be that it is not tolerated in part because it is not understood. And, interestingly, it is often those engaged in state integration that display intolerance of sub-state nationalism as we saw in the interventions by EU figures in the Scottish referendum debate discussed above. Is sub-state nationalism really bucking the trend of international integration, or is it in fact asking the hard questions of this trend: how democratic, pluralistic and inclusive is this trend? If state sovereignty is declining why not open up space below it rather than accrue all of the power to unaccountable institutions above the state?

# IV. Conclusions

It is perhaps surprising that, in spite of the fierce grip which it has held over political praxis throughout the passing 'ages'[43] of the post-enlightenment period, nationalism developed as a subject of rigorous study by social scientists only in the last century and more specifically in the post-war period. Since then, however, its importance to the development of the modern world has been scrutinised at length, with nationalism being elevated on occasion to dizzying heights of importance. Smith for example, is assured of the pre-eminent role of the nation as a focus of identity: 'To date, we cannot discern a serious rival to the nation for the affections and loyalties of most human beings'.[44] Tom Nairn in the same vein elevates nationalism as *the* pre-eminent topic of humanistic and social scientific study, suggesting that, 'the true subject of modern philosophy might be, not industrialisation … but its immensely complex and variegated aftershock—nationalism'.[45]

Nationalism also took on new meaning after World War Two. It is easy to forget as we turn to consider a post-state age that often we have in mind those states that have existed for centuries. But these are mainly European states, the vast majority of the world's states are still in their relative infancy as are the nation-building projects which they have adopted. Nation-building processes are still playing themselves out, and the assumption that they will be subsumed within some form of political globalisation is simply not borne out by the evidence. The terrain for sub-state territories seeking to exert a stronger international presence

---

[43] EJ Hobsbawm, *Age of Revolution: Europe, 1789–1848* (London, Weidenfeld and Nicolson, 1962); EJ Hobsbawm, *Age of Capital, 1848–1875* (London, Weidenfeld and Nicolson, 1975); EJ Hobsbawm, *Age of Empire 1875–1914* (London, Weidenfeld and Nicolson, 1987); EJ Hobsbawm, *Age of Extremes: the Short Twentieth century, 1914–1991* (London, Michael Joseph, 1994).

[44] Smith, *Nationalism and Modernism* (n 16) 195.

[45] T Nairn, *Faces of Nationalism: Janus Revisited* (London, Verso, 1997) 1 (see also 17).

is, therefore, complex and challenging. On the one hand sub-state nationalists are alive to globalisation and seek to rub along with the new realities of the weakening state, but on the other hand they find the political space they wish to occupy is also space that the host state may be seeking to protect or even reclaim, retrieving such components of sovereignty it can, components which it is then reluctant to share with its own internal national societies.

I have tried to revisit the sub-state nationalist challenge to plurinational states in the context of wider forces which today operate to constrict the existing politico-constitutional capacity and competence of the nation-state. In one sense the classical Westphalian formulation of the state as a politically self-contained and legally autonomous unit was always a caricature that failed to reflect international inter-dependence and the relative strengths and weaknesses of different states at different times; and that this characterisation also served to under-estimate the existing role of sub-state territories in limiting central state authority. But this is not the whole story. This historical reality requires to be tempered by an appreciation that in many other ways the power of the nation-state endures in important respects. It is, therefore, within this complex environment of wider global change set against the endurance of state power, that the constitutional agendas of sub-state national societies require to be reformulated. Sub-state national societies are perhaps in a useful position to produce imaginative governmental strategies, given the predisposition towards constitutional change which has long informed their political practices, and given the practical opportunities which increasingly fluid normative sites now seem to offer to flexible political operators. But the terrain upon which to build these alternative approaches to sovereign power is, for now at least, less than welcoming.

# 5

# Re-Thinking Nationalism After Yugoslavia: Multi/Plurinational Regionalisms as Alternatives to Statehood

DEJAN STJEPANOVIĆ

## I. Introduction

Mention of post-Yugoslav politics in the 1990s and early-2000s evokes images of ethnic conflict, sectarian nationalism and political volatility. However, there also exist(ed) political projects in the former Yugoslav countries, in Croatia and Serbia in particular, which illustrate that the construction of polities based on exclusive and ascriptive ethnic membership was not the only way of engaging in the creation and maintenance of political peoplehood. Neither did all of these territorial projects aim at the establishment of independent states or secession in order to join neighbouring countries.

Departing from the usual 'ethnic politics' frame for analysing territorial developments in the post-Yugoslav space this chapter is a contribution to theories of nationalism and regionalism. The argument based on the references to the regionalist politics of historic regions of Dalmatia and Istria (in today's Croatia) and Vojvodina (in today's Serbia) differs from some of the literature in the field that considers autonomy as a slippery slope to secession; that the politicisation of identities by regionalist parties is likely to stimulate conflict and secessionism; that the design of a state's institutions is the key factor determining whether politicians will muster sufficient support for independence as well as from the assumption that there is a straight-line historic development from regionalism into nationalism. I call these various tendencies in the literature, for the purpose of this chapter, the 'teleology of total exit' argument. This is a theoretical issue which is intimately related to the other, more empirically informed question of this chapter. Namely, why in the cases of post-Yugoslav sub-state political projects in which membership was not defined as ethnically exclusive, the demands for the creation of sub-state polities were not voiced in terms of nationalist claims for self-determination, simultaneously ruling out independence as an option. This is a particularly pertinent question since in the West European context, despite the processes of de-ethnicisiation of membership, sub-state nationalist demands are becoming more vociferous.

The chapter shows that unlike the West European cases of stateless nationalisms, nationalism in the post-Yugoslav context is delegitimised and is associated with secession and oftentimes violence. Multinational and plurinational regionalisms instead offered an alternative compatible with the plurality of opinion in the globalised integrationist setting.

# II. Theoretical Considerations

That nationalism is above all a form of politics is widely accepted in the literature. Mann[1] and Breuilly[2] inform us that the political appeal and strength of nationalism can be explained by its institutionalisation. Furthermore, nationalism as a political ideology draws its normative power from the principle of self-determination (external or internal). Rather than trying to identify nations in social reality and reify them by adopting them as units of analysis, Brubaker[3] suggests that we should account for the ways and conditions under which politicians are successful in the process of reification of their groups and subsequent mobilisation. Nation-building is influenced by previous historical experiences. The evocation and interpretation of histories, but also historical developments of territorialised institutions, play important roles in this process. Nationalism aims at the construction of 'imagined communities', to use Anderson's term.[4] The politicisation and mobilisation of members of the putative nation is a way of gaining support for the political project.

Most of these points hold true for political regionalism as well. Functional and economic regionalism might differ in that sense from nationalism. Yet, regionalism is about politics and regions are imagined communities: the interpretation of history and politicisation of identity are therefore just as important. Unlike nationalism, the principle of self-determination is not necessarily used to legitimise regionalist projects. Thus, the normative context defines different opportunities for region and nation-building projects and helps us understand the differences between regionalism and nationalism on the theoretical plane but also actual choices political elites are confronted with.

---

[1] M Mann, 'The Emergence of Modern European Nationalism' in JA Hall and IC Jarvie (eds), *Transition to Modernity: Essays on Power, Wealth, Belief* (Cambridge, Cambridge University Press, 1992).

[2] J Breuilly, *Nationalism and the State* (Manchester, Manchester University Press, 1993) 64.

[3] R Brubaker, *Ethnicity without Groups* (Cambridge MA and London, Harvard University Press, 2004) 10.

[4] B Anderson, *Imagined Communities: Reflections on the Origin and Spread of Nationalism* (London & New York, Verso, 1983) 6.

To illustrate this, one might look at the Basque case in which the Basque collective political project straddling the borders of Spain and France has differentiated spatially defined manifestations: as a nation-building project on the Spanish side of the border and as a regional project in France. Political opportunities in the Spanish Basque case based on the invocation of historic territorial privileges such as *fueros* provided 'realistic' and 'legitimate' ideas while the institutional build-up and devolved nature of the Spanish state served as an opportunity structure for successful expression of collective claims within a nationalist paradigm. Claims to self-determination which would not have been successful in the context of the French state were muted. Instead, following the principles of 'new regionalism' and focusing more on economic development, institutional reform and recognition of cultural particularities, regional Basque elites chose to rally support for the creation of a Basque *département*[5] rather than to focus on nation-building as is the case in the Spanish Basque country. Thus, one could claim that Basqueness has been marked by two territorial political movements, regionalism in France and nationalism in Spain.

There is an argument related to the territorial basis of regional politics as opposed to ethnonationalism which entails a belief in common historical descent, namely that territory-centred political projects allow for a more civic conception of group identity. But, just as nations can have an ethnic basis, territories of regions can be constructed on ethnic grounds. However, the latter is less frequently the case. Although often true for nationalism, regionalism is by definition a territorial political project. Regionalism starts from the assumption that there is a specific territory over which it makes political claims. The fact that territory is the primary point of reference for regionalism explains the cases in which regionalism can accommodate more nationalist projects, be supplementary and/or compete against them. Territory, on the other hand, should not be considered as bounded and exclusive but as a political and social construct. Unlike space, which has a predominately geographic basis, territory includes a specific pattern of social, economic and political relations within it.[6]

Regionalism could then be defined as a political project within and across substate territory that relies on an existing or invented culture, identity and history, but also other cleavages such as patterns of production or region-specific economies. However, culture, identity and history should be considered as 'thin' concepts and just as with the creation of nations, can be invented, rediscovered and are in most cases given specific meaning by regional entrepreneurs.

There is a strand in the literature describing the declining role of the nation-state using the 'Europe of the regions' paradigm. More recently, the appeal of the 'Europe of the regions' is losing ground especially in the cases of stateless nations

---

[5] Z Bray and M Keating, 'European Integration and the Basque Country in France and Spain' in TJ Mabry, J McGarry and B O'Leary (eds), *Divided Nations and the Expanded European Union* (Philadelphia, University of Pennsylvania Press, 2013).

[6] M Keating, 'The Political Economy of Regionalism' in M Keating and M Loughlin (eds), *The Political Economy of Regionalism* (London, Frank Cass, 1997) 38.

such as Scotland and Catalonia in which there is a growing demand for independence. Related to the debate on Europe and sub-state politics is the issue of *new regionalism*. Keating distinguishes between traditional regionalisms and a new, modernising type of regionalism.[7] 'Regional traditionalists' resembling nineteenth-century conservative regionalists are usually uninterested in regional autonomy and prefer more informal ways of representation in central state structures. On the other hand, '[m]odern regionalists will be more outward-looking and see the region as a dynamic force for economic and social change'.[8] The development of *new regionalism* which encompasses identity politics, economic development and demands for autonomy is primarily a product of economic restructuring, globalisation and in the European context, European integration. Some have argued that the new regionalism is,[9] for the time being, an exclusively Western European phenomenon, something I have argued against elsewhere.[10]

Bourdieu recognised the entanglement of ethnic, regional and national projects and challenges the analysis of these by saying that '[s]truggles over ethnic or regional identity … are a particular case of the different struggles over classifications, struggles over the monopoly of the power … to impose the legitimate divisions of the social world and, thereby, to *make and unmake groups*'.[11] If we consider nationalism and regionalism as political projects that make claims over a population often using similar references it becomes obvious that both ideologies and their manifestations as political projects have a lot in common.

## III. The 'Teleology of Exit options' Argument

Disregarding the rough-and-ready argument made by Louis Snyder that regionalism is simply a nationalism on a smaller scale or 'mini-nationalism,'[12] there is a dominant position in the literature spanning disciplinary boundaries that the processes of construction of regional political community are inherently linked to the ideology of nationalism and eventually lead to the demands for, or actual establishment of an independent nation-state. Owing to the constraints of the chapter, I can only discuss and illustrate these tendencies briefly. All of these are related arguments but differ somewhat in focus.

[7] M Keating, *The New Regionalism in Western Europe: Territorial Restructuring and Political Change* (Cheltenham, Edward Elgar, 1998) 89.

[8] ibid 89.

[9] See R Pasquier and C Perron, 'Régionalisations et régionalismes dans une Europe élargie: les enjeux d'une comparaison Est-Ouest' (2008) 39(3) *Revue d'études comparatives Est-Ouest* 5.

[10] D Stjepanović, 'Regions and Territorial Autonomy in Southeastern Europe' in AG Gagnon and M Keating (eds), *Political Autonomy and Divided Societies: Imagining Democratic Alternatives in Complex Settings* (Basingstoke, Palgrave Macmillan, 2012).

[11] P Bourdieu, *Language and Symbolic Power* (Oxford, Blackwell Publishing, 2003) 221.

[12] LL Snyder, *Mini Nationalisms: Autonomy or Independence* (Greenwood Press, 1982); LL Snyder, *Encyclopedia of Nationalism* (London, St James Press, 1990).

The first one is the straight-line argument and it is particularly dominant in historical and sociological analyses of the development of nationalism. The argument is that regionalisms are either absorbed by the central state nationalisms or that they eventually become national projects in their own right. This is often illustrated by prominent examples such as the Catalan regionalism, which over the course of centuries but especially in the early-twentieth century has become a national project. Region-building is not necessarily an opposite process to nation-building. Historically, region-and-nation-building in Spain and Catalonia were inseparable. National and regional collective identities complemented each other as the result of dynamic historical process.[13] In many cases nationalist movements strengthened local and regional identities as a form of a 'grass-root' national identification. My argument is that the reverse was possible as well; nation-building could develop into regionalism and could seek legitimacy from the same building material (histories, identities, economy). However, because of such salient instances in which regional political projects preceded the national project, the Catalan case being exemplary of regional political collective claims transformed into a (stateless-)national one, it is often assumed, even by authors such as Núñez Seijas,[14] that regionalism somehow precedes nationalism. This is an argument that can be found, albeit in somewhat different form, in the work of a Marxist-leaning historian Miroslav Hroch who considers the creation of modern nations as a linear process (coupled with a predefined set of stages of development) and a *telos* represented by the 'fully developed' nation.[15] Although Hroch is explicit about the '*degree of completeness*'[16] of nations other prominent theories of nationalism, such as the one proposed by Ernest Gellner,[17] often imply that nation-building is a one-way process too.

Equally prominent is the understanding, primarily in the fields of international relations, conflict studies and law that the institutionalisation of territorial autonomy (or other types of decentralised/devolved sub-state regions) is a stepping stone to secession, thus contributing to the slippery slope argument. Arendt Lijphart, for example, in the defence of consociationalism, argues not only that regional autonomy strengthens intra-ethnic cohesiveness increasing the likelihood of inter-ethnic conflict, but also that establishing regional autonomy is a slippery slope to independence.[18] A more developed argument along similar lines

---

[13] X Núñez Seijas, 'The Region as Essence of the Fatherland: Regionalist Variants of Spanish Nationalism (1840-1936)' (2001) *European History Quarterly* vol. 31 no. 4.

[14] ibid.

[15] M Hroch, *Social Preconditions of National Revival in Europe: A Comparative Analysis of the Social Composition of Patriotic Groups among the Smaller European Nations* (New York, Columbia University Press, 2000).

[16] ibid 26.

[17] E Gellner, *Nations and Nationalism* (Oxford, Blackwell, 1983).

[18] A Lijphart, 'The Wave of Power-sharing Democracy' in A Reynolds (ed), *The Architecture of Democracy: Constitutional Design, Conflict Management, and Democracy* (Oxford, Oxford University Press, 2002).

is that by Erin Jenne, who locates autonomy claims on a continuum where cultural autonomy is referred to as less extreme, territorial autonomy moderately extreme, and secession/irredentism as representing the most extreme claim.[19] This sort of argument could be questioned on both theoretical and empirical grounds. We could consider that, for example, the demands for maximum devolution (falling short of independence) in the negotiations between Holyrood and the Westminster government in 2012 could be considered as a more extreme claim than the demands for independence.[20] This was confirmed by the agreement of the Westminster government to allow the independence question in the Scottish referendum of September 2014 and exclude the maximum devolution one in spite, or probably because, of the fact that the majority of Scottish electorate supported maximum devolution rather than the outright secession.[21]

There is another argument in the literature, more nuanced and qualified, about the influence of autonomous institutional precedents in the creation of independent states. According to the main proponent of this approach, Philip Roeder, the design of a state's institutions is the key factor that determines whether politicians will muster sufficient support for independence.[22] Based largely on the study of post-Soviet space Roeder argues that those likely to secede are those that benefit from territorially defined structures or as he calls them segment-states.

Finally there is an argument that regional (sub-state identities) and their politicisation incite secessionist demands. Dawn Brancati argues claims for 'autonomy are more likely to lead to instability if they are made by regional parties'.[23] The 'negative' effects associated with decentralisation are, according to her, caused by regional parties that are likely to stimulate conflict and secessionism by promoting regional identities and advocating legislation that can be harmful to other regions or minorities.[24]

---

[19] E Jenne, *Ethnic Bargaining: The Paradox of Minority Empowerment* (Ithaca and London, Cornell University Press, 2007) 39–44.

[20] Maximum devolution in the UK could be seen as a bigger challenge to the state's constitution than secession. It is also worth emphasising that this qualification is context specific and depends on position of the opposing camps and the party platforms. Maximum devolution as proposed by the Scottish government would have required major constitutional changes, within the UK and among its nations. Thus, although it might seem paradoxical at first sight, secession could be more readily acceptable by the central government than maximum devolution.

[21] S MacNab, 'Scottish independence: Most Scots back "devo max"' *The Scotsman* (19 February 2014).

[22] PG Roeder, *Where Nation-States Come from: Institutional Change in the Age of Nationalism* (Princeton, NJ, Princeton University Press, 2007).

[23] D Brancati, 'Pawns Take Queen: The Destabilizing Effects of Regional Parties in Europe' (2005) 16(2) *Constitutional Political Economy* 156.

[24] It must be noted that although not explicitly referring to Brancati, Jonathan Bradbury shows that there is no necessary causal relation between promotion of sub-state identities by political parties and increased demands for independence. Thus, my argument in theoretical terms is not original. Bradbury shows that in the Welsh case the increased assertion of Welshness has not led to a rise in support for independence. See J Bradbury and R Andrews, 'State Devolution and National Identity: Continuity and Change in the Politics of Welshness and Britishness in Wales' (2010) 63(2) *Parliamentary Affairs* 229.

Prima facie, many of these arguments falling under the 'teleology of exit options' are common sense, especially Roeder's reference to institutional structures. We can take the recent example of Ukraine's autonomous region of Crimea to confirm most of the above claims in the literature—an autonomous region of a sovereign state (albeit with the interference of a kin-state) unilaterally seceded while the previously existing institutional framework was used for those aims. Regional identity was mobilised against the central state especially as regards the language policies etc. However, accepting these arguments at face value could have normative implications, which might be used to justify central state nationalist elites' suspicion of autonomy as a stepping-stone to secession and towards the possible suppression of minority claims. But, most importantly many of these arguments in literature are marred by 'selecting on the dependent variable'. This refers to the process in which a number of observations are restricted to the cases in which a phenomenon did indeed occur, in our case secession or nation-building, rather than to a set of possible cases in which a phenomenon was possible but was not observed. Thus, it might be worth looking at cases in which secession was possible, there were institutions in place, regional identities were mobilised and claims were made for the establishment/maintenance of a regional polity, but neither independence featured as a prominent exit option[25] nor the right to self-determination was evoked; hence, we cannot speak of nationalist projects but rather of particular kinds of regionalisms.

## IV. Nations, Regions and Territories in the Post-Yugoslav Space

Before moving onto the case of regionalism it is worth contextualising the development of nationalism and state in particular Croatian and Serbian cases of nation-building as the most relevant ones. Modern Croatian and Serbian national projects are intricately intertwined. Attempts at the creation of Yugoslav nation(s) at times were related to both and the boundaries between them were not clearly defined throughout most of the nineteenth and early-twentieth centuries. The current definition of Croatian national membership was in many ways a response to Serbian nationalism as defined by ethnoreligious criteria. However, this was not necessarily the case historically. The mid-nineteenth-century Illyrian

---

[25] Bartolini offers a concept of exit that can be used both for analysing non-secessionist demands by the sub-state regions as well as the territorial management strategies by the central state. Bartolini suggests that territories can exit from within state organisations, creating various forms and levels of partial exit that can be exercised within (and across) territories and is radically different from the total exit options such as secession. See S Bartolini, *Restructuring Europe: Centre Formation, System Building and Political Structuring between the Nation State and the European Union* (Oxford, Oxford University Press, 2005).

movement, which was in some ways a predecessor to a conception of Yugoslavism and Croatian nationalism, was not religiously coloured. Broadly speaking it was primarily driven by ethnic considerations, with the aim of uniting all the South Slavs (or at least those living within the Habsburg domains) in the former case. In the latter case legitimacy was mainly sought in the historical tradition of the Croatian territorial institutions, often referred to as the Croatian state right[26] and Croatia's (quasi-)autonomous status during Hungarian and Habsburg rules. With the nineteenth-century Serbian state adopting and institutionalising membership criteria which were largely ethnoreligious (adherence to the Serbian Orthodox Church) in their nature, coupled by Habsburg Serbs' gradual turn towards Serbia as their kin-state, Croatian nationalism slowly drifted in a similar direction. The outcome of the process was the way in which Croatian national membership came to be defined in ethnoreligious terms. Thus, Catholic religious identity became one of the cornerstones of Croatian national identification.[27]

In a context in which national membership started to be defined by ascriptive and exclusive ethnic and religious markers, regional identities, memberships and politics that were legitimised by territorial references, historical institutions and multiple allegiances, more often than not clashed with the predominant national projects. Historically speaking, and especially in the period of classical modernity most historical regions or imperial administrative units in Southeastern Europe were strongly influenced by the arrival of enlightenment ideas of nationalism. These territories served either as political spatial foci for the construction of nation-states (independent or autonomous) as was the case of Croatia-Slavonia and the Belgrade Pashalik; were assimilated into nation-states such as Dobrudja;[28] or became multi-ethnically legitimised territories with their own institutions as was the case with the historic Dalmatia[29] and to some extent Macedonia in the nineteenth century.

In the cases of Croatia and Serbia in the twentieth century, with the establishment of national projects tainted by ethnoreligious definition of nations, the historically established territories lost some of their earlier clout. The dominance of the principle of self-determination in the (post-) World War One era underscored this development. Territory was important and contested nevertheless, but in another way. The arguments in favour of self-government were mainly justified

---

[26] F Veliz, 'Nationalism and the International Order: Re-interpreting the Politics of Banal Croatia, 1908–1918' (Florence, European University Institute, 2010).

[27] There were a few exceptions nevertheless, one of them being the Croat fascist Ustashe ideologists who claimed Bosnian Muslims were in fact Croats of Islamic faith, something that was done for strategic reasons and expediency. See SK Pavlowitch, *Hitler's New Disorder: The Second World War in Yugoslavia* (New York, Columbia University Press, 2008).

[28] Absorbed into the Romanian and Bulgarian nation-states in the late-19th century.

[29] It must be noted that, despite having different understandings of the region at different points in time, a significant segment of Dalmatian elites advocated its institutional independence (most often under Habsburg crown) despite having different ethnic origins and rising ethnonational projects in neighbouring territories.

by ethnic and religious reasons and historic territories were often gerrymandered as to create ethnically 'homogenous' territories. On many occasions, this development was matched by forced assimilations and expulsions of entire populations. One of the very few examples of regionalism and territorially based movements which were not ethnically marked was a demand for economic decentralisation of the Yugoslav Kingdom, coming from Vojvodina elites as well as certain Croatian (including Croatian Serb) political circles.

In the post World War Two period, the Yugoslav state was re-established as a federation in which units of the federal state often served as nation-states for their constitutional peoples.[30] The borders between the republics respected historical and ethnic lines in varying proportions. After the adoption of the 1974 Constitution, the federal state was further decentralised and the republics were given an opportunity to decentralise and devolve their competencies towards the 'self-managing' communities. Autonomies of Vojvodina and Kosovo were elevated to match those of the constituent entities of the Yugoslav federation. Yugoslavia was something of an odd case owing to its decentralised system of territorial management. Some went even further claiming that Yugoslav self-management represented 'the most extreme form of democratic participation in the economy, public services and local government in the world'.[31] Certainly, this position could be challenged by the fact that the system had limited mechanisms for the democratic participation of ideological opposition.

The Autonomous Province of Vojvodina was a case in point of Yugoslav uniqueness because the autonomy settlement was established in a historically multi-ethnic territory where Serbs constituted a plurality or majority. Territorial autonomy was given to an ethnically plural region, with a national majority (Serbs in this case), but unlike in other similar autonomous regions of Communist countries Vojvodina did not have a titular nation or nations.[32] In that sense, Dalmatia in Croatia was in a similar situation to Vojvodina; it was a historic territory with a Croat majority, not a region of or for ethnic 'Dalmatians' but rather for Dalmatians in the regional sense who happened to be Croats, Serbs or the few remaining Italians. The 1974 Constitution of the Socialist Republic of Croatia foresaw the

---

[30] This was not a constitutional fact but rather a perception; eg Croats were a constituent 'people' or nation in both Croatia and Bosnia-Herzegovina while Serbs were constituent in Bosnia-Herzegovina, Croatia and Serbia. See SL Burg, 'Republican and Provincial Constitution Making in Yugoslav Politics' (1982) 12 (Winter) *Publius: The Journal of Federalism* 131.

[31] S Woodward, 'Varieties of State-building in the Balkans: A Case for Shifting Focus' in M Fischer et al (eds), *Berghof Handbook in Conflict Transformation*, vol 2 (Berlin, Berghof Center, 2010) 326.

[32] The Constitution of the Socialist Autonomous Province of Vojvodina (1974), unlike other substate constitutions of the Yugoslav Federation at that time, does not explicitly mention any national group or groups as titular nation(s) of the province. Instead, there is a reference to the equality of Serb-Croat, Hungarian, Slovak, Romanian and Ruthenian languages and their respective scripts/alphabets. In the Soviet Union there were autonomous republics in which the state-wide ethnic majorities were regional majorities as well but the autonomous republic had a titular nation at least symbolically. One such example is the Karelian ASSR, established for the Karelian ethnic group which was a regional minority.

creation of the so-called *Zajednice općina*[33]—Associations of Municipalities with relatively far-reaching competencies established through bottom-up initiatives and Dalmatia was one of those. Istria, unlike Dalmatia and Vojvodina, did not possess distinct territorial units under the Yugoslav system.[34]

With the turn to multi-party politics in Croatia in 1990, the ruling nationalist HDZ (Croatian Democratic Union) party abolished the constitutional law on the Associations of Municipalities, thus practically removing all the decentralised competencies. Vojvodina's autonomous competencies following the adoption of the 1990 Serbian Constitution were reduced to linguistic and cultural rights protection and remained symbolic through the 1990s.

# V.  Multi/Plurinational Regionalisms vs Centralising Nation-States

Serbian president Milošević's curbing of the autonomies of Kosovo and Vojvodina are well researched and documented.[35] Less frequently mentioned is the fact that centralisation drives did not stop there but were fully implemented in Serbia proper as well. What is further obfuscated in the literature is that (the Croatian president) Tuđman, in the context of Croatia, adopted a set of measures of centralisation that had a similar effect on sub-state structures. While the driving logic and the outcomes were comparable, the means and strategies used differed somewhat.

There is a noticeable departure from the decentralised self-management of Yugoslav times towards more territorial centralisation from the late-1980s and early-1990s in Serbia initially, followed by Croatia. This is coupled by the strengthening of ethnonational criteria of political membership and 'nationalisation' of the state to borrow Brubaker's[36] term, which served primarily to strengthen and empower a single titular nation of each republic. These developments have, especially in polities that used to be defined as bi/multi-national in the pre-1990 Yugoslavia such as Croatia and Serbia, caused significant tensions. Serbia, from being the most decentralised republic of socialist Yugoslavia, became highly

---

[33]  Ustav Socijalističke Republike Hrvatske (Zagreb, Narodne novine, 1974).

[34]  There were nevertheless some territory-specific institutional arrangements such as the provisions for the use of Italian language in certain municipalities of Istria.

[35]  See eg SP Ramet, *Balkan Babel: The Disintegration of Yugoslavia from the Death of Tito to the War for Kosovo* (Boulder, Colorado, Westview Press, 1999); D Conversi, 'The Dissolution of Yugoslavia: Secession by the Centre?' in J Coakley (ed), *The Territorial Management of Ethnic Conflict* (London, Franck Cass, 2003); N Vladisavljević, *Serbia's Antibureaucratic Revolution: Milošević, the Fall of Communism and Nationalist Mobilization* (New York, Palgrave Macmillan, 2008).

[36]  See R Brubaker, 'National Minorities, Nationalizing States, and External National Homelands in the New Europe' (1995) 124(2) *Daedalus* 107.

centralised in the 1990s. Croatia adopted a façade decentralisation which served, actually, to strengthen the centralist grip of the ruling party.

In 1990, Croatia was a relatively ethnically heterogeneous polity. A new constitution was adopted soon after the HDZ's victory and transformed the bi-national republic[37] into a Croat nation-state, with explicitly ethnic criteria for membership. Serbs lost their privileged status as a constituent people (*narod*), which was 'downgraded' to that of a national minority. Initially supported by Milošević, ethnic Serb leaders in Croatia declared a Serb autonomous region (Krajina) but de facto seceded from the independent Croatia. Hence, demands for autonomy became increasingly associated with separatism.

In 1992, in the midst of the war, Croatia was divided (and remains so until today) into 20 (de jure) symmetrically organised counties (*županije*) and the city of Zagreb. Each of these has a directly elected government. Since 2009, heads of counties (*župani*) have also been directly elected. Counties nevertheless have limited powers. At first sight, the establishment of counties under Tuđman's rule is surprising considering that his vision of Croatia was based on a unitary and homogenous nation. But, gerrymandering the territory into counties without historic institutional precedents, all of them with ethnic Croat majorities, was aimed at offsetting Krajina Serb secessionist drives and regionalisms in Istria and Dalmatia. The Habsburg crown lands of Croatia, Slavonia, Dalmatia and the March of Istria had distinct institutional existences which were not necessarily based on ethnicity. Therefore, endowing these regions with even little powers was vehemently opposed by the central state. It was feared that decentralisation based on historic regions would 'have [had] negative effects on the still unfinished process of national integration'.[38] No less importantly, the system of territorial division into counties was conceived also as one of the safeguards to HDZ's dominance in the parliament, specifically in the upper chamber, the House of Counties. That the HDZ government was not genuinely promoting decentralisation could be seen in the earlier decision to abolish the Associations of Municipalities through constitutional amendments.[39] Apart from the apparent desire to centralise the state and pre-empt the possible creation of a regionally based opposition, Tuđman feared armed resistance to his rule (not unfoundedly as it turned out) which could be

---

[37] Dejan Jović suggests that, Croatian Serbs, although numerically significantly smaller, were made 'constitutionally' equal to Croats because of their suffering under the fascist Ustashe regime as well as owing to their overrepresentation in the partisan movement and the Communist Party ranks. See D Jović, 'Reassessing Socialist Yugoslavia 1945-1990: The Case of Croatia' in D Djokić and J Ker-Lindsay (eds), *New Perspectives on Yugoslavia: Key Issues and Controversies* (Abingdon, Routledge, 2011) 117.

[38] J Vrbošić, 'Povijesni pregled razvitka županijske uprave i samouprave u Hrvatskoj' (1992) 1 *Društvena istraživanja* 66.

[39] *Odluka o proglašenju Ustavnog zakona za provođenje Amandmana LXIV. do LXXIV. na Ustav Socijalističke Republike Hrvatske* (Zagreb, 25 July 1990).

upheld by a particular reading of the Constitution on the competences of the associations in the areas of defence and public security.[40] In the post-Tuđman era, the territorial structure remained unaltered while the House of Counties was abolished. The only obvious measures towards (limited) decentralisation in that period took place in the Istrian County.

The territorial structure of Serbia is largely the legacy of Milošević's rule and its overt centralisation in the 1990s. In that period the state was formally defined as civic, but a huge discord existed between the official founding documents and the actual ethnonationalist policies on the ground.[41] The veneer of 'civic-ness' coupled with the purported danger of secessionism was used as a legitimation for unprecedented centralisation measures. Not only were the autonomous provinces of Vojvodina and Kosovo significantly limited or dismantled, but regional associations, just as in Croatia, within Serbia proper were abolished too. The underlying aim was to limit any possible opposition to the regime, be it territorial, ethnic or other. Further augmenting centralisation, in 1995, all the previously socially owned property that has been used by the municipalities/autonomous provinces became the property of the central state, thus curtailing the already limited self-governing capacities of municipalities/autonomous provinces.

Following the change of the regime in 2000, some measures towards decentralisation of the state were taken, while the formal political membership definitions were changed to correspond closely to the ethnic policies applied in practice. The 2006 Constitution reflected that reality and defined Serbia as a nation-state of the Serb *narod*. Nationhood was conceived primarily in ethnic terms and Serbia's role as a kin-state of all ethnic Serbs was confirmed. According to the 2006 Constitution, Serbia is organised as a unitary state, nevertheless with two asymmetric autonomous provinces, Kosovo and Metohija, and Vojvodina. However, since 1999, Serbia has had no control over Kosovo, which declared independence in 2008. Apart from Vojvodina and its elected meso-level government, other units of territorial government in Serbia are municipalities and cities. The 2006 Constitution allows for the creation of other autonomous provinces but under difficult conditions.[42]

## A. Istrian Regionalism of the IDS

In the midst of the transition to multiparty politics, on 14 February 1990 a new party was formed with an Istrian rather than Croatian denominator, the Istrian

---

[40] Ustav Socijalističke Republike Hrvatske [Constitution of the Socialist Republic of Croatia] 1974, Art 184.

[41] J Vasiljević, 'Citizenship and Belonging in Serbia: in the Crossfire of Changing National Narratives' CITSEE Working Paper Series 2011/17, 11.

[42] For more details on sub-state polities in the former Yugoslav countries (including the cases analysed here), see D Stjepanović, 'Territoriality and Citizenship: Membership and Sub-State Polities in Post-Yugoslav Space', CITSEE Working Paper Series 2012/22.

Democratic Assembly (IDS).[43] The IDS did not contest elections in 1990 lacking party infrastructure and having insignificant membership. At least formally, the party programme stressed liberalism as its main ideological principle. The name of the party consciously referred to the historic Istrian Diet or Assembly, while three goats on a green field symbolised the Croat, Italian and Slovene nature of the region but also reflected the historic coat of arms of the Istrian March which represented the emblem of the party.

The party defined its goal as being the development of 'all the particularities and richness of Istria and its islands as a *regional entity shaped by its immense ethnic, economic and cultural wealth and uniqueness*'(emphasis added).[44] In order to achieve that goal, the IDS proposed an extensive autonomy and consciously shied away from mentioning anything that could be interpreted as secession.[45] The party has won all the regional and state elections in Istria since 1992. After the change of Tuđman's regime in 2000, the IDS managed to push through a statute of the Istrian region in the Croatian parliament, which mainly protects Istria's cultural and linguistic specificities. Apart from the statute, Istria is one of the 21 Croatian counties. The regionalist project promoted by the IDS could be charac-terised primarily as *plurinational*, as it considered identities and histories context-specific and not mutually exclusive. For the same reason, every-day, historically rooted bilingualism was elevated to a political level and the IDS promoted the institutionalisation of Italian (alongside Croatian) in the entire county despite the fact that only around 7 percent of the population identified as Italian (see Table 1) and that in many of the areas of Istria (primarily in the hinterland) Italian was not widely used even historically. The IDS relied almost exclusively on the regionalist variant of historiography and projected a particular vision of Istria's past, that is, the one of *convivenza*, tolerance and hybridity of identities.[46] This interpretation of the past also cut across cleavages in Istrian society and appealed to nearly all political, cultural and ethnic groups. In the Istrian case, the fluctuation and per-meability of national group identification as well as a prominent regional Istrian identity (as a second element here) expressed in censuses of certain periods, shows the plurality of and contextual dependence of group identification in Istria. Consequently, we can talk about a *plurinational* regionalism and a plurinational regional polity. Particular interpretations of inter-group relations in conjunction with specific interpretations of the past create distinct constitutive stories that are

---

[43] The party initially and still officially uses the trilingual (Croatian, Italian and Slovene) name: *Istarski demokratski sabor-Dieta Democratica Italiana-Istarski demokratski zbor* (Statut Istarskog demokratskog sabora).

[44] Statut Istarskog demokratskog sabora, 1992, 1.

[45] Interview with Emil Soldatić, former secretary general of the IDS, Motovun/Montona, 21 February 2009.

[46] See P Ballinger, '"Authentic Hybrids" in Balkan Borderlands' (2004) 45(1) *Current Anthropology* 31; JE Ashbrook, *Buying and Selling the Istrian Goat: Istrian Regionalism, Croatian Nationalism, and EU Enlargement* (Brussels, Peter Lang, 2008).

plurinational in their character. This was used as a symbolic and legitimising narrative against the central state's aggressive nationalism especially in the 1990s, but also as an internally homogenising factor. Further, the conception of the Istrian regional polity of the Italian minority representatives largely corresponded to the vision of the self-governing Istrian region as promoted by the IDS.

## B. Dalmatian Regionalism of the DA

It is worth mentioning this case of failed multi/plurinational regionalism for two reasons, the first being the fact that it is a negative case, where a regional project for the establishment/maintenance of a regional polity was possible but did not materialise (neither does Dalmatia exist as a single political unit nor is there a credible regionalist political option), but also because it differs on institutional grounds from that of Istria, Dalmatia having an immediate institutional precedent in the form of Association of Municipalities.

The Dalmatian Action (Dalmatinska akcija—DA) was the chief regionalist party of the 1990s. The party declared its social democratic character and regionalism as its main ideology. The programme of the party demanded regional restructuring of Croatia based on its historic provinces in which Dalmatia would be a self-governing unit sharing prerogatives with the central government. Regional history, identity and the multinational character of the region (Croat and Serb primarily) were the key features, according to the DA, that set it apart from the rest of Croatia. The party programme, nevertheless, asserted the territorial integrity of the Republic of Croatia and it was in many crucial points similar to the IDS programme on the regionally based territorial restructuring of Croatia. Indeed, many other points in the programme echo the IDS party programme in its demands. According to the programme, the DA 'represents the interests of all Dalmatians wherever they live, as well as all those who live in Dalmatia despite their religion and nationality'. Article 2 of the programme said that the DA is fighting for the protection of Dalmatian ethnic, cultural and linguistic uniqueness.

But for a party that claimed to represent the interests of all Dalmatians, its aim paradoxically referred only to the coastal and island areas of Dalmatia and within those areas to very few and specific economic sectors such as tourism. Other concerns such as shipbuilding as one of the main industrial sectors of coastal Dalmatia were not mentioned either.

The DA's poor electoral performance was conditioned by various forms of state oppression strategies but more importantly by the decision to emulate politics of the IDS, believing that the successful programme of the IDS could be replicated in Dalmatia. The DA opposed both of the exclusive nationalist projects and advanced the demands for federalisation of Croatia based on historic regions— crown lands. However the support for the party remained limited to few specific, littoral social elements and included a specific, regionalist, understanding of history. The DA did not manage to achieve larger congruence of interests and to impose itself as a pivot for those. For these reasons primarily, I have characterised this type of regionalist politics as *sectional* regionalism. The argument in favour of this characterisation is that despite the declared aims of representing the entire territory of the historic region, through its policies Dalmatian regionalist entre-preneurs explicitly addressed only a small section of the regional population and interests.

## C. Vojvodina's Regionalism of the LSV and DS

Unlike Istria and Dalmatia, Vojvodina's range of successful regionalist parties is somewhat broader. The League of Social Democrats of Vojvodina (Liga socijal-demokrata Vojvodine—LSV) dominated the political scene in the 1990s while the regionalist wing of the state-wide Democratic Party (Demokratska stranka—DS) was more prominent in the 2000s and early-2010s.

Following the Second World War, and especially with the constitutions of 1963 and 1974, Vojvodina was established as an autonomous province with compe-tences that, in most respects, equalled those of the federal units of Yugoslavia catering at the same time for the specific interests of various ethnic and linguistic groups in the province (see Table 2). The multi-ethnic autonomous institutions were early victims of centralising nationalism in the 1990s under Milošević.

Since 2000 and the regime change in Serbia, there is a growing support for decentralisation among Vojvodina's electorate regardless of the ethnonational divide.[47] This support for decentralisation nearly never translates into demands for independence which only a marginal section of Vojvodina's population (never surpassing 5 per cent) seems too support. Apart from multiculturalism and references to historical institutions of Vojvodina, the DS and LSV rely on economic arguments to support their autonomist claims. With the support of the Alliance of Vojvodina Hungarians (VMSZ), they have controlled the major-ity of Vojvodina's 120-seat assembly since 2000. Together these parties promote a multinational membership concept in Vojvodina with clearly defined group boundaries, unlike in Istria where the regional identity promoted by the IDS is more fluid and hybrid.[48] Their demands for autonomy were partly met by the

---

[47] Scientia, Novi Sad, 1995; GEOTAKT project, Novi Sad, 2001; Dragomir Jankov, Vojvodina, Propadanje jednog regiona: podaci i činjenice (Novi Sad, Graphica Academica, 2004); Scan, Novi Sad, 2010.

[48] It is worth comparing census figures on national identification in both regions. Vojvodina's national groups are relatively stable over time and the only significant change comes through migra-tion. In the Istrian case, on the other hand, there is a relatively high fluctuation of national identifica-tion in censuses which is not caused by migration but by changes in individual self-declaration which is compatible to the plural and hybrid identity politics of the IDS. See appendix.

adoption of the Statute of Autonomy which is based on Serbia's Constitution from 2006. Despite the fact that the territory of Vojvodina and its identity references are differently constructed and perceived by various ethnic and national groups, institutional frameworks and economic interests are highly territorialised and serve as a pivotal point for the mobilisation against the central state. I suggest calling this regionalism—*multinational regionalism*. The maintenance and protection of various communities' interests were used as tools for the accommodation of various group interests. Several modes of self-government for national and ethnic groups in Vojvodina were achieved at the regional level. Multinational regionalism differs from the Istrian case of plurinational regionalism, as in Vojvodina, political identities are organised in a more hierarchical fashion and are ethnonationally divisive with a secondary Vojvodinian regional identity. The DS was more successful in breaching various ethnic and national divides by promoting the economic interests of the region while advocating the protection of cultural rights and had a wider appeal to the electorate than the LSV.

# VI. Conclusion

The outcomes of regionalist claims varied across the cases mentioned. What is similar in all of them is that no devolved competencies or autonomy was achievable in the 1990s under overtly undemocratic regimes in either Serbia or Croatia. Dalmatia is an unsuccessful case in which regional multi-or plurinational polities do not formally exist. In the 2000s, with the introduction of more pluralistic and democratic politics, in the cases of Istria and Vojvodina regional competences were somewhat expanded. In those two cases we can characterise the outcome as the existence of clearly identifiable regional polities, constructed on *plurinational* principles in the former and *multinational* principles in the latter case.

It must be noted that central state elites were still wary of regionalist mobilisations and often resorted to nationalist rhetoric as a justification for the alleged protection of the state's integrity against fictional regionalist secessionism. Weller claimed that in the context of Southeastern Europe autonomy will be tolerated only if 'independence has been firmly precluded as a potential option'.[49] Regionalist politics in most of these cases excluded independence as a potential

---

[49] M Weller, 'Enforced Autonomy and Self-governance: the Post-Yugoslav experience' in M Weller and S Wolff (eds), *Autonomy, Self-governance and Conflict Resolution* (London and New York, Routledge, 2005) 72.

option in their respective constructions of regional political space. However, state elites' intransigence and the fact that these regionalist projects were not secessionist in their nature does not fully explain significant differences in their outcomes.

The outcomes were not only conditioned by central elites' attitudes towards decentralisation and the failure of regional entrepreneurs in Dalmatia to offer a viable alternative to exclusive nationalist projects by capturing the symbolic, cultural and economic interests of the populations on their territories, but also by offering an alternative politics in the form of regionalism.

Regarding the theoretically informed question, on the relations between regionalism and nationalism, we can confirm the initial proposition that nation- and region-building processes are contingent, interrelated and reversible. Nations and regions are constantly being made and remade. There is no *telos* to these processes and we should not assume any type of finiteness of either. We could also observe that the claims made in the name of the examined cases of regionalisms differed from those of nationalisms and related more to histori- cally emerging territorialised institutions and economic needs and less to post- territorial ethnonational forms of political belonging in the construction of their polities. Thus, at least in this context, it is worth utilising a conceptual distinction between regionalism and nationalism. One should not forget that the regional- ist entrepreneurs operated in a broader political context and were affected by the wider normative environment and not only by the opportunity structures of domestic political systems. This points to two related factors. First, to the fact that nationalism in the (post-)Yugoslav space relied on ethnic exclusiveness unlike in some of the West European cases where there is a process of de-ethnicisation of membership (for example Scotland). Second, the regionalist political projects analysed here were consciously constructed as being inclusive of ethnonational groups and accommodating of competing claims to self-determination. Thus, nationalism was ruled out as an ideological option. Instead politics similar to those of *new regionalism* in Western Europe were the obvious choice. Yet again, this shows that we cannot brand this type of politics as mini-nationalism but rather as plurinational and multinational regionalism, accommodating several national projects that could otherwise be in conflict, constituting a viable alter- native to statehood.

Finally, this chapter serves as a corrective to the 'teleology of exit options argu- ment'. The establishment of regional autonomy is not a slippery slope to inde- pendence; the maximalist demands in these cases are those for autonomy rather than for secession; the development of regionalism is not unidirectional; the polit- icisation of regional identities does not stimulate conflict and secessionism but actually serves the purpose of accommodation of diversity while the existence of an institutional framework (current, immediately preceding or historical) does not make claims for independence necessarily the most salient and successful exit option.

*Dejan Stjepanović*

# Appendix

**Table 1:** Historic census in Istria

| Year | Croats | Slovenes | Italians | Germans | 'Regionals' | Others | Total |
|------|--------|----------|----------|---------|-------------|--------|-------|
| 1880 | 81,175 | 6,995 | 79,155 | 4,231 | N/A | 6,825 | 178,381 |
| % | 45.5 | 3.9 | 44.4 | 2.4 | | 3.8 | 100 |
| 1910 | 126,478 | 10,254 | 98,520 | 12,452 | N/A | 17,132 | 264,836 |
| % | 47.7 | 3.8 | 37.2 | 4.7 | | 6.5 | 100 |
| 1921 | / | / | / | / | / | / | 240,221 |
| 1931 | / | / | / | / | / | / | 251,065 |
| 1945 | 160,872 | 2,771 | 58,681 | N/A | N/A | 10,443 | 232,767 |
| % | 69.1 | 1.2 | 26.2 | | | 4.5 | 100 |
| 1948 | 155,701 | 4,606 | 42,727 | N/A | N/A | 3,619 | 206,653 |
| % | 75.3 | 2.2 | 20.7 | | | 1.8 | 100 |
| 1953 | 155,063 | 5,552 | 23,934 | N/A | N/A | 14,729 | 199,278 |
| % | 77.8 | 2.8 | 12 | | | 7.4 | 100 |
| 1981 | 157,112 | 3,434 | 7,859 | N/A | 3,691 | 45,510 | 217,606 |
| % | 72.2 | 1.6 | 3.6 | | 1.7 | 20.9 | 100 |
| 1991 | 135,170 | 3,671 | 15,627 | N/A | 37,654 | 42,023 | 234,145 |
| % | 57.7 | 1.6 | 6.7 | | 16.1 | 17.9 | 100 |
| 2001 | 148,328 | 2,020 | 14,284 | 180 | 8,865 | 32,667 | 206,344 |
| % | 71.9 | 1.0 | 6.9 | 0.09 | 4.30 | 15.83 | 100 |
| 2011 | 142,173 | 1,793 | 12,543 | N/A | 25,203 | 26,343 | 208,055 |
| % | 68.33 | 0.86 | 6.03 | | 12.11 | 12.66 | 100 |

(Sources: Klemenčić et al, *Promjene narodnosnog sastava Istre 1880-1991*; M Bertoša, *Istarska enciklopedija*; DZS, *Stanovništvo prema narodnosti, po gradovima/općinama, POPIS 2001, POPIS 2011*; G Perselli, *I censimenti della popolazione dell'Istria, con Fiume e Trieste, e di alcune città della Dalmazia tra il 1850 e il 1936*)

**Table 2: Ethnic/linguistic/national identification of population on the territory of modern day Vojvodina (1880–2002)[50]**

| Year | Total population | Hungarians | | Germans | | Serbs | | Croats, Bunjevci | |
|---|---|---|---|---|---|---|---|---|---|
| | number | number | % | number | % | number | % | number | % |
| 1880 | 1,172,729 | 265,287 | 22.6 | 285,920 | 24.4 | 416,116 | 35.5 | 72,486 | 6.2 |
| 1890 | 1,331,143 | 324,430 | 24.4 | 321,563 | 24.2 | 457,873 | 34.4 | 80,404 | 6 |
| 1900 | 1,432,748 | 378,634 | 26.4 | 336,430 | 23.5 | 483,176 | 33.7 | 80,901 | 5.6 |
| 1910 | 1,512,983 | 425,672 | 28.1 | 324,017 | 21.4 | 510,754 | 33.8 | 91,016 | 6 |
| 1921 | 1,528,238 | 363,450 | 23.8 | 335,902 | 22 | 533,466 | 34.9 | 129,788 | 8.5 |
| 1931 | 1,624,158 | 376,176 | 23.2 | 328,631 | 20.2 | 613,910 | 37.8 | 132,517 | 8.2 |
| 1941 | 1,636,367 | 465,920 | 28.5 | 318,259 | 19.4 | 577,067 | 35.3 | 105,810 | 6.5 |
| 1948 | 1,640,757 | 428,554 | 26.1 | 28,869 | 1.8 | 827,633 | 50.4 | 132,980 | 8.1 |
| 1953 | 1,701,384 | 435,210 | 25.6 | / | / | 867,210 | 51 | 127,040 | 7.5 |
| 1961 | 1,854,965 | 442,560 | 23.9 | / | / | 1,017,713 | 54.9 | 145,341 | 7.8 |
| 1971 | 1,952,533 | 423,866 | 21.7 | 7,243 | 0.4 | 1,089,132 | 55.8 | 138,561 | 7.1 |
| 1981 | 2,034,772 | 385,356 | 18.9 | 3,808 | 0.2 | 1,107,375 | 54.4 | 119,157 | 5.9 |
| 1991 | 2,013,889 | 339,491 | 16.9 | 3,873 | 0.2 | 1,143,723 | 56.8 | 97,644 | 4.9 |
| 2002 | 2,031,992 | 290,207 | 14.3 | 3,154 | 0.2 | 1,321,807 | 65 | 76,312 | 3.8 |
| 2011 | 1,931,809 | 251,136 | 13 | 3,272 | 0.2 | 1,289,635 | 66.8 | 63,502 | 3.3 |

[50] The census data is compiled from various sources and is only illustrative. It must be noted that until 1941, the data was gathered on the basis of linguistic/mother tongue identification. The census categories in Socialist Yugoslavia used self-identified *nacionalnost* [nationality] or ethnicity. Croats and Bunjevci are placed in the same column as some of previous censuses did not recognise a separate Bunjevac language/nationality. According to the 2002 census, there are 19,776 self-declared Bunjevci and 16,469 in 2011. Other significant self-declared groups include Slovaks (50,321 or 2.60% in 2011), Roma (42,391 or 2.19% in 2011), Romanians (25,410 or 1.32%) and Montenegrins (22,141 or 1.15% in 2011). Sources: Kocsis and Kocsis-Hodosi, 1995; Jankov, 2004; Census 1991 and 2002, 2011; Vojvodina-CESS, 2010; Đurić et al, 1995.

# 6

## Southphalia or Southfailure? National Pluralism and the State in South Asia

ASANGA WELIKALA

## I. Introduction

The unifying premise of the essays in this book is the hypothesis that the nation-state, while still the central organising principle of international order, is in a state of flux brought about by the dual processes of sub-state nationalisms and supra-state globalisation. In exploring this premise, this chapter considers the concepts of state and nation in South Asia, a region that represents a very different set of historical, political, economic, social, and cultural circumstances to the Western conditions that form the backdrop for most other chapters in this book. I undertake this exploration by looking at how two South Asian states—India and Sri Lanka—have responded to competing nationality claims by groups within their borders. This issue of 'national pluralism' is a complex type of constitutional challenge that poses fundamental questions for the Westphalian conception of the nation-state even in older Western states that are in an advanced state of constitutional development.[1] It is a challenge that has proved even more intractable in the younger post-colonial states of India and Sri Lanka, often causing protracted conflict, and cementing, in Mahmud Ali's vivid description, a 'fearful state' in South Asia.[2] But as Ayesha Jalal remarks pertinently

> South Asian states and societies have kept a march ahead of the rest of the world in at least one important respect. The recent surge in assertions on 'ethnic' identity and demands

---

[1] See eg W Kymlicka, *Multicultural Citizenship: A Liberal Theory of Minority Rights* (Oxford, Oxford University Press, 1996); M Keating *Plurinational Democracy: Stateless Nations in a Post-Sovereignty Era* (Oxford, Oxford University Press, 2001); AG Gagnon and J Tully (eds), *Multinational Democracies* (Cambridge, Cambridge University Press, 2001); S Tierney, *Constitutional Law and National Pluralism* (Oxford, Oxford University Press, 2004); W Norman, *Negotiating Nationalism: Nation-Building, Federalism and Secession in the Multinational State* (Oxford, Oxford University Press, 2006); M Burgess and J Pinder (eds), *Multinational Federations* (London, Routledge, 2007); F Requejo and M Caminal (eds), *Political Liberalism and Plurinational Democracies* (London, Routledge, 2011).

[2] M Ali, *The Fearful State: Power, People, and Internal War in South Asia* (London, Zed Books, 1993).

for national sovereignty in the erstwhile Soviet Union, Eastern Europe, the Middle East, the United Kingdom, Canada and elsewhere is an old and familiar occurrence in the subcontinent. Indeed, the dialectic between centralism and regionalism has played a pivotal part in the more dramatic developments in subcontinental history.[3]

Among other multinational South Asian polities (most prominently, Nepal), the choice of these two countries makes for particularly interesting comparative insights because their historical processes of state-formation and constitutional development bear striking similarities. They share ancient cultural and civilisational ties, their modern state tradition commenced as British colonies during the nineteenth and early-twentieth centuries, they achieved independence at the same time in the first wave of British decolonisation in the late-1940s, both are common law jurisdictions with a shared heritage of British constitutionalism, both were founders and then prominent members of the Non-Aligned Movement during the Cold War era, and while both have experienced internal upheavals, they are the only two states in South Asia that have an unbroken record of post-colonial electoral democracy.[4]

On the other hand, these two countries' post-colonial pathways of nation and state building have diverged significantly, and in particular, their constitutional responses to ethnic and religious pluralism have been radically different. The Indian state has adopted a generally accommodating attitude in discharging its democratic commitments in a large and bewilderingly plural polity.[5] In building a strong constitutional culture of 'unity in diversity',[6] it not only adopted traditional constitutional mechanisms such as a justiciable bill of rights and a federal structure for the state, but also imaginatively used a wide array of policies such as multilingualism, affirmative action and federal re-territorialisation in the management of pluralism.[7] Sri Lanka, by contrast, has progressively mutated into an intolerant majoritarian 'ethnocracy' that has sought to contain its Tamil minority nation almost exclusively through political and military repression.[8] While these differences must be appreciated, it is apparent nonetheless that post-colonial

---

[3] A Jalal, *Democracy and Authoritarianism in South Asia: A Comparative and Historical Perspective* (Cambridge, Cambridge University Press, 1995) 157.

[4] See generally H Tinker, 'South Asia at Independence: India, Pakistan and Sri Lanka' in AJ Wilson and D Dalton (eds), *The States of South Asia: Problems of National Integration* (New Delhi, Vikas, 1982) ch 1.

[5] K Bajpai, 'Diversity, Democracy, and Devolution in India' in S Baruah (ed), *Ethnonationalism in India: A Reader* (New Delhi, Oxford University Press, 2010) ch 1.

[6] C Jaffrelot, 'Nation-Building and Nationalism: South Asia, 1947-90' in J Breuilly (ed), *The Oxford Handbook on the History of Nationalism* (Oxford, Oxford University Press, 2013).

[7] A Stepan, JJ Linz and Y Yadav, *Crafting State-Nations: India and Other Multinational Democracies* (Baltimore, John Hopkins University Press, 2011) chs 2, 3, 4; H Kumarasingham, *A Political Legacy of the British Empire: Power and the Parliamentary System in Post-Colonial India and Sri Lanka* (London, IB Tauris, 2013) ch 4; L Tillin, *Remapping India: New States and their Political Origins* (London, Hurst, 2013) ch 2.

[8] O Yiftachel, *Ethnocracy: Law and Identity Politics in Israel/Palestine* (Philadelphia, PA, University of Pennsylvania Press, 2006) 22–25; J Uyangoda, 'Travails of State Reform in the Context of Protracted Civil War in Sri Lanka' in K Stokke and J Uyangoda (eds), *Liberal Peace in Question: Politics of State and Market Reform in Sri Lanka* (London, Anthem Press, 2011) ch 2.

India's fundamental commitment to the overarching Westphalian conceptual and doctrinal framework has rendered it incapable of specifically accommodating multiple nations within the state.

What the comparison of India and Sri Lanka in relation to their national pluralism reveals therefore is the persistence of a hard—in European terms, early modern—conception of the state in South Asia. Globalisation and especially sub-state nationalisms may challenge the South Asian state, but unlike its Western European counterparts, these challenges have entrenched rather than retrenched its role and power. Thus both states' primary response to sub-state national challenges in Kashmir and with regard to the Tamils has been one of military suppression (involving counter-insurgency tactics that have resulted in serious human rights violations) rather than any constitutional concession of the state's primacy.

While there are many ways of explaining the divergence, perhaps for constitutional lawyers the most salient difference in the state-formation histories of the West and South Asia is the issue of colonialism. In South Asia, constitutional modernity was introduced by the colonial power, and this in turn has significant implications for the way ideas about the state, the nation and nationalism developed in the modern era. While anti-colonial sentiments pervasively influenced post-colonial nation-building, the path-dependent trajectory of the post-colonial state had been set by the autocratic colonial state. Thus the flipside of Sri Lanka's deceptively tranquil transition to independence was that, effectively, the colonial state continued unchanged, albeit with new owners and managers putting the old state to new authoritarian uses.[9] Even in India, where a much more self-conscious attempt was made to break with the past, essential coercive elements of the colonial state continued intact.[10]

The nation, on the other hand, had to be constructed anew, so that the post-colonial state was invested with the democratic legitimacy crucial to its stability and viability. Drawing upon the unifying experience of its independence struggle, India achieved this with a mixture of modernist idealism, pragmatic communal compromises, and in some cases such as the princely state of Hyderabad or the Portuguese exclave of Goa, forced incorporation. Partition had also removed most of the large minority of Muslims to the separate state of Pakistan. Among the peripheries that have defied integration into the Indian nation-state, the most prominent has been the remaining Muslim majority region within India, Kashmir.

---

[9] D Udagama, 'The Sri Lankan Legal Complex and the Liberal Project: Only Thus Far and No More' in TC Halliday, L Karpik and MM Feeley (eds), *Fates of Political Liberalism in the British Post-Colony: The Politics of the Legal Complex* (Cambridge, Cambridge University Press, 2012); H Kumarasingham, '"The Jewel of the East yet has its Flaws": The Deceptive Tranquillity surrounding Sri Lankan Independence' (2013) Heidelberg Papers in South Asian and Comparative Politics Working Paper No 72.

[10] H Alavi, 'The State in Post-Colonial Societies: Pakistan and Bangladesh' (1972) 1(74) *New Left Review* 59; J Alam, 'The Nation and the State in India: A Difficult Bond' in Z Hasan, E Sridharan and R Sudharshan (eds), *India's Living Constitution: Ideas, Practices, Controversies* (London, Anthem Press, 2005).

In Sri Lanka, no comparable process of modernist nation-building was attempted, and instead, the majority Sinhala-Buddhist nation took control of the state, triggering a sub-state national challenge from the Tamils, which remains constitutionally unresolved to this day.

In what follows, I elaborate on these initial observations to: (i) set out a theoretical history of modern state-formation in South Asia; (ii) explain the implications of colonial modernity for our understanding of the contemporary South Asian state; and (iii) illustrate the resilience of the South Asian state in the context of the sub-state national challenge. There are vigorous scholarly debates among political scientists, historians, sociologists and anthropologists in a vast literature on India and (to a lesser extent) Sri Lanka, as well as on imperial Britain itself, with regard to the multifarious issues raised by the first two of these concerns. I do not intend either to rehearse those debates or to narrate histories, but to rely on those explanatory accounts that I find most persuasive in theorising these processes.

By contrast, the focus of my third concern, the peculiar constitutional issues that arise from the existence of multiple nations within the territorial and historical space of the contemporary South Asian state are either wholly neglected by constitutional lawyers, or inadequately theorised in the existing literature. The principal focus of my argument with regard to the resilience of the South Asian state therefore is devoted to exploring the relationship between national pluralism and the constitutional structure of the nation-state. Going beyond the 'negative' aim of demonstrating the resilience of the nation-state, this part of the discussion also hopes to contribute to a clarification of the terms of South Asian debates on states and nations.

The history, political science and sociology literature that exists, while in many ways highly sophisticated, in my view fails to address several of the key, specifically *constitutional*, issues that arise from claims for accommodation from multiple nations within the state. This is epitomised in the way many social scientists and most lawyers commonly pigeonhole—often with a pejorative subtext of ethnic revanchism—sub-state national claims in the category of ethnonationalist separatism, whereas the nation-state is implicitly regarded as the apogee of progressive civic modernity.[11] The use of terminology therefore is instructive: positive ideas like nationhood, patriotism and citizenship are usually associated with the state; terms that have negative connotations like ethnonationalism, secessionism and

---

[11] For particularly striking illustrations of this prejudice in the Sri Lankan literature, see A Bandarage *The Separatist Conflict in Sri Lanka: Terrorism, Ethnicity, Political Economy* (London, Routledge, 2009); HL De Silva, *Sri Lanka a Nation in Conflict: Threats to Sovereignty, Territorial Integrity, Democratic Governance and Peace* (Colombo, Visidunu Prakasakayo, 2008); D Jayatilleka, *Long War, Cold Peace: Conflict and Crisis in Sri Lanka* Rev edn (Colombo, Vijitha Yapa, 2014). See also I Ahmed, *State, Nation and Ethnicity in Contemporary South Asia* (London, Pinter, 1996). For a penetrating critique of these assumptions in the Indian context, see A Nandy, *The Romance of the State—And the Fate of Dissent* (New Delhi, Oxford University Press, 2003). I have also attacked this approach in A Welikala, *Beyond the Liberal Paradigm: The Constitutional Accommodation of National Pluralism in Sri Lanka* (2014, PhD Thesis, University of Edinburgh).

conflict are often reserved for sub-state groups and movements. By using the analytical and normative insights of plurinational constitutionalism, I ask questions
that have not yet been either fully understood or answered clearly even by South
Asian scholars who have discerned in national pluralism a discrete category of
political and policy challenges. Even more so than elsewhere in the fully modern
world, I suggest that there is nothing in the South Asian experience that justifies the assumption of a moral superiority of the nation-state against sub-state
national claims.

   The persistence of Westphalian nostrums in the historical and cultural conditions of South Asia, and how that dominance precludes adequate constitutional
responses to national pluralism, can be characterised as a 'Southphalian' model
of state.[12] This discussion serves to sound a note of caution against drawing over-
hasty generalisations from constitutional developments in the West (and especially Europe) with regard to nationalism and globalisation, and in the context
of these dynamics, about the nature and future of the nation-state. The robust
survival of the South Asian nation-state, I argue, should give pause in particular
to those scholars of global constitutionalism and constitutional pluralism who
assume the irreversible decline of the Westphalian model.[13] Whether or not South
Asian conceptions of state and nation would over the *longue durée* evolve in the
post-sovereign and post-modern directions of the Western European nations and
states remains to be seen. But what can concretely be asserted for now in this
region is that there is little sign of the nation-state's retreat, and contingently, that
minority *nationality* claims would find constitutional resistance, even if they find
accommodation as *minority* claims. Although it is a matter for normative judgement rather than a description of the strength and vigour of the South Asian state,
we might in this context ask if 'Southphalia' actually implies 'Southfailure'.

## II. State and Nation in South Asia: Colonial Constitutional Modernity

'Bonaparte made kings; England makes nations'—Lord William Bentinck[14]

'Euro-American Selves and Indian Others have not simply interacted as entities
that remain fundamentally the same. They have dialectically constituted one
another'—Ronald Inden[15]

---

[12] Thanks to Stephen Tierney for suggesting this deft neologism, analogously to how other scholars
have characterised the rise of an 'Eastphalia' in international law, see: DP Fidler, 'Eastphalia Emerging?
Asia, International Law and Global Governance' (2010) 17(1) *Indiana Journal of Global Legal Studies* 1.

[13] For a sophisticated attempt to track and theorise these changes, see N Walker, *Intimations of
Global Law* (Cambridge, Cambridge University Press, 2014).

[14] J Rosselli, *Lord William Bentinck: The Making of a Liberal Imperialist, 1774-1839* (London, Sussex
University Press, 1974) 155.

[15] R Inden, *Imagining India* (Oxford, Basil Blackwell, 1990) 3.

Constitutional lawyers generally assume that modern constitutional government began in Sri Lanka with the Colebrooke-Cameron Reforms of 1832–34, and in the subcontinent with the Government of India Act 1858.[16] While valid for most purposes including the present discussion, some qualifications to this assumption are also important. The first is that these reforms and other British colonial influences during the nineteenth century did not 'invent' either state or nation in these polities.[17] This proposition is contrary to influential theories of state and nation advanced, for example, by the Subaltern Studies Collective on India and the post-Orientalist school on Sri Lanka.[18] Indigenous ideas of state and nation, while quite distinct from both contemporaneous European conceptions as well as what we understand by those terms today, in fact have a long pedigree in South Asia.[19]

The work of CA Bayly in relation to India and Michael Roberts in regard to Sri Lanka is especially instructive in establishing this thesis. These scholars do not deny the introduction of new ideas through colonialism. Neither do they argue that pre-colonial ideas remained immutable. The more important point, in their view, is to understand how pre-colonial and colonial ideas with regard to nation and state interacted: 'What [colonial] modernity did was to transform and redirect these emergent identities rather than to invent them *ex nihilo*'.[20] Therefore when we consider the question of the colonial establishment of the modern constitutional state, in addition to the obviously dominant motivations of the imperial power,[21] we must always bear in mind the voice of local political actors and the agency of local political forces.[22] These views were central to the way categories like community and nation were understood, and in this way, they had a strong

---

[16] A Berriedale Keith, *A Constitutional History of India, 1600-1935* (London, Methuen, 1926) ch VI; GC Mendis, 'Introduction' in GC Mendis (ed), *The Colebrooke-Cameron Papers: Documents on British Colonial Policy in Ceylon, 1796-1833* vol I (Oxford, Oxford University Press, 1956) ix–lxiv; CR de Silva, *Ceylon under British Occupation, 1795-1833* vol 2 (Colombo, Apothecaries, 1962) 594; HM Seervai, *Constitution of India: A Critical Commentary* vol 1, 4th edn (New Delhi, Universal Law Publishing, 1991) 3; CL Anand, *Constitutional Law and History of Government of India* 8th edn (revised by HK Saharay, New Delhi, Universal Law Publishing, 2008) 102–04.

[17] CA Bayly, *Origins of Nationality in South Asia* (New Delhi, Oxford University Press, 1998) chs 2 and 4.

[18] J Spencer (ed), *Sri Lanka: History and Roots of Conflict* (London, Routledge, 1990); R Guha, *The Subaltern Studies Reader* (Minneapolis, University of Minnesota Press, 1997); N Silva (ed), *The Hybrid Island: Culture Crossings and the Invention of Identity in Sri Lanka* (London, Zed Books, 2002); P Jeganathan and Q Ismail (eds), *Unmaking the Nation: The Politics of Identity and History in Modern Sri Lanka* 2nd edn (New York, South Focus Press, 2009); V Chaturvedi, *Mapping Subaltern Studies and the Postcolonial* (London, Verso, 2012).

[19] See eg KM de Silva, 'Nineteenth Century Origins of Nationalism in Sri Lanka' in KM de Silva (ed), *History of Ceylon* vol 3 (Colombo, Apothecaries, 1973); H Scharfe, *The State in Indian Tradition* (Leiden, EJ Brill, 1989); D Rothermund, 'Nationalism and the Reconstruction of Traditions in Asia' in D Rothermund, *The Role of the State in South Asia and Other Essays* (New Delhi, Manohar, 2000).

[20] Bayly, *Origins of Nationality* (n 17) 3.

[21] A Thompson, 'Empire and the British State' in S Stockwell (ed), *The British Empire: Themes and Perspectives* (Oxford, Blackwell, 2008) 42–51.

[22] CA Bayly, *Recovering Liberties: Indian Thought in the Age of Liberalism and Empire* (Cambridge, Cambridge University Press, 2012) 1–25.

bearing on how governing institutions were designed.[23] This view stands in opposition to the Subaltern or post-Orientalist and even orthodox Marxist accounts of South Asian nation- and state-formation, in which constitutional modernity is depicted as a wholly European imposition, or at best, an elitist (comprador) enterprise.[24]

One of the important ways in which the state changed with the arrival of colonialism however was in becoming a permanent presence in society.[25] Previously, as Javeed Alam recalls, 'The state as a centralised institution, though not absent, was an episodic presence, with very long periods intervening without any such presence'.[26] Even though pre-colonial kingly states and empires in South Asia routinely made hyperbolic sovereignty claims to vast territories, the physical absence of the state in the life of the community for long periods of time allowed cultural communities an autonomy of existence upon which the modern state could now intrude with impunity. The modern state could do so not only because it had unprecedented coercive power and technology at its disposal, but also by calling upon the devices of ideological legitimation provided by Westphalian discourse. Against the assimilating tendencies of this more entrenched incarnation of the state, those collective memories of past autonomies feature heavily in the mobilising ideologies and legal claims to self-government by ethno-territorial communities and state-seeking nations in today's South Asia.[27]

The other point to note is that by the time the British colonial state was established in India and Sri Lanka, not only had British ideas about the British state and nation already crystallised into something resembling the modern sense of those concepts, but as Andrew Thompson notes, 'across the period from the later eighteenth to the later twentieth centuries, the British state has been inseparable from the idea of empire'.[28] Moreover, a homogenised conceptualisation of these ideas was transmitted across the Empire through the 'centripetal jurisprudence'[29] of its judicial institutions. As Rohit De reminds us, 'the British Empire was tied together in a web of law, through which precedents, documents, statutes, and personnel circulated across five continents'.[30] But the more important point for our purposes,

[23] ibid; Mendis, 'Introduction' in Mendis (ed), *The Colebrooke-Cameron Papers* (n 16); S Sivasundaram, *Islanded: Britain, Sri Lanka and the Bounds of an Indian Ocean Colony* (Chicago, Chicago University Press, 2013) chs 1, 3, 8.

[24] Bayly (n 17) chs 2, 4; M Roberts, *Sinhala Consciousness in the Kandyan Period: 1590s to 1815* (Colombo, Vijitha Yapa, 2004) ch 1.

[25] S Hettige, 'Building Citizenship in Sri Lanka: The Dynamics of State-Action and Ethnic Conflicts' in H Bhattacharyya, A Kluge and L König (eds), *The Politics of Citizenship, Identity and the State in South Asia* (New Delhi, Samskriti, 2012) 207.

[26] Alam 'Nation and the State in India' (n 10) 88.

[27] S Krishna, *Postcolonial Insecurities: India, Sri Lanka, and the Question of Nationhood* (Minneapolis, University of Minnesota Press, 1999) xvii–xviii.

[28] Thompson, 'Empire and the British State' (n 21) 40. This is incidentally contrary to most functionalist accounts of modern nation-formation, which hold that this process occurred only after industrialisation and democratisation. See also Roberts, *Sinhala Consciousness* (n 24) ch 6.

[29] M Sharafi, *Parsi Legal Culture in British India* (Cambridge, Cambridge University Press, 2014).

[30] R De, '"A Peripatetic World Court" Cosmopolitan Courts, Nationalist Judges and the Indian Appeal to the Privy Council' (2014) 32(5) *Law and History Review* 821, 821.

and one that lawyers generally are ill-equipped to adequately appreciate, is that the British conception of the state that informed the design of the colonial state was one forged in the crucible of the French Revolutionary and Napoleonic Wars and the establishment of the 'Second British Empire'.[31] As Bayly observes, this 'new expansion was set in motion by the ferocious reaction of the state and its military apparatus to external challenge and internal revolt'.[32] Thus, 'Empire was the expression of re-vivified nation-state operating at an international level according to general principles—the protection and glorification of Crown, Church, law and trade'.[33] In the construction of the colonial state, therefore, 'The wider Burkean formulation of the 'glories of the British constitution' was inappropriate where indigenous peoples were to be denied their own 'constitutions'.[34] In the colonies, the Crown rather than the Constitution was the emblem of order and the 'wide and philosophic principle' at the heart of the Empire.

These factors are critical to understanding the authoritarian and quasi-militaristic nature of the colonial state, and indeed, the overtones of bellicosity and ethno-cultural superiority that characterised the British idea of nationality and nationalism at the time. In this way, local elites in the South Asian colonies were acculturated at the very moment of their early nationalist reawakening to an authoritarian, hierarchical and racially segregated conception of *modern* constitutional order. Ironically, this notion of the 'modern' state also resonated in many ways with recent memories of the nature of *pre-colonial* indigenous socio-political orders to which absolutist monarchism and casteism as well as hierarchy and differentiation were central.[35] It is hence perhaps unsurprising that these elites would continue this colonial state tradition after independence, and thus the inherited legacy reflected not the liberal imperialists' cherished constitution of law, liberty and justice,[36] but a thoroughly hard-edged and potentially aggressive state, which was more concerned with order and control than with freedom and equality.[37]

Seen in this light, colonial constitutional modernity reflected two key departures from European modernity. As Terence Halliday and Lucien Karpik observe,

> British colonies shared a fundamental contradiction. On the one hand, British imperial authorities and jurists insisted that the British colonial project was built upon a foundation not merely of force, but of the *universality* of the rule of law. On the other side, the

[31] VT Harlow, *The Founding of the Second British Empire, 1763-1793* vols 1 and 2 (London, Longmans Green, 1952 and 1964).
[32] CA Bayly, *Imperial Meridian: The British Empire and the World, 1780-1830* (London, Longman, 1989) 102.
[33] ibid.
[34] ibid 108.
[35] Roberts (n 24) chs 1, 3.
[36] Bayly, *Recovering Liberties* (n 22) ch 2; K Mantena, *Alibis of Empire: Henry Maine and the Ends of Liberal Imperialism* (Princeton, Princeton University Press, 2011) ch 1; Sivasundaram, *Islanded* (n 23) 286–92.
[37] Alavi, 'The State in Post-Colonial Societies' (n 10); Alam (n 10); J. Uyangoda, 'The United Front Regime of 1970 and the Post-Colonial State of Sri Lanka' in T Jayatilaka (ed), *Sirimavo: Honouring the World's First Woman Prime Minister* (Colombo, The Bandaranaike Museum Committee, 2010) 31–45.

colonisers insisted upon two reservations to law's radical equality and universality: (a) a reservation in the form of a *law of exception* and (b) a reservation embodied in a *rule of difference*. (emphasis in original)[38]

The law of exception related to the arbitrary and dictatorial emergency powers, often involving the invocation of martial law, when and if there was a threat to the colonial order. But in revealing 'the iron fist that lay behind the velvet glove of law', these occasions 'not only threaten[ed] the normative foundations of the colonial order, but question[ed] the very legitimacy of the law's universality'.[39] Thus, the relationship between the rule of law and the use of emergency powers in British colonies represented 'an intractable tension'.[40] The difference in the application of exceptional powers between the colonies and within Britain was not only the extent of those powers and the frequency of their use, but also that in the colonies they were used by a foreign power in defence of an imperial order against a native population.

Likewise, the rule of difference contaminated the pristine ideal of the rule of law with racial discrimination in the British colony. As Halliday and Karpik argue, 'While the rule of law was premised on universality, colonial rule depended on particularity ... at one and the same time [the British] insisted on a universality and neutrality of law and asserted a rule of racial difference'.[41] The rule of difference was manifested in a gallimaufry of practices across the empire, and in Bayly's view, these were

> reinforced by the 'governing race' principle which emphasised the fitness of Britons to rule by virtue of their 'moral independency' and their understanding of the rule of law; an institutionalised and philosophical racism thus became an increasingly important part of the project.[42]

Replicated and expanded after independence, both these central qualifications to legal equality at the heart of the modern state were to have as much or more pernicious consequences than under colonialism.[43] In Sri Lanka, the rise of Sinhala-Buddhist nationalism and its claims to the ownership of the post-colonial state reproduced the rule of difference with regard to minorities, and the resulting tension and extra-institutional violence has necessitated recourse to the law of exception, moreover as the norm rather than the exception.[44] Thus the distorted

---

[38] TC Halliday and L Karpik, 'Political Liberalism in the British Post-Colony: A Theme with Three Variations' in Halliday, Karpik and Feeley (eds), *Fates of Political Liberalism* (n 9) 11–12.

[39] Halliday and Karpik, 'Political Liberalism in the British Post-Colony' (n 38) 12–13.

[40] N Hussain, *The Jurisprudence of Emergency: Colonialism and the Rule of Law* (Ann Arbor, University of Michigan Press, 2003) 133.

[41] Halliday and Karpik (n 38) 13.

[42] Bayly, *Imperial Meridian* (n 32) 109.

[43] Halliday and Karpik (n 38) 15; Udagama, 'The Sri Lankan Legal Complex and the Liberal Project' (n 9). See also Alavi (n 10); Uyangoda, '*The United Front Regime of 1970* (n 37).

[44] See O Gross and F Ní Aoláin, *Law in Times of Crisis: Emergency Powers in Theory and Practice* (Cambridge, Cambridge University Press, 2000) 220–27; A Welikala, *A State of Permanent Crisis: Constitutional Government, Fundamental Rights and States of Emergency in Sri Lanka* (Colombo, Centre for Policy Alternatives, 2008) 96–99.

modernity introduced by the colonial state instantiated a state tradition that was continued after independence, owing to the new uses to which the rule of differ-ence and the law of exception could be put by the post-colonial Sinhala-Buddhist owners of the state. In Halliday and Karpik's typology of British post-colonies, this has made the Sri Lankan state a 'despotic order',[45] although as will be seen below, its characterisation as an 'ethnocratic' regime is more appropriate. In post-colonial India this process was more subtle and complex, which enables it to be characterised as a 'liberal-legal order'[46] in Halliday and Karpik's scheme. But as Charles Epp notes,

> Like many such post-colonial societies, India retains strong elements of a colonial legal system originally designed to facilitate control of the population. India's Constitution authorises the government to detain without charge or trial individuals considered a threat to security and to declare a national emergency and rule by decree. The police operate under a colonial-era statute (The Police Act 1861) adopted by the British in response to the Indian uprising of 1857.[47]

The central point that emerges from this brief discussion of the theoretical impli-cations of colonialism for the evolution of the post-colonial state is that, however much lip-service is paid to it, the overarching idea of equality that is the defining characteristic of Western modernity from the nineteenth century onwards does not have the same historical significance, social traction or normative force in the constitutional tradition of the post-colony. India sought to address this very deliberately through its post-colonial nation-building efforts in which its vener-ated constitution has played a key role. But even then, deep legal inequality is still endemic in that country and because of the very Westphalian normative assump-tions that are at the heart of these efforts, the Indian nation-state's capacity to recognise sub-state nations *qua* nations is severely limited, although it has success-fully deployed other policies and institutional devices in addressing other varieties of ethnic and cultural diversity. In Sri Lanka, the absence of the norm of equality in the nation-building discourse facilitated the Sinhala-Buddhists' claims to pri-macy in relation to both polity and state, and to all manner of discriminatory legislation and practices from citizenship to language rights that followed from that constitutional self-understanding.

It is important, however, for the reasons mentioned above that we do not see the state and its coercive apparatus as an entirely or exclusively 'derivative' inheritance, for that would be to oversimplify the historical continuities and the social founda-tions of the South Asian state within its pre-colonial, colonial and post-colonial continuum. While we must have a nuanced understanding of the implications of colonial constitutional modernity, the liberal normative critique of Southphalia will not prosper if all it can do is flog the dead horse of colonialism. Culture and

---

[45] Halliday and Karpik (n 38) 15–16, 26–35.
[46] ibid 14–15, 18–26.
[47] CR Epp, '*The Legal Complex in the Struggle to Control Police Brutality in India*' in Halliday, Karpik and Feeley (n 9) 92–93.

history are of tremendous importance in understanding this model of constitutional order, and these issues are played out in the discourse of nations and nationalism.

## III. State and Nation in the British Post-Colony: The Divergent Trajectories of Nation-State Building in India and Sri Lanka

'The unity of India was no longer merely an intellectual conception for me, it was an emotional experience which overpowered me'.—Jawaharlal Nehru[48]

'History precisely designed to assuage the sufferings of the people often does exactly the opposite because it is so easily assimilated into the rhetoric of righteous tyranny'.—Sir Christopher Bayly[49]

The preceding section has given us an inkling of the South Asian state's constitutional character and the significance of colonialism to its evolution, but what of the nation? This is the aspect in which the post-colonial development of our two case studies diverges significantly, albeit *within* the overall Westphalian framework of nation-state. Both drew deeply from pre-colonial history, but India undertook a highly self-conscious process of modernist nation-building including through the making of its constitution in which, whilst successfully deploying historical and cultural resources in its support, modernity rather than tradition was unmistakably privileged. Thus the transition to independence was seen in terms of three revolutions. First, a political revolution in overthrowing colonial rule. Second, a social revolution that would salvage India from 'the medievalism based on birth, religion, custom, and community and construct her social structure on modern foundations of law, individual merit, and secular education'.[50] And third, an economic revolution that would permit, '[t]he transition from primitive rural economy to scientific and planned agriculture and industry'.[51]

This manifestly modernising agenda was however given a unifying embrace not only by the shared experience of the independence struggle (and institutionally the role of the Congress party),[52] but also cultural content by the idea of India as an 'immemorial nation'. Alam cites Nehru as saying, 'In ancient and medieval

---

[48] J Nehru, *The Discovery of India* (Calcutta, Signet Press, 1948) 38.

[49] Bayly (n 17) 127.

[50] Member of the Indian Constituent Assembly and Editor of *The Hindustan Times*, K Santhanam, cited in G Austin *The Indian Constitution: Cornerstone of a Nation* (New Delhi, Oxford University Press, 2004) 26.

[51] K Santhanam, cited in Austin *The Indian Constitution* (n 50) 26.

[52] SK Mitra, '*The Nation, State and the Federal Process in India*' in U Wachendorfer-Schmidt (ed), *Federalism and Political Performance* (London, Routledge, 2000) 54.

times, the idea of the modern nation was non-existent, and feudal, religious or racial or cultural bonds had more importance', only to assert immediately that, 'Yet I think that at almost any time in recorded history an Indian would have felt more or less at home in any part of India'.[53] Alam's assessment of these sentiments bears reproduction:

> The key words in looking at the immemorialness [sic] of the Indian nation is not simply that the people here are marked by an imprint that is characteristically Indian but that this has been characterised *throughout the ages*, as an overarching *national heritage* over the individual, linguistic features of the various people who have been living in India. What is observed today as the intersection of the regional-national and pan-Indian features is not a modern phenomenon but has always existed. It is being clearly suggested that this Indian nation is immemorial in the sense that what has unified the innumerable, distinct, linguistic-cultural groups in India has been a national heritage for hundreds of years. (emphasis in original)[54]

Such views were not by any means confined to India's dominant political leader, but constituted a vision of the country that was widely shared by its cultural and political elites. In one of the earliest descriptive accounts of the new Indian nation, the eminent Indian historian BG Gokhale observed,

> The most outstanding characteristic of the history of India during the last hundred years has been the emergence of Indian nationalism and nationhood in the place of the regional 'patriotism' and statehood of the past. The unexpressed but vividly felt sense of cultural unity making itself manifest through the entity called the Indian nation that has emerged on the stage of human history.[55]

Thus when tradition was being engaged to furnish the spiritual and emotional content to the conceptual idea of the immemorial Indian nation, the subcontinent's vast demographic diversity dictated that this be articulated in inherently pluralistic terms. Jacobin-style homogenisation, or national unity without the open recognition of communal and regional diversity, was therefore never a viable option in the post-colonial reconstruction of the Indian nation. And yet, the overarching aim here was to articulate the Indian nation as a unified, monistic concept, and one that was exclusively attached to the Indian state. At this stage of political development, a multinational federation was never in contemplation, and while the Indian state has made various concessions to sub-state claims in practice over the whole course of its post-colonial history including through the territorial reorganisation of its federal states in response to linguistic and cultural claims, its constitutional structure remains strongly conceptually wedded to the original notion of a monistic Indian *demos*.[56] As Rajeev Bhargava notes, 'the governing elite in

---

[53] Alam (n 10) 92.

[54] ibid 93.

[55] BG Gokhale, *The Making of the Indian Nation* 2nd edn (London, Asia Publishing House, 1960) 5. See also Bayly (n 17) ch 1.

[56] See for a history of the Indian states reorganisation process, Tillin, *Remapping India* (n 7) ch 2.

India, perhaps even the larger political elite, has always had a conceptual block about recognizing multiple nationalities in India'.[57] That it is a multinational state capable in practice if not in theory of accommodating multiple nations within the state therefore remains very much in the realm of the academic imagination rather than constitutional practice.[58]

In Sri Lanka (or Ceylon as it was then known) by contrast, classical modernist assumptions unambiguously underpinned the thinking of the architects of its post-colonial constitutional order such as DS Senanayake and Sir Ivor Jennings, and the elitist mode of transition also assumed the existence of a 'Ceylonese' nation.[59] No attempt was made to elaborate on its political and cultural content through a popular constitution-making exercise or otherwise.[60] In contrast also to the communal carnage and nationalist hysteria of the subcontinent's moment of independence, the Ceylonese elites were rather proud of their peaceful transfer of power, and they constantly associated themselves and sought political inspiration, not from the Indian struggle, but from modes and models of constitutional change provided by the older settler Dominions.[61]

Moreover, while the island polity was characterised by ethnic and religious pluralism, its relative compactness in terms of both territory and population in comparison to the teeming multitudes of the Indian subcontinent, made for a much more reluctant attitude to constitutionally recognise communal pluralism. The overwhelming evidence is that both British officials and Ceylonese leaders (and their advisors like Jennings) took the view that the best approach should encourage civic homogenisation around an implicit Ceylonese *demos*, rather than encourage disintegration by institutionalising distinct ethnoi and their fissiparous constitutional claims. This did not prevent limited recognition of pluralism however. As Jennings authoritatively declared,

> Communal representation … encourages communalism; and what a self-governing country must develop is not communalism but common loyalty. Even so, the first step towards common loyalty is inter-communal co-operation; and to develop that co-operation it is necessary to recognize communal distinctions and to enable each

---

[57] R Bhargava, 'The Crisis of Border States in India' in J Bertrand and A Laliberté (eds), *Multination States in Asia: Accommodation of Resistance* (Cambridge, Cambridge University Press, 2010) 51.

[58] See eg Alam (n 10); H Bhattacharyya, 'Federalism and Competing Nations in India' in Burgess and Pinder (eds), *Multinational Federations* (n 1); H Bhattacharyya, 'Ethnic and Civic Nationhood in India: Concept, History, Institutional Innovations and Contemporary Challenges' in SC Saha (ed), *Ethnicity and Socio-Political Changes in Africa and other Developing Countries* (Lanham, Lexington, 2008) ch 8.

[59] A Welikala, '"Specialist in Omniscience"? Nationalism, Constitutionalism and Sir Ivor Jennings' Engagement with Ceylon' in H Kumarasingham (ed), *Constitution Making in Asia: Decolonisation and State-Building in the Aftermath of the British Empire* (London, Routledge, 2015) (forthcoming).

[60] A Welikala, 'The Failure of Jennings' Constitutional Experiment in Ceylon: How "Procedural Entrenchment"' Led to Constitutional Revolution' in A Welikala (ed), *The Sri Lankan Republic at 40: Reflections on Constitutional History, Theory and Practice* (Colombo, Centre for Policy Alternatives, 2012) 150–67.

[61] Kumarasingham, *A Political Legacy* (n 7) ch 5; KM de Silva, '"The Model Colony": Reflections on the Transfer of Power in Sri Lanka' in Wilson and Dalton (eds), *The States of South Asia* (n 4) 77–88.

community to play its part in national development. At this stage of affairs it is impossible to hope for integration, but partnership is not impossible.[62]

Part of the explanation for this approach in Ceylon, then, was the practical convenience of expeditiously establishing the new state without opening up difficult constitutional problems, but more normatively, most of the important decision-makers sincerely believed that the most progressive of modern statecraft required this approach. As we know from subsequent Sri Lankan history, however, this was a tragically erroneous choice of policy, for it only allowed the empty vessel of the Ceylonese nation to be occupied by the historically and numerically dominant Sinhala-Buddhist ethnic nation to the exclusion of all others. As Siri Hettige observes,

> the Sri Lankan state—despite the universalistic approach adopted in the provision of public services to the wider population such as education, health and social security—did not evolve as a modern welfare state leading to the creation of social citizenship, capable of transcending identities based on ethnicity and religion.[63]

This story is well documented elsewhere, but for our purposes what is important is how we conceptualise the Sri Lankan nation-state.[64] Beneath the veneer of an outwardly modernist form, the distortion of key Westphalian principles such as the monistic *demos* and the unitary conception of sovereignty have transmogrified the nation-state into a Sinhala-Buddhist 'ethnocracy'. The leading theorist of ethnocracy, Oren Yiftachel, defines this regime-type in the following way:

> Ethnocracy denotes a type of regime that facilitates and promotes the process of ethnicisation, that is, expansion and control. It surfaces in disputed territories, where one ethnonational group is able to appropriate the state apparatus and mobilise its legal, economic, and military resources to further its territorial, economic, cultural, and political interests. The struggles over the process of ethnic expansion become the central axis along which social and political relations evolve.[65]

Moreover, according to Yiftachel,

> not only does it denote the dominance of a specific ethnic group, it also denotes the prominence of ethnicity in all aspects of communal life. This is due to the elevation of the ethnos over the demos as a principle of political organisation. Ethnocracy legitimises the use of ethnicity (that is, cultural identity based on belief in a common past at a specific place) as a tool for intranational [ie intra-state] group stratification and marginalisation.[66]

---

[62] WI Jennings, *The Approach to Self-Government* (Cambridge, Cambridge University Press, 1956) 97. For a much more strident statement of these views, see WI Jennings, 'Ceylon: Inconsequential Island' (1946) 22(3) *International Affairs* 376, 388.

[63] Hettige 'Building Citizenship in Sri Lanka' (n 25) 210.

[64] See eg CR de Silva, 'The Sinhalese-Tamil Rift in Sri Lanka' in Wilson and Dalton (n 4); KM De Silva, *Managing Ethnic Tensions in Multi-Ethnic Societies, Sri Lanka 1880-1985* (Lanham, MD, University Press of America, 1986); N DeVotta, *Blowback: Linguistic Nationalism, Institutional Decay and Ethnic Conflict in Sri Lanka* (Stanford, Stanford University Press, 2004).

[65] Yiftachel, *Ethnocracy* (n 8) 295.

[66] ibid 295–96.

Once the public sphere is pervaded in this way by a dominant ethnicity through the capture of the state, then there is little space for any normative conception of pluralism to survive, although sociological pluralism may be allowed to exist subject to minorities accepting an ethnic hierarchy in which they are firmly subordinate. What is more, such a constitutional order is not merely unaccommodating but is also actively and especially hostile to any nationality claims that minority groups might make, as the Sri Lankan Tamils do. It follows that the ethnocratic state's response to such claims are policies of control and suppression, not accommodation and management, and the result is that an ethnocracy is 'chronically unstable and replete with ethnic conflicts and tensions'.[67]

In comparing the divergent trajectories of nationalism and nationhood in India and Sri Lanka, therefore, four issues seem analytically important. I will however only flag the first three issues. My attention in what follows is focused on the fourth, which relates to the dominant model of nationhood in the mid-twentieth century. First, the style of political leadership as between Nehru and Senanayake could not have been more different. Nehru was a Harrow and Cambridge educated intellectual who had thought deeply and written widely about the idea of independent Indian nationhood long before he assumed power. His complex personality that straddled Anglophile liberalism and Indian nationalism is neatly encapsulated in the way he described himself to John Kenneth Galbraith as 'the last Englishman to rule India'.[68] Senanayake was a landowner more given to country pursuits than learned discourse—in Jennings' description, 'a rugged farmer with a sense of humour'[69]—who relied on his instincts and a trust in British-style institutions to provide the practical solutions to his country's problems. He was very far from a man of letters and being a poor public speaker, his preferred metier of constitutional negotiation was quiet discussion with similarly clubbable British officials with shared notions of gentlemanly discretion and confidence. In Ceylon therefore the independence leader was uninterested in the learned tomes and the soaring rhetoric with which his Indian counterpart led the struggle. The two very different approaches to the question of independent nationhood in these countries therefore mirrored the contrasting leadership styles of these two leaders.

Second, the nature of the process of decolonisation was also very different as already noted. The Indian nationalist struggle was itself a nation-building process, which only needed to be formally institutionalised upon achieving independence, even though that was in itself a complex task. In Sri Lanka by contrast, every incremental step of the way to independence was a matter of elite constitutional negotiations, which while avoiding the political drama and violence of the

---

[67] ibid 296.

[68] Kumarasingham (n 7) 50. See also J Brown, *Nehru: A Political Life* (Oxford, Oxford University Press, 2004).

[69] WI Jennings, *The Road to Peradeniya: An Autobiography* (Colombo, Lake House, 2005) 175. See also H Kumarasingham, *Constitution-Maker: Selected Writings of Sir Ivor Jennings* (Cambridge, Cambridge University Press, 2015) 19–23.

subcontinent, nevertheless ensured that there had been no broader societal conversation whatsoever about what independent nationhood would entail. Thirdly,
and again as noted, political geography was also important in the way the nation
was conceived. The vast territory and the diversity of its peoples determined that,
notwithstanding the monistic fashion in which the Indian nation was imagined,
it had to be built on a pluralism of social foundations.[70] Sri Lanka's much smaller
size and lesser diversity persuaded its leaders that a more homogeneous model of
nationhood should be pursued.

But in considering how these otherwise dissimilar nation-building exercises
impacted on the constitutional claims of sub-state minority nations from the
perspective of constitutional theory, what is most important by far is the dominant model of post-colonial nation-statehood they both drew upon. Decolonising
states in the mid-twentieth century all tried, or were encouraged by the departing
imperial power, to adopt a stylised version of the Westphalian nation-state as the
sure path not only to their political emancipation, but also as their ideal-type for
post-colonial political, social and economic development. This model of classical
modernist post-colonial nation-building saw the nation-state as 'intrinsic to the
nature of the modern world and to the revolution of modernity'.[71] Proponents of
the model sought to 'build', 'forge', 'mould' and 'construct' territorial, civic, nations
corresponding to states through a wide array of techniques, including communications, mass education, political mobilisation and constitution-making, in much
the same way, in the words of Anthony D Smith, as 'one might speak of building
machines or edifices through the application of design and technical devices to
matter'.[72] As he further notes,

> It was a question of institutionalisation, so as to create good copies of the Western model
> of the civic participant nation. This became a technical question of appropriate recipes
> for national development, [...] well organised and responsive publics, and mature and
> flexible elites. This was the way to replicate the successful model of the Western nation-
> state in the ex-colonies of Africa and Asia.[73]

Smith's influential conceptualisation of modernist nation-building sets out five
key contentions made by proponents of the model, of which the first two are
especially important to this discussion. The first proposition was that 'nations
[are] essentially territorial political communities. They [are] sovereign, limited
and cohesive communities of legally equal citizens, and they were conjoined with
modern states to form ... unitary "nation-states"'.[74] Secondly,

> nations [constitute] the primary political bond and the chief loyalty of their members.
> Other ties—of gender, region, family, class and religion—[have] to be subordinated

---

[70] H Bhattacharyya, '"A Nation of Citizens" in a Fragmented Society? Citizenship as Individual and
Ethnic Entitlements in India' in Bhattacharyya, Kluge and König (eds), *The Politics of Citizenship, Identity and the State* (n 25) 24.
[71] AD Smith, *Nationalism and Modernism: A Critical Survey of Recent Theories of Nations and
Nationalism* (London, Routledge, 1998) 3.
[72] ibid 3.
[73] ibid 3.
[74] ibid 20.

to the overriding allegiance of the citizen to [the] nation-state, and this [is] desirable because it [gives] form and substance to the ideals of democratic civic participation.[75]

It is true as Smith notes that in the world of social science scholarship the model 'achieved its canonical formulation in the 1960s'[76] in the context of the proliferating processes of decolonisation in Asia and Africa. In South Asia, however, it has a pedigree as long as that of Europe, because in both Sri Lanka and India, it was the model that was adopted as the anti-colonial vehicle of emancipation as well as the aspirational form of that emancipation by educated elites and the burgeoning middle classes from at least the mid-nineteenth century. Especially in Ceylon, which by the 1940s was considered the constitutional 'pioneer of the non-European dependencies' and the 'senior colony of the new empire',[77] British policy from the early-twentieth century actively encouraged the development of a civic Ceylonese *demos* transcending ethnic differences as a prelude to forthcoming self-government.[78]

As Walker Connor reminds us, John Stuart Mill had instituted the dominant liberal paradigm on the coincidence of nationality and state in 1861, a view that Elie Kedourie considered the best exposition of 'the Whig theory of nationality'.[79] Mill declared in *Considerations on Representative Government* that, 'it is in general a necessary condition of free institutions that the boundaries of government should coincide in the main with those of nationality'.[80] Mill's detractor was no less eminent a Victorian liberal authority. Mounting a strong defence on liberal grounds of multinational states in 1862, Lord Acton contended in *On Nationality* that,

> The presence of different nations under the same sovereignty … provides against the servility which flourishes under the shadow of a single authority, by balancing interests, multiplying associations and giving the subject the restraint and support of a combined opinion.[81]

In his nuanced reappraisal of Mill's position on nationality, Georgios Varouxakis suggests that Mill and Acton (as well as others like Bagehot and Arnold) were much closer in their thinking than is implied by the quotations above, and he is right in cautioning us against 'anachronistic misreadings'.[82] However, without denigrating Varouxakis' important critique, we can plausibly take these views as

---

[75] ibid 20.

[76] ibid 3.

[77] M Wight, *The Development of the Legislative Council, 1906-1945* (London, Faber and Faber, 1946) 74.

[78] These issues are discussed at length in Welikala, *Beyond the Liberal Paradigm* (n 11) ch 5.

[79] E Kedourie, *Nationalism* (London, Hutchinson, 1985) 131–33.

[80] Cited in W Connor, *Ethnonationalism: The Quest for Understanding* (Princeton, Princeton University Press, 1994) 6.

[81] ibid 6.

[82] G Varouxakis, *Mill on Nationality* (London, Routledge, 2002) ch 1, see esp 5–6. See also R Beiner (ed), *Theorizing Nationalism* (Albany, State University of New York Press, 1999) 3; HS Jones, *Victorian Political Thought* (Basingstoke, Macmillan, 2000) 62–63; D Miller, *Citizenship and National Identity* (Cambridge, Polity Press, 2000) 34.

merely articulating two counterposing ideal-types of mono-national and multi-national states for the purposes of the present discussion.

Connor describes how the Mill-Acton debate within liberalism was continued by others such as Sir Ernest Barker and Alfred Cobban in the first half of the twentieth century.[83] More recently, this is of course a debate that is directly engaged within plurinational constitutionalism, through its reliance on the political philosophy of Liberalism II and liberal nationalism, to show that: (i) liberalism and non-state nationalisms are not mutually incompatible; (ii) that the sociological reality of many of the states in the world today do not conform to the classical modernist ideal as articulated by Mill and others; and (iii) that multination states are a discrete category of polity that can be defended on liberal democratic grounds.[84]

For present purposes what is interesting about this debate is that it raises the tantalising counterfactual possibility that had the multi-national as opposed to the mono-national perspective informed British colonial policy in South Asia, then the development of the colonial state, and the constitutional inheritance that it would possibly have left behind, could have assumed a fundamentally different character. Again however it is important to emphasise a difference, which has salience for post-colonial nation-building in the two countries. In India, the British constitutional inheritance involved a federal-type institutional structure reflecting the country's size and diversity, whereas in Ceylon, it left behind a highly orthodox constitutional model that enshrined the unitary state and parliamentary supremacy.[85] In the former case, this contributed to not only the continuation of the federal-type structure (albeit with some highly centralising features)[86] but also a tendency to post-colonial policies of accommodation; whereas in the latter, the

---

[83] Connor, *Ethnonationalism* (n 80) ch 1, esp 5–8.

[84] See C Taylor, 'The Politics of Recognition' and M Walzer, 'Comment' in A Gutmann, *Multiculturalism: Examining the Politics of Recognition* (Princeton, Princeton University Press, 1994) 25–73, 99–103; Kymlicka, *Multicultural Citizenship* (n 1) chs 4 and 9, esp at 52, 186; Norman, *Negotiating Nationalism* (n 1) 1–9; Keating, *Plurinational Democracy* (n 1) ch 2; N MacCormick, *Questioning Sovereignty: Law, State, and Nation in the European Commonwealth* (Oxford, Oxford University Press, 1999); A Stepan, 'Modern Multinational Democracies: Transcending a Gellnerian Oxymoron' in A Stepan, *Arguing Comparative Politics* (Oxford, Oxford University Press, 2001); Tierney, *Constitutional Law and National Pluralism* (n 1) chs 2, 3, 4; M Guibernau, *Belonging: Solidarity and Division in Modern Societies* (Cambridge, Polity Press, 2013).

[85] The horizontal institutional structure and distribution of powers between the centre and the states in the Constitution of India (1950) was substantially based on the Government of India Act 1935: see DD Basu, *Commentary on the Constitution of India* vol 1 (Calcutta, SC Sarkar, 1955) 4; PM Bakshi, *The Constitution of India: Selective Comments* 6th edn (New Delhi, Universal Law Publishing, 2005) 4. On the unitary state and parliamentary sovereignty in Sri Lanka, see Welikala, 'The Failure of Jennings' Constitutional Experiment in Ceylon (n 60).

[86] D Verney, 'How Has the Proliferation of Parties Affected the Indian Federation? A Comparative Perspective' in Hasan, Sridharan and Sudharshan (eds), *India's Living Constitution* (n 10) 137–40.

British legacy in centralising power authorised the unbridled ethnic majoritarianism in both constitutional form and discourse.[87]

Nevertheless, the serving model at independence was the 'unitary nation-state' the central thesis of which was that there could only be one nation within the state.[88] In the context of not merely ethnic but also national pluralism, this has been unhelpful in two interrelated respects. Firstly, this theoretical model espoused a normative dogma of centripetal and unitary discourse of nationality, sovereignty and statehood against the sociological reality in decolonising multinational states. Secondly, the application of this model has been analytically misleading, in that it has served to obscure a proper appreciation of the cultural bias inherent in the nation-state towards a dominant group(s) at the cost of the cultural distinctiveness of minority nations. This has been managed relatively successfully in India through various policies of accommodation, as illustrated by the way in which Tamil nationalist secessionism, which was severe at the inception of the Indian republic, was gradually neutralised.[89] On the other hand, the Indian state's accommodative capacity has demonstrated its limits in its inability to successfully address the Kashmiri claim.[90]

Much more starkly in Sri Lanka, the nation-state has hidden the ideological project of majoritarian hegemony—or ethnocracy—undertaken by Sinhala-Buddhist nationalism behind relatively benign explanations like democratic majoritarianism, with the implication that to the extent this is problematic in a plural polity, it could be addressed through standard counter-majoritarian solutions like bills of individual rights and other minority protection devices. The sub-state national demands of the Sri Lankan Tamils, however, require constitutional responses that go far beyond the protection of individual and group rights, and call for a major renegotiation of the Sri Lankan state's constitutional foundations.[91]

[87] J Uyangoda, 'Sri Lanka's State Reform Debate: Unitarism, Federalism, Decentralization and Devolution' in J Uyangoda (ed), *State Reform in Sri Lanka: Issues, Directions and Perspectives* (Colombo, Social Scientists Association, 2013) ch 2; A Welikala, 'The Sri Lankan Conception of the Unitary State: Theory, Practice and History' in A Amarasingham and D Bass (eds), *Post-War Sri Lanka: Problems and Prospects* (London, Hurst, 2015) (forthcoming).

[88] See eg KW Deutsch and W Folz (eds), *Nation Building* (New York, Aldine-Atherton, 1966); SN Eisenstadt and S Rokkan (eds), *Building States and Nations* vols 1 and 2 (London, Sage, 1973).

[89] A Kohli, 'India: Federalism and the Accommodation of Ethnic Nationalism' in UM Amoretti and N Bermeo (eds), *Federalism and Territorial Cleavages* (London, John Hopkins University Press, 2004) 285–88; S Ramaswamy, *Passions of the Tongue: Language Devotion in Tamil India, 1891-1970* (Berkeley, University of California Press, 1997); MR Barnett, *The Politics of Cultural Nationalism in South India* (Princeton: Princeton University Press, 1976).

[90] Kohli, 'India: Federalism and Ethnic Nationalism' (n 89) 292–97; L Tillin, 'Unity in Diversity? Asymmetry in Indian Federalism' (2007) 37(1) *Publius* 45; A Varshney, 'Three Compromised Nationalisms: Why Kashmir has been a Problem' in Baruah (ed), *Ethnonationalism in India:* (n 5); S Ganguly, 'Explaining the Kashmir Insurgency: Political Mobilization and Institutional Decay' in Baruah (n 5); S Bose, 'The Kashmir Conflict in the Early 21st Century' in Baruah (n 5).

[91] See eg AJ Wilson, *The Break-Up of Sri Lanka: The Sinhalese-Tamil Conflict* (London, Hurst, 1988); AJ Wilson, *Sri Lankan Tamil Nationalism: Its Origins and Development in the 19th and 20th Centuries* (New Delhi, Penguin, 2000).

Either way, owing to the limitations plurinational constitutionalists have high-lighted in the Westphalian nation-state to be discussed below, the model has a fundamental conceptual incapacity to meet the specific normative and institutional challenges of national pluralism, which continues to consistently disallow the best possible response to the claims of sub-state nations. It also reminds us that the prevalence of the monistic conception of nationality, territory and sovereignty in South Asia makes for a procrustean nation-state whose tolerance of internal pluralism is not open-ended, but strictly limited.

# IV. The Multinational Conundrum

'Much nonsense is talked as to the principle of nationalities, as about all approximate practical precepts which claim to be first philosophical principles.'—Walter Bagehot[92]

'Modern social science has been thirled to a model of the nation state, from which it has difficulty in escaping.'—Michael Keating[93]

The condition of 'national pluralism', which denotes the existence of more than one group claiming a *national* identity within the territory and space of a state, raises fundamental questions for the Westphalian nation-state. The constitutional claims that flow from the assertion of national status by territorially based and historically defined groups are both different from, and more difficult to address through, conventional concepts of democratic constitutionalism than are claims to recognition and representation made by 'minority' groups.[94] Within a burgeoning social science literature addressing the multifarious issues raised by national pluralism, I am here interested in drawing upon some of the analytical and normative arguments of a body of constitutional theory known as 'plurinational constitutionalism' in interrogating the South Asian state.

But before I commence my discussion of the insights of plurinational constitutionalism in relation to South Asia, however, it is necessary to briefly discuss the widely cited recent work of Alfred Stepan, Juan Linz and Yogendra Yadav in addressing these very concerns, and to explain the reasons for my chosen preference for the former approach, or more precisely, the qualifications with which Stepan et al must be treated from a constitutional law point of view. Their unique contribution is to theorise two dichotomous models of political organisation: the

---

[92] N St John-Stevas (ed), *The Collected Works of Walter Bagehot: The Political Essays*, vol VIII (London, The Economist, 1974) 157.

[93] M Keating, *The Independence of Scotland: Self-government and the Shifting Politics of Union* (Oxford, Oxford University Press, 2009) 10. Note: Keating uses the word 'thirled' in the Scots sense to mean 'enslaved' rather than the Old English to mean 'pierced'.

[94] Tierney (n 1) 4–5; Keating (n 1) 3–6; Kymlicka (n 1) ch 2; AD Smith, 'Nations in Decline? The Erosion and Persistence of Modern National Identities' in M Young, E Zuelow and A Sturm (eds), *Nationalism in a Global Era: The Persistence of Nations* (London, Routledge, 2007) ch 2.

'nation-state' and the 'state-nation'.[95] Despite the terminological resemblance, the latter concept is very different from both the French concept of *état-nation*[96] and the way state-nation is sometimes used to highlight the state's antecedence to the nation in Third World contexts.[97] Through a 'nested policy grammar'[98] reflecting seven key state policy choices, the argument is that state-nations are more capable of institutionalising 'multiple but complementary identities' in plural societies and of preserving territorial unity consistently with democracy:

> State-nation policies involve crafting a sense of belonging (or 'we-feeling') with respect to the state-wide political community, while simultaneously creating institutional safeguards for respecting and protecting politically salient sociocultural diversities.[99]

While acknowledging serious deficiencies in past practice, these authors argue plausibly that India has more or less followed state-nation policies in its management of diversity.[100] This is contrasted, again persuasively, with the pursuit of 'hard nation-state policies' in Sri Lanka, which led to secessionism and armed conflict.[101] In this regard, their critique of the teleological and substantive monism that characterised the older post-colonial nation-building discourse (discussed above) is entirely valid.

Stepan et al argue that the state-nation is capable of accommodating national pluralism in the manner defined above but this claim is undermined in a number of ways, mainly by a far too perfunctory dismissal of the serious questions raised by plurinational constitutionalists with regard to the constitutional implications of national pluralism. In trying to distinguish the state-nation from 'pure multinationalism',[102] they fail to appreciate the explanatory theses advanced by plurinationalist constitutionalism in arguing that the existence of multiple nations within the state makes for a discrete type of polity that is categorically different from multi-ethnic or multicultural polities. The recognition of this discreteness in turn requires political practices and constitutional structures to be reconceived in order to meet national pluralism's specific challenges. On the contrary, however, Stepan et al indiscriminately cluster the claims of sub-state nations with other types of 'politically salient sociocultural diversities'. This in the view of plurinational constitutionalism constitutes a category error.[103]

---

[95] Stepan, Linz and Yadav, *Crafting State-Nations* (n 7) ch 1.

[96] W Swenden, 'The Territorial and Non-Territorial Management of Ethnic Diversity in South Asia' (2012) 22(5) *Regional & Federal Studies* 613, 620.

[97] See M Guibernau, *Nationalisms: The Nation-State and Nationalism in the Twentieth Century* (Cambridge, Polity Press, 1999) ch 6; P Saravanamuttu, 'Sri Lanka: The Intractability of Ethnic Conflict' in J Darby and R MacGinty (eds), *The Management of Peace Processes* (London, Macmillan, 2000); P Saravanamuttu, 'Governance and Plural Societies: Sri Lanka' in PR Chari (ed), *Security and Governance in South Asia* (Colombo, Regional Centre for Security Studies, 2001) 130–34.

[98] Stepan, Linz and Yadav (n 7) 17–22.

[99] ibid 4–5.

[100] ibid ch 2.

[101] ibid ch 5.

[102] ibid 11.

[103] Tierney (n 1) 13.

It seems that the reason for this scepticism is that they view the plurinational ideal as

> a model in which a nationalist vocabulary is used by groups who conceive of their nationalities as nation-states *in potentia* and aim at reducing the state to a bare minimum, with the result, intended or not, of bringing about an extremely weak 'we feeling'—if any.[104]

In other words, the criticism is that plurinationalism is effectively tantamount to disintegration through secessionism. Yet this seems too simplistic a reading of plurinational principles. As Ferran Requejo and Miquel Caminal (two authors that Stepan et al are highly critical of)[105] argue,

> the key question for a plurinational democracy is to establish, not how the *demos* can become a *cratos*—that would be the traditional view of democracy—but how different *demoi* (majorities and minorities) that co-exist within the same democracy can be politically and constitutionally recognised and accommodated on equal terms.[106]

Going further in his review of Stepan et al, Wilfried Swenden cites a large number of well-known scholars who have contributed to our understanding of plurinationalism, and while highlighting the many parallels in this work with state-nation policies, he also points out that 'not all of these authors are favourably disposed to realising the "state" aspirations of these minority nations'.[107] While therefore the contribution of Stepan et al is exceedingly valuable for their empirical comparativism and as a toolkit for policy-makers in negotiating competing claims in multinational societies, their refusal to engage with plurinational constitutionalism in any adequate depth means that they leave many questions that are crucial from a *constitutional* viewpoint unanswered. Put another way, it seems to me that their unmistakable *descriptive* clarity in understanding 'robustly politically multinational'[108] polities as a distinctive type of state is not matched by due attention to the necessary *normative* consequences that ensue from that analysis. It is to these questions that I now turn.

The 'plurinational state' is a liberal democratic model of constitutional accommodation for national pluralism. It is distinct from other models of pluralism such as multiculturalism and minority rights, or the wide variety of models of territorial and institutional pluralism such as federalism and devolution, in terms of the political phenomenon that it seeks constitutionally to accommodate. The distinctiveness of the issue arises from the fact that the sub-state national challenge

---

[104] Stepan, Linz and Yadav (n 7) 11. Of course, many scholars argue against granting state-like institutional apparatuses to sub-state nations on the grounds that it leads to the break-up of states and international instability. For noted expositions of arguments in this vein, see J Snyder, *From Voting to Violence* (New York, WW Norton, 2000); PG Roeder, *Where Nation-States Come from: Institutional Change in the Age of Nationalism* (Princeton, Princeton University Press, 2007).

[105] See Stepan, Linz and Yadav (n 7) 12–13.

[106] F Requejo and M Caminal, 'Liberal Democracies, National Pluralism and Federalism' in Requejo and Caminal (eds), *Political Liberalism and Plurinational Democracies* (n 1) 5.

[107] Swenden, 'Territorial and Non-Territorial Management of Ethnic Diversity' (n 96) 620.

[108] Stepan, Linz and Yadav (n 7) xii.

is one conceived in specifically *national* terms, which means that they carry with them normative claims to recognition, autonomy and representation that are more fundamental than claims made by 'minority' groups. Minority ethnic nationalists may also make similar claims, but often, because such movements can be 'nationalist' without actively promoting a 'nation' (or seeking a state), these can be addressed within the state without fundamentally questioning the host nation-state's monistic conception of nationality and sovereignty.[109]

However, the demands of those stateless nations with which we are concerned—such as the Kashmiris and the Tamils—are not likely to be fulfilled by mere self-government that does not carry with it an acknowledgement of their nationality claim. Short of a nation-state of their own, which for broader geopolitical reasons is not and has never been realistically on the agenda in either of these cases, the challenge then is to devise constitutional frameworks for the full expression of these claims in the governing arrangements of the state within which they are located, as nations and not as minority groups. Michael Keating posits the basic rationale of the plurinational state in straightforward terms:

> The argument is that we cannot resolve nationality issues by giving each nation its own state, but neither can, nor should we seek to eliminate nationality as a basis for political order. Rather we need to embrace the concept of plural nationalities and shape political practices and institutions accordingly.[110]

As noted before also, plurinational constitutionalists therefore do not assume that sub-state nationalism is always synonymous with separatism, and in fact they argue that 'from a legal perspective, constitutional accommodation *within* the plurinational state in fact raises more interesting questions on the nature of sovereignty and its potential for divisibility than does secession'.[111] Plurinational constitutionalism accordingly presents a number of descriptive and normative critiques of the theoretical foundations, political practices and constitutional arrangements of the nation-state, which as noted above, is traditionally conceived in unitary terms with regard to nationality, territory and sovereignty. In suggesting radically pluralist alternatives to dominant narratives of constitutional self-understanding in the light of those critiques, plurinational constitutionalism is concerned with both the reinterpretation of existing constitutional arrangements of the host state as well as in their structural amendment, in appreciation of the state's plurinational character.

A key ground of normative critique presented by plurinational constitutionalism against the Westphalian nation-state model concerns the 'monistic *demos* thesis', ie, the notion that operates as both postulate and presumption that the

---

[109] This is the way federalism is often advocated as a method of ethnic conflict regulation: see eg N Bermeo, 'Conclusion: The Merits of Federalism' in Amoretti and Bermeo (eds), *Federalism and Territorial Cleavages* (n 89); K Scott, *Federalism: A Normative Theory and its Practical Relevance* (New York, Continuum, 2011) 128–32.

[110] Keating (n 1) ix.

[111] Tierney (n 1) 18–19, 18 fn 52.

'nation' is synonymous with the 'state'.[112] By their very existence, sub-state nations challenge the monistic presupposition that there is, or can only be, one nation within the state.[113] A closely related contention is that regarding 'host state societal dominance', ie, that the conceptualisation of the nation in both unitary terms and in exclusive association with the state not only prevents the fullest constitutional recognition of national pluralism, but that it also serves to privilege in effect a majority or otherwise dominant cultural identity to the disadvantage of minority nations.

This is vividly demonstrated in the Sri Lankan case not merely by the assertion of Tamils to a distinct national identity and territory throughout its post-colonial history, but also by the Sri Lankan state's equally rigid refusal to accept that there can be anything other than one nation in the state. Exacerbating this, the Sinhala-Buddhist majority have not merely taken political control of the state, but also pervasively infused the state with its own cultural identity, thereby negating the cultural neutrality that is a purported strength of the modernist nation-state.

In India the picture is more nuanced, but as we have seen, the active adoption of the mid-twentieth-century nation-building model in its constitution-making process has meant that an Indian nation defined in monistic terms has become both entrenched and romanticised.[114] The post-colonial state has perpetuated and reproduced this 'monolithic definition of nation, nationalism, and national unity'[115] due to its critical significance for the state's own legitimacy and survival in a pluralistic polity. Alam is right in reminding us that, 'This monolithic definition is not a recent creation of Hindutva as is assumed but with a different set of meanings and content has also been the basis of secular politics'.[116] He goes on to note:

> From pre-Independence times the secularist-nationalist leadership has refused to even countenance the possibility that different people with varying 'national compositions' could have different notions of what it means to be Indian. It has thoughtlessly insisted on treating India as a nation in the sense in which Portugal or Sweden or Germany are nations. This kind of transferred a priori understanding of what it means to be a nation is obviously out of tune with the specificities of India. It has come to be met with varying degrees of resistance in different parts of the country.[117]

---

[112] 'Monistic *demos* thesis' is Tierney's term, as is 'host state societal dominance: Tierney (n 1) 230, 128–29.

[113] Taylor, 'The Politics of Recognition' (n 84).

[114] Nandy, *The Romance of the State* (n 11) 1–14.

[115] Alam (n 10) 101.

[116] Alam (n 10) 101-02. Bhattacharyya, Kluge and König (n 25) at xv, define 'Hindutva' as 'literally, "Hinduness"; the quality of being a Hindu. A social concept developed by VD Savarkar which has been politicized by Hindu nationalist forces'. It challenges India's 'four founding mythologies: democracy, socialism, secularism, and federalism': S Corbridge, 'Federalism, Hindu Nationalism and Mythologies of Governance in Modern India' in G Smith (ed), *Federalism: The Multiethnic Challenge* (London, Longman, 1995). This movement is at the heart of India's present Bharatiya Janata Party (BJP)-led government. See C Jaffrelot, *The Hindu Nationalist Movement and Indian Politics, 1925 to 1990s* (London, Hurst, 1996). On the BJP, TB Hansen and C Jaffrelot (eds), *The BJP and the Compulsions of Politics in India* (New Delhi, Oxford University Press, 1998).

[117] Alam (n 10) 102.

This critique of the monism of the modernist, secular Indian nationalism resonates closely with the plurinational critique of traditional liberalism, which points
to the imperviousness with which the existence of plural *demoi* within the state
and their attendant claims have been treated, rendering sub-state nations 'voice-
less and faceless'.[118] As Requejo has noted in relation to the work of liberal scholars
such as Rawls and Habermas, national pluralism 'is a question that is not so much
badly resolved as completely unaddressed by the premises, concepts and normative questions of these theorists'.[119] Stephen Tierney goes further in pointing out a
more insidious consequence of this deficiency in traditional liberalism:

> What is particularly debilitating about this gap in the conceptual precepts of traditional
> liberal theory is that it has led to a false assumption that the liberal democratic state is
> neutral in cultural and societal terms. Whereas in reality, as Requejo contends, 'practi-
> cally speaking, all liberal democracies have acted as nationalising agencies for specific
> cultural particularisms.' Accordingly, many of the normative prescriptions emerging
> from traditional liberal accounts have been built on epistemological error, or at least,
> imprecision.[120]

The assumption that the collective identificatory function of nationhood rests
only with the statal nation denies the possibility of multiple conceptions of
national identity that are commonly held by citizens of plurinational polities. For
example, an individual may consider himself a member of both a Tamil nation
and a Sri Lankan nation. By the failure to acknowledge this important dimension
of individual identity and autonomy, the nation-state denies to individual members of sub-state nations, for whom the sub-state societal space is an important
means of political self-expression, such cardinal commitments of democracy as
the freedom of choice, equality and justice. On the other hand, the pretence that
the state national society is a culturally neutral entity held together by purely normative values of citizenship (sometimes accompanied by the disparaging implication that sub-state nations are not and cannot be similarly modern, progressive
and inclusive entities),[121] hides the reality that the state-national identity is more
often than not associated with a dominant societal or cultural influence within the
plurinational polity. The failure to apprehend the homogenising consequences of
the unitary nation-state results in states in multinational polities failing to fulfil
basic normative dictates of the democratic ideal.

In addressing this conceptual deficit, the methodology of plurinational constitutionalism places emphasis not only on the sociological fact of plural
national spaces within the state, but also on such nationalisms as a form of
'normal politics'.[122] It recognises that sub-state nations are deliberative spaces for

---

[118] Tierney (n 1) 10.

[119] F Requejo, 'Introduction' in F Requejo (ed), *Democracy and National Pluralism* (London,
Routledge, 2001) 4. See also Kymlicka's observations on Rawls and Dworkin in Kymlicka (n 1) 128.

[120] Tierney (n 1) 10.

[121] See M Canovan, 'Sleeping Dogs, Prowling Cats and Soaring Doves: Three Paradoxes in the Political Theory of Nationhood' (2001) 49(2) *Political Studies* 203, 204–06.

[122] Keating (n 1) viii.

individuals' participation in civic and political life, through which they play an essential intermediary role in the relationship between the citizen and the state. The sub-state nation rather than the nation-state is often the foremost vehicle of identity and agency for the individual member of the sub-state nation, and accordingly,

> the value which he finds in the democratic process can be more fully explained by appreciating these ties, and by understanding the preferences felt by this citizen for the location of his right of *individual* self-determination within the broader condition of *collective* self-determination for his primary *demos*'.[123]

The meaningful realisation of democratic commitments in respect of citizenship in plurinational polities therefore requires the empirical reality of national pluralism to be fully acknowledged and accommodated in symbolic, normative and institutional terms by the plurinational state. Even the multicultural concept of state-nation propounded by Stepan et al does not meet these requirements, rendering the Southphalian state remote and forbidding, and often violently repressive, from the point of view of sub-state nations.

A related challenge to the nation-state's orthodox constitutional discourse inheres in plurinational constitutionalism's critique of 'narrow positivism' on two fronts: narrow positivism's promotion of a unitary model of legal sovereignty, and its 'artificial distinction' between legal and political sovereignty, both of which it is argued, 'fit nicely with, and share the same flaws as, unitary conceptions of the *demos*'.[124] The result is the close association of narrow positivism with unitary or centralised models of constitutional form fundamentally at odds with sub-state national aspirations within multinational polities. As Tierney argues,

> This notion of sovereignty has been a central ideological device in legitimising the dominant, monistic vision with which the plurinational state has masqueraded as the nation of the state ... The dominant society has been able to crystallise political power at the centre of the state, presenting it in the guise of legal legitimacy, and hence entrenching political hegemony in purportedly objective constitutional form.[125]

One of the issues with narrow positivism is that it purports to offer a self-contained account of pristine legal sovereignty that is divorced (indeed, liberated) from politics. Although the validity of this claim to political neutrality is heavily disputed,[126] taken at face value, this also means that narrow positivism is divorced from the 'social reality'[127] of which legal institutions are a part, and from which flow the legitimacy of both institutions and power. By contrast to narrow positivism, more sophisticated positivist accounts call for a fuller understanding of the relationship between social conditions and legal institutions, and especially the relationship between political power and legal sovereignty. As Martin Loughlin has pointed out,

---

[123] Tierney (n 1) 11.
[124] ibid 13.
[125] ibid 16.
[126] ibid 13–15.
[127] MacCormick, *Questioning Sovereignty* (n 84) 106.

Sovereignty is essentially an expression of a political relationship and, from a juristic perspective, sovereignty constitutes the essence of the modern state ... Sovereignty ... is the name given to express the quality of the political relationship that is formed between the people and the state ... This relational aspect of sovereignty is highlighted by Croce. 'In the relationship between the ruler and the ruled', he argues, 'sovereignty belongs to neither but to the relationship itself'.[128]

Plurinational constitutionalists rely upon this relational conceptualisation of sovereignty that stresses the interrelationship between the political and the legal, albeit by extending this insight to the plurality of peoples or nations within the plurinational state.[129] It follows from the application of the relational understanding of sovereignty to the reality of multiple nations within the state that both the idea of sovereignty and the legal form of governing institutions must also be pluralistic. The challenge of national pluralism to the nation-state with regard to the divisibility of sovereignty therefore is to develop the discursive and conceptual capacity to provide for plurinational institutional requirements. This is well illustrated in the Indian case where, despite innovative experiments with linguistic re-territorialisation and asymmetric federalism—or in other words, the use of an array of 'state-nation' policies—the idea of sovereignty has remained classically Westphalian. The centralising features of India's original quasi-federalist post-colonial constitutional settlement are both anchored in, and further sustain, the exclusive and unitary sovereignty claimed by the Indian nation and state.[130] Sri Lankan constitutional discourse has proved totally resistant to any pluralisation of sovereignty, flowing from its unshakeable commitment to the formal and substantive centralisation of political power and legal authority embodied in the unitary state.[131]

Taken together, these and other theses of plurinational constitutionalism represent a major critique and call for a fundamental re-conceptualisation of the Westphalian conception of the sovereign nation-state, in terms of its internal constitutional norms, doctrines and structures. From the perspective of constitutional law and theory, the essence of the plurinational challenge may be summarised in Tierney's words as follows:

central to the challenge presented by sub-state national societies to the host state is a call for the disaggregation of the terms 'state' and 'nation'; those who adhere to the traditional conceptualisation of the 'nation-state' as one politico-constitutional territory encapsulating a unitary national society are charged with the task of reconceiving the plurinational state in appreciation of its essential societal plurality.[132]

---

[128] M Loughlin, *The Idea of Public Law* (Oxford, Oxford University Press, 2003) 83, citing B Croce *Politics and Morals* (SJ Castiglione tr, New York, Philosophical Library, 1945) 17.

[129] Tierney (n 1) 102–04.

[130] But see for a sophisticated argument about how sovereignty can be historicised and rearticulated consistently with pluralist norms in the Indian context, LI Rudolph and SH Rudolph, 'Federalism as State Formation in India: A Theory of Shared and Negotiated Sovereignty' (2010) 31(5) *International Political Science Review/Revue internationale de science politique* 553.

[131] Welikala, 'Sri Lankan Conception of the Unitary State' (n 87).

[132] Tierney (n 1) 5.

This disaggregation of the nation from the state allows territory, sovereignty and institutions to be completely rethought and redesigned with not merely the plural social, cultural or ethnic, but the plural *national* foundations of the state in mind. Without such an overhaul of the nation-state, national pluralism is bound to produce tension and conflict, which so far in Sri Lanka with the Tamils, and India in the case of Kashmir especially, have been dealt with by force. In doing so, these states have expanded their control potential and entrenched their claims to ultimate sovereignty even further, and as much if not more lamentably, sought to legitimise the associated excesses by emotionally charged appeals to the romanticised unity of the monistic nation.

While at the normative level the debates mentioned above are conducted within liberalism in the current literature on the plurinational state, the broader arguments about the monistic *demos*, cultural dominance and unitary sovereignty are obviously of much wider application, directed as it is to the Westphalian nation-state, of which the Southphalian state is an amplified version. Moreover, while paying pharisaic homage to the nation-state, particularly as a means of denying sub-state national claims, post-colonial states like Sri Lanka have actively undermined its principles. Westphalian concepts like the unified *demos* have, as noted before, been pervasively ethnicised in Sri Lankan constitutional practice, thereby negating the model's normative dictates, and distorting its emancipatory potential as a conceptual conduit for social progress from ethnic hierarchy to civic equality as envisaged in the early literature on post-colonial nation-building.[133] In the decolonisation era, Westphalian doctrines, endorsed for example by the Five Principles of Peaceful Coexistence embodied in the Sino-Indian Agreement of 1954,[134] were seized upon by weak emerging states as safeguards as much against internal ethno-territorial challenges as against external interference. In this internal sense, Westphalian principles have become ideological weapons in the state's armoury in the rejection of sub-state national claims to territorial accommodation, as seen constantly in the Indian state's inability to successfully address the Kashmiri claim.

# V. Conclusions

My modest aim in this chapter has been to demonstrate the resilience of a very orthodox conception of the Westphalian nation-state in South Asia—which

---

[133] Smith, *Nationalism and Modernism* (n 71) ch 1.

[134] Agreement (with exchange of notes) on trade and intercourse between Tibet Region of China and India (29 April 1954) *United Nations Treaty Series* (1958) 299 UNTS 57. It is noteworthy that the signatory states to this treaty are in today's world the two rising global powers of Asia, with the political and economic capacity to influence the content of international law and practice, including in relation to concepts of state- and nation-hood and sovereignty. This again points to a revival of orthodox doctrines within the international system rather than their terminal decline.

I have called 'Southphalia'—by focusing on the Southphalian state's response to the major constitutional challenge of national pluralism. The argument about the rigidity of the Southphalian state's fundamentalist conception of key principles like nationality, sovereignty and territoriality proceeded in three steps. In the first step I tried to explain how the influence of colonialism instantiated a particular type of soft authoritarian state, and its post-colonial path dependency. I then discussed how the legal power of the juridical state was politically buttressed by a monistic conception of the nation (in both its Indian civic and Sri Lankan ethnic avatars), which while providing majoritarian legitimacy for the state, entailed major injustice, exclusion and even suppression for minority nations. In the third stage of the discussion I brought to bear certain analytical insights and normative perspectives associated with plurinational constitutionalism, so as to further reveal the inadequacies of the Southphalian nation-state when confronted with the challenge of national pluralism. Aside from the violence against sub-state national challenges mounted by the 'fearful state', what this served to prove was its lack of conceptual malleability, which has been further reinforced rather than softened in response to the claims of the periphery.

I hope this part of the discussion has also raised some theoretical questions for comparative South Asian constitutional law and politics, which have so far not been adequately debated in the literature. These questions deserve more sustained scholarly attention if Southphalia is not to represent a Southfailure in terms of the cardinal requirements of the basic democratic ideal to which both India and Sri Lanka seem ostensibly committed.

Two recent political developments require brief mention in this regard. In May 2014, the National Democratic Alliance (NDA), dominated by leading Hindu chauvinist parties and personalities (including Narendra Modi who became Prime Minister), assumed power in India raising widespread concern about the future of India's secular democracy. Among other things, Modi is opposed to Article 370 of the Indian Constitution, which, while originally conceived as a transitional provision but remains improperly unimplemented, grants a special autonomous status for Jammu and Kashmir.[135] More generally, LK Advani, another prominent BJP luminary has expressed views which, notwithstanding Modi's frequent invocations of 'co-operative federalism', can be taken to describe this political tradition's approach to the nature of the Indian state and nation even today:

> The BJP rejects this thesis of a multi-national state. India is multi-lingual, it is multi-religious; but it is still one nation. Indians are one people. The Indian Constitution is also based on this acceptance. It is, therefore, that our Constitution-makers made the Indian Republic federal in form but essentially unitary in content.[136]

---

[135] See especially Tillin, 'Unity in Diversity?' (n 90) 52–55. See also HK Saharay. *The Constitution of India: An Analytical Approach* 3rd edn (Kolkata, Eastern Law House, 2002) 979–83; AG Noorani, *Article 370: A Constitutional History of Jammu and Kashmir* (Oxford, Oxford University Press, 2011).

[136] Cited in Tillin (n 7) 60.

In Sri Lanka, President Mahinda Rajapaksa's ultra-Sinhala nationalist government militarily crushed the armed separatist Liberation Tigers of Tamil Eelam (LTTE) in May 2009. In the triumphalist aftermath of the war victory, President Rajapaksa introduced constitutional changes, not to address the root causes of the conflict, but to institutionalise a regime of populist authoritarianism and hyperpresidentialism. In a ceremonial address to Parliament upon the conclusion of the war, he controversially declared that there were no more ethnic minorities or majorities in Sri Lanka; only those who love the country and those do not.[137] As Nira Wickramasinghe remarked,

> The President's vision merges nation and state and promotes a love of country based on a particular reading of the history and foundation myth of the Sinhala people, where all other groups … are present merely as shadows and not as constitutive elements of a common political culture.[138]

The subsequent record of the regime followed this interpretation closely, but President Rajapaksa was, however, unexpectedly defeated in the presidential election of January 2015, with the common opposition platform promising major constitutional reforms to restore democratic governance. It is interesting to note that notwithstanding the widespread support he enjoyed among the minorities, the new President Maithripala Sirisena was careful to avoid any specific commitments with regard to Tamil aspirations to territorial autonomy, so as not to alienate the majority Sinhalese from his candidacy.

The Modi government has not yet undertaken any precipitous action in pursuit of its ideological beliefs, while the Sirisena government is only beginning its democracy reforms. Nevertheless, these developments in the two countries serve to underscore the fact that the central precepts of the Southphalian settlement that stand in the way of a normatively rigorous response to national pluralism remain undisturbed. Consistent with the limited objective of the chapter as outlined above, I have not tried to articulate a positive theory of the Southphalian state. This work remains to be done, but I would conclude by reiterating the caution I voiced at the beginning about the danger of generalising too much from the retreat of the Western nation-state. In this sense, the Southphalian state is not post-sovereign, post-national, post-modern, or post-anything, except postcolonial. The European situation especially represents a historically contingent experience which does not hold true in other regions of the world, at least for now.

---

[137] Verbatim extract cited in N Wickramasinghe, 'After the War: A New Patriotism in Sri Lanka?' (2009) 68(4) *Journal of Asian Studies* 1045, 1046.

[138] N Wickramasinghe, '*Producing the Present: History as Heritage in Post-War Patriotic Sri Lanka*' (2012) ICES Research Paper No 2, 2.

Part 2

# Constitutional Globalisation:
# The Settings for National Pluralism

International Law: Accommodating
Pluralism?

# 7

# Modelling Democratic Secession in International Law

STEVEN WHEATLEY*

## I. Introduction

The focus of this chapter is the possibility of developing a model of democratic secession consistent with the emergent teleology of an international law system increasingly focused on the idea of legitimate political authority. A right of democratic secession is understood as the right of a group to a state by virtue of the fact that its political leaders have been able to mobilise majority support around a nationalist case in favour of independence. In order to develop an argument for recognising a such a right, the work develops an abstract conceptual model of world society to explain the emergence of new states. Drawing on developments in the natural sciences through an application of the third wave of systems theory thinking know as complexity, it outlines a model of state as the framing of the emergent patterned communications of co-evolved and co-existent law and politics systems. In contradistinction to much of the systems theory literature, law and politics are understood to be complex systems: the patterned communications of the systems are a consequence of the actions of constituent agents; their interactions with each other; and interactions with other actors and systems in the external environment. A focus on the nature of the politics systems—understood through the cognitive frame of international law—allows us to develop an argument that supports the right of democratic secession in three related steps: the rejection of the sovereign authority of the territorial state by certain subjects; the acceptance of the authority of emergent systems of law and politics of the new political entity; and observation (or 'recognition') of the political entity as possessing legitimate political authority.

The chapter proceeds as follows. It first outlines the way in which international law responds to claims for recognition of the right of national self-determination—understood here as the claim to a sovereign and independent state. The extant

* My thanks to Robert Geyer, James Summers and Tom Webb for comments on an earlier draft.

incoherence in the existing doctrine and practice of political self-determination and statehood suggests a requirement for a new conceptual model to make sense of this problem. In common with a long tradition in the social sciences (including law), the chapter looks to developments in the natural sciences to make sense of the social world—in this case by reference to a variant of systems theory known as complexity, which is focused on emergent systems that represent the patterned communications of networks of agents, without any central controller or guiding hand. The rationale for relying on complexity is the perceived advantages of an approach that can illuminate debates in international law, clarifying its underlying conceptual base, while being consistent in its application. Law and politics systems are understood to be *like* the complex systems we observe in the natural world—and are therefore amenable to an application of the insights of complex systems theory thinking. Whilst there is an emerging literature that seeks to apply the insights from complexity to domestic law systems,[1] hitherto, complexity has had limited impact on international law scholarship, and there has been no attempt to apply complexity to the law on national self-determination.[2] Following the insights from complexity, we can develop an abstract model of *state* as the observation of the patterned communications of the co-evolved and co-existent law and politics systems. The third part of the chapter relies on this abstract model to outline a right of democratic secession. The work concludes by reflecting on the implications of the analysis for the events of 2014 in the Crimea, Donetsk and Luhansk regions of Ukraine.

## II. The International Law on National Self-Determination

The nationalist argument is that each nation has the right, if it so chooses, to its own state. The justification for the position lies in the claim that nations and their cultures are both valuable in themselves and important to individuals in terms of identity, well-being and flourishing, and that the nation and those marked by the national culture are best protected within a sovereign and independent

[1] See eg HM Babcock, 'Democracy's Discontent in a Complex World: Can Avalanches Sandpiles, and Finches Optimize Michael Sandel's Civic Republican Community?' (1996–97) 85 *Georgetown Law Journal* 2085; GT Jones, 'Dynamical Jurisprudence: Law as a Complex System' (2008) 24(4) *Georgia State University Law Review* 873; J Webb, 'Law, Ethics, and Complexity: Complexity Theory & the Normative Reconstruction of Law' (2005) 52 *Cleveland State Law Review* 227; T Webb, 'Tracing an Outline of Legal Complexity' (2014) 27(4) *Ratio Juris* 477.
[2] Lars-Erik Cederman applies the insights from complexity in an attempt to explain the processes that lead to the establishment of new nation-states: L Cederman, *Emergent Actors in World Politics: How States and Nations Develop and Dissolve* (Princeton, NJ, Princeton University Press, 1997). See also L Cederman and L Girardin, 'Growing Sovereignty: Modeling the Shift from Indirect to Direct Rule' (2010) 54 *International Studies Quarterly* 27.

nation-state. Where this is not already the case, the literature suggests that the group has the right to establish a state on one of three grounds: that each nation has the right to a state on its territorial homeland; that individual members of the nation have a choice-based, or democratic, right of secession; and that, in cases of extreme injustice, the group has a remedial right of secession. This section briefly outlines the ways in which international law responds to these claims.

Nationalism, in the words of Anthony Smith, is the belief that all those who share a common history and culture should be 'autonomous, united and distinct in their recognised homelands'.[3] Nationalism concerns, generally speaking, the demand by a group for a state, by virtue of the fact that the group is a 'nation'. The claim by sub-state groups is advanced in two related steps: first, that each nation is, if it so chooses, entitled to its own state, and, second, the territorial state in which the nation is located enjoys limited, if any, authority over certain subjects, by virtue of the ethnic, religious and linguistic differences between the centre and the relevant group.[4] The manifestation of a sentiment of national self-determination is seen as a reaction by the periphery to the homogenising efforts of the language and culture of the centre, and a conflict over the assertion of political authority and the place and meaning of the boundary between the centre and the nation.

A cursory glance at the different maps drawn since 1900 might suggest that the nationalist argument has proven highly effective, as the world has changed from a handful of largely European empires to over two hundred sovereign and independent states.[5] This interpretation would be mistaken. The process by which new states have emerged—in particular in the period since the inception of the United Nations—has in fact undermined the distinctive claim of nationalism, ie the right to a 'nation-state'. This conclusion may appear paradoxical as many would claim that it was nationalism that replaced empire as the organising principle of world political society, and we continue to see new states emerge in response to the nationalist demands—a state of Montenegro for Montenegrins, for example. An examination of the international law doctrine and practice demonstrates, however, that when questions of legitimacy supplemented the criterion of effectiveness for the establishment of new states, political authority was framed in terms of a consent-based or 'democratic' self-determination, and not any nationalist principle. This is explained by reference to the turn to ethics in international law that accompanied the introduction of the United Nations as an organisation of global governance capable of giving expression to the inchoate values of the international community, and which has resulted in arguments for

---

[3] AD Smith, *Nationalism in the Twentieth Century* (Oxford, Martin Robertson, 1979) 2.

[4] See generally E Gellner, *Nations and Nationalism* (Oxford, Blackwell, 1983); J Breuilly, *Nationalism and the State* 2nd edn (Manchester, Manchester University Press, 1993).

[5] New states have emerged in a number of *waves*, notably at the time of the United Nations decolonisation movement in the 1960s, during which decade 42 states were admitted to UN membership; and the partial collapse of the Soviet Empire and dissolution of Yugoslavia in the 1990s, when 32 new members were admitted. Since the turn of the 21st century, only 5 new states have been admitted to the United Nations (a significant decrease on the average).

significant modifications to the 'Montevideo checklist' for the identification of new states and revised understandings as to the required conditions for the establishment of statehood.

The term 'nation' in international law can refer either to the state (the international *Law of Nations*), or to groups within the state or that cross state borders. For reasons of clarity, this work will use the more common international law terminology of 'state' and 'people'. The distinctive claim of nationalism, ie the right of a nation to a state, is then reformulated in terms of the right of peoples to political self-determination, statehood and independence. The traditional position of international law has been that the establishment of a sovereign political community is a question of fact: an effective political power under the rule of law has a prima facie claim to be accepted as a state. Outside of the state-of-nature, international law recognised a right of sovereignty where a political community was able to establish its independence 'safely and permanently' (in the words of the Lassa Oppenheim) from the previous sovereign power.[6] The position remains largely unchanged in the present day: an entity that can, by its own efforts, establish itself 'safely and permanently' within a territory has a claim to be accepted as a state.

Whilst there is consensus in the literature that effectiveness (the exercise of independent government functions over a territory and population) is a necessary, and often the most important, criterion of statehood, there is disagreement as to whether it is a sufficient criterion as a consequence of the non-recognition of certain state-like entities, including Southern Rhodesia and Turkish Republic of Northern Cyprus. A revised understanding is developed in one of two ways. First, as a modification of the 'Montevideo checklist':[7] a prohibition on statehood where independence results from an unlawful act of military intervention (Turkish Republic of Northern Cyprus), or where independence is achieved through a violation of the rights of people to self-determination based on political equality (Southern Rhodesia). Secondly, that certain principles related to an idea of legitimacy can support or undermine the claim to 'effectiveness': an ineffective but legitimate political community may be recognised as a state (Guinea-Bissau, Croatia, Bosnia and Herzegovina), whilst an effective but illegitimate political community may not be recognised (Southern Rhodesia, Turkish Republic of Northern Cyprus and Transdniestria).

The normal mechanism by which a new state is established is through its separation from the territorial state. This is a consensual process. Where the territorial state accepts and recognises the newly independent state, the international community will normally follow its lead, unless the new state is established in

---

[6] L Oppenheim, *International Law: A Treatise*, vol I 'Peace' 1st edn (London, Longmans, Green, and Co, 1905) 112–13.

[7] According to Art 1 of the Montevideo Convention on the Rights and Duties of States (adopted 26 December 1933) 165 LNTS 19. Reprinted (1934) 28 (Supplement) *American Journal of International Law* 75), *state* as legal person in international law should possess the following qualifications: (a) permanent population; (b) defined territory; (c) government; (d) and the capacity to enter into relations with other states (usually understood as independence).

violation of an international law norm of *jus cogens* standing. Where the territorial state does not consent to the establishment of the new state, the relevant process is unilateral secession. This can be achieved in one of two ways: through effective control of the territory 'safely and permanently' or by virtue of the right of peoples to self-determination. A positive application of the right to self-determination would logically accord a right to statehood in the absence of effective political control. Consider, for example, the practice of creating nation-states following World War One, when the *Peacemakers* (*pace* Margaret Macmillan) sought, on objective criteria, to identify nations and to establish their sovereign and independent existence—a process foreshadowed in President Woodrow Wilson's 'Fourteen Points' address to Congress in 1918, in which he called for the establishment of a state of Poland, 'which should include the territories inhabited by indisputably Polish populations'.[8]

The United Nations decolonisation project took a different approach to the post World War One settlement, establishing a right of political self-determination and statehood only for non-contiguous colonised territories.[9] 'Colonised' peoples were defined by their relationship to the territory, and not any racial, ethnic, cultural, religious or linguistic characteristics. The territorial approach to defining 'peoples' was confirmed by the application of the principle of *uti possidetis*: the requirement for the recognition of colonial administrative borders as the boundaries of political self-determination. As Hurst Hannum explains, in the UN decolonisation process, '[t]erritory, not "nationhood," was the determining factor'.[10] The negative aspect of the international law right of peoples to self-determination developed by the United Nations denies political legitimacy in cases of colonial rule and accords a right to independence and statehood to non-self-governing *territories*.

The fact that the overwhelming majority of non-self-governing territories have achieved political self-determination by way of independence, integration or association does not exhaust the application of the right of peoples to self-determination. According to general, customary and conventional international law: '*All peoples* have the right to self-determination. By virtue of that right they freely determine their political status'.[11] Whilst, there is no agreed international law definition of 'people', four general criteria are normally considered to be relevant in the identification of peoples: some identity characteristic that differentiates members of the group from others, based on race, ethnicity, culture, language, religion, or common economic life etc; historical continuity, understood in terms that peoples

---

[8] Point XIII. Woodrow Wilson, 'An address to a Joint Session of Congress' (The Fourteen Points Address)', 8 January 1918, reprinted as AS Link et al (eds), *The Papers of Woodrow Wilson*, vol 45 (Princeton NJ, Princeton University Press, 1984) 534.

[9] Declaration on the Granting of Independence to Colonial Countries and Peoples (adopted 14 December 1960) UNGA Res 1514 (XV).

[10] H Hannum, *Autonomy, Sovereignty, and Self-Determination: The Accommodation of Conflicting Rights* (Philadelphia, University Pennsylvania Press, 1990) 36.

[11] Art 1(1) common to International Covenant on Economic, Social and Cultural Rights (adopted 16 December 1966) 993 UNTS 3 and International Covenant on Civil and Political Rights (adopted 16 December 1966) 999 UNTS 171 (emphasis added).

have a history and an imagined future; that the group is associated with a particular territory, or 'homeland'; and the self-conception of the group as an actual or potential unit of self-determination. Self-evidently these criteria can encompass ethno-cultural groups within the state, and it is accepted that the international law category of 'people' can be applied to groups within a state that *ipso jure* enjoy a right to political self-determination. It is less clear what the consequences of such a recognition entail, although there is general agreement in the international law doctrine and literature that the right of peoples to political self-determination does not (alone) accord a right to statehood for sub-state groups.

Whilst self-determination does not establish a right to statehood, this does not preclude the possibility of a group within the state declaring its independence,[12] or achieving statehood through the establishment of effective control over a territory and its population—as secession is neither lawful, nor unlawful, as a matter of international law.[13] The right of the state to its territorial integrity is opposable to (ie valid against) other states, not peoples and groups within the state. Where a politically effective people becomes de facto autonomous and independent, without external military support, it has a claim to be a state. But what about politically ineffective peoples? Outside of the colonial context, three possible scenarios can be identified for accepting a right of independence for groups seeking statehood, but which are unable to establish effective control: in cases of serious human rights abuses ('remedial secession'); the internationalisation of promises of independence in certain circumstances ('promissory secession'); and following a positive vote in an independence referendum or its functional equivalent ('democratic secession').

In relation to the first possibility ('remedial secession'), where there are serious human rights abuses following the exclusion of one part of the population from the political process, a number of authors identify a right of secession through a reverse reading of the so-called 'saving clause' in the Declaration on Friendly Relations,[14] and the emergence of Bangladesh as a sovereign and independent state. Whether the remedial right of secession establishes a right of independence opposable to the territorial state and all other states *erga omnes*, or simply negates the proscription on achieving statehood with the support of external military forces is unclear given the limited doctrine and practice. Whilst recognised by a number of authors, the existence of the remedial right of secession is disputed by many scholars as a matter of international law.

The second possibility for recognising a right to statehood for politically ineffective peoples is where a domestic constitution or international peace

---

[12] See *Accordance with International Law of the Unilateral Declaration of Independence in Respect of Kosovo* (Advisory Opinion) [2010] ICJ Rep 403, [122].

[13] J Crawford, *The Creation of States in International Law* 2nd edn (Oxford, Oxford University Press, 2006) 390.

[14] Declaration on Principles of International Law Concerning Friendly Relations and Co-operation among States in Accordance with the Charter of the United Nations (adopted 24 October 1970) UNGA Res 2625 (XXV).

agreement promises independence following the holding of a valid referendum ('promissory secession'). The relevant state practice concerns South Sudan, whose right to statehood via a democratic referendum was guaranteed under the Comprehensive Peace Agreement of 9 January 2005 and the domestic laws of Sudan;[15] the separation of Montenegro in accordance with the Constitution of Serbia and Montenegro;[16] and (arguably) the Edinburgh Agreement between the United Kingdom government and the Scottish government, which provided that the independence referendum should 'deliver a fair test and a decisive expression of the views of people in Scotland *and a result that everyone will respect*'.[17] The domestic or international guarantee is understood to 'trigger' a particular application of the right of peoples to political self-determination, in the form of a right to an independent state. International law scholars take different positions as to whether this argument can be sustained and there is limited evidence for the position in the relevant jurisprudence, although the Canadian Supreme Court did conclude that secession should be the result of a negotiated process between the relevant parties, and that the way in which the parties engaged with the process would influence the question of recognition by outside states.[18] In other words, the (internal) promise made by the state government (expressly or impliedly) to engage in a process leading to independence may well create (external) international law obligations opposable to the territorial state.

The third possibility is to recognise that a positive vote in support of independence in a valid referendum can create an international law right of secession for politically ineffective peoples ('democratic secession'). The mainstream international law position holds that the right of peoples to self-determination does not accord a right to statehood, even when there is a democratic vote for independence or its functional equivalent.[19] Certain writers claim, however, that a vote for independence is not irrelevant in the process of creating states.[20] Reflecting on recent events in Crimea, Anne Peters concludes that contemporary international law is moving towards a position of requiring that all territorial realignments should be justified by democratic means, preferably through a territorial referendum.[21] There is then an emergent literature highlighting the relevance of democratic

---

[15] See J Vidmar, 'Explaining The Legal Effects Of Recognition' (2012) 61 *International and Comparative Law Quarterly* 361, 368–69.

[16] S Mancini, 'Rethinking the Boundaries of Democratic Secession: Liberalism, Nationalism, and the Right of Minorities to Self-determination' (2008) 6 *International Journal of Constitutional Law* 553, 582.

[17] Agreement between the United Kingdom Government and the Scottish Government on a referendum on independence for Scotland (15 October 2012) (emphasis added).

[18] *Reference re Secession of Quebec* (1998) 2 SCR 217, [103] and [143].

[19] Crawford, *Creation of States* (n 13) 417.

[20] See S Murphy, 'Democratic Legitimacy and the Recognition of States and Governments' (1999) 48 *International and Comparative Law Quarterly* 545, 580; J Vidmar, *Democratic Statehood in International Law: The Emergence of New States in Post-Cold War Practice* (Oxford, Hart, 2013) 200.

[21] A Peters, 'The Crimean Vote of March 2014 as an Abuse of the Institution of the Territorial Referendum' in C Calliess (ed), *Liber amicorum Torsten Stein* (forthcoming, 2015), available at SSRN: http://ssrn.com/abstract=2463536, 8.

decisions-making by the affected population in determining the future of any territory.

How are we to resolve the differences of scholarly opinion on the possibilities for statehood for politically ineffective peoples? In dealing with the problems that face the discipline, international lawyers often rely on abstract models of the international system, and they consider that these models should not only, or not merely, be of theoretical interest, but also helpful in answering the practical questions that face the discipline.[22] The dominant way in which international lawyers have modelled the state has been by reference to the idea of *State as Person*, which explains the reliance on *birth* to describe the emergence of new states.[23] The International Court of Justice has, for example, referred to the '*birth* of so many new States'.[24] The idea of *State as Person* also underpins the reliance by most international lawyers on the declaratory approach to the recognition of new states. Just like natural persons, states are *born*, and it is contrary to common sense to conclude that an artificial legal *person* can exist, or not exist, depending on the conclusions of another party.[25]

On the 'state as simple fact of the world' understanding, the democratic legitimacy (or otherwise) of a secessionist movement would be irrelevant to any claim to statehood. The problem for this model is that it cannot easily explain why effectiveness is no longer the only relevant criterion in the identification of new states (colonial states could not maintain authority over territory simply by virtue of effective control and new states cannot emerge only be seizing control of the territory from the previous sovereign power) or explain certain inconvenient facts like the existence of Abkhazia, Nagorno-Karabakh, Somaliland, Southern Rhodesia, Transdniestria and Turkish Republic of Northern Cyprus. The presence of de facto regimes in world society suggests that the *State as Person* model no longer functions effectively to explain the international law on statehood—a point reflected in the ever more complicated and controversial modifications of the definition of 'state' that seek to explain why certain 'state-like' entities are not, in fact, 'states', but without reference to the criterion of recognition, given that academic international lawyers, with few exceptions, follow the declaratory position on statehood: 'An entity is not a State because it is recognised; it is recognised because it is a State'.[26]

---

[22] A Riles, 'Models and Documents: Artefacts of International Legal Knowledge' (1999) 48 *International and Comparative Law Quarterly* 805, 808.

[23] G Lakoff and M Johnson, *Metaphors We Live By* (Chicago, University of Chicago Press, 1980) 117.

[24] *Legal Consequences for States of the Continued Presence of South Africa in Namibia (South West Africa) notwithstanding Security Council Resolution 276 (1970)* (Advisory Opinion) [1971] ICJ Rep 16, [52] (emphasis added).

[25] The anthropomorphic metaphor is clearest in the work of Stefan Talmon: '[m]uch like the *birth* of a child, the creation of a State is predominantly a question of fact' (emphasis added): S Talmon, 'The Constitutive Versus The Declaratory Theory of Recognition: *Tertium Non Datur?*' (2004) 75 *British Yearbook of International Law* 101, 125.

[26] J Crawford, 'State' (2011) *Max Planck Encyclopedia of Public International Law*, para 44.

The challenge, then, is to find a way of modelling *state* that helps solve the problem of the identification of new states. Rather than begin with the image of *Leviathan* emerging as a natural and adult *body politic*, the proposition here is that we should build on developments in understandings in the natural sciences, as applied to the social sciences, specifically the third wave of systems theory thinking known as complexity theory, to frame *state* as the observation of the emergent patterned communications of co-evolved and co-existent law and politics systems. The justification for this approach lies in the fact that since Hugo Grotius and Emmerich de Vattel, *state* has been conceptualised by international lawyers (if not by others) as an independent political community, organised in a particular territory, under a coercive system of government under the rule of law, which is not subject to the authority of any other political entity. *State*, in other words, is imagined as the co-evolved and co-existent systems of law and politics, where the politics system is understood in terms of the adoption of collectively binding decisions that will be coercively enforced. This understanding is generally reflected (albeit expressed in different terms) in the international law literature and forms the basis of the Montevideo formula that defines 'state'.[27]

## III. Systems Theory Thinking

This chapter seeks to develop an argument for recognising a right of democratic secession in international law. In doing so, it builds a model of 'state' grounded in a variant of systems theory known as complexity theory. The argument from general systems theory is that we can think of any collection of interacting objects, actors or agents as a 'system', and that all systems have certain shared characteristics, whether we are looking at the Solar System or Criminal Justice System. The objective in both cases is to observe, frame and explain the patterned behaviours of the objects, actors or agents in the system. Given its focus on relationships between actors or agents, systems theory thinking has proved influential in developing our understandings of the functioning of human social systems. Before moving on to consider the implications of an understanding of the emergence of new states grounded in complexity theory, this chapter first looks to the insights from another variant of communications systems theory: *autopoiesis*. The closed systems theory of *autopoiesis*, developed by Niklas Luhmann, has resonated with a number of legal academics, given its understanding of 'law' as a self-producing system of law communications. It makes sense then to look to the established literature on closed systems theory on the conceptualision of the state, before turning to the insights from the nascent theory of complexity.

---

[27] See above n 7.

*Steven Wheatley*

Luhmann's closed systems theory imagines world society as a system of self-creating, self-maintaining and self-organising—*autopoietic*—systems of communication.[28] These social systems are distinguished from the background noise of world society by virtue of the fact that each has its own functional specialism and its own binary coding that provides a positive and a negative value and through which the system creates its own understanding of the world from a perspective that is internal to the system.[29] The only relevant perspective is that of the system and the only relevant observer is the system. Examples of *autopoietic* social systems include the law system, the politics system, the economic system, science, the education system and the media. Systems of the same type may have different programmes, but each will have the same binary code. Law and politics are, according to Luhmann and others,[30] *autopoietic* systems of communication that build themselves from their own communications, which then constitutes the possibilities of future communications. The functional specialism of law is to maintain expectations in the face of disappointment. The binary coding is lawful/unlawful, or law/non-law. There can be different systems of law (different programmes in the language of systems theory), but all will have the same binary code. The function of the politics system is to provide society with a means of making (collectively) binding decisions on political questions. The binary coding is governing/governed, or authority/subject. The politics system is comprised of communications on those issues identified as requiring the adoption of collectively binding decisions that will be coercively enforced. Again, there can be different types of politics systems, but all with the same binary code: (coercively) governing/governed.

Law and politics are, in Luhmann's terms, *structurally coupled* under the state constitution:[31] politics establishes the scope of effective law norms through executive enforcement; law translates power into legitimate political action. *State*, following the logic of *autopoiesis*, can then be modelled as the space *occupied* (metaphorically) by an effective law system (law, structurally coupled with politics) and a legitimate politics system (politics, structurally coupled with law): *state is a self-willed or self-producing entity, constituted through the emergence of co-evolved and co-existent systems of law and politics, coupled structurally under a constitution.* Consequently, the boundaries of the state are not the lines we observe on a world

---

[28] The argument is self-evidently not a literal description of the world, but a way of modelling the complexities of human social existence by drawing on insights from science: *autopoietic* social systems of communication are self-creating, self-organsing and self-reproducing—just *like* biochemical systems (the standard example is the biological cell).

[29] See generally N Luhmann, *Theory of Society*, vol 1 (R Barrett tr, Stanford, Stanford University Press, 2012); N Luhmann, *Theory of Society*, vol 2 (R Barrett tr, Stanford, Stanford University Press, 2013).

[30] See esp G Teubner, *Constitutional Fragments: Societal Constitutionalism and Globalization*, (G Norbury tr, Oxford, Oxford University Press, 2012); C Thornhill, *A Sociology of Constitutions: Constitutions and State Legitimacy in Historical-Sociological Perspective* (Cambridge, Cambridge University Press, 2011).

[31] N Luhmann, 'Operational Closure and Structural Coupling: The Differentiation of the Legal System' (1991–92) 13 *Cardozo Law Review* 1419, 1436.

political map or manifested in our experiences at passport control, but the juris-dictional space occupied by the overlapping system boundaries of politics and law.

This closed systems model of *state* resonates to some extent with the traditional accounts of statehood that have tended to understand the state to be a self-willed or self-producing entity. The idea can be seen in the works, inter alios, of Thomas Hobbes, John Locke and Emmerich de Vattel that seek to explain the establishment of sovereign authority in the state-of-nature. It can also be seen in the declaratory accounts of recognition, which conclude that a community that understands itself to be a state and which establishes its factual political and legal independence *is* a state, subject only to the *factual* limits imposed by nature and other systems. The problem for the model from *autopoiesis* is that it proves deficient when con-trasted with the extant practice of the international community, which does not accept that new states can emerge on their own terms (consider, for example, the statehood claims of Nagorno-Karabakh and Transdniestria); admits the possibil-ity of limited recognition by neighbouring and other states (Turkish Republic of Northern Cyprus, Abkhazia and South Ossetia); and in the case of Kosovo allows significant disagreement as to whether the territory is a state, or not. In other worlds, whilst the model from *autopoiesis* might be able to explain how a law or politics system can make sense of the world in its own terms, it can no longer (if it ever could) help us to solve the practical question of the emergence of new states in world society. We require, then, another model.

## IV. Complexity Theory

Niklas Luhmann's theory of *autopoiesis* forms part of what Keith Sawyer calls the 'second wave' of systems theory thinking. Sawyer concludes that this second wave has been of limited utility in explaining the functioning of social systems, but that a 'third wave' developed since the 1990s has proved more useful. This third wave of systems theory thinking is focused on micro level agents, communication and social emergence, with a particular concern with 'complex' systems whose pat-terned behaviours cannot be understood to be the result of some 'guiding hand'.[32] This chapter now turns to outline the insights from the third wave of systems theory thinking to develop a model of *state* as the coupling of *complex* systems of law and politics.

'Complex adaptive systems theory', or 'complexity theory', or simply 'complex-ity' emerged as a body of scientific thinking about certain systems in the second half of the twentieth century to further challenge the paradigm of a Clockwork

---

[32] RK Sawyer, *Social Emergence: Societies as Complex Systems* (Cambridge, Cambridge University Press, 2005) ch 2.

Universe that could be taken apart and subjected to analysis. The prior assumption of Newtonian science was that all systems, even highly complicated systems, were 'the sum of their parts', and, like a clock, they could be understood by examining the component elements. The insight from scientists working on the weather and those looking at cells and the brain, etc was that certain (chaotic and complex) systems could not be understood in this reductionist way. It is not possible, for example, to understand an ecosystem (the patterned behaviour of organisms within a particular space) simply by examining its constituent parts. The properties of chaotic and complex systems were seen to be the result of the behaviours of the individual components, *and* their interactions with each other, *and* their interactions with the environment outside of the system: the whole (of the system) was 'greater than the sum of its parts'.

Chaos theory observes that the elements of certain systems, the weather is the standard example, sometimes combine to produce unpredictable consequences and that small inputs can have disproportionately large outputs (non-linearity)—the, so-called, *Butterfly effect*, whereby the weather in Texas can be influenced by the flapping of the wings of a butterfly in Brazil. Both chaos and complexity have in common the idea that the patterned behaviour of a 'system' can be the result of a relatively simple set of laws followed by a large number of agents. In chaos theory, those laws produce unpredictable outcomes. In complexity, the actions and interactions of agents result in complex patterned behaviour at the *edge of chaos*: the place between entropy (where the system decays) and chaos (too much activity). The problem for the science of complexity is that complex systems cannot be modelled accurately because they cannot be simplified without losing some of their complexity. Any reductive description fails to capture the full complexity and adaptability of the system, or loses some important element, meaning that predictions of the future shape and form of complex systems become impossible to make with any certainty.

Complexity is more firmly established in the natural sciences, where it has been applied, for example, to ecosystems and the brain. The insights from complexity have also been relied on by social scientists to examine economic systems, the internet, and the functioning of human societies, from the phenomenon of the standing ovation in the concert hall, to the organisation of nation-state societies. In all of these cases, observed patterned behaviour is the result of the actions and reactions of agents following rules. Consider the example of a game of chess: agents (the players) operate within a relatively simple set of rules; develop strategies within those rules; and respond to how the other players develop their strategies. No two games are ever the same (notwithstanding the limited set of rules) as the patterns on the board emerge from the actions and reactions of the players. The same can be said about human societies—and the social systems that result from the actions and interactions of human agents. Drawing on the insights from complex systems theory, this chapter now turns to develop a model of *state* as the framing of the emergent patterned communications of co-evolved and co-existent law and politics systems.

## V.  Complex Adaptive Systems

The dynamic character of a complex system is provided by the facts of emergence and self-organisation. Emergence reflects the idea that patterned behaviour is a consequence of the actions of individual components following certain rules; self-organisation that patterned behaviour is not the result of some central controller or guiding hand, but a consequence of individual agents responding to the unpredictability of emergence in a search for stability.[33] The capacity for self-organisation allows complex systems to change their internal structures in response to developments within the system and events in the external environment. The structure of the system (the positions, actions and reactions of agents) occurs spontaneously as the result of the interactions of the parts of the system as they react to the flow of information through the system. The capacity for self-organisation is the property of a complex system that enables it to process and make sense of information in order to develop or change in response to changes in the environment.

*Emergence* is the key attribute of complexity. The patterns observed in a complex system are the result of the actions and interactions of networks of agents. It is important to be clear that emergence is not random patterned behaviour: emergence reflects the idea that the interactions between the component agents and their interactions with actors outside the system and the wider environment can produce unexpected consequences. This is particularly the case as complex systems are *non-linear*—small inputs can have disproportionately large effects (the *Butterfly effect*), and an apparently stable system can change suddenly in unpredictable ways. Emergence is, then, focused on the properties of the system that cannot be deduced from examining the component elements.[34]

The basic components of a complex adaptive system are called *agents*. The term refers to actors able to respond to other agents and to the external environment. The key point is that agents are, to some degree, autonomous, whilst operating in accordance with certain rules.[35] When agents 'react' they do so in a *thinking* way, based on a collective memory contained within the system. Complex systems learn through the processing of information by agents and the presence of negative and positive *feedback* loops. Complex systems are also *learning systems*. This is an emergent property of the system: as the interactions of agents create new patterns in response to new information, the system can be said to have 'learnt' and adapted

---

[33] See generally M Mitchell, *Complexity: A Guided Tour* (New York, Oxford University Press, 2009) 12–13. See also N Johnson, *Simply Complexity: A Clear Guide to Complexity Theory* (London, Oneworld Publications, 2009) 13–16; P Cilliers, 'What Can We Learn from a Theory of Complexity?' (2000) 2 *Emergence* 23, 24.

[34] J Goldstein, 'Emergence as a Construct: History and Issues' (1999) 1 *Emergence* 49, 58.

[35] F Heylighen, P Cilliers, and C Gershenson, 'Philosophy and Complexity' in J Bogg and R Geyer (eds), *Complexity, Science and Society* (Oxford, Radcliffe, 2007) 117, 125.

and evolved. In order to adapt, evolve and change—and not simply 'mirror' its environment, the system must have a memory, and therefore a history.[36] Learning is not possible without some form of *memory* that contains information important to the existence of the system, which is stored and dispersed throughout the system (even the most simple social animal must be able to distinguish friend from foe). The *history* of the system helps to determine its structure, representing the memory of the system of the processes of self-organisation that resulted in its extant structure and processes. That memory also constrains the system's possible futures: the idea of *path dependency*.

As well as cooperating and competing with other agents within their locale, agents may be influenced directly by external actors and elements. In other words, complex systems are *open* systems. This makes the identification of the boundaries of a complex system particularly problematic. Take the example of the paradigmatic complex system: a rainforest. As a result of the incompressibility (a complex system cannot be simplified without losing some element that makes them complex) and openness of the system (agents in the ecosystem sometimes interact directly with elements in the external environment), any description of the rainforest ecosystem and its boundaries inevitably involves the making of choices as to what is 'system' and what is 'not system'. This process of separating is called framing—and it is undertaken by an observer.[37] Any description of a complex system concerns, then, both the fact of patterned behaviour and the making of choices by those framing the system.

# VI.  The Complex Systems of Law and Politics

Complex systems have the following characteristics: agents follow rules, but act with some autonomy; agents are in a network of relationships; the patterned behaviours of agents can be framed as a system; system characteristics are not derived only from the actions of agents; agents act and react, relying on information within and outside system; the system evolves without any guiding hand; system memory constrains future possibilities. The argument here is that systems of law and politics can be understood as complex systems and modelled as patterned communications between authorities and subjects. Consider the law system. Law is self-organising: there is no central controller or guiding hand—neither the legislature nor supreme court is able to control the shape and form of the entire system. The law system is the emergent, undirected, pattern of normative communications framed in terms of law adopted by authorities and applied to

---

[36] P Cilliers, *Complexity and Postmodernism: Understanding Complex Systems* (London, Routledge, 1998) 91–92.
[37] ibid 4.

subjects. It is the result of the communicative actions of a large network of agents (legislatures, courts, judges, lawyers, litigants and others) capable of responding to other actors and other systems, which operate with no overall guiding hand. The law system can, then, be mapped, or modelled, as a pattern of law normative communications between legal authorities and the subjects of the law regime: 'It is unlawful for X to kill Y', 'It is unlawful for A to break their contractual arrangement with B', etc, etc.

The patterned communications of the law system are a consequence of the actions and reactions of law-actors, with the legal system representing the 'memory' of previous actions and interaction, providing 'feedback' to law agents who operate in accordance with certain rules: higher courts bind lower courts, rules are interpreted logically and in accordance with precedent, etc. Information flows through the system; its source can be internal or external. Memory is distributed throughout: in statutes, court judgments, academic textbooks, etc. That memory of the law system limits the possibilities of future communications (path dependency).[38] This is clearest in the practice of the common law,[39] and related judicial principle of stare decisis.[40] A law system evolves and maintains its fitness by adapting to developments within the system and in the wider environment, and by accommodating itself with other law systems. Law agents exchange information and the law system is able to rely on feedback loops and use information from within the system and from other law systems in order to adapt and change (consider the way in which legal systems in Europe have accommodated themselves to the emergence of the law system of the European Union). In its evolution, the law system builds on the collective memory of the system, but in ways that cannot be predicted as constitutions are revised or replaced,[41] legislatures adopt radical law reform, and supreme courts overturn long-established precedent. Any event (often unforeseen events) can influence the future shape of the law system in unexpected and significant ways. Finally, law systems are open systems: their boundaries have the characteristic of porous legality and it is not always easy to determine to which system a law norm communication belongs.[42]

---

[38] JB Ruhl, 'Law's Complexity: A Primer' (2007–08) 24 *Georgia State University Law Review* 885, 894–95.

[39] On the idea of the common law as a complex system, see D Katz et al, 'Social Architecture, Judicial Peer Effects and the "Evolution" of the Law: Toward a Positive Theory of Judicial Social Structure' (2007–08) 24 *Georgia State University Law Review* 977 (and references cited). See also JB Ruhl, 'The Fitness of Law: Using Complexity Theory to Describe the Evolution of Law and Society and Its Practical Meaning for Democracy' (1996) 49 *Vanderbilt Law Review* 1407, 1471.

[40] On path dependency and stare decisis, see O Hathaway, 'Path Dependence in the Law: The Course and Pattern of Legal Change in a Common Law System' (2000–01) 86 *Iowa Law Review* 601.

[41] DT Hornstein, 'Complexity Theory, Adaptation, and Administrative Law' (2005) 54 *Duke Law Journal* 913, 932.

[42] The idea of porous legality, or interlegality, is common in the literature on legal anthropology. The phenomenon has also been observed in colonial and post-colonial settings; in relation to new forms of pluralism within the state; and in the areas of transnational and other forms of global governance. The term 'interlegality' is taken from B de Sousa Santos, *Toward a New Legal Common Sense: Law, Globalization, and Emancipation* 2nd edn (London, Butterworths, 2002).

The politics system at the level of the state can also be understood as a complex system.[43] The politics system is the emergent patterned system of communications adopted by those in power to the subjects of the political regime. Politics is the pattern of regulatory communications concerned with the adoption of collective binding decisions by the government in relation to the governed. There is no single guiding hand or omnipotent power in the state: regulations can be adopted by legislatures, executives and administrative bodies. Collectively binding decisions emerge through the processing of information by agents within the system, often relying on feedback loops. The politics system has its own memory, which limits the possible scope of future decisions, and its own ways of thinking. Political systems can, though, change in unexpected ways (often quickly)—consider the democratic revolutions during the so-called 'Arab Spring'.[44] To survive, a politics system must adapt and evolve with the systems of world society. Politics systems are also open systems, interacting with other politics systems and political communications at one level can form part of the politics system at another—consider the way in which global political communications are part of domestic political communications, concerning, for example, military and humanitarian interventions, climate change, and commitments for overseas development assistance.

## VII. Modelling 'State' as Complex Systems of Law and Politics

This chapter has outlined the similarities in the approaches of systems theorists and international lawyers to the idea of the 'state' in world society. Both sets of scholars conceptualise the state in terms of an independent political community under a coercive system of government under the rule of law, which is not subject to the authority of any other political entity. Expressed in the particular language of systems theory: state is understood in terms of co-evolved and co-existent law and politics systems. The insight from complexity is that these law and politics systems are emergent, undirected *complex* systems. How, then, do we model 'state' against the background noise of world society in conditions of complexity?

The first requirement is to separate each system from the environment of world society. The idea of a complex *system* presupposes the existence of a boundary that distinguishes 'system' and 'not-system'. If we understand world society in terms of communications, we can observe patterns of communications that we would recognise as 'law' and 'politics'. We can, further, frame networked communications

---

[43] For a useful introduction to complexity applied to the politics system, see R Geyer and S Rihani, *Complexity and Public Policy: A New Approach to 21st Century Politics, Policy and Society* (Abingdon, Routledge, 2012).

[44] See generally S Gunitsky, 'Complexity and Theories of Change in International Politics' (2013) 5 *International Theory* 35.

as law systems and politics systems. The boundaries of these systems are not, however, to be understood as enjoying an 'objective' reality, or as being established only by the operations of the system (in contradistinction to *autopoiesis*). Boundaries are simultaneously a function of the activity of the system (there must be patterned behaviour that can be observed) and the product of the strategy of description involved in the act of observation when separating the system from its environment.

Any description of a complex system involves the making of choices by those observing the system. Different observers may frame the patterned communications differently, depending on their strategic and cognitive frames: constitutional lawyers see domestic law norms; international lawyers see international law norms, for example. Where there is more than one observer, there may be different perspectives on the existence and scope of the system, and no reason to conclude that each observer will *see* the same version of the system—or to prefer one version or vision of the system and its boundary to another. It is then difficult to be absolutely certain of the position of the boundaries of law and politics systems in world society. Importantly, there are no objective boundaries—the act of framing involves the making of choices—and it is impossible for the observer to avoid the responsibility of choosing, ie deciding which communications are inside the system and which are outside. Once we recognise that law and politics are complex systems, we must reject (as an observed reality) the argument that a political entity (represented by the co-evolved and co-existent systems of law and politics) which is capable of establishing its independence and has the will to be a state *is* a state. *State* is not a fact of the world simpliciter: it is fact of the world *observed* through the cognitive frame of international law.

In the identification of new states, the following insights from complexity theory emerge. First, there must be *patterned communications*. Complex systems are not merely a function of observation. We must be able to *see* co-emergent and co-existent systems of law and politics. Second, there must be an *observer* to distinguish the patterned communications of the law and politics systems from the background noise of world society. This is done through the framing of communications of the same type, that is by framing the pattern of law communications coded lawful/unlawful (or law/non-law) issued by authorities to subjects and the pattern of communications issued by the government to the governed on collective binding decisions that will be coercively enforced. It follows that the 'existence' of the complex systems of law and politics is both a function of the system (reflected in patterned communications) and the fact of observation. Third, given the inherent indeterminacy in the modelling and observation of complex systems, there may be multiple perspectives on the system and its boundary, and no reason to privilege the perspective of one observer over any other.

*State*, following the logic of complexity, is the *observation of the patterned communications of the co-evolved and co-existent law and politics systems*. Where the law system and politics system are *observed* to be co-existent, then, according to the Montevideo formula, the territory subject to the normative communications of the law and politics systems has a prima facie claim to be a state. Where they are not observed to be co-existent, the political entity is not a state. Given the incompressibility and open nature of the complex systems of law and politics, different actors may come to different conclusions, depending on their cognitive frame and interpretation of the observed patterned communications, ie as to whether an emergent 'sovereign' entity can be seen. The approach from complexity leads, then, inevitably to a defence of the constitutive position on statehood: the legal status of *state* is constructed by way of recognition by already existing states.[45] State is the *observation* of the law and politics systems 'coupled' under a constitution.

# VIII.  Legitimate Political Authority and Democratic Secession

We have, then, our abstract model of *state*: the *observation of the emergent patterned communications of co-evolved and co-existent law and politics systems*. To observe a state, international lawyers must be able to 'see' co-evolved and co-existent systems of law and politics against the background noise of world society. This is achieved through the identification of communications systems by observing their function and binary coding. The law system is the pattern of normative communications coded lawful/not-lawful, which are promulgated by recognised authorities and applied to subjects. This definition is clearly contestable, but, for the most part, controversies in relation to the international status of a political entity do not concern the question as to whether it has a system of 'law'—although this argument has been made before the European Court of Human Rights in relation to Turkish Republic of Northern Cyprus.[46] The focus, then, is on the politics system—as observed by state and non-state actors in the international community.

From the time of Hugo Grotius, it has been accepted that the overall approach of the international law system to the regulation of world society emerges through the exercise of sovereigns' wills, ie there is no guiding hand (international law is the paradigmatic complex law system). In the period since the adoption of the United Nations Charter, the emergent teleology of the international law system has undergone a process of transformation, in part through the recognition of the right of peoples to political self-determination, but also in the adoption of numerous international human rights law instruments, indicating a move away from a Hobbesian notion of politics, to considerations of legitimate political authority manifested in the adoption of positive laws accepted (unthinkingly) by subjects. To be accepted by subjects, authority systems must develop, and act in a manner

---

[45] See H Kelsen, 'Recognition in International Law: Theoretical Observations' (1941) 35 *American Journal of International Law* 605.
[46] See eg *Protopapa v Turkey*, App no 16084/90 (ECtHR, 24 February 2009).

consistent with, a legitimation narrative. Without this, government is nothing more than the exercise of naked power.

The idea of practical authority developed by Joseph Raz explains the way in which the legitimation narratives of political authorities function. This account of practical authority relies on four interrelated theses: the dependence thesis, which provides that authority is legitimate where undertaken in accordance with the reasons that already apply to subjects; the pre-emption thesis—the directives of legitimate authorities establish content-independent reasons for action; the normal justification thesis, which establishes that the exercise of normative power is only legitimate where the authority is better placed than subjects to establish regulatory directives; and the independence thesis—on some issues it will be more important for individuals to decide for themselves than to decide correctly. The key is the normal justification thesis. Raz argues that the normal way of establishing authority is to demonstrate to the subjects of authority directives that they would better conform to the reasons that already apply to them by following the directives of the authority than by acting independently.[47] The reasons for accepting the authority of another include that the authority is more knowledgeable; is more likely to make a correct decision; and accepting the authority of another allows for effective co-ordination. Once established, the directives of a legitimate authority are binding on those subjects within its jurisdiction.

The requirement for practical authority is a consequence of the identification of co-ordination and collective action problems. It follows that before an actor, institution or system can satisfy the normal justification criterion (ie regulate in the interests of subjects), it must be recognised or accepted as an authority by a large number of persons who do actually accept that the relevant actor, institution or system satisfies the normal justification criterion in cases of co-ordination over matters of common concern. The exercise of normative power by the state is, then, legitimate where the state is more likely than the individual to establish a social norm or convention that regulates the behaviour of the individual and others in accordance with the background reasons that already apply to the subjects of authority directives taken individually. Where the individual subjects accept the authority of the politics system of the state, the state is an authority for them.[48]

Raz's account of the justification for authority establishes a significant break with the social contract tradition that has dominated the discourse around legitimate political power. Authority is not established at some hypothetical foundational moment of agreement that binds subsequent generations. According to Raz's account, subjects will only accept the authority of the regime where it governs, or at least claims to govern, in their interests at *this* point in time. The only reasons

---

[47] J Raz, *The Morality of Freedom* (Oxford, Oxford University Press, 1986) 53.

[48] In the case of the political authorities of the state, Raz concludes that the requirement to solve co-ordination problems means that they should be in a position of 'real power', ie de jure political authorities should also be de facto authorities, and that this will require the use of coercive force to ensure compliance with authority directives: J Raz, 'The Problem of Authority: Revisiting the Service Conception' (2006) 90 *Minnesota Law Review* 1003, 1036.

that an authority may take into account in determining the content of authority directives are those that already apply to actually existing subjects, including the requirement for cooperation on a wide range of issues—and that subjects recognise this is the case.

Raz's idea of practical authority allows us to develop a model a democratic secession in three related steps:[49] first, the rejection of the sovereign authority of the territorial state by certain subjects; second, the acceptance of the authority of the emergent, undirected, systems of law and politics of a new political entity; and, finally, the observation (or 'recognition') of the political entity as possessing legitimate political authority in relation to its 'subjects'. The arguments are considered in turn.

## A. The Rejection of the Authority of the State

Legitimate political authority depends on the development of a legitimation narrative by the politics system—and the acceptance of that narrative by the subjects of the regime taken individually. There are two parts to the equation, and both can provide the grounds for secession: the state can repudiate the bonds of authority by failing to govern in the interests of some or all of the subjects of the regime; or some or all of the subjects can reject the authority of the state. In relation to the first possibility (government *not* in the interests of subjects), self-evidently where the exercise of power makes no pretence to be in the interests of those targeted by the regulatory regime (tyranny, occupation, etc), 'subjects' are released from the bonds of authority by the simple fact that the political institutions are not an authority for them. This is explained in legal doctrine and political theory in terms of a right of revolution, or right of rebellion, etc.

The idea that 'subjects' are released from the bonds of authority where the state manifestly makes no attempt to govern in their interests resonates with the 'remedial right' of secession outlined by Allen Buchanan, which concludes that such a right exists in cases of persistent and grave injustice, defined in terms of genocide or massive violations of basic human rights.[50] Buchanan later supplements these criteria with that of the persistent violation of intra-state autonomy agreements, which he links to serious ethnic conflict.[51] In a similar vein, Alan Patten's 'failure of recognition' criterion concludes that a claim to secede should be accepted where

---

[49] *cf*, however, Raz's well-known position recognising a collective right to self-determination for those (ethno-cultural) groups that provide secure identity and belonging to members. The objective is to establish and guarantee the necessary conditions for the prosperity and self-respect of the group. The right to self-determination is limited only by the requirement that the encompassing group commit itself to the protection of basic human rights and exercises its right to self-determination in a manner that limits any damage to already existing states: A Margalit and J Raz, 'National self-determination' (1990) 87 *The Journal of Philosophy* 439.

[50] A Buchanan, 'Theories of Secession' (1997) 26 *Philosophy & Public Affairs* 31.

[51] A Buchanan, *Justice, Legitimacy, and Self-Determination: Moral Foundations of International Law* (Oxford, Oxford University Press, 2004) 351–52.

the state has failed to introduce constitutional arrangements that accommodate the distinctive ethno-cultural identity of the relevant group.[52] In both cases (and in the language of practical authority), the state cannot claim authority in relation to certain persons within the state, for the reason that the legitimation narrative established by the politics system makes no attempt to govern in their interests or to accommodate the distinctive identity of those persons—distinguished from the majority on national, ethnic, religious or linguistic grounds.

The second possibility is to recognise a right of the subjects of the state (taken individually) to reject the authority of the state. Secession can then be understood in terms of the repudiation of the political authority of the territorial state by certain subjects of the regime, ie it is a challenge to the boundaries of its authority. (This also explains why the constituency in any self-determination referendum comprises those persons in the self-determination unit only, and not the population of the territorial state as a whole.) Buchanan and Patten both reject the idea of a choice-based or democratic right of secession, which is triggered by the decision of a group to leave the state, with nothing more required. This stance is common in the literature, and few writers argue for the recognition of what Susanna Mancini refers to as a political–territorial right to secession 'legitimated by aggregated individual choices'.[53] Harry Beran, for example, concludes that liberal political philosophy permits secession where it is desired by a territorially concentrated group, provided that the secession 'is morally and practically possible'.[54] Practical considerations might include the size of the group and whether the group is located on the periphery of the territorial state. Moral considerations are often grounded in empirical, risk-based considerations: the dangers to peace and security; the possibility of unjust terms of separation; and the unpredictable and possibly deleterious consequences of establishing a precedent for non-voluntary secession. Where justice is a relevant criterion, it often concerns the obligations that flow from the secessionist unit to the remainder of the territorial state,[55] including the obligations from social justice to other citizens where the separatist territory is wealthier than the rest of the state. The logic of secession is also said to point to a prohibition on secession from liberal states by illiberal groups.

Whilst it would be naïve not to recognise the potential dangers to peace and human security in accepting a democratic right of secession (and likewise in the repression of separatist movements—the opposing empirical, risk-based consideration), the burden of proof, as Kai Nielsen observes, is on those arguing that

---

[52] A Patten, 'Democratic Secession from a Multinational State' (2002) 112 *Ethics* 558, 563.

[53] S Mancini, 'Secession and Self-Determination' in M Rosenfeld and A Sajo (eds), *The Oxford Handbook Of Comparative Constitutional Law* (Oxford, Oxford University Press, 2012) 481, 484–85.

[54] H Beran, 'A Liberal Theory of Secession' (1984) 32 *Political Studies* 21, 23. See also D Philpott, 'In Defense of Self-Determination' (1995) 105 *Ethics* 352, 382.

[55] See eg CH Wellman, 'A Defense of Secession and Political Self-Determination' (1995) 24 *Philosophy & Public Affairs* 142, 161–62: 'any group may secede as long as it and its remainder state are large, wealthy, cohesive, and geographically contiguous enough to form a government that effectively performs the functions necessary to create a secure political environment'.

the moral right of democratic secession should be overridden.[56] To put it another way: the burden rests with those seeking to justify the imposition of coercive governmental authority on unwilling subjects. By way of contradistinction, the argument here follows the logic of *legitimate* political authority: the state must govern in the interests of subjects and develop a legitimation narrative to explain how it is governing in their interests—and the subjects of the politics system must recognise that this is the case. Where the subjects of the politics system do not accept that this is the case, then the state is not an authority for them. The decision to accept or reject the authority of the state is one for each individual targeted by the authority directives of the state. The choice cannot be made by others, especially not by a majority of the citizens of the state as a whole. This ability to accept or reject the authority of the state operates on a simple binary divide. Where a subject accepts the authority of the co-evolved and co-existent systems of law and politics, the state is an authority for them. Where they do not, the state is not an authority.[57] It is, then, possible for a number of subjects to reject the authority of a government that enjoys legitimate authority in relation to other parts of the population. The basis for this lies in the rejection of the legitimation narrative developed by the constitutional state: nothing more is required.

## B. The Establishment of New De Facto Authorities

There are three circumstances in which the idea of legitimate authority allows for the subjects of the state to be released from the bonds of authority. First, where the state has undergone a process of dissolution, for example in the case of the Socialist Federal Republic of Yugoslavia. In these exceptional circumstances, there is factually no politics system claiming authority over the subjects of the state—in other words, there is an authority vacuum that can be filled by other systems of authority. Second, where the state makes no pretence to govern in the interests of some or all of the population, the government is not an authority for the relevant subjects. Third, any subject of an authority regime can reject the legitimation narrative of the politics system as it is applied to them—subjects can create an authority vacuum in relation to themselves.

Within the unoccupied governance space created by the loss of authority of the territorial state, it is possible for subjects to recognise and accept emergent systems of law and politics under a new constitution: this is the way in which constituent power is exercised by subjects. Whilst the acceptance (or rejection) of authority is a question for the individual, the establishment of authorities must be seen as a collective endeavour, as the requirement for practical authorities follows the identification of co-ordination and collective action problems by a group of

---

[56] K Nielsen, 'Liberal Nationalism, Liberal Democracies, and Secession' (1998) 48 *University of Toronto Law Journal* 253, 253.

[57] The argument applies both to the fact of authority and the scope of authority. For the implications of this, see S Wheatley, 'Conceptualizing the Authority of the Sovereign State over Indigenous Peoples' (2014) 27 *Leiden Journal of International Law* 371.

individuals. Given that Raz's conception of practical authority concerns the exercise of normative power in relation to individuals capable of deciding whether, and on what grounds, they should accept a claim to authority (ie it concerns subjects capable of understanding and responding to arguments supported by reasons), the collective determination to accept a new authority must logically be undertaken on the basis of reasoned deliberation. This applies both as between the authority and subjects, and between subjects themselves: the determination to establish or recognise an authority follows a collective act of political will-formation grounded in reasoned public deliberations in which all voices count equally.

In practical politics, the determination by a group of persons to establish an authority regime will normally be made by way of an independence referendum, although other proxy measures may be permitted in exceptional circumstances— a declaration of independence by a representative body with popular support, or the results of a general election showing popular support for autonomy or independence. In relation to the standards required of the referendum, the international law on elections can be taken as establishing the basic principles and procedures.[58] There are, though, particular requirements in relation to referendums.[59] The question on the ballot paper must be sufficiently clear to establish the will of the people. The process should specify in advance what majority of the vote will be required and the required turnout of voters. There should also be international observation of the vote and the period of democratic debate preceding the vote. In the period leading up to the vote on independence there is a need for inclusive, informed and effective public debate, requiring a free media; the neutrality of political institutions; the participation of as many citizens as possible; limited involvement of external forces; and a long timescale leading up to the vote.[60] This period of time may also allow for the territorial state to revise its constitutional narrative of political legitimacy in a way that is able to accommodate the aspirations of the members of the group making the decision on separation.[61]

## C. International Recognition

An emergent political entity in world politics can be modelled in terms of a constitutional order that represents the co-evolved and co-existent systems of law and

---

[58] Y Beigbeder, 'Referendum', *Max Planck Encyclopedia of Public International Law*, para 46.

[59] On the conditions for independence referendums, see The Venice Commission's Guidelines for Constitutional Referendums at National Level CDL-INF (2001)10; and Guidelines on the Holding of Referendums CDL-AD(2007)008.

[60] See S Tierney, *Constitutional Referendums: The Theory and Practice of Republican Deliberation* (Oxford, Oxford University Press, 2012) ch 10. Whilst Tierney is primarily concerned with referendums in democratic states, the conclusions can also be applied more generally to the conduct of independence referendums.

[61] Consider, eg, the promises of greater autonomy and devolution of powers made by the leaders of the main political parties in the United Kingdom in the run-up to the vote on independence in Scotland: S Carrell, 'Scotland promised extra tax and legal powers for referendum no vote' *The Guardian* (5 August 2014).

politics, with coercive institutions of government. A political entity has a prima facie claim to be accepted as a state where its law and politics systems are observed to be co-existent. An absence of controversy concerning statehood reflects a consensus between the political entity, the territorial state and other already existing states, and the wider international community on the observation of co-existent law and politics systems. Divergent positions reflect different conclusions on the claims of the law and politics systems to autonomy and authority.

The identification of new states requires that we distinguish the patterned communications of law and politics (coupled under a constitution) from the background noise of world society. The analysis developed from complexity demonstrates the importance of the third party observer in the 'recognition' of the systems of law and politics—and consequently in the recognition of new states. In the identification of new states, the requirement to distinguish the patterned communications of the law and politics systems from the background noise of world society requires a conception of how international law understands the politics system. The traditional doctrine and practice of international law has understood the politics system in terms of the coercive enforcement of binding decisions. This is no longer the case. The period of the United Nations has seen the reconceptualisation by international law of the politics system in terms of legitimate political power, reflected inter alia in the development of international laws on the self-determination of peoples and human rights of individuals.

The emergence of the right of peoples to self-determination signalled an ethical turn in international law, from 'statehood as effectiveness' to 'statehood as legitimate political authority'. Politics is observed as a system of communications with an underlying legitimation narrative framed in terms of government in the interests of the subjects of the regime. (Where this is not the case, international law speaks in terms of occupation forces, illegal regimes, etc.) Where politics is understood in terms of a legitimate authority accepted by subjects, certain regimes will simply not count as politics systems—the racist political regime in Southern Rhodesia following its Unilateral Declaration of Independence in 1965 is the paradigm case. The international community (or at least a majority of the members of the international community) does not *see* a pattern of *political* communications between government and governed, ie a politics systems (properly understood)—and consequently cannot *see* a state, even if it can see the exercise of coercive power and an effective legal regime.

*State* is the observed fact of emergent systems of law and politics, coupled under a constitution. International law no longer understands the politics system only as the coercive enforcement of governmental power, but *also* in terms of legitimate political authority. Whilst the international law system does not impose substantive requirements on the politics systems of the government of new states (with the possible exception of regimes underpinned by a racist ideology, for example Southern Rhodesia and the South African 'Bantustans'), it does require that new states emerge with the consent of the population to be governed by the new regime. It follows, then, that in order to be recognised as a new state, a political entity must demonstrate that its politics system enjoys the support of the relevant population. The only way in which this can be definitively established is through the holding of an independence referendum, or its functional equivalent. In other words, the international law system restricts the possibility for the establishment of sovereign independence to political communities established in accordance with the popular or 'democratic' will of the people: 'We the people' being defined by reference to a political community of deliberative equals, and not the ethnic, religious and linguistic ties that bind human societies. That being the case, the conclusion raises the question as to the salience of nationalism in the structuring of political power in world society, beyond that of an organising principle of domestic politics— albeit a highly effective organising principle.

# IX. A Choice-Based or Democratic Right of Secession

The arguments developed in the previous sections lead inevitably to the conclusion that the emergent international law teleology, focused increasingly on the idea of legitimate political authority, can accommodate a right of democratic secession. First, the authority of the territorial state can be 'removed' by way of an independence referendum held in conditions of considered, open and free democratic debate. The requirement is straightforwardly applied in the normal conditions of democratic politics. In situations of violence and civil war, and only where an authority vacuum is created by the collapse of the central authorities or operation of the remedial 'saving clause' (when political institutions make no attempt to function as legitimate authorities), proxy measures to determine the will of the people may be relied upon, including the results of previous elections and decisions of representative bodies with popular support.

Second, a positive vote in the independence referendum can be taken as expressing the desire of a majority of the population of the territory to establish a sovereign and independent state—and to accept the authority of law and politics systems of the new state. This new political entity must not only demonstrate that it has the support of a majority of the population of the relevant territorial group, but also that its legitimation narrative can be accepted by all those that are to be subjected to its regulatory directives—hence the importance of minority guarantees when new states are established. Where the proposed legitimation narrative of the new state does not seek to accommodate the interests of all putative subjects, there is a strong argument for the holding of a fragmentary plebiscite, in which different parts of the self-determination unit can opt for different outcomes,[62] mindful of

---

[62] See eg the 'separation' of the canton of Jura from that of Bern in Switzerland in 1979: Mancini (n 16) 580–81.

the requirement of territorial contiguousness and cohesion for the territorial state and any new state. The possibilities of 'fragmenting' the separatist territory should be clearly outlined in advance of any vote on independence.[63]

The international law right of peoples to political self-determination is a fundamental norm of the international community. The scope and content of the norm remain opaque, however, when applied beyond the colonial context. The argument here is that the decision to hold a referendum on independence gives concrete meaning to the content of the right *in the particular context*, ie it cannot be read across to other situations. A positive vote for independence signals the rejection of the authority of the state by one part of the population, and the determination to establish a new state. That population—or 'people'—has an international law right to political self-determination *now* understood as a presumptive claim to statehood, opposable to the territorial state, which must engage with the separatist territory in a meaningful way, in order to facilitate its right to political self-determination, understood as sovereign independence, or some other status acceptable to a majority of the population. The obligation on the state to facilitate the right of peoples to political self-determination is owed both to the relevant population and to all other states in the international community, *erga omnes*.[64]

The international law obligation of the state to engage with the separatist territory cannot be understood as according a right to statehood. *State* is the observed fact of co-existent law and politics systems, where the politics system is framed in terms of communications on collectively binding decisions *that will be coercively enforced*. In the absence of de facto coercive power over the subjects of the politics system, an entity does not have a claim to statehood. The right of a people that has voted for independence is the right to a process leading to the establishment of a sovereign and independent state. Where the territorial state rejects the possibility of independence or imposes unreasonable conditions or restrictions on the establishment of sovereign independence, it is in breach of its international law obligation to engage in good faith with the separatist entity. This cannot be understood as authorising the use of force by outside states to facilitate the sovereignty and independence of the territory, except in the exceptional circumstances envisaged by the 'saving clause' doctrine. The use of military force under the Charter of the United Nations is regulated by its own *lex specialis* and, with the exception of an application of the (related and contested) 'saving clause' and humanitarian intervention doctrines, the right to use military force is not triggered by a violation of the international law right of peoples to self-determination. A violation of the right, through a failure to engage in the process leading to independence, will, though, engage the responsibility of the territorial state, and allow other states to

---

[63] At a late stage in the independence referendum campaign in Scotland, it was suggested that Shetland might be treated differently from the rest of the territory: E Addley, 'Shetland may reconsider its place in Scotland after yes vote, says minister' *The Guardian* (17 September 2014).

[64] *Legal Consequences of the Construction of a Wall in the Occupied Palestinian Territory* (Advisory Opinion) [2004] ICJ Rep 136, [88].

introduce non-forcible measures ('sanctions') in support of the establishment of the independence of the territory.

# X. Conclusion

This chapter developed and defended an argument for recognising a right to democratic secession. In doing so, it drew on the insights from a particular variant of communications systems theory: complexity. The work began from the premise that international lawyers share a foundational conception of *state* as an independent political community under a coercive system of government that operates through law and which represents the community with similar communities. Reformulated in the language of communications systems theory, *state* was understood as the symbolic space occupied by the coevolved and coexistent systems of law and politics. A key insight developed in this chapter is that law and politics are complex systems. The idea of *state*, following the third wave of system theory thinking known as complexity, was formulated as the *observation of the patterned communications of the coevolved and coexistent law and politics systems coupled under a constitution*. Where the law system and politics system are observed to be coexistent, the population and territory subject to the overlapping normative communications of the two systems has a claim to be statehood. A focus on the nature of the politics systems—understood through the cognitive frame of international law—allowed us to develop a right of democratic secession in three related steps: the rejection of the sovereign authority of the territorial state by certain subjects; the acceptance of the authority of emergent systems of law and politics of the new political entity; and observation (or 'recognition') of the political entity as possessing legitimate political authority. The argument is that this 'model' of democratic secession underpins and explains the extant international law on statehood.

At the time of writing,[65] three self-determination events focused on the idea of democratic separation or secession are dominating the media: the referendum on Scottish independence has produced a vote in favour of Scotland remaining part of the United Kingdom;[66] Crimea has seemingly become a federal subject within the Russian Federation, following a referendum, although this possibility has been rejected by the international community;[67] and the Donetsk People's Republic and

---

[65] September 2014.

[66] BBC News, 'Scottish referendum: Scotland votes "No" to independence' *BBC News Online* (19 September 2014).

[67] See UNGA 'Territorial Integrity of Ukraine' (27 March 2014) UNGA Res 68/262, para 5, which asserted that the independence referendum for Crimea, 'having no validity, cannot form the basis for any alteration of the status of the Autonomous Republic of Crimea': also, Council of Europe's Venice Commission's Opinion on 'Whether the decision taken by the supreme council of the autonomous republic of Crimea in Ukraine to organise a referendum on becoming a constituent territory of the Russian federation or restoring Crimea's 1992 constitution is compatible with constitutional principles' CDL-AD(2014)002.

Luhansk People's Republic in eastern Ukraine have declared their independence (again following hastily arranged and badly organised referendums), although neither has been recognised by any state, including Russia.[68] Had Scotland voted for independence, it would not seem implausible to argue that the people of Scotland would enjoy a right to statehood opposable to the United Kingdom. Yet, no serious academic argues that the Ukrainian regions of Crimea, Donetsk or Luhansk have a right to statehood, and (subsequently and consequently) the right to determine their own status, including by way of union with Russia. This is the case notwithstanding the fact that the regions have voted for independence.[69] How, then, do we evaluate the claims of the Crimea, Donetsk or Luhansk regions: deny any right of democratic secession; reject the idea of a remedial right of secession in case it is misused (as seems the case here);[70] or simply ask whether the regions have 'safely and permanently' managed to exclude the authority of Ukraine, without the level of external support prohibited by international law?[71]

An application of the model developed in this chapter would recognise a general right of democratic secession for the populations ('peoples') of Crimea, Donetsk and Luhansk, but reject the claims to independence by those regions by way of democratic secession in the particular circumstances—not because the populations do not have a right to self-determination or must subject themselves to the authority of the Ukrainian state, but as a consequence of the failure of the authorities and the populations to engage in reasoned, democratic deliberations concerning the allocation of political authority in the region. Simply put: the situation in the Crimea, Donetsk or Luhansk regions cannot be understood as an example of choice-based or democratic secession, as the only force permitted in the context of the democratic right of secession is the force of the better argument—and that is certainly not the case here.

---

[68] It is not clear that the electorate voted for independence, as the referendum question used a Russian word, *samostoyatelnost*, which could mean independence or greater autonomy: S Walker, 'East Ukraine goes to the polls for independence referendum' *The Observer* (11 May 2014).

[69] The position in Crimea is complicated by the question asked in the 16 March referendum, which provided voters with two choices: (1) reuniting Crimea with Russia as a subject of the Russian Federation; or (2) retaining the status of Crimea as part of Ukraine. The case of Crimea may then be an example of association rather than secession. In either case, the same principles would apply in relation to the requirement to deliberate on the future of the territory over a period of time.

[70] A UK parliamentary committee has accused Russia of using 'ambiguous warfare' tactics in Ukraine: Defence Committee, 'Towards the Next Defence and Security Review: Part Two—NATO' (HC 2014–15 358).

[71] Under the rules of general international law, a state is responsible for the actions of a non-state actor outside of its territory where the relationship is 'one of [complete] dependence on the one side and control on the other': *Application of the Convention on the Prevention and Punishment of the Crime of Genocide* (Bosnia and Herzegovina v Serbia and Montenegro) (Judgment) [2007] ICJ Rep 43, [391]. Such a finding will be exceptional.

# 8

## Beyond Secession? Law in the Framing of the National Polity

NEIL WALKER

## I. Introduction: Three Sets of Questions

The independence referendum of 18 September 2014 offered a democratic[1] opportunity for the people of Scotland, or at least its resident population[2]—to end the 307-year-old legal and political Union latterly known as the United Kingdom of Great Britain and Northern Ireland (UK).[3] In the event, the Scottish elector- ate voted against independence by a narrow but clear majority of 55 per cent to 45 per cent. Yet this unarguably remains one of the most significant episodes in the modern constitutional history of the British nation and nations. In addition, the Scottish story has a broader relevance for anyone interested in the causes and pat- terns of national formation and transformation as viewed through a constitutional optic. For it is a story that is generally instructive of and—in certain respects— consequential for the evolving role of law in the shaping and situating of political community across the European region and in the wider global context.

Notwithstanding an unusually robust indigenous legal framework for manag- ing the secession question, from the very beginning of a referendum campaign that would span almost three years[4] an outward-looking perspective was present and pertinent. In particular,[5] the question of an independent Scotland's prospective

---

[1] On the democratic credentials of referendums, see S Tierney, *Constitutional Referendums: The Theory and Practice of Republican Deliberation* (Oxford, Oxford University Press, 2012) ch 2.

[2] Scottish Independence Referendum (Franchise) Act 2013, s 2.

[3] First known as Great Britain after the 1707 Treaty of Union joining England and Scotland; then with the addition of Ireland in 1800, the United Kingdom of Great Britain and Ireland; and finally, following the formation of the Irish Free State in 1922, the United Kingdom of Great Britain and Northern Ireland.

[4] For a useful timeline of events, see Scottish Constitutional Futures, 'The Independence Referen- dum: Timeline of Events' at: www.scottishconstitutionalfutures.org/Resources/Timeline/tabid/1658/ Default.aspx. See also, T Mullen, 'The Scottish Independence Referendum 2014' (2014) 41 *Journal of Law and Society* 627.

[5] While this chapter concentrates on EU membership, we should note that other questions concerning an independent Scotland's global role were also controversial, especially the issue of NATO membership and the retention of a nuclear defence capacity. See the Scottish government's

membership of another larger political entity, namely the supranational European Union (EU), loomed large, figuring amongst the most hotly and persistently contested issues of the whole campaign. The supporters of independence were keen to emphasise the benefits of continued participation in the EU's common market and system of supranational governance[6] for a 'small nation'[7] of five million and, in stark contrast to their opponents, to insist upon the strength of Scotland's candidature.[8] Many points were at issue. In shorthand, we can call these 'what', 'how' and 'whether' questions.

The 'what' questions were much to the fore. They concerned the terms on which a newly independent Scotland might assert or be offered membership of the European Union. Could and should Scotland retain the UK's historic opt-outs on matters such as membership of the Euro currency or inclusion within the Schengen area of open borders, or even inherit a share of the UK's controversial rebate on contributions to the EU's budget?[9] Predictably, as the retention of these opt-outs was forecast to be generally beneficial to Scottish interests, many supportive of independence argued strongly in favour of what they coined 'the principle of continuity of effect',[10] while many in the pro-UK 'Better Together'[11] camp took the opposite view. They painted a much less optimistic picture of the membership negotiations, and the conditions a new Scottish state would be required to accept.

The 'how' questions were also much disputed. If a mandate were secured for independence in the referendum, would the emerging new Scottish state, as in the regular case of a candidate state from beyond the territorial boundaries of the EU, be required to follow the dedicated accession route under Article 49 of the Treaty on European Union (TEU)? Or did the fact that the Scottish case contemplated an unprecedented 'internal enlargement'—involving the separation of a state already within the EU in circumstances where the seceding part sought to remain within the EU[12]—suggest that the general Treaty revision procedures under Article 48

---

independence blueprint: Scottish government, *Scotland's Future: Your Guide to an Independent Scotland* (26 November 2013) ch 6, esp 224–51.

    [6] See *Scotland's Future* (n 5) ch 6, esp 216–24.
    [7] See M Keating and M Harvey, *Small Nations in a Big World: What Scotland Can Learn* (Edinburgh, Bell and Bain, 2014) esp 69–73.
    [8] See S Tierney and K Boyle, 'An Independent Scotland: The Road to Membership of the European Union' (2014) ESRC Scottish Centre on Constitutional Change, Briefing Paper, 20 August 2014; D Kenealy and S MacLennan, 'Sincere Cooperation, Respect for Democracy and EU Citizenship: Sufficient to Guarantee Scotland's Future in the European Union?' (2014) 20 *European Law Journal* 591.
    [9] For discussion, see J Kerr, 'The Other Union; Scotland and the EU' (*Scottish Constitutional Futures Forum Blog*, 30 January 2013).
    [10] *Scotland's Future* (n 5) 221.
    [11] The official name of the pro-UK campaigning organisation set up to contest the referendum.
    [12] In previous cases of internal separation, Algeria from France in 1962 and Greenland from Denmark in 1979 (in the latter case achieving autonomous status rather than independent sovereign statehood) the leaving part sought to exit the EU rather than remain within it. See eg J Crawford and A Boyle, 'Opinion: Referendum on the Independence of Scotland: International Law Aspects' in UK government, *Scotland Analysis: Devolution and the Implications of Scottish Independence* (Cm 8554, 2013) para 146.

TEU, crafted for dealings amongst existing members, should be used instead? Since both revision mechanisms were intended for already established sovereign states, whether EU members (TEU, Article 48) or non-members (TEU, Article 49), neither provision was well suited to the circumstances of a state-in-waiting seeking to complete the post-referendum process of negotiating independence from the 'parent' state and obtaining international recognition. And whichever route—both formally awkward—might be chosen, was there any special duty on the part of the EU institutions or its Member States to smooth the passage, and so facilitate or even expedite Scotland's joining the Union? Again, unsurprisingly, those well disposed towards independence tended to argue for a fast-track channel, while those ill-disposed warned of a more difficult journey ahead.

Finally, and most basically, there was the 'whether' question. Would an independent or prospectively independent Scotland's claim to EU membership be one of right, or at least of legitimate expectation? Or was the claim somewhat less than that, perhaps involving no presumption either way? Or, at the other end of the spectrum, should the sundering of an existing Member State actively count against EU membership for the seceding part, perhaps even debar such membership? For reasons discussed below, during the referendum campaign this question was rarely explicitly addressed by those who would be directly authorised in the legal process for securing Scottish membership, still less given a definitive answer, although many others did express their views.

Yet it is the 'whether' question, I argue, that holds the key to the broadest understanding, and so provides our point of departure. In particular, the 'whether' question bears upon three closely connected matters, each explored below. These matters we can situate in ascending order of abstraction, and also of generality of ramification.

To begin with, most obviously and most concretely, the 'whether' question, and how it was (or was not) addressed, had significant implications for the unfolding and outcome of the Scottish case. There is a narrow and a broad dimension to this. Narrowly, how the 'whether' question might be addressed would have an important bearing on the advance treatment of the 'what' and 'how' questions of Scottish membership of the EU. On the one hand, the existence of a strong case in principle for Scottish membership would, in affirmation of such a principled case, tend in favour of a more welcoming path in terms of 'what' (conditions) and 'how' (easily). On the other hand, and in more practical vein, the implicit beliefs and explicit utterances of involved actors on each side concerning the proper approach of the EU to the merits of the Scottish claim, whether these beliefs were in principle justifiable, were bound to have—and in fact did have—a motivating and mobilising effect on the approaches taken to the detailed 'what' and 'how' questions.

More broadly, how the 'whether' question was addressed, together with the closely associated 'what' and 'how' questions, was also intimately tied up with the overall fate of the independence project. Past and future tense are both important here. Not only would we have expected the attitude of the various parties to the 'whether' question to have coloured their 'how' and 'what' arguments in the event of a 'Yes' vote, and during the inevitably complex and precarious double-stream secession-and-accession negotiations with the remaining UK (rUK) and the EU itself that would have followed. In addition, and—especially in view of the 'No' vote—more pertinently, arguments about the general merits and the particular strengths and weaknesses of the Scottish case for membership, and the reaction of the EU to these arguments, also had a tangible influence on voting behaviour, and so affected the outcome of the referendum itself.[13] This, indeed, was only to be expected, for, as already noted, these arguments were from the beginning of the campaign part and parcel of competing narratives of the anticipated costs and benefits of independence.

In the second place, the Scottish case has ramifications for secessionist movements and similar fragmentary tendencies elsewhere within the EU, or otherwise pertinent to the EU, and also for what would count as an appropriate response by the EU to these movements. The obvious and topical cases in point here are Catalonia in relation to Spain, and Flanders in relation to Belgium. But there are other less developed intra-EU secession movements as well as a vivid contemporary history of turbulent nationalist politics with secessionist implications in the EU's near neighbourhood.[14] Once more, what is at stake is both normative and practical. For reasons developed below, the EU ought to endeavour to strike a coherent attitude and develop a consistent approach to the different dissolution scenarios it confronts, though such an aspiration encounters profound difficulties. And in practical terms, the EU's position in respect of the Scottish independence process would in any case inevitably set an important precedent, and so the adoption of any such position was bound to be influenced by the EU's advance appreciation of its precedent-setting potential. That is to say, the EU's approach to the lead case of Scotland, inasmuch as it contributed to the shaping of a general institutional orientation, would clearly have implications for how it would be minded to act in the face of similar scenarios, just as (and partly because) it would be bound to affect the expectations and incentives of those politically engaged in

---

[13]  The findings are still raw, but early analysis indicates that uncertainty over Scotland's place in the EU was a factor of not inconsiderable importance in the 'No' vote. One immediate post-referendum poll by Lord Ashcroft, for example, found that 47% of 'No' voters cited the 'too great' risks of independence (amongst which were numbered those associated with future EU membership) as their main reason for voting that way. When isolated as a factor, only 15% of 'No' voters and 12% of 'Yes' voters cited EU membership as one of the two or three most important issues bearing upon how they cast their votes. Tellingly, however, as many as 57% of 'No' voters (and as few as 7% of 'Yes' voters) cited 'the pound' (in particular, we can reasonably infer, uncertainty over its retention in an independent Scotland with EU membership) as one of the two or three most important issues. See Lord Ashcroft Polls, *Post-Referendum Scotland Poll* (19 September 2014). See also G Hassan, 'Anatomy of a Referendum—and its Aftermath' *Scottish Review* (24 September 2014).

[14]  Most recently, events in Eastern Ukraine before and after the Russian annexation of Crimea in March 2013. The accompanying referendum was deemed unconstitutional in an Opinion issued by the Council of Europe's European Commission for Democracy Through Law (Venice Commission): Venice Commission, Opinion 762/2014, CDL-AD(2014)002 (Venice, 21–22 March 2014).

these other independence struggles and debates. That, indeed, is why the rest of Europe watched the Scottish debate so closely.[15]

Just because it is the Scottish case that has provided the occasion, and the prompt, for sustained reflection on other European secession scenarios, the first and second matters are entangled. And so they are treated together in the following section. That leaves for consideration in the final section the bearing of the Scottish case on the more general question of the relationship between the law and politics of independence internal to a political community on the one hand, and the broader transnational legal environment—with particular reference to the normative capacity and reception of the EU as a supranational entity. These questions may be less urgent, but they are of deep and lasting significance. Let me introduce them in bare outline.

The EU, as a regional system of legal governance, and so as an intermediate site within the multi-level pattern of planetary legal relations, offers a clear point of intersection of global and local legal norms and institutions.[16] The legal context of independence struggles provides one specific but highly consequential and more generally illuminating test of how the EU might mediate the relationship between the global-in-general and the local. On the one hand, state-making and state-breaking questions engage a particularly important domain of law—one that supplies both a limiting and a precarious instance of law's steering capacity. On the other hand, and notwithstanding the fragility of law in this domain, the EU, despite its reluctance to take a strong stance in the Scottish case, or in any other particular case, retains a distinctive, indeed, unprecedented role in the legal fashioning of political community.

Why is this so? Note that, situated above and below the EU's continental regime, the global and the local juridical levels are here represented respectively by the international law of self-determination and by a cluster of national constitutional law principles associated with collective autonomy—with secession located at the end point of a spectrum of possibilities. Yet, as we shall explain, self-determination and secession have the status of *liminal* concepts within their respective legal fields. They necessarily operate at and around the threshold of legality, so to speak, located both within and outside the boundary of legal authority. This restricts the effectiveness of each, as well as the terms of their mutual engagement. However, once the EU enters the picture as a 'third player', a more fertile set of possibilities emerges. By dint of its very interposition of a new level of legally coded political community, it can do more than offer a third stream of regulatory principle. That is to say, as well as adding its own (very tentative) voice to constitutional law and international law as a regulator of the terms of political community within its territory, and so contributing to the appropriate legal conditions and procedures

---

[15] See eg C Marshall, 'World's eyes on Scottish independence referendum' *The Scotsman* (19 September 2014).

[16] See more generally N Walker, 'The Place of European Law' in G de Burca and J Weiler (eds), *The Worlds of European Constitutionalism* (Cambridge, Cambridge University Press, 2012) 57–104.

of state-making, recognition and dissolution, EU law is in addition constitutively involved in the basic 'framing'—or reframing—of legal community. For its very emergence as a legally constructed political entity alters the elementary calculus through which we attribute value—both instrumental and expressive—to forms of political life at, above and below the level of the state. And while the full consequences of this reframing exercise remain unsettled and unpredictable, they are already reshaping political expectations and aspirations in ways that alter our very sense of the relevance of secession and associated statuses.

# II. Europe in Scotland, Scotland in Europe

The Scottish independence debate revealed a highly distinctive, indeed unprecedented, pattern in the relevant legal 'division of labour'. In a nutshell, constitutional law played a role that was unusually facilitative of the basic claim of secession, though not at all conducive to settlement of its detailed terms; international law was largely consigned to the margins; and European law, never before called upon to address the question of secession within its own borders, was, in consequence, offered an unwanted prominence. How should we account for this, and what difficulties followed from that distribution of authority?

## A. Begging the European Question

For reasons we discuss in due course,[17] most constitutional traditions are hostile to the prospect of the secession of any part of their territory. Few contemporary state constitutions make explicit provision for secession—only Ethiopia, St Kitts and Nevis, and Liechtenstein—or even indirectly countenance its prospect—only Austria and Singapore.[18] And in all these cases the procedural route to legitimate secession is formidable. A far greater number of state constitutions adopt the opposite posture, enshrining ideas, such as state 'indivisibility', 'national unity' and 'territorial integrity', that are more or less emphatically inconsistent with the idea of secession.[19] And while both open-ended constitutional amendment procedures[20]

---

[17] See section III.A below.

[18] Although there have also been some prominent cases in the past. For example, in its 1924, 1936 and 1977 Constitutions, the USSR recognised the right of each of its constituent republics to secede. See C Sunstein 'Constitutionalism and Secession' (1991) 58 *The University of Chicago Law Review* 633.

[19] For an extensive listing, see P Radan, 'Secession in Constitutional Law' in A Pavkovic and P Radan (eds), *The Ashgate Research Companion to Secession* (Farnham, Ashgate, 2011).

[20] See ibid. The relationship between open-ended constitutional amendment procedures on the one hand and eternity clauses and other strongly entrenching terms within the same constitutional text on the other, is complex. On the increased attention of constitutional courts worldwide, in light of this complexity, to the possibility of 'unconstitutional constitutional amendments', see Y Roznai, 'Unconstitutional Constitutional Amendments: The Migration and Success of a Constitutional Idea' (2013) 61 *The American Journal of Comparative Law* 657.

and the creative interpretive work of constitutional courts[21] can mitigate the impact of prohibitive words, or allow contemplation of secession where the constitutional text is silent, the possibilities offered here have tended to remain moot. In practice, with very few exceptions,[22] where secession does take place, therefore, it follows an *extra-constitutional* route, consensual or otherwise. Either it is a 'voluntary disassociation', as in Bangladesh, Eritrea or Czechoslovakia, where the very fact that all internal parties, with or without a period of prior conflict, come to agree to separation, renders the constitutional settlement of the previously unseparated state redundant; or it involves a non-consensual 'dissolution', as in the case of the former Yugoslavia, where the strength of disagreement, and its violent expression, reflects and reinforces the failed authority of the previous constitutional settlement. In the Scottish case, however, the existing framework of constitutional authority was neither redundant nor discredited. Rather, it retained a significant though loose structuring role. The explanation for this turns on certain peculiar features of British constitutional history and context.

We should begin with the UK's distinctively 'unwritten' constitution—it's rare, if not unique,[23] standing as a national constitutional arrangement lacking a canonical textual authority. Discovering and comprehending British constitutional law instead involves exploring the evolved legislative record, as well as the common law, judicial precedents, conventions and practices of a flexible order arranged under the narrow sign of parliamentary sovereignty. And, ironically, the very flexibility of constitutional content allowed by the bare doctrine of parliamentary sovereignty has encouraged a striking continuity of constitutional form. For its very capacity to accommodate radically different political arrangements and legal forms has helped immunise the 'top rule' itself from challenge and change since it became established in the seventeenth century.[24]

There exists, then, no positive constitutional document, or at least none broadly recognised as such,[25] that might have ruled in, or much more likely, ruled out secession, as so many other foundational texts have. Rather, within the shifting

---

[21] See esp *Reference re Secession of Quebec* [1998] 2 SCR 217.

[22] Arguably, many of the secessions from the Soviet Union, beginning with the Baltic States, followed a constitutional path under the extant Soviet Constitution of 1977. However, as the process gathered pace it assumed more of the character of an extra-constitutional 'voluntary disassociation'. On matters of categorisation, see S Mancini, 'Secession and Self-Determination' in M Rosenfeld and A Sajo (eds), *The Oxford Handbook of Comparative Constitutional Law* (Oxford, Oxford University Press, 2012).

[23] The idea of an unwritten constitution fuses (and sometimes confuses) two notions. It can refer to a scenario where there is no single document named as the constitution, but where one or more fundamental legal texts are nevertheless recognised as such (as in Israel or Saudi Arabia). Or it can refer to a scenario where there is a single document named as the constitution, but where that document does not possess the standing of basic or fundamental law (as in New Zealand). Only in the UK is there neither a nominate written constitution nor otherwise recognition of fundamental legal text(s).

[24] See N Walker, 'Our Constitutional Unsettlement' (2014) *Public Law* 529.

[25] The Treaty of Union, by which agreement the Union was established in 1707, held in Art I that 'the two Kingdoms of Scotland and England shall upon the first day of May next ensuing the date hereof, *and for ever after*, be united into One Kingdom by the Name of Great Britain'. However, at least before the development of the new view of the Union state, this document was not broadly regarded as having constitutional standing. See further n 29 below.

mosaic of British constitutional thought and practice, a new self-understanding
of what is entailed by the idea of a 'Union state' has gradually taken hold in recent
years.[26] This differs from the constitutional orthodoxy which for a long time saw
the 1707 Union as an unconditional settlement. According to that understanding,[27]
the British project was understood as an 'incorporating Union', with the Celtic
nations absorbed within the institutional structure of the previously English
state—in particular the Westminster Parliament—without constitutional remainder. The new view instead revives and extends an even older understanding of the
foundational pact(s)[28] in which the different national parts of the Union retain
something of their legal and political identity, and, it follows, some continuing
measure of independent influence over their constitutional condition.

Certain glimpses of this development can already be seen in constitutional case-
law and commentary from the mid-twentieth century onwards,[29] but it was only
through executive and parliamentary initiative in response to deeper social transformation—so often the driving forces in the unwritten constitution[30]—that real
constitutional change came about. In particular, we should look to the resolution of
deep-set political conflict between British loyalists and Irish nationalists in Northern
Ireland, which had simmered since the partition of Irish territory in the formation
of the new (southern) Irish state in 1920[31] and boiled over into sustained violence
from the late 1960s onwards, as the (largely unacknowledged)[32] impulse behind the
broader relaxation of Unionist thinking. For after numerous failed initiatives, the
continuation of the troubles in the North eventually drew the negotiated concession
from the British government, recorded in the 1998 Good Friday Agreement,[33] that

> it is for the people of the island of Ireland alone, by agreement between the two parts
> respectively, to exercise their right of self-determination on the basis of consent, freely and
> concurrently given, North and South, to bring about a united Ireland, if that is their wish.[34]

---

[26] See esp C Kidd, *Union and Unionisms: Political Thought in Scotland, 1500-2000* (Cambridge,
Cambridge University Press, 2009). And for the general intellectual background to the contemporary
idea of the Union state, see S Rokkan and D Urwin, *Economy, Territory, Identity. Politics of West European Peripheries* (London, Sage, 1983).

[27] See esp A Dicey and R Rait, *Thoughts on the Union between England and Scotland* (London,
MacMillan, 1920).

[28] See eg Kidd, *Union and Unionisms* (n 26).

[29] In particular the dictum of Lord President Cooper in the Scottish case of *MacCormick v Lord
Advocate* 1953 SC 396, in which he ventures that an unqualified version of parliamentary sovereignty,
taking no account of the 1707 Articles of Union, has never been the law of Scotland.

[30] And one reason why 'political constitutionalism' provides such an influential framing theme in
the appraisal of the UK Constitution. See eg G Gee and G Webber, 'What is a Political Constitution?'
(2010) 30 *Oxford Journal of Legal Studies* 273.

[31] Itself an instance of non-consensual dissociation or secession.

[32] On the widespread tendency to fail to explicitly acknowledge the lines of mutual influence
between the British mainland and Northern Ireland 'parts' of the UK Constitution, see C McCrudden,
'Northern Ireland and the British Constitution since the Belfast Agreement' in J Jowell and D Oliver
(eds), *The Changing Constitution* 6th edn (Oxford, Oxford University Press, 2007). See also Walker,
'Our Constitutional Unsettlement' (n 24) 531.

[33] Concluded with the Irish government and all (8) political parties in Northern Ireland—
nationalist, unionist and unaligned.

[34] Good Friday Agreement 1998, 3.

This entitlement was subsequently reflected in Westminster legislation (re)estab-lishing devolved government in Northern Ireland, and, crucially, allowing for peri-odical referendums on the question of independence.[35]

In the very same year, in response to peaceful (and quite unrelated) political pressure towards greater autonomy in Scotland, emanating from a broad front of Scottish National Party (SNP) and more modestly decentralising forces, a devolved Scottish Parliament and Executive with significant and wide-ranging powers was established under the Scotland Act. And from this point onwards it was uncontested amongst key political actors and constitutional commenta-tors, albeit typically only tacitly or tersely conceded, that there should be no UK constitutional impediment to the Scottish people exercising a right to self-determination—just as had recently been so vividly recognised of the people of Northern Ireland—if and when a viable platform of support for such an option were to emerge.[36]

That platform began to form just a decade later. Growing electoral backing for the SNP saw them break new ground to form the devolved Scottish government in Edinburgh under the leadership of Alex Salmond, first in 2007 as a minority administration, and subsequently in 2011 with an overall majority in the Scot-tish Parliament. In part because support for the nationalists' ultimate objective of independence had remained consistently lower than had backing for the SNP as the custodians of devolved Scottish government in Edinburgh,[37] the UK gov-ernment under David Cameron took the pre-emptive step early in the life of the 2011 Scottish government of insisting that Salmond deliver sooner rather than later on his electoral mandate promise of an independence referendum. With both sides now committed to a plebiscite, intense debate was joined between London and Edinburgh over matters of process. Alongside the precise schedul-ing of the referendum (the SNP government preferred to wait until later in their administration to allow time to build up support), key issues included the range of options on the table (the SNP were open to the inclusion of a third option of

---

[35] Northern Ireland Act 1998, s 1. This requires a period of at least 7 years between referendums.

[36] See eg S Tierney, *Constitutional Law and National Pluralism* (Oxford, Oxford University Press, 2006) 323. Certainly, the Scottish claim to self-determination had a long history quite independently of developments. In Northern Ireland, the Royal Commission on the Constitution (Kilbrandon Commission) comes close to acknowledging such a right (see *Report of the Royal Commission on the Constitution, 1969-73* (Cmnd 5460, 1973) esp paras 433, 468 and 497). See also Campaign for a Scottish Assembly, 'A Claim of Right for Scotland' in OD Edwards (ed), *A Claim of Right for Scotland* (Edinburgh, Polygon, 1989), from which emerged the Scottish Constitutional Convention and the popular front leading to the Scotland Act 1998, and which contained a robust claim of Scottish popular sovereignty. Yet the claim only becomes unanswerable in constitutional reason, and is only conceded in constitutional practice, after the Northern Ireland developments.

[37] While at that stage backing for independence had rarely risen above one-third in opinion polls, the SNP had succeeded in winning 45% of the popular vote in the 2011 Scottish parliamentary elections.

'Devo Max' between independence and the status quo ante, while the UK government was not), and the extent of the franchise (the nationalists sought, with eventual success, to give a referendum vote to 16- and 17-year-olds).[38] In addition, and of some practical importance given the extent of disagreement over terms and conditions—views also differed over who possessed ultimate 'constitutional' title to validate the exercise by the Scottish people of their 'constitutional' right to choose their own 'constitutional' destiny.[39]

As this way of posing the issue indicates, difficult questions of regressive constitutional authority arose. On the one hand, it was arguable that if the claim of popular sovereignty of the Scottish people was truly a claim of constitutional *right*, as appeared to be generally accepted under the recently revised understanding of the Union state, then permission to exercise that right should not reside within the effective gift of the UK Parliament. On the other hand, it also remained persuasively arguable that the resilient doctrine of parliamentary sovereignty simply allowed of no other answer in strict law to the question of final authority and constitutional title, in which case the Scottish claim could only consist in a strong moral and political direction to the legal sovereign at Westminster.

The impasse threatened by these differing perspectives was overcome in the so-called Edinburgh Agreement of October 2012 between the two governments.[40] By its authority each party bound itself to respect the outcome of a referendum to be held in September 2014, and also to generate a legislative plan—to be ratified by both Parliaments under the existing (Westminster parliamentary) authority of the Scotland Act—resolving and specifying the basic terms of that referendum. Yet again, therefore, the suppleness of the British Constitution allowed a certain type of creative solution without conceding or compromising its traditional fundamental rule of parliamentary sovereignty. The Edinburgh Agreement was itself an unidentifiable constitutional object, neither international treaty (in the absence of two contracting states) nor of any formally elevated constitutional standing, but instead joining the loose category of so-called 'constitutional concordats'[41] between different levels of government by which a decentralising UK had begun to regulate its newly quasi-federal arrangements.

Certain important consequences follow from this improvised solution. In particular, exploiting the mutability of the unwritten constitution to carve out a constitutional path to secession—one where, to repeat, the existing constitutional order is neither rendered redundant nor discredited—allowed the contest

---

[38] Scottish Independence Referendum (Franchise) Act 2013, s2(1)(a).

[39] For the competing governmental views, see Scottish government, *Your Scotland, Your Referendum* (Edinburgh, 2012); UK government, *Scotland's Constitutional Future* (Cm 8203, 2012). See also Scottish Affairs Select Committee, *Making the Process Legal* (HC 2012–13, 542). For the accompanying academic debate, see eg G Anderson et al, 'The Independence Referendum, Legality and the Contested Constitution: Widening the Debate' (*UK Constitutional Law Blog*, 31 January 2012).

[40] The Edinburgh Agreement (October 2012). For the subsequent joint agreement under the Scotland Act 1998, s 30, see Scotland Act 1998 (Modification of Schedule 5) Order 2013, SI 2013/242.

[41] See eg R Rawlings, 'Concordats of the Constitution' (2000) 116 *Law Quarterly Review* 257.

to proceed in circumstances where the UK government could operate according to two distinct registers of constitutional legitimacy. While conceding the legitimacy of the secession-contemplating *process* in line with the revised self-understanding of the Union state, as defenders of the continuing integrity of the UK constitutional order the UK government could also legitimately continue to argue against a secessionist *outcome*. In practice that meant that although London was bound to play by the rules as jointly agreed in the Edinburgh Agreement and consequential legislation, as the representative of the interests of rUK it had no incentive to let these rules be cast in generous terms or otherwise to facilitate the subsequent pathway to Scottish independence or encourage the view that such a pathway would be free of significant obstacles. Instead, the concession of constitutional principle was heavily qualified by a political strategy on the part of the British government and the 'Better Together' campaign of pro-Unionist political parties that sought two connected ends, or at least entailed two connected consequences: first, to emphasise the uncertainty and fragility of the terms on which an independent Scotland would acquire sovereign statehood; and secondly, the adoption of a negotiating stance, backed both by its standing and control of resources as the recognised 'external' sovereign in international law and by its effective retention through its parliamentary majority of those levers of 'internal' sovereignty required to 'sign off' the various stages of disassociation leading to eventual Scottish divorce,[42] which, in its vigorous assertion of rUK interests, would contribute to that very uncertainty and fragility.

Nowhere was this two-pronged approach more evident than with regard to the question of EU membership. On the one hand, the British government warned that Scotland's pathway to the EU 'could be complex and long, and the outcome could prove less advantageous than the status quo'[43]—a message emphatically reinforced by the Better Together campaign. On the other hand, the British government's own negotiating position made its prediction only more plausible. It made much of the claim, hardly controversial though it was in international law,[44] that rUK rather than Scotland would be treated as the successor state to the UK for the purposes of membership of international organisations. Consequently, the burden of applying to rejoin the EU would fall on Scotland, and on Scotland alone. London also endorsed the view that, prior to Scotland completing the process of securing independence from the UK after a referendum victory, any advance negotiations with the EU on the terms and conditions of any new membership application in the ambitiously narrow 18-month window between a referendum 'Yes' vote and the nationalists' projected 'Independence Day',[45] if

---

[42] In the event of a 'Yes' vote, the nationalists would have requested in the first instance from the Westminster Parliament a revision of the Scotland Act to provide a 'constitutional platform' of transferred powers allowing them to prepare for Independence Day. See *The Scottish Independence Bill: A Consultation on an Interim Constitution for Scotland* (Scottish government, 2014).

[43] UK government, *Scotland Analysis: EU and International Issues* (Cm 8765, 2014) 55.

[44] Crawford and Boyle, *Opinion* (n 12).

[45] Namely, 24 March 2016.

pursued at all, would have to be through the formal medium of the British government as the existing Member State. One additional, and more pointed negotiating posture on London's part assumed increasing significance as the campaign reached its climax. By refusing, against vehement nationalist protests, to countenance the continuation of a formal sterling currency Union between rUK and an independent Scotland—an arrangement that would require the extension of the UK's Euro currency opt-out to the new Scottish state, the British government sharply exposed the reluctance of the nationalists to embrace what has been a normal condition of membership for all EU candidate states since the advent of Economic and Monetary Union.[46] In so doing, they not only achieved notable success in tapping into voter concerns about losing the pound,[47] but also shone unwanted light on what was bound to be one of the most vulnerable aspects of Scotland's bargaining position vis-a-vis the EU.

As intimated, the approach of the Scottish government and its sympathisers was quite different. From their perspective, certain special features of the EU and its deep penetration of its Member States' legal and political systems argued for a largely seamless accommodation of Scotland's newly independent standing. 'Continuity of effect' should apply because Scotland's five million citizens were already citizens of the EU under EU law [48] and should be deprived neither of such citizenship and its consequential rights, nor of the specific terms and conditions associated with their collective membership, just on account of their having registered a desire to leave *another* entity, namely the UK. Indeed, as a case of 'internal enlargement' Scotland should benefit from the normal insider channel of Treaty reform—TEU, Article 48—to settle the terms of its independent membership. And in any event, regardless of the procedurally proper route—TEU, Article 48 revision or TEU, Article 49 accession—Scotland should not be treated like a new applicant. It should not be expected to take its place in the queue behind existing candidate states;[49] or to undergo 'due diligence' to ensure that it met the threshold criteria of respect for EU values—human dignity, freedom, democracy, equality, the rule of law and human rights[50]—and of readiness to assume the institutional responsibilities of membership;[51] or to begin its negotiations from the premise

---

[46] In the original Treaty on European Union, signed at Maastricht in 1992. See (current) Treaty on European Union, Art 3(4); Treaty on the Functioning of the European Union (TFEU) pt 3, Title VIII. See also Copenhagen criteria (below n 51).

[47] See above n 13.

[48] TFEU, Arts 20–25.

[49] See eg D Edward, 'Scotland and the European Union' (*Scottish Constitutional Futures Forum Blog*, 17 December 2012).

[50] See TEU, Arts 2 and 49.

[51] In accordance with the so-called Copenhagen Criteria (named after the city where the European Council Presidency Conclusions were drafted in 1993) established in anticipation of Eastern Enlargement. These conclusions, which continue to represent the general 'eligibility criteria' stipulated by the European Council under TEU, Art 49 require 'that a candidate country has achieved stability of institutions guaranteeing democracy, the rule of law, human rights, respect for and protection of minorities, the existence of a functioning market economy as well as the capacity to cope with competitive pressure and market forces within the Union. Membership presupposes the candidate's ability to take on the obligations of membership including adherence to the aims of political, economic and monetary union'.

that its historical participation in the 'opt-outs' and other special provisions of UK membership had been rendered irrelevant. Rather, referring to fundamental Treaty commitments to democracy and minority rights[52] and respect for 'national identities',[53] and to the principle of 'sincere cooperation'[54] between the Union and its members, nationalists and those sympathetic to their legal case argued that there was a positive duty on the part of all interested parties to enter into good faith and timely negotiations to secure Scotland's continuing membership.[55]

The strategic lines of the parties became increasingly entrenched as the campaign progressed. Both stances, however, were profoundly question-begging. Neither side had an interest in finding common ground on the other's preferred terms, and, as we have seen, there was no domestic constitutional requirement to pursue an advance settlement, nor even a mechanism, such as a constitutional advisory jurisdiction,[56] which might have provided the basis for a shared legal understanding in subsequent negotiations with Brussels. However confidently they might predict the likely course of an independent Scotland's negotiations, therefore, in the absence of an independent authoritative resolution, the legal narratives of the British and Scottish government on the prospects of EU membership for an independent Scotland remained as speculative as they were polarised. But where else, if anywhere, might such an authoritative resolution be forthcoming?

## B. The Sidelines of International Law

Might international law fill the gap? The short answer is no, and the reasons can be briefly stated. Quite simply, the domestic constitutional concession of the basic legality of a negotiated accession, combined with international law's reticence before the special case of the EU, meant that general international law had little to contribute.

On the one hand, on the substantive question of secession and its relationship to the broader norm of self-determination, the Scottish case had no need for what international law had to offer. International jurisprudence concerning a possible but much disputed right to 'remedial secession'[57] as a last resort to counter the oppression of a minority population was clearly not applicable to the democratically entitled and socially and economically protected circumstances of Scotland

---

[52] TEU, Art 2.

[53] TEU, Art 4(2).

[54] TEU, Art 4(3).

[55] See S Douglas-Scott, 'Why the EU should welcome an independent Scotland' (*Scottish Constitutional Futures Forum Blog*, 11 August 2014). See also Edward, 'Scotland and the European Union' (n 49); Kenealy and MacLennan, 'Sincere Cooperation' (n 8).

[56] As in the Canadian case; see *Reference re Secession of Quebec* [1998] 2 SCR 217.

[57] For discussion, see eg P Radan, 'International Law and the Right of Unilateral Secession' in Pavkovic and Radan (eds), *Research Companion to Secession* (n 19). For suggestive dicta, see esp Judge Yusuf's opinion in *Accordance with International Law of the Unilateral Declaration of Independence in Respect of Kosovo* (Advisory Opinion) [2010] ICJ Rep 141, [618]. See also *Reference re Secession of Quebec* [1998] 2 SCR 217.

in the UK. Equally, reference to an emerging broader duty in international law on all parties to negotiate where there was a well-founded aspiration for political autonomy[58] was unnecessary, or at least premature, given the willingness in principle of the British government to acknowledge a referendum-centred legal path to independence.

On the other hand, where international law is in point, as to the law of state succession, its guidance was far from definitive. The general rule, as reflected in the 1978 Vienna Convention on Succession of States in Respect of Treaties,[59] attaches continuing treaty obligations to all successor states covering the territory of the predecessor state, but this formula is subject to a broad exception for international organisations. The Convention applies 'without prejudice to the rules concerning acquisition of membership and any other relevant rules of the organization',[60] which, in the case of an organisation as deeply and complexly integrated as the EU, are closely tailored to the circumstances of existing club members and their mutual accommodation. General international law re-enters the picture only at the margins. It is required simply to indicate which entity in a post-separation context should be the single 'continuator state', thereby automatically inheriting the existing rights and obligations of club membership and avoiding the burden of any special rules and procedures associated with acquisition. Given that rUK would retain the vast majority of the population and resources, a narrow majority of the territory, and possess the seat of government and control of most of the state institutions, there is little doubt under current international law and practice that it, rather than Scotland, qualifies as the default successor to EU membership.[61]

## C. The EU's Conservative Neutrality

Given the limits of domestic constitutional law, and the deferential attitude of international law to the accession procedures of international organisations, the obvious place to look for answers to the detailed legal form and consequences of sustained or renewed membership of the EU in the case of Scotland's internal separation is to the law and institutional orientation of the EU itself. When we do, however, we find the response of the EU distinctly muted. This attitude we can summarise as one of *conservative neutrality*. It tries to avoid taking sides either in individual cases or in terms of general policy towards internal enlargement, but stresses instead the need to cleave to the existing framework of rules

---

[58] For discussion, see section III.A below.

[59] Although this had not been widely ratified (and not by UK, Spain or Belgium) it does reflect the mainstream approach by international organisations to questions of membership.

[60] Vienna Convention on Succession of States (adopted 3 August 1978, entered into force, 6 November 1996) 1946 UNTS 3, Art 4.

[61] See Crawford and Boyle (n 12); sees also MP Scharf, 'Musical Chairs: The Dissolution of States and Membership in the United Nations' (1995) 28 *Cornell International Law Journal* 29; C Connolly, 'Independence in Europe: Secession, Sovereignty and the European Union' (2013) 24 *Duke Journal of Comparative and International Law* 51.

and practice as a template of disinterested process. The practical expression of conservative neutrality in the Scottish case was one of reluctant involvement, and of a restrained and cautious pattern of intervention. This, first, tended towards a prudential minimalism in which the state-centred aspects of the accession procedures were emphasised and their close adherence promised; secondly, declined to engage in detailed discussion of particular cases, including the terms and conditions of any possible Scottish accession; and thirdly, produced inconsistencies over time that its laconic formulations left unexplained.

As this summary implies, the actual record of EU institutional involvement was a spare one. The only institution to pronounce on the question was the Commission—the Union's permanent executive, and even it spoke seldom and briefly. On a handful of occasions the incumbent Commission President Barroso reiterated without elaboration the concise opinion of his predecessor Romano Prodi in 2004[62] that a new state created by secession from an existing Member State would have to apply for membership following the dedicated TEU, Article 49 route for all new candidates.[63] On the last occasion he addressed the matter, in February 2014, Barroso attracted much controversy by adding the view, again in brief and narrowly technical terms, that, looking to these formal procedures and equating the Scottish case to the more typical one of external accession, it would be 'extremely difficult if not impossible' for an independent Scotland to join the European Union.[64]

This stance was somewhat softened by Jean-Claude Juncker shortly after being elected Barroso's successor in the summer of 2014. The purpose of Juncker's intervention in fact lay elsewhere, as an inaugural statement of intent to the current five candidate states for Enlargement,[65] and others in more distant ante-rooms,[66] that there would be no new accessions until 2019. And it was only in response to renewed speculation of what this implied for Scotland that his office moved to issue a clarification, reporting that as an internal applicant a newly independent Scotland would be deemed already to meet 'core-EU requirements' and so, to that very limited extent, be treated as a special and separate case.[67] However, this last intervention was again reluctantly drawn and lacking detailed specification,

---

[62] Answer given by Mr Prodi on behalf of the Commission, 1 March 2004 [2004] OJ C84E/422.

[63] See esp and most expansively, his letter in response to a request from Lord Tugendhat, chair of the House of Lords Economic Affairs Committee inquiry into 'The Economic Implications for the United Kingdom of Scottish Independence': Letter from Jose Manuel Barroso to Lord Tugendhat (10 December 2012).

[64] Stated on UK nationwide television in the BBC's *Andrew Marr Show* on 17 February 2014. For comment, see N Walker, 'Hijacking the Debate' (*Scottish Constitutional Futures Forum Blog*, 18 February 2014).

[65] Macedonia, Iceland, Montenegro, Serbia and Turkey.

[66] Albania, Bosnia and Herzegovina and Kosovo have been promised 'the prospect of joining when they are ready' (European Commission, *EU Enlargement*, 4 January 2014). Other more or less obvious candidates include Norway, Switzerland, Armenia, Azerbaijan, Georgia, Belarus, Moldova and the Ukraine. For discussion, see F Emmert and S Petrovic, 'The Past, Present and Future of EU Enlargement' (2014) 37 *Fordham International Law Journal* 1349.

[67] A Whitaker, 'Independence: Juncker "sympathetic" to Scots EU bid' *The Scotsman* (20 July 2014).

rendered less weighty by its reactive form and indirect attribution, and typically unwilling to look beyond the existing procedural matrix in search of solutions and justifications.

This sequence of responses had certain ironic consequences. Minimal engagement and a disinclination to countenance creative interpretation of the rules was intended to communicate an attitude of studied impartiality and respect for the internal democratic and constitutional processes of the states involved. But given that the conservative interpretation so clearly favoured the strategy of the Unionist side, the opposite impression was in fact created—and of course reinforced by Barroso's gloomy prognosis delivered in his final statement. Minimal engagement was also intended to eliminate or reduce the risk of sending confused or conflicting signs—again in the spirit of non-interference. But once again the opposite effect was achieved when Juncker effectively contradicted his predecessor without explicit acknowledgement or explanation.

Yet however perverse its actual effect, if we look more deeply into the reasons for the strategy of conservative neutrality we can identify three cumulative sets of factors which pulled strongly in its direction. Considered together, as we shall see, they provide a more sympathetic account of the EU's predicament. Yet they also indicate the current sharpness of that predicament. These factors are in turn institutional, constitutional and strategic.

Institutionally, we begin by noting the *acephalous* quality of the EU polity. There are many departments in the EU political system. Executive leadership is shared between the permanent Commission, the Council of Ministers (with a revolving membership, comprising different government ministers from each Member State depending on the policy areas under consideration) and the European Council (comprising the national heads of state or government). The impression of a multipolar and decentred polity is reinforced by a broader diffusion of functions. The European Parliament, and more recently the national parliaments,[68] join the Council and Commission in initiating, developing or checking legislation, as well as performing broader tasks of executive scrutiny. National administrations assume much of the burden of executive implementation alongside the Commission and a number of independent agencies, and in the judicial branch, too, the Court of Justice is supported by a wider network of national and supranational courts. In significant part, this institutional spread and complexity reflects the 'compound'[69] quality of the EU polity. It indicates the manner in which it combines separate 'estates'[70]—national (Council and European Council), supranational (Commission, Court of Justice) and popular (European Parliament)—with the interests of these distinct constituencies only partially reconciled in a political

---

[68] Since the Treaty of Lisbon 2009, Protocol 2.

[69] See eg S Fabbrini, *Compound Democracies: Why the US and Europe are Becoming Similar* (Oxford, Oxford University Press, 2010).

[70] G Majone, 'Delegation of Regulatory Powers in a Mixed Polity' (2002) 8 *European Law Journal* 319.

form which possesses no uncontested core of sovereignty[71] and whose use of the integrative and state-familiar language of constitutionalism, as we shall shortly explain, remains controversial.[72]

Nowhere is this acephalous quality more apparent than in the procedures for Treaty revision in general (TEU, Article 48) or accession of new members in particular (TEU, Article 49), both being broadly equivalent to constitutional amendments provisions. For TEU, Article 49 decisions, which are even somewhat *less* baroque than general Treaty revisions under TEU, Article 48, all of the institutional actors in the executive and legislative branches listed above are implicated in the procedure, as also are the variety of internal constitutional mechanisms required by the Member States for ratification of international treaties.[73] And the role of the Commission in this complex process is actually the comparatively modest one of requiring consultation by the Council prior to the latter reaching a decision in principle, made with the consent of the European Parliament, to proceed with the membership application.

So the Commission is just one institutional player amongst many, and not even a particularly important one, in the accession process. Granted, unlike any other branch its function is to 'promote the general interest of the Union', and it has a continuity, and a visibility and familiarity born of continuity, that the other branches lack.[74] That, indeed, is why it is understood, and self-understood, as the default spokesperson for the Union as a whole in this and many other contexts. Yet in interpreting the generality of its remit we do better to understand the Commission—the only unelected body of the major executive and legislative institutions—as servant of the Treaty framework rather than its master.[75] Indeed, its very centrality both to the daily business of the EU and to the Union's symbolic

---

[71] See eg N Walker (ed), *Sovereignty in Transition* (Oxford, Hart Publishing, 2003).

[72] See eg N Walker, 'The EU's Unresolved Constitution' in Rosenfeld and Sajo (eds), *Oxford Handbook of Comparative Constitutional Law* (n 22).

[73] Art 49 reads: 'Any European State which respects the values referred to in Article 2 and is committed to promoting them may apply to become a member of the Union. The European Parliament and national Parliaments shall be notified of this application. The applicant State shall address its application to the Council, which shall act unanimously after consulting the Commission and after receiving the consent of the European Parliament, which shall act by a majority of its component members. The conditions of eligibility agreed upon by the European Council shall be taken into account. The conditions of admission and the adjustments to the Treaties on which the Union is founded, which such admission entails, shall be the subject of an agreement between the Member States and the applicant State. This agreement shall be submitted for ratification by all the contracting States in accordance with their respective constitutional requirements'.

[74] TEU, Art 17.

[75] This conclusion is reinforced by an examination of the Commission's functions. TEU, Art 17 continues by specifying the Commission's role in ways that reflect and confirm its status as the EU's administrative college. Its responsibilities are largely downstream. They include the monitoring of the application of European law, the performance of various budgetary, management, executive and management functions, as well as the power to initiate (but not decide) legislation under the Treaties. In all of this the Commissioners, including the President, like civil servants everywhere, are charged to act independently of external influence.

representation to the world[76] is best understood as a form of compensation for and a corrective to the centrifugal tendencies within the Union structure as a whole. In that very broad respect, moreover, the authority of the Commission is not dissimilar to that of the Court of Justice. Both are elevated by their fiduciary responsibility to the Union as a whole, but both are also limited by the terms of that trust, with the Court even more marginal than the Commission to the 'high politics' of Treaty reform—possessing no abstract jurisdiction to consider such reform in advance.[77]

The point here, however, is not merely one of institutional dilution or confusion. It is not just that the Commission, as one of a number of voices, has no exclusive right to speak for the Union, and on that account alone should best understand its role modestly. In addition, now moving to our second level of explanation of the posture of conservative neutrality, we observe a deeper structural dynamic at work. For there are profound limits to the capacity of *any* institution of the Union to develop a persuasive 'constitutional' narrative for the Union as whole, *regardless* of the number or variety of other voices striving to be heard. For their part, the political institutions are hamstrung by the partiality of their constituency, and by the corresponding partiality of perspective—or at least deemed partiality of perspective—that follows from their representation of that particular constituency alone within the acephalous polity of 'estates'. Meanwhile, the non-political institutions—the Commission and Court (but also, of enhanced significance over the recent years of financial crisis, the Central Bank), are hamstrung by the opposite weakness, by their failure to represent *any* particular constituency and by the derivative and constricted nature of their claim to represent the Union in its entirety.

This means that, particularly with regard to matters of deep internal structure, where the relevant questions are collectively *self*-referential in focus—at issue the very political nature and purpose of the Union as a singular entity and the correspondingly appropriate balance and relationship between the institutional forces of that entity—it is difficult to develop a 'constitutional' narrative that stands above sectional interests, or for any particular sectional voice to claim to articulate such a narrative. For constitutional revision or amendment, including the questions at stake here concerning the territorial limits of a polity, the basic conditions of leaving and joining, and the proper relationship between its 'federated' parts, is

---

[76] To some extent now challenged by the 5-year Presidency of the European Council, a position inaugurated under the Treaty of Lisbon 2009. However, the Commission, with its permanent staff and permanent seat of power in Brussels, remains the more publicly visible role. By contrast, the President of the European Council operates through a (changing) body of national heads of government, displaying just the kind of centrifugal tendencies to which the Commission offers itself as a corrective.

[77] The Court of Justice does possess abstract jurisdiction elsewhere, being authorised to decide whether the Union's envisaged external agreements are compatible with the Treaties: TFEU, Art 218(11). There are also various ways in which the actions of various institutions or the status and claims of European citizens might have come to the Court's attention *after* Treaty negotiations on Scottish membership had been concluded, or perhaps even after they had begun, but not in advance of that. See Tierney and Boyle, 'An Independent Scotland' (n 8).

always an intensely reflexive affair. It is a process in which the partial interests of the very institutional branches engaged in the reform process are themselves often at stake, together with, and inevitably in tension with the interests of the whole. Even for a state polity, where there often is a longstanding common constitutional narrative to build upon, this type of political collective action problem can often lead to a bargained or stalled process in which the sectional interests prevail. All the more so in the acephalous polity of the European Union, which lacks both that strong historical narrative and a set of central institutions that could offer the authentic voice of such a narrative. And all the more reason, in the face of such strong sectional forces, for its central institutions to play down the holistic constitutional dimension of the accession debate and revert instead to the narrow formalism of conservative neutrality.

In turn, this leads onto the third, strategic aspect of our explanation of conservative neutrality. For beyond—and exacerbating—the general problem of the proper allocation of authority in the decentred European polity, in the treatment of the Scottish question there have been significant concrete state interests at stake and a particularly strong 'partial' narrative that runs in support of these concrete state interests and in opposition to secession. This oppositional sentiment grew out of the anxieties of various states other than the UK about their own secessionist movements. Their concern, only occasionally made explicit in their own public pronouncements but much discussed, anticipated and reported as 'hearsay' by influential others,[78] was as follows: that the combination of a receptive approach by the European institutions to the Scottish case for membership and the successful realisation of Scottish independence—eventualities separately feared but also widely assumed to be causally connected—might provide the catalyst for a chain of further secessionist struggles.

As already noted, the most immediate concerns centred upon Catalonia in Spain and, at a less critical stage, Flanders in Belgium. But in Corsica, the Basque Country and Northern Italy, other strong secessionist movements and their host states also observed the Scottish Play with rapt attention. These specific fears of fragmentation, furthermore, fed off and into a deeper and broader anxiety in the European historical memory about the sometimes destabilising and destructive force of nationalism, most recently stoked by conflict on the EU's expanding eastern border after 1989. It is instructive, for example, and regularly cited by those who emphasise the depth of European opposition to current secessionist movements in Scotland and elsewhere, that despite active EU involvement in the securing and stabilising of Kosovo's autonomy from Serbia,[79] there are still five EU states—Spain, Cyprus, Greece, Romania and Bulgaria—some with only remote

---

[78] As in Barroso's own televised intervention; above n 64.

[79] In the continuing form of the European Union Rule of Law mission in Kosovo, established in 2008 under the umbrella of the UN Interim Administration Mission in Kosovo (UNMIK) (UN Security Council Resolution 1244).

secessionist concerns in their own territory, who continue to refuse to recognise Kosovo as an independent state on account of the example it might set.[80]

However the Catalan case best illustrates the way in which the Scottish case became closely connected in the European political imagination to the other secessionist struggles. The Spanish Constitution offers a quite different background context to the United Kingdom, and this supplies the comparison with its sharpest edge. There is a written constitution, the post-Franco Spanish Constitution of 1978, which allows greater governmental autonomy to those regions with 'common historic, cultural and economic characteristics', including Catalonia. Yet the constitution also proclaims the 'indissoluble unity of the Spanish nation' in Article 2, and as it fails to guarantee to the regions any particular set of distinct competences, it lacks at least the formal attributes of a federal system. In recent years, in opposition to Madrid's centralism, the autonomist movement in Catalonia has grown, and constitutional disputation has reflected an increasingly intense struggle. The Spanish Constitutional Court sought to curtail the ambitions of the regional government in Barcelona, first by ruling against significant parts of a revised Statute of Autonomy which had been approved by a referendum of the Catalan people in 2006 and more recently, in 2013, by striking down a declaration on Sovereignty and the Right to Decide of the Catalan People that sought to pave the way for a binding referendum on independence.[81] These and other rejections of Catalan autonomy were met by widespread public protest in the region, embracing both those pro-independence and those merely asserting a constitutional right to choose. As it is precisely that right to decide that has been forthcoming in the Scottish case, the example of Scotland, for long a point of comparison and a focus for solidarity amongst Europe's regional nationalists, has been regularly cited with approval and followed with close interest in Barcelona, just as it has been treated as a cautionary tale by the Spanish government in Madrid.[82]

Matters came to a head when the Constitutional Court again intervened to hold that a regional independence referendum planned for 9 November 2014, on account of its failure to embrace the whole Spanish people, was illegal.[83] When the referendum was reframed as an informal consultation, the Court continued to offer objections,[84] although neither this nor threats of more specific legal reprisals

[80] In Cyprus, the palpable concern is Turkish North Cyprus; in Greece, the somewhat less immediate concern is its Macedonian province; and in Bucharest and Sofia there are less focused worries about 'greater Hungary' rhetoric in Budapest, and their own ethnic Hungarian communities. See Kerr, 'The Other Union' (n 9).

[81] See Connolly, 'Independence in Europe' (n 61) 55–59.

[82] See eg A Kassam and I Traynor, 'Spain says it could take independent Scotland years to win EU membership' *The Guardian* (17 September 2014).

[83] See J Vintro, 'Legality and the Referendum on Independence in Catalonia' (Institut de Dret Públic Blog, 23 October 2012).

[84] See eg N Casals and N Krisch, 'Using Spanish law to block Catalonia's independence consultation may simply encourage Catalans to construct their own "alternative legality"' (*EUROPP Blog*, 4 November 2014). See also I Sanz and S Morris, 'Spanish court blocks second bid for Catalan independence vote' *Reuters* (Madrid, 4 November 2014).

from Madrid was enough to deter the Catalan government from proceeding to hold the ballot.[85] And, in the course of this struggle, so close had become the symbolic connection with the Scottish case, that the key vote of the Catalan Parliament approving the November referendum was scheduled for the day following the Scottish referendum. As matters stand, the Catalan government continues to use the Scottish case, even though it ended in defeat, as the benchmark for an unflattering comparison with Madrid.[86]

In these circumstances, the strategy of conservative neutrality may prove a double-edged sword. On the one hand, while far from endorsing the case for Scottish independence, or promising the new state a safe and untroubled passage into the EU, the Commission did not question the legitimacy of the Scottish referendum as a consensual product of the UK's internal constitutional arrangements. And even the government in Madrid—in the separate voices of the Prime Minister and of the Foreign Minister[87]—has emphasised the distinction between the constitutional permissiveness of the British arrangement (while taking care to deplore the prospect of a result favourable to independence) and the constitutional bar on secession and secessionist processes such as referendums in the 'indissoluble' nation of Spain.

From the perspective of the conservative neutralist, this might be seen to draw some of the sting from the Scottish case. Its atypical backdrop of agreement in national constitutional law could be seen as reducing its precedential value. In particular, Article 4 TEU of the Treaty on European Union, which requires respect for 'fundamental structures, political and constitutional' at state level, and also for 'the essential state function [of] ensuring the territorial integrity of the State', could, notwithstanding other textual terms arguably more supportive of sub-state autonomy,[88] be pled in favour of an approach that defers entirely to the different particularities of national constitutional arrangements. On this view, if the 'fundamental constitutional structures' point one way in the UK, and another in Spain, that should be the end of the story in terms of EU recognition of the primary constitutional 'facts on the ground'. And even if the reluctance to comment on moot cases means that the Commission itself will not be easily minded to make such a position explicit, others, in particular interested national governments, have been and will remain only too willing to fill the silence.

On the other hand, however, such an approach will not sit well with the sub-state nations themselves. As so often in law, the high abstraction of formal

---

[85] In which 80% of 2.2 million votes were cast in favour of independence, with a further 3.2 million eligible voters not participating. Predictably, the low turnout led the Madrid government to denounce the result as meaningless: R Minder, 'Catalonia Overwhelmingly Votes for Independence from Spain in Straw Poll' *The New York Times* (9 November 2014).

[86] See eg M Vargas, 'Scotland Got its Referendum, but all Catalonia Gets is Threats and Repression' *IB Times* (26 September 2014).

[87] See G Murray, 'Spain will not veto an independent Scotland joining EU' *Scottish Express* (26 February 2012).

[88] See TEU, Arts 2, 3(4), 4(2) and 4(3) and TFEU, pt 3, Title VIII and Arts 20–25.

equality—in this case the maxim 'treat all national constitutions alike'—delivers marked substantive inequality. The Catalan nationalist parties, like those of Scotland, and also of Flanders, are strongly pro-EU. In many ways, indeed, their viability as nationalist political movements, and the manner in which they understand the autonomy of nationalist politics in the modern European age, depends upon and presupposes the EU—a point to which we will return. Yet despite the similarity of motivation, and despite the comparable justifiability of their claim in terms of criteria of political morality such as level and persistence of support, strength of national identity and viability in terms of size and natural resources, not to mention practical considerations such as the prior existence of robust institutions of regional governance, under the strategy of conservative neutrality the Catalan case will be treated quite differently from the Scottish case. The Scottish case might have encountered all sort of problems, might even have been significantly damaged by the self-interest of existing Member States and the cautious deference of the Commission, but the Catalan case would not even reach base camp.

The strategy of conservative neutrality becomes further conflicted if we contemplate the Belgian situation. Here the case for independence is led by the Flemish North, which is increasingly divided linguistically, culturally, economically and (due to previous rounds of devolution) in terms of political institutions from the French-speaking Walloons in the South. Yet even though the Belgian Constitution is no more hospitable to secession than the Spanish Constitution, there are several non-constitutional differences which make it unlikely that the European fate of an internally enlarged Belgium would be the same as that of Catalonia.

First, there is a dynamic of mutual estrangement in Belgium. A break-up, if it happens, may take the form of a Czechoslovakia-style voluntary disassociation, with two successor states. Secondly, even if Flanders takes the sole initiative, and Wallonia as the continuing party makes exclusive claim to successor statehood, because Flanders makes up the majority of Belgian territory, population and (increasingly) economic resources, it, rather than Wallonia, would in fact 'be the most obvious candidate to inherit Belgium's legal personality'.[89] And thirdly, the difficult case of Brussels—which as the bi-cultural capital is the most obvious source of conflicting territorial claims between the two communities—is further complicated by its also supplying the seat of government of the EU itself. Its exclusion, therefore, seems inconceivable. In a nutshell, then, despite having no stronger a claim in political morality than the Catalans, nor there being any right to secede in Belgian constitutional law, the combination of the possibility of a 'velvet divorce' between the two estranged parts, the strength of Flanders within the Belgian polity and the strategic importance of Brussels to the EU, suggests that a mechanism would likely be found to accommodate this particular internal enlargement.

---

[89] See Connolly (n 61) 89, and also, more generally, 62–66 and 89–93.

If that were so, the strategy of conservative neutrality would have produced three quite different results in three cases: accommodation in the last analysis in the Scottish case in light of local constitutional permissiveness; exclusion in the Catalan case in light of local constitutional prohibition; and accommodation, perhaps even expedited accommodation in the Belgian case, in light of local extra-constitutional considerations together with the strategic self-interest of the 'federal' level EU polity.

## III.  Reframing Community Through Law

One reading of the difficulties confronted by the European Union when faced with secessionist struggles is that they are indicative of the broader limitations of law when faced with questions about the birth, marriage, divorce and death of states or similar political communities. The involvement of the EU in the direct regulation of these questions turns out to be very modest and highly derivative. It does not seek to contribute to any substantive standard by which we might assess the legality of secession, nor to specify procedures for resolving secession questions that might compensate for what is not available within the constitutional contemplation of its Member States or augment what (little) is available. Instead, the Commission tacitly endorses the diversity of national constitutional contexts and orientations through the incentive of not withholding—but hardly encouraging or facilitating—the privilege of club membership from those secession claims that do not violate national constitutional norms.

Viewed in a global horizon, the limitations faced by the EU in developing a strong and consistent legal narrative on matters of secession might appear to reflect and to reinforce the limitations faced by other streams of law, both international and constitutional. Let us first say something about these difficulties before returning to the case of the EU and exploring the other forms of influence that it might possess.

## A.  Self-Determination and Secession: The Limitations of Two Liminal Concepts

The concepts of self-determination in international law and secession in constitutional law exhibit a similarly unusual structure. They operate as liminal concepts, situated both within and outside the boundary of legality. On the one hand, they may be seen as fundamental jurisgenerative principles. In that role, they are located on the inside boundary, so to speak, framing and ordering the basic edifice of the international legal system. On the other hand, they are claims whose expansive recognition would undermine that same basic edifice. To that extent, they often register, if at all, as inchoate bids, incapable of realisation in any legal effective form, and so sounding outside the boundary of legality.

Take, first, the concept of self-determination. Originating in its modern form in Woodrow Wilson's Fourteen Points, it assumed the status as a foundational right of 'peoples' in a number of seminal post-war instruments. This is seen most vividly in Article 1(2) of the UN Charter, then—elevated from principle to right— in the common Article 1(1) of the two global human rights treaties adopted by the UN in 1966, and, in the colonial context, in the General Assembly's Resolution 1541(XV) of 1960 and in its later Declaration on Friendly Relations of 1970. In these and subsequent texts, and also in the jurisprudence of the International Court of Justice (ICJ), there is clear recognition that self-determination is a cornerstone of the international legal system.[90] It is that cornerstone which allows us to identify the legitimate subjects of international law—those collective state actors to whom sovereignty is attributable and whose territorial integrity is to be respected. Yet there is also clear recognition of the limits to that right. Except, perhaps, in the extreme case of remedial secession, self-determination does not imply an 'external' right to sovereign statehood, and so to secession from an existing state, but only an entitlement to 'internal self-determination', and the lesser forms of recognition of autonomy *within* an existing sovereign state form that this implies.[91]

One notable consequence of this liminal structure is that it severely limits how self-determination might intervene as a form of positive law. To the extent that the self-determination principle is recognised as located at the inside boundary of legal relations, framing and shaping the international system of state sovereignty, it is largely as a presupposition or confirmation which grounds a system of positive law rather than as an actively posited norm in live legal questions. That is to say, its presentation as an effective norm in any particular instance tends to function as a signal that it is a status already achieved or (in the colonial context) generally recognised as legitimate, rather than as providing an effective argument for the realisation of a new status in a contentious case. In short, the work that the concept does within the boundary of law is often rhetorical rather than instrumental, confirmatory rather than constitutive, assumed rather than argued. Yet equally, given the extensive limits to any right of external self-determination failing any such already achieved status, the right to self-determination quickly loses any practical traction, as unarguably absent—and so stranded outside the boundary of viable legal recognition—as it is unarguably present in the privileged case.

One important caveat to this characterisation concerns recent attempts to proceduralise the norm of self-determination. Drawing upon the landmark decision of the Canadian Constitutional Court in *Reference re Secession of Quebec*[92]

---

[90] See eg Radan, 'International Law and the Right of Unilateral Secession' (n 57).

[91] See eg Mancini, 'Secession and Self-Determination' (n 22); A Buchanan, 'Theories of Secession' (1998) 27 *Philosophy and Public Affairs* 31; DH Doyle (ed), *Secession as an International Phenomenon: From America's Civil Wars to Contemporary Separatist Movements* (Athens, University of Georgia Press, 2010).

[92] *Reference re Secession of Quebec* [1998] 2 SCR 217.

concerning the duty to negotiate in good faith in the event of an unambiguous statement by Quebec of a wish to secede, as well as the recent jurisprudence of the ICJ and the work of the Badinter Commission in helping the European Union formulate its policies towards the dissolution of Yugoslavia, some jurists have begun to reformulate the right to self-determination as something like 'a right to be taken seriously'.[93] While this is undoubtedly a trend of some significance, it does little to overcome the basic structural limitation of self-determination as a liminal legal concept. A right to be taken seriously is, of course, no guarantee that one's preferred outcome will be forthcoming, but that is the basic restriction of any procedural right. More significantly, given that the procedural context within which a claim to be taken seriously might be made tends, with few exceptions, to remain within the gift of the very actors whose cooperation and procedural engagement is sought, then it risks precisely the same redundancy as the substantive version of the right. The danger is that the right to be taken seriously will only ever be articulated and respected *as* a right in contexts where the significant actors (in most cases exclusively local actors with a direct stake)[94] are already predisposed to 'take seriously'—so to speak—such a procedural imperative, so rather limiting its credentials as a generalisable legal entitlement.

If we turn to secession and to its status in constitutional law, a similar scenario presents itself. Many new states have emerged and continue to emerge from a more or less peaceful or consensual act or process of secession, including, of course, the first modern constitutional state—the United States itself. So secession, too, possesses a jurisgenerative quality, standing as a framing self-assertion at the inside boundary of national legal order. In that sense, the idea of secession poses, and sometimes answers, 'the most fundamental'[95] of constitutional questions. Yet, like self-determination, it carries two opposing implications. It is simultaneously 'the most revolutionary and the most institutionally conservative of political constructs'.[96] As the United States' own history testifies, it may be assumed as the deep background premise of one's own established constitutional order but be denied to others within the terms of that established constitutional order—thereby placing *their* claims outside the boundary of any recognised legality.[97] To allow otherwise would not simply be deeply destabilising of existing states. It

---

[93] See esp J Klabbers, 'The Right to be Taken Seriously: Self-Determination in International Law' (2006) 28 *Human Rights Quarterly* 186; C Bell, 'What we Talk about when we Talk about International Constitutional Law' (2014) 5 *Transnational Legal Theory* 241.

[94] But not all cases. In Kosovo, for instance, the close attention of the international community and the presence of UNMIK (see above n 79) in support of Kosovan autonomy seemed to influence the ICJ to 'take more seriously' the claim of Kosovo to independence. *Kosovo Advisory Opinion* [2010] ICJ Rep 141 (Radan (n 57)).

[95] See S Levinson, '"Perpetual Union", "Free Love" and Secession: on the Limits of "The Consent of the Governed"' (2004) 39 *Tulsa Law Review* 457, 461. See also AR Amar, 'Abraham Lincoln and the American Union' (2001) *University of Illinois Law Review* 1109; AR Amar, *America's Constitution: A Biography* (New York, Random House, 2005) ch 1.

[96] Mancini (n 22) 481.

[97] *Texas v White* (1869) 74 US 700.

would also run counter to a dominant conception of modern constituent authority which sees it inhere in the entire people, as reflected and cemented in the indi-
visible sovereignty of their 'constituted' state, rather than remain latent in various
sub-state populations.

Of course, as we have seen, there have been and still are exceptions to this constitutional orthodoxy, the British conception of the Union state being our key
case in point. However, as we have also seen, these exceptions are quite rare, and
where they do obtain, their authority stems from the peculiarity of the local constitution itself, with little reference to wider international or supra-constitutional
principles.[98] And so, once again, like the right to self-determination, the 'right'
to secede has a conservatively circular quality, reliant upon the terms of the very
constitutional system from which secession is sought. Or in the language of limi-
nality, where the right to secede cannot be located within a plausible domestic
constitutional narrative then it inevitably languishes beyond the boundaries of
legal viability.

## B. The EU as Reframer

The EU, in adopting the role of conservative neutrality, may be seen as reflecting and reinforcing the brute fact that, rather than meeting an oft-proclaimed
more ambitious 'Rule of Law' standard as a general mode of regulation of public
power,[99] our available legal forms remain broadly acquiescent before the power
of those particular public political forms known as states in the liminal legal zone
of the norms and practices of state-making and state-breaking. Just as international law tends to defer to those already self-determined in developing the rules
of self-determination, and just as constitutional law tends to defer to those already
seceded or otherwise already constituted in developing its rules on secession, so
too the attitude of the European institutions is to defer to decisions that flow from
these very same state-conservative rule regimes in its managing of the relationship
between sub-state nationalism and EU membership.

Have we, therefore, reached the end of the legal road? I have already pointed to
the anomalies and inconsistencies, as seen from the perspective of the sub-state
nations of Scotland, Catalonia and Flanders, of the EU's adopting such a state-
deferential attitude of conservative neutrality. But perhaps the only perspective
that matters is the sovereign perspective of the States themselves, who as Masters

---

[98] In *Reference re Secession of Quebec* [1998] 2 SCR 217 there clearly was an attempt by the local
court to 'delocalise' the question through bringing international law into the Canadian constitutional
discussion in a quite central way. For that effort, and the imagination with which it was pursued,
that decision has—quite rightly—attracted a lot of attention, especially in academic circles. However,
although the Court provides an elegant methodology for attending to international law in the context
of the national legal argument for any court minded so to do, it cannot provide authority for any court,
or indeed any other constitutional actor, *not* so minded.

[99] See eg J Waldron, 'Are Sovereigns Entitled to the Benefits of the International Rule of Law?' (2011)
22 *European Journal of International Law* 315.

of the Treaties, remain the basic building blocks and the sole recognised unit of membership of the EU. Yet that would be a reductive approach, one that simply affirms the deep bias within the prevailing legal structure. For if we acknowledge that sub-state nations, too, like nation (or multi-national) states, are entities which are morally significant to their individual members—and, indeed, given that both categories define themselves as 'nations', are morally significant to their members in many of the same ways as states—then we must continue to try to embrace *both* perspectives, state and sub-state, in examining the adequacy of the overall legal regime of recognition of claims to autonomy.

Re-engaging this more inclusive perspective, what more can we say about the EU's contribution, and what more can we expect from that contribution? We should begin by acknowledging that the EU does already relate to sub-state nations in many and significant ways other than through directly treating (or not treating) their claims to independence. Since the Maastricht Treaty of 1992, a Committee of the Regions has emerged as a consultative body to the other institutions. Its somewhat marginal (and marginalised) early role was improved under the Lisbon Treaty of 2009, which requires the Commission, Council and Parliament to consult it on matters concerning local or regional government, and which also allows the Committee to challenge EU laws that may fall foul of the broadly framed principle of subsidiarity.[100] Regions also benefit from their legal recognition *as* regions through access to European structural funds administered through their Member States, and through rights-based and anti-discrimination measures that guarantee linguistic and cultural protection for minority groups. More generally, the economic and political structure of a supranational union can provide avenues of opportunity to regions not available within the solitary state. Regions now have free access to a community-wide market of five hundred million people, and these open frontiers can help promote joint economic activity and encourage cultural connections between regions. And alongside this horizontal network of 'para-diplomacy',[101] there are also new political ties in the vertical structures of European governance, particularly through the European Free Alliance (of nationalist, regionalist and autonomist parties) in the European Parliament and the establishment of the informal Conference of European Regions with Legislative Power.

Crucially, all of these factors speak not to a directly prescriptive role of the EU in matters of polity-making, but to a more subtly (re)constitutive role. The emerging structure of regional opportunities we have described testifies to the ways in which the EU, just by providing a new level of political community, begins to reframe the terms on which we conceive of political membership. The instrumental value of regionalism and sub-state nationalism is altered by the changing matrix of opportunities for voice and resource-acquisition that the EU provides. And by

---

[100] For an overview, see Directorate-General for Internal Policies, 'The Role of National Parliaments in Regional Policy under the Treaty of Lisbon' (European Parliament Committee on Regional Development, 2010).

[101] See eg F Aldecon and M Keating (eds), *Paradiplomacy in Action: The Foreign Relations of Subnational Governments* (London, Frank Cass, 1999).

pooling ever more of the economic and social powers previously associated with national sovereignty at the supranational level, the EU also continues to moderate the instrumental significance of statehood itself. This means that, owing to the depth and breadth of the EU's insinuation into the patterns of political life, new calculations of value require to be made across and between different political forms. Judgements of the shifting benefits of regional autonomy are not made in absolute terms, but relative to the similarly unmoored value of statehood.[102]

Alongside the instrumental dimension, there is also an expressive dimension to the reframing work of the EU. By supplying a new level of political identity, including a form of citizenship whose membership may be state-derivative but whose portfolio of associated rights and referential institutions is quite different,[103] the EU also alters the symbolic significance of national sovereignty and its alternatives. To take one brief example from our focal setting of the United Kingdom, just as 'independence in Europe'—as in the Scottish nationalists' longstanding slogan—conveys a very different meaning and sense of collective identity than would 'separatism outside Europe's Northern edge', so too 'Britain in Europe' is much less isolationist than without its qualifier (whose elimination the United Kingdom Independence Party and some parts of the Conservative Party are currently avidly seeking),[104] and 'Scotland-in-Britain-in Europe' suggest a much less subordinate and more broadly assimilated native political identity than merely 'Scotland in Britain'. In short, to the extent that the affective dimension of political belonging—the investment we make and the vindication we receive—varies with the range of available forms of political community, their possible combinations and their changing instrumental significance—the emotional meaning of independence, relative autonomy and the like will change as the underlying matrix of objective possibilities alters.[105]

As our examples imply, the arguments here can cut both ways in terms of the political forces that may be released. The presence of the EU, by offering new forms of access to resources and new platforms of recognition to sub-state forms—though still short of those it offers to states, can provide a spur to new projects of national sovereignty. Or it can offer a relief valve, a means of reducing the gap in benefits between statehood and its alternatives, and thereby also reducing state sovereignty's symbolic allure.[106]

For some, the very fact that the reframing role of the European Union changes the calculus of instrumental and symbolic value associated with statehood and its alternatives, and that, in turn, this has brought about a new balance of subnational forces in Europe, is reason enough for us to revisit the question of the EU's direct

---

[102] See eg Tierney, *Constitutional Law and National Pluralism* (n 36) ch 4.

[103] See eg the recent special issue of the *German Law Journal* on 'European Citizenship: Twenty Years On' (2014) vol 15(5).

[104] See Walker (n 24).

[105] See eg A Mason, *Community, Solidarity and Belonging: Levels of Community and their Normative Significance* (Cambridge, Cambridge University Press, 2000).

[106] See Connolly (n 61) esp 99–105.

regulatory role in these matters, and to argue for a less neutral stance. On the one side, it is claimed that the very ethos of integration, reconciliation and continental solidarity that has fed the European project from its post-War beginnings should cause the EU, and all those who endorse the best understanding of its foundations, to take a dim view of any separatist impulse that seems to betray these founding virtues. From this perspective, therefore, far from having a stronger claim than external candidates who have benefited from the post-Cold War enlargement, those sub-state nations such as Scotland and Catalonia that are already comfortably nested in the EU's Western European heartland should be refused a safe supranational haven if they insist on the path to independence.[107] On the other side, a quite different message is drawn from the history and contemporary dynamics of the European Union. On this view, the EU's historical mission to accommodate national differences within an unprecedented supranational synthesis is best achieved by respecting and recognising new national claims, just as it once recognised the claims of its founding members, and just as it recognised and continues to recognise the nation-building claims of its recent new members and present candidate members in Eastern Europe.[108]

Yet there are good reasons not to be tempted down this path. In the first place, as these arguments demonstrate, opinion is acutely divided over which is the better interpretation of the EU's historical purpose. There can be no strong position on sub-state nationalism that does not sharply disavow one of these two versions, and so disappoint and alienate those who subscribe to that version. Secondly, we must in any case recall the wider political backdrop to the present strategy of conservative neutrality. For all its limitations, it is the product of the state-centred balance of forces within the acephalous European polity, and the lack of a shared constitutional narrative of constitutional purpose. The more committed positions taken by those who would have the EU offer either strong regulatory encouragement or discouragement to the aspirations of sub-state nations may be a reaction against the limitations of conservative neutrality, but their polarisation also offers a cautionary tale of the difficulties of moving beyond that position.

Thirdly, and more positively, the reconstitutive effect of the EU's supranational innovation, in any case, is surely in significant measure its own reward, whether or not accompanied by a new regulatory approach. Wherever one stands on the merits of this or that sub-state national case for independence, or on their merit in general, the EU has succeeded in making the question of political membership much less of a zero sum game, and so considerably less likely to excite violent passions in its own territorial space. It may seem ironic that one drawback of the EU's defusion of the possibility of major conflict over national belonging in Western Europe, precisely because the weight of its supranational presence reduces the costs and consequences of state-*making* as much as it enhances the possibilities of sub-national

---

[107] See esp JHH Weiler, 'Scotland and the EU: A Comment' (*Verfassungsblog*, 8 September 2014).
[108] See Douglas-Scott, 'Why the EU should welcome an independent Scotland' (n 55). See also N MacCormick, *Questioning Sovereignty* (Oxford, Oxford University Press, 1999) esp 191.

accommodation within existing states, may have been to increase the possibility of the type of comparatively minor conflict we are presently witnessing. Yet it remains a relatively small irony, and one that is worth the contemporary price.

In a nutshell, in the theatre of nationalist politics in Europe, the EU, at least as presently constituted, may lack the legitimising presence to play a directorial role. But whether or not this should be considered a matter of regret, and whether or not we can imagine it developing such a role in the future,[109] its background work of stage redesign has already had quite profound, and, on balance, beneficial effects.

One final point can be made in favour of a European approach that seeks to manage and defuse the problems of secession by reframing rather than direction. In recent years much has been said for and against the idea of 'normative power Europe'[110]—the notion that the European way of dealing with internal and external conflict is to be celebrated and offered as a model for the rest of the world. Even if we thought this a good idea, however, 'we can hardly proclaim the Europeanization of the world'.[111] The historical circumstances of the European continent are highly particular, the opportunities for replicating the favourable aspect of its relatively peaceful model of continental 'enmeshment' limited and to be treated with caution.[112] And precisely because its example should be offered with modesty, it is best offered *as* an example. The reason why European states, old and new, actual and potential, East and West, want to join or remain in the EU, and the reason they will, in general,[113] respect its model of deep rule-based integration, is because of the advantages it offers of peaceful and productive interdependence, not because of its espousal of a strongly directive constitutional philosophy. The continuing possibility of Europe exerting influence in its near neighbourhood and beyond over basic questions of the viability and terms of co-existence of different political collectivities would seem to depend upon its maintaining its stress on example over dogmatic declaration.

---

[109] Even if the EU lacks the legitimate authority to adopt a strong substantive position on sub-state independent membership, there may still be scope to develop the policy of conservative neutrality in procedural terms. Just as there is presently a general withdrawal clause for Member States (TEU, Art 50), we might envisage a new Treaty provision to regulate internal secessions-and-readmissions (for example, specifying the timescale, insisting upon a referendum). That would reduce uncertainty, take the pressure off the Commission in responding to particular cases, and, most importantly, introduce a more equal playing field for different sub-state applicants. However, as I was reminded when I recently discussed these possibilities with a number of EU 'insiders', the political forces set against such a course remain formidable. At a time when the consensus necessary to achieve any Treaty reform in the EU seems a distant prospect, intervention in an area such as this will likely win little support. Indeed, given the national sensitivities involved, even the most modest procedural provision may be summarily dismissed as a form of unwanted encouragement to the forces of disorderly nationalism.

[110] I Manners, 'Normative Power Europe: A Contradiction in Terms?' (2002) 40 *Journal of Common Market Studies* 235.

[111] P Kahn, *Putting Liberalism in its Place* (Princeton, Princeton University Press, 2005) 306.

[112] See eg R Kleinfeld and K Nicolaidis, 'Can a Post-colonial Power Export the Rule of Law? Elements of a General Framework' in G Palombella and N Walker (eds), *Relocating the Rule of Law* (Oxford, Hart Publishing, 2009).

[113] A recent exception being Victor Orbang's Hungary. See eg K Lane Scheppele, 'The Rule of Law and the Frankenstate: Why Governance Checklists Do Not Work' (2013) 26 *Governance* 559–62.

# 9

## Which Pluralism? External Self-Determination at the Intersection of National, Social and Geopolitical Emancipation

ZORAN OKLOPCIC

## I. Introduction

During the better part of the twentieth century, 'self-determination of peoples' existed as a central organising principle of the international political order, structuring the political imagination both of the defenders and the challengers of the international territorial status quo. Codified as a 'right', it reached its apogee in the early-1960s by providing justification for the creation of new independent states from the crumbling European colonial empires. From its outset, however, self-determination, particularly in its 'external' incarnation, was always in a state of existential crisis. Especially since the end of the Cold War, international law scholars have repeatedly decried its logical inconsistency and inflammatory effects on nationalist politics, and have either prognosticated its demise, suggested paths to its reform, or simply suspended judgement about its meaning.

The recent impasse in international jurisprudence hasn't helped. Over the last 20 years, the vocabulary of external self-determination in international legal and paralegal forums has been both *elusive* and *allusive*. The controversial Badinter Opinions on the legal aspects of Yugoslav dissolution evaded giving a clear answer on the meaning of self-determination, while simultaneously demanding a republic-wide referendum as a condition for international recognition of the Yugoslav republics as independent states.[1] That has led some scholars to infer that the right to external self-determination in the post-Cold War setting, under certain restrictions, belongs to 'the people' of an identifiable autonomous territorial

---

[1] A Pellet, 'The Opinions of the Badinter Arbitration Committee: A Second Breath for the Self-Determination of Peoples' (1992) 3 *European Journal of International Law* 178.

unit. The Five Experts' Opinion commissioned by the Québécois National Assembly—though following Badinter as an exemplar of the emergent *lex ferenda*—rejected this view, arguing that Quebec doesn't enjoy the right to external self-determination, yet can still count on international law to protect its territorial integrity in the case of a unilateral secession.[2] Likewise, the Supreme Court of Canada's Quebec Secession Reference rejected Quebec's putative right to external self-determination, but unlike the Five Experts, hinted that Quebec's territorial integrity would be put in question as the mandated negotiations about secession unfold.[3] While not having a right to external self-determination, the Court argued, the population of Quebec has a right to internal self-determination including the right to *pursue* secession within the Canadian constitutional order. Equally, in what would become an important signpost in jurisprudential debate, the Court speculated about the emergence of the remedial right to external self-determination. While admitting that it 'remains unclear whether this third proposition actually reflects an established international law standard', the Court hazarded that external self-determination may be permissible in the case of gross oppression and discrimination of a minority group. Finally, continuing the pattern of elusiveness and allusiveness, the International Court of Justice in the Advisory Opinion on Kosovo's unilateral independence sidestepped the question of self-determination altogether, while still, unnecessarily, citing the signatories of the Kosovo Declaration of Independence as 'the representatives of the people of Kosovo.'[4]

The resilience of the vocabulary of self-determination must be understood as resulting not only from the fact that new states continue to be formed, often with great cost to lives and livelihoods, but also from the ambiguities and silences in international jurisprudence about its meaning.

In good measure owing to these factors, over the last two decades external self-determination has attracted remarkable interest in normative political theory. Theorising it, however, has always been embedded in the particulars of the *Zeitgeist*. The demise of communism, the apparent ultimate triumph of liberal democracy, and optimism about a 'new world order' based on the rule of law, brought about the first wave of normative theories—*theories of secession*—all of which were firmly entrenched in liberal political morality. But the political

---

[2] 'The Territorial Integrity of Quebec in the Event of the Attainment of Sovereignty' ('L'integrite territoriale du Quebec dans l'hypotese de l'accession a la souverainete') in AF Bayefsky, *Self-Determination in International Law: Quebec and Lessons Learned* (The Hague, Kluwer Law International, 2000).

[3] *Reference Re Secession of Quebec* [1998] 2 SCR 217, [135].

[4] *Accordance with International Law of the Unilateral Declaration of Independence in Respect of Kosovo* (Advisory Opinion) [2010] ICJ Rep 141, [109]. In the cases in which the ICJ squarely addressed self-determination in the years following the Cold War, it didn't venture further than restating the meaning of self-determination inherited from the decolonisation context: *Case Concerning East Timor (Portugal v Australia)* [1995] ICJ Rep 90; *Legal Consequences of the Construction of a Wall in the Occupied Palestinian Territory* (Advisory Opinion) [2004] ICJ Rep 136, [88], [122] and [156]. *Sovereignty over Pulau Ligitan und Pulau Sipadan (Indonesia v Malaysia )* (Application for Permission to Intervene, Separate Opinion of Judge Franck) [2001] ICJ Rep 575, 654–58.

events in the first decade of the 2000s have implicated external self-determination in a larger set of concerns—such as regional integrations, external interventions and international migrations—and de-emphasised state-building as the master-concern of the international legal order. Equally, new legal phenomena, such as the fragmentation of international law and the emergence of functional, competing constitutional regimes, have increasingly shaped the outlook of international legal theorising. New waves of normative treatment of self-determination—such as *theories of territorial rights and democratic theory*—have risen in prominence, in part because they have spoken to these new phenomena as well.

The purpose of this essay is not to hazard another theoretical account of external self-determination, nor to offer a new juridical interpretation by extrapolating from the present legal material. Rather, by mapping the state of the theoretical debate in section II, I wish to set the stage for unearthing political considerations that have (re-)surfaced as increasingly relevant in theorising self-determination. Specifically, in section III of the chapter, I will focus on recent pluralist contributions to the field. I will focus on three specific pluralisms that are closest to the *problématique* of self-determination—those where one would have expected to find, if not enthusiasm, then at least a limited defence of external self-determination. However, theorists of *bounded*, *constitutional* and *radical* pluralism have all abandoned the reconstructive potential of external self-determination.[5] Bounded pluralism has supplanted external self-determination with the interplay of effectivity and state recognition; constitutional pluralism has interpreted self-determination to justify territorial status quo in face of external intervention; and radical pluralism has recast it not as a norm but rather as a multifaceted 'practice of public autonomy' with unclear territorial implications.

Mapping recent pluralist moves at the intersection of international law and political theory will also unearth two distinct considerations that were previously submerged in the normative 'wave' of theorising self-determination in the 1990s and 2000s. The work of secession, territorial rights, or democratic theorists in that period featured an explicit or implicit commitment to liberal democracy, and was not particularly interested in the machinations of great powers. Recent pluralists, in contrast, are concerned both with great power hegemony (or hegemony in general), and are more keen to provide normative space for different political ideologies and projects of social emancipation.

This, in turn, raises another principled question that has been submerged in the previous debates about self-determination: do the registers of national, social and geopolitical emancipation have to be pitted against each other? In other words, will heightened concern for national pluralism in international law provide a springboard for great power interference? Equally, will concern for national pluralism

---

[5] Global legal pluralism is a burgeoning field. However, little attention is devoted to territorial reconfigurations and self-determination even when territoriality is an explicit focus of the scholarly attention; *cf* PS Berman, 'Dialectical Regulation, Territoriality, and Pluralism' (2006) 38 *Connecticut Law Review* 952.

within the state undermine state-wide projects of social emancipation that depart from liberal ideology? Or is there a way to reconcile them, and make them work in tandem? The last part of the chapter is devoted to briefly exploring these concerns.

## II. External Self-Determination in Normative Theory: The People and the Territory Between Moral Rights and Affectedness

The first wave of theorising external self-determination (secession) has its origin in the early-1990s, and over the subsequent decade produced a lively body of scholarship. Over time, three broad theories crystallised: the remedial, nationalist and choice theories of secession. Remedial theories have argued that only groups that have suffered serious oppression or discrimination have a right to secede. More at variance with positive international law are nationalist and choice theories of secession, which argue that any group that forms a nation, and is viable, has a right to secede. Choice theories have been the most lax among the three, as they don't attach any objective or subjective conditions to the group's exercise of self-determination. Any group that is viable and capable of protecting the human rights of its members has a moral right to form its independent state.[6]

Early on, however, some theorists argued that in order to be complete, the moral right of a group to secede must be accompanied by a complementary *territorial* right to a *particular* piece of land.[7] For example, if the Québécois have a moral right to secede, they don't enjoy it *in abstracto*, or over the Côte d'Azur, but over the land of present-day Quebec. What gives them a right to secede is their putative territorial right. Over the last decade, the idea of territorial rights—as an extension of the moral right to secede—has captured an important intuition that there must be some relevant moral link between *this* people and *this* space, and not some other. Here, as well, several theoretical approaches crystallised. One approach holds that rights to a territory are generated either by a pre-political nation endowing the land with material value or symbolic meaning.[8] A second, in accordance with the Kantian conception, suggests the land belongs to a territorial, self-governing people.[9] Thirdly, left-libertarians inspired by Locke take the view that the state's territory emerges as the aggregate of private properties of the would-be fellow citizens.[10]

---

[6] CH Wellman, *A Theory of Secession: The Case for Political Self-Determination* (Cambridge, Cambridge University Press, 2005).

[7] L Brilmayer, 'Secession and Self-Determination' (1991) 16 *Yale Journal of International Law* 177.

[8] D Miller, 'Territorial Rights: Concept and Justification' (2012) 60 *Political Studies* 252.

[9] A Stilz, 'Why Do States Have Territorial Rights?' (2009) 1 *International Theory* 185.

[10] H Steiner, 'Territorial Justice' in S Caney et al (eds), *National Rights, International Obligations* (Boulder, Westview Press, 1996) 139.

The third wave of theoretical contributions to the debate about external self-determination—coming from the field of democratic theory—has been cresting over the last couple of years. For a number of years, many democratic theorists have argued that the scope of the *demos*, let alone its *territorial* scope, is impossible to determine from within democratic theory. Early on, however, Robert Dahl and Frederick Whelan suggested that 'the people' (*demos*) should be understood as the body of individuals affected by a certain decision.[11]

Conceived in this way, the vocabulary of the 'will of the people' becomes 'the will of all those affected'. Initially, such reinterpretation of the principle of popular sovereignty has had seemingly little to offer to the issue of secession. Theorists such as Robert Goodin have claimed that the all-affected-interests principle should apply to every person on the globe, which should consequently lead to the establishment of some form of a global democracy.[12] Some scholars have admitted a more limited role for the principle of affected interests, arguing that those who are affected ought to have a say in reaching a political decision, but only if their basic human rights are affected.[13] Others have argued that 'being affected' should not be understood causally—where X causally affects the interests of Y—but rather juridically, where those who are 'being affected' are affected simply because they are 'subject to the government and its laws.'[14]

However, recent contributions suggest that instead of restricting the meaning of 'being affected', we should recognise its fundamental openness to diverging interpretations.[15] According to this view, since we cannot know in advance who is legitimately affected by creating a new state—and many will claim to be so affected—all those who lay such a claim should have a democratic say in a decision to create an independent state. This, the most recent contribution of democratic theory, has direct implications for external self-determination, but in the process it turns our intuition about self-determination on its head: the 'self-determining' 'people' on this account is not a group whose moral agency we are bound to recognise, but rather the product of the decision of a wider group (potentially the entire 'international community') about who is affected, and how, by a proposal to create an independent state.[16]

---

[11] R Dahl, *After the Revolution?: Authority in a Good Society* (New Haven and London, Yale University Press, 1970); FG Whelan, 'Democratic Theory and the Boundary Problem' in JR Pennock and JW Chapman (eds), *Nomos XXV: Liberal Democracy* (New York, New York University Press, 1983).

[12] RE Goodin, 'Enfranchising All Affected Interests, and its Alternatives' (2007) 35 *Philosophy and Public Affairs* 40.

[13] C Gould, 'Self-Determination Beyond Sovereignty: Relating Transnational Democracy to Local Autonomy' (2006) 37 *Journal of Social Philosophy* 55.

[14] L Beckman, 'Democratic Inclusion, Law and Causes' (2008) 21 *Ratio Juris* 350.

[15] H Agné, 'Why Democracy Must be Global: Self-founding and Democratic Intervention' (2010) 2 *International Theory* 381.

[16] ibid 389.

# III. 'New' Pluralists and External Self-Determination

The first three waves' approaches to external self-determination have generally not been concerned with international law. With the notable exception of Allen Buchanan's work, other normative approaches have either not been concerned with the extant international legal framework, or have seen their theories as a horizon towards which international law ought to strive.[17]

The fourth, explicitly pluralist, wave that has emerged over the last few years situates accounts of external self-determination, or its cognates, at the intersection of different disciplines, simultaneously paying keen attention to both political theory and to the extant international legal and political order. The 'new' pluralists' normative arguments about self-determination are implicated in larger arguments about the *telos* of the international legal order, such as the respectful accommodation of ideological differences, as in Brad Roth's 'bounded pluralism'. Or, in the perspective of Jean Cohen's 'constitutional pluralism', they are inseparable from concerns about recent corrosive developments in international law, such as great powers' abuse of their position in the UN Security Council. Finally, self-determination ends up being radically re-crafted—such as in Nico Krisch's 'radical pluralism'—to accommodate other developments in international law that are not immediately related to state-formation, such as the verticalisation, functionalisation and fragmentation of the international legal order.

Besides engaging self-determination with a keen eye on the purpose, challenges and developments of *positive* international law, new pluralists have built their argument in conversation with constitutional theory. Roth's 'bounded pluralism', for example, has relied on a particular account of 'popular sovereignty'. Cohen's 'constitutional pluralism' has utilised Carl Schmitt's concept of the *Bund* as a promising template for the reform of the United Nations.[18] Finally, Krisch's 'radical pluralism'—which understands self-determination as a 'practice of public autonomy'—critically depends on an explicit engagement and rejection of the vocabulary of constitutionalism, as inadequate to deal with new social movements and global legal phenomena.[19]

Equally, in contrast to most normative theories of secession, territorial rights and democratic theories, pluralists seem to have been more concerned with the feasibility of their proposals. Roth, who has argued in favour of going back to the 'original promise' of sovereign equality, has called for 'sound application of the most essential liberal premises about morality, in light of a *sober* recognition of the limitations

---

[17]  eg Wellman, *A Theory of Secession* (n 6) 181 for his 'hopeful prediction' that we are not 'far away' from the day when international actors embrace a generous account of the right to self-determination.

[18]  J Cohen, *Globalization and Sovereignty: Rethinking Legality, Legitimacy and Constitutionalism* (Cambridge, Cambridge University Press, 2012) 121.

[19]  N Krisch, *Beyond Constitutionalism: The Pluralist Structure of International Law* (Oxford, Oxford University Press, 2010) 17.

of moral absolutes in international politics' (emphasis added).[20] Equally, Cohen—who is proposing a far-reaching set of amendments to the United Nations Charter that would deny the veto to the 'permanent five' in the Security Council—explicitly situates this project against both 'infeasible utopias' and 'unimaginative realism'.[21] Finally, Krisch, whose project is most radical in its rejection of constitutionalist vocabulary, relies on the reality of the non-hierarchical interaction between various normative orders in the international arena.

Curiously, however, the reality of political nationalism doesn't register prominently in the recent wave of pluralist thinking. The reason for that may be not only that nationalism now has to compete for attention with other international legal and political phenomena that have captured the imagination of international lawyers, legal and political theorists over the last two decades, but also that the secessionist fever of the early-1990s has somewhat abated. After the dissolution of communist federations, Western liberal democratic federal or union states, such as Canada and the United Kingdom, seem to have found ways to accommodate secessionist impulses without the need to resort to the vocabulary of international law.[22] But the most important reason why external self-determination is short-changed in recent pluralist accounts appears to be a conscious privileging of other forms of political emancipation that depart from the conventional view of external self-determination as an ultimate vehicle for a nation's self-government.

## A. Empty Self-Determination: Bounded Pluralism, Ideological Diversity and Moral Dignity of Effectivity

Brad Roth's bounded pluralism 'empties' self-determination at three, mutually reinforcing levels: teleological, normative and doctrinal. From the teleological point of view, abandoning external self-determination's prescriptive content is a consequence of Roth's overarching understanding of the *telos* of the international legal order—the respectful accommodation of ideological differences among sovereign states, where the smaller among them are always under threat by the hegemonic designs of great powers. While bounded pluralism still grounds territorial integrity and sovereign equality of states in the norm of self-determination, that justification remains formal—divorced both from nationalism and the democratic ideal of the consent of the governed. Respectful accommodation of ideological differences is best accomplished if challenges to legitimacy are fought

---

[20] B Roth, *Sovereign Equality and Moral Disagreement: Premises of a Pluralist International Legal Order* (Oxford, Oxford University Press, 2011).

[21] Cohen, *Globalization and Sovereignty* (n 18).

[22] eg Secession Reference (n 3); An Act to give effect to the requirement for clarity as set out in the opinion of the Supreme Court of Canada in the Quebec Secession Reference, SC 2000 c 26; Agreement between the United Kingdom Government and the Scottish Government on a referendum on independence for Scotland (Edinburgh, 15 October 2012).

out internally; where the test of legitimacy is the principle of effectivity, not an independent normative standard that would provide a springboard for the self-serving and damaging meddling of powerful external actors.[23] In Roth's provocative statement, self-determination should be understood 'with much irony but little exaggeration, as a right of territorial populations to be ruled by their own thugs and to fight their civil wars in peace'.[24]

But elevating the principle of effectivity cannot be justified only in terms of its contribution to preventing external meddling in the affairs of polities at the brink of, or torn by, civil war. Though Roth doesn't explicitly say so, the teleologically justified principle of effectivity must likewise be understood as having a deeper, normative justification. Given all of the potential brutality implicated in achieving effectivity, it must be capable of being redeemed by more than a project of simply putting great powers in their place.

Indeed, Roth argues that banishing external meddling would disincentivise local insurgents who occasionally choose to militarily engage a state's authorities in hope that it will react disproportionately and provoke external intervention. The international legal order can ill afford to tolerate the human cost of such insurgent strategies.[25] Equally, if not more important, the mixed motives of the interveners may lead 'to cut-rate and irresolute methods that leave the situation worse off than it was before the action was undertaken'.[26] Aerial bombing as a safe(r) policy option than a full-on ground invasion might exacerbate rather than mitigate human suffering.[27] One of the tacit bets of bounded pluralism is that the principle of effectivity is more effective in reducing human suffering than an outright external intervention. Tacitly dignified for its role in minimising violence, locally circumscribed and sometimes violent 'trial by ordeal' supplants, in part, normative arguments in favour of this or that interpretation of popular sovereignty and self-determination.

Nationalism, or national accommodation, is not the explicit target of Roth's work. However, his explicit rejection of cultural pluralism as the normative basis of bounded pluralism equally applies to recent sophisticated defences of national self-determination.[28] Roth argues that to embrace the role of culture, and by implication nationalism, in justifying the international legal order would logically lead us to embrace oppressive practices that would in the process silence 'local liberal dissidents'.[29] While these claims are relatively familiar in recent literature, Roth's contribution lies in pitting the ideological (in effect, 'the social') against the national: culture-based pluralism should also be rejected because it privileges

---

[23] Roth, *Sovereign Equality and Moral Disagreement* (n 20) 81 throughout.
[24] ibid.
[25] ibid 161.
[26] ibid 126.
[27] ibid 127.
[28] Y Tamir, *Liberal Nationalism* (Princeton, Princeton University Press, 1995) 36 throughout.
[29] Roth (n 20) 100.

'traditional-hierarchical non-liberalism [against] revolutionary-egalitarian non-liberalism'.[30] For Roth, 'culture is not worthy of special standing, analytically independent of and morally privileged over garden-variety ideological difference. The proper focus is on ideological difference, irrespective of its (always-contested) relationship to cultural difference'.[31]

Finally, external self-determination's prescriptive content is emptied through a doctrinal analysis. Roth has argued that 'self-determination' has historically been the result of the principles of effectivity and non-intervention. Over time, doctrines have developed requiring states not to recognise entities formed through external intervention, nor to 'prematurely' recognise entities that emerged as independent polities. This latter requirement, argues Roth, has been interpreted stringently: no state has become a member of the United Nations without the consent of the parent state, and states have generally been reluctant to recognise the independent statehood of entities where the parent state didn't abandon claim(s) to that territory. According to this view, the effective internal boundaries created through an internal struggle are not sanctioned by the principle of effective control, until they, at some point in this division, become 'mature'. Roth emphasises that in this case, too, 'sovereignty is "earned" by effective struggle, with a very strong presumption in favor of the forces that earned it first'.[32]

No jurisprudential developments, during or after the Cold War, point towards the development of the norm of external self-determination that could be used outside of its colonial context.[33] The 1970 *Friendly Relations Declaration*, for Roth, was not intended to create a right to remedial secession for oppressed or discriminated groups. Rather, it should be understood in its context: as a victory for the Third World countries seeking to deny legitimacy to the apartheid regimes of South Africa and Israel, while at the same time legitimising the sovereignty of other Third World, non-liberal democratic polities.[34] Equally, more recent jurisprudential developments that have tackled state dissolution have left the principle of self-determination vague and inoperative. The Badinter Committee Opinions, hailed as the 'advent of the self-determination of peoples', are for Roth nothing more than a well-intentioned 'improvisation' with no actual bearing on the principle of self-determination.[35] Finally, the recent International Court of Justice Advisory Opinion on Kosovo's unilateral declaration of independence corroborates 'the ad hoc nature of the international order's solutions' to state-formation, rather than the advent of a new post-colonial understanding of self-determination.[36]

---

[30] ibid.

[31] ibid 102.

[32] ibid 178.

[33] But cp A Peters, 'Does Kosovo Lie in the *Lotus*-Land of Freedom?' (2011) 24 *Leiden Journal of International Law* 95, 105. Contra Roth, Peters maintains that international legal scholarship predominantly supports remedial account of external self-determination.

[34] Roth (n 20) 182.

[35] ibid 186.

[36] ibid 199.

As a result, the doctrinal demise of external self-determination dovetails with the restored dignity of effectivity as the best bulwark against great power machinations in an international order committed to respectful accommodation of ideological, not national, differences.

## B. Conservative Self-Determination: Constitutional Pluralism and the Taming of Great Power Hegemony

Roth's bounded pluralism affirms statist, constitutionalist assumptions in the context of a domestic order, yet it does not succumb to the temptation to seek constitutional(ist) solutions to territorial conflicts, external interventions, and attempts at great power domination. In contrast, while Cohen's *constitutional pluralism* embraces sovereign states as the arch-stones of the international legal order, in her desire to curb great power hegemony she moves past Roth's bounded pluralist version, enthusiasm for unreformed sovereign equality, and agnosticism over the normative import of self-determination.

Instead, Cohen's brand of pluralism—while still building on states' sovereign equality—seeks to enframe itself within a more legitimate, federalised, international legal architecture which would democratise decision-making in the United Nations, removing the veto of the five permanent members of the Security Council both in the amending procedure to the United Nations Charter and in the Council's decision-making itself.[37] While her project is more ambitious than Roth's, she doesn't contemplate strengthening legal mechanisms that would empower certain bodies within the UN structure—either the General Assembly or the International Court of Justice (ICJ)—to arbitrate in cases of territorial conflict, thus endowing territorial self-determination with a more dynamic, constructive role in situations of territorial conflict.

Instead, Cohen primarily understands self-determination as a conservative principle, an ideal that provides a normative firewall that protects weaker polities from the self-serving impulses of great powers that might seek to exploit a situation and mould the constitutional order of an intervened-upon country according to its political image. Thus the only legitimate form of intervention is one that seeks to establish conditions for the internal self-determination of an existing polity. The occupier has to pursue 'inclusiveness, but that cannot mean the imposition of a particular regime'.[38] Like Rousseau's Lawgiver, the occupier must enable—but not 'intrusively regulate'.[39]

But the spectre of territorial legitimacy haunts Cohen's conservative self-determination. The 'inclusiveness' she prescribes is not a neutral, minimal moral desideratum, but a momentous—and contentious—political question that

---

[37] Cohen (n 18) 19.
[38] ibid 254.
[39] ibid 251.

predefines many other constitutional choices. The political conflict in many countries intervened upon has not been about inclusion, but rather about various degrees of exclusion. In fact, many brutal acts of governmental suppression have begun in response to secessionist demands. To require an inclusive process is to stack the deck against the aspirations of the minorities trapped under an existing territorial status quo. And even if 'inclusiveness' is understood purely in procedural terms, as setting a procedure where the domestic political actors will debate and decide on a constitutional settlement that may include secession, it is naïve to believe that a political majority in an intervened country would ever agree on this.

But perhaps more importantly, Cohen's commitment to conservative self-determination is in tension with the *telos* of constitutional pluralism, which cannot simply be circumscribed to the level of international politics. Historically, constitutional pluralism has been articulated not only in the context of supranational integrations such as the European Union, but also in the context of multinational polities and union states, such as the United Kingdom.[40] While constitutional pluralists have been agnostic about how far the demands of ultimate constitutional authority on behalf of different national communities should proliferate, they have recognised the legitimacy of nationalist claims for constitutional accommodation. Neil MacCormick, for example, though silent on 'further' constitutional pluralism within a union state, seems to have embraced further nesting of territorial autonomies under the aegis of the 'communal' subsidiary. More recently, Neil Walker seems to have also accepted the legitimacy of recursive or countervailing nationalist aspirations in the context of radical reconstruction of a constitutional order. While not directly linking it to the project of constitutional pluralism, Walker has argued that liberals 'must be concerned to show due liberal respect and concern for others … who champion *other and potentially inconsistent* national projects'.[41]

Finally, there is nothing in Cohen's account that would prevent her from extending constitutional pluralism all the way down. She understands federal structure (as one of the manifestations of constitutional pluralism) as being composed of two 'layers' but there is nothing in the federal principle as such that would prevent us from seeing federal unions as being composed of three, four and more levels of government. Since protecting diversity is one of the central normative justifications of federalism, it remains unclear why the federalist logic wouldn't be extended—and the member states federalised—where there is a demand for such recognition of national plurality.[42] Equally, there is nothing in the idea of constitutional pluralism that would prevent these nested-federal units entering into constitutional relations with other constitutional orders in various symmetric

---

[40] N MacCormick, *Questioning Sovereignty: Law, State and Nation in the European Commonwealth* (Oxford, Oxford University Press, 1999).

[41] N Walker, 'Scottish Nationalism For and Against the Union State: the vision of Neil MacCormick' (2011) 25 University of Edinburgh School of Law Working Paper 8, 14.

[42] Cohen (n 18) 62.

or asymmetric ways. For example, the constitution of Bosnia and Herzegovina gives constituent entities a right to establish 'special parallel relations' with neighbouring countries Croatia and Serbia. Equally, the structures created by the Belfast Agreement provide for a variable geometry of political relations between Northern Ireland, Ireland and Great Britain.

The reason Cohen's conservative self-determination cannot be reconciled with constitutional pluralism that seeks to accommodate national pluralism is because it interferes with the register of social and geopolitical emancipation. Constitutional pluralism on an international level works in tandem with the denial of constitutional pluralism on a local level: fending off 'liberal imperialism' and the 'neo-imperialist efforts of the sole existing superpower and … re-emerging great powers'.[43] Such a selective embrace of constitutional pluralism and a similarly reductive idea of the normative content of self-determination may rest on dubious assumptions, however. They presuppose that territorial reconfigurations generally favour the interests of great powers, or that such powers would be more likely to intervene if there existed a norm of self-determination—or an understanding of constitutional pluralism—that would lend certain dignity to nationalist demands. The validity of these tacit assumptions is not obvious, and I will question them toward the end of this essay.

## C. Ethereal Self-Determination: Radical Pluralism and the 'Practice of Public Autonomy'

Both bounded and constitutional pluralism are devoted to the territorial status quo among currently existing, independent states. They either tacitly accept (Roth) or complicate (Cohen)—but in any event never abandon—the constitutionalist premises of the modern international legal order. In contrast, Krisch's radical pluralism abandons constitutionalism, finding it implicated in hegemonic practices at all levels. The ossification of power relations occurs not only at the international level of constitutional orders, but also at the domestic level. All constitutions 'stabilise and immunise' existing social structures; they are 'tools for powerful groups to protect their vision of society from challenge'.[44] Perhaps because he is concerned with the 'social hegemony' of constitutionalism and not explicitly with great power hegemony and external interventions, Krisch's embrace of radical pluralism comes with a rich argument in favour of self-determination, which exists not as a norm of international law, but rather as a 'practice of public autonomy'.

In highlighting the role of affected interests, Krisch's pluralism is perhaps the only one that reaches towards the vocabulary of normative and democratic theory. In doing so, it takes on board not only the trope of 'all affected interests', but also, although indirectly, the value of actual consent in forming political community.

---

[43] ibid 17 and 243 respectively.
[44] Krisch, *Beyond Constitutionalism* (n 19) 79 and 259 respectively.

I say indirectly, because Krisch's prescriptions about the legitimacy of a new *demos* glances over consent by saying that the institution of a new *demos* should not be '*mere* expression of attitudes or will by citizens'; suggesting that expression of individual political attitudes *remains* a critical component of the 'exercise of public autonomy'.

In exercising public autonomy, however, mobilised citizens will have to show the appropriate level of other-awareness. They have to seriously engage the outsiders' desires to be included on the one hand, and the insiders' claims to create their own political structures on the other.[45] An inability to provide an account of the 'balance' between these two concerns will not count as exercise of public autonomy. Finally, their collective claim should be judged according to the 'strength of its social grounding of the participatory practices that support it'.[46]

Krisch doesn't say this explicitly, but this malleable *practice* of public autonomy effectively supplants the *norm* of self-determination. While territorial self-determination exists to be conclusively interpreted by an authoritative body, the exercise of public autonomy remains open to everyone's judgement.[47] Equally, in contrast to territorial self-determination, where the designation of a group as 'the people' predetermines the scope of the political options available to it, in exercising political autonomy, the *demos* emerges as the result of legitimate political choices and the quality of public participation itself.

Does this ethereal practice of public autonomy prevent the emergence of territorially bounded polities? Seemingly aware of this problem, Krisch writes that 'if participation is thought to extend to all questions of a constitutional character, it also has to apply to the scope of the polity—the reach of the constitutional frame—itself'.[48] Like normative theorists of self-determination, Krisch is aware of the problem of the scope of the polity, but never confronts it at the territorial level.

As a result, there are two ways in which we can extrapolate from Krisch's 'public autonomy' argument and make it speak to the context of territorial reconfigurations. On the one hand, most plausibly, I think, we can conceive of it as a normative *challenge* to the zero-sum territorial politics of self-determination. The practice of public autonomy, on this account, should yield non-territorial functional *demoi*, superimposed on already existing, unscathed, territorial jurisdictions. The solution to territorial conflict would be not in the reapportionment of territory, but in the creation of non-territorial jurisdictions. The Opinions of the Badinter Committee, mentioned earlier, could be seen as an exemplar of such an approach. In an attempt to solve the conundrum between ethnic and demotic self-determination, the Committee suggested giving Serbian minorities in Croatia and Bosnia and Herzegovina a right to choose their nationality, which would have enabled them to continue to act simultaneously as citizens of the territorial polities of Croatia and

---

[45] ibid 101.
[46] ibid.
[47] For a general critique of the role of the principle of affectedness in justifying public autonomy, see A Somek, 'The Constituent Power in a Transnational Context' (2012) 3 *Transnational Legal Theory* 31.
[48] Krisch (n 19) 93.

Bosnia, and as political members of the Serbian nation, a non-territorial political community stretching over the territorially reconstituted Yugoslav space.

While such an interpretation of Krisch's project is more plausible, we could still use it to seek a productive engagement with territorial reconfigurations in the key of national pluralism. In fact, it is Iris Marion Young's later work that has provided a sketch of territorial solutions to national conflict, and showed how radical pluralism's tacit sympathy for proliferating jurisdictions can be grafted onto the sphere of territorial politics.[49] In her relational model, territorial self-determining jurisdictions keep proliferating and nesting within larger units without an imperative to be large or territorially contiguous. What distinguishes her model from the first-wave theories—more specifically, choice and nationalist theories of secession—is her attention to the externalities that nascent polities produce for their environment. As a result, some patterns of geo-demographic distribution may simply call for an ongoing constitutional arrangement between different political communities. Unlike for Jeremy Waldron, however, for whom mutual proximity and affectedness is a reason to dismiss self-determination's reconstructive potential,[50] Young's solution has been to revive federalism as a response to multiplying territorial complexity. For her, non-contiguous national territories would maintain their nominal unity but be bound to align themselves with other adjacent units, which may surround or pockmark the national territory.

This, however, is not the tack pursued by Krisch, irrespective of his approving nods in Young's direction.[51] Somewhat ironically, then, the richest account of self-determination (though under a different name) among the three contemporary pluralisms has an *ethereal* presence in the struggles over the territorial scope of nationalist aspirations and democratic politics. Krisch's account of the practice of public autonomy makes visible criteria that can be used to redraw territorial boundaries, but, without explicit acknowledgement of their role in territorial self-determination, we can never be certain whether we can grasp and apply them for the purposes of territorial self-determination.

## IV. External Self-Determination: Reconciling National, Social and Geopolitical Emancipation beyond the Disciplinary Silos?

Empty, conservative, ethereal: these are the new pluralist understandings of external self-determination. For different reasons, the three pluralisms have

---

[49] IM Young, *Global Challenges: War, Self-Determination and Responsibility for Justice* (Cambridge, Polity, 2008) 7.

[50] J Waldron, 'Two Conceptions of Self-Determination' in S Besson and J Tasioulas (eds), *The Philosophy of International Law* (Oxford, Oxford University Press, 2010) 410.

[51] Krisch (n 19) 87.

abandoned self-determination's reconstructive potential. Rejecting nationalism as the legitimating principle of the international legal order, Roth's bounded pluralism has moralised the principle of effectivity, which, together with the principle of non-intervention, allegedly structures the international legal response to secessionist mobilisation. In such a way, Roth's bounded pluralism has explicitly sought to create more breathing room for ideological pluralism and new projects of social emancipation, but also, implicitly, to minimise political violence implicated in state-formation. Cohen's constitutional pluralism hasn't abandoned self-determination, but has made it largely inoperative in the context of territorial reconstructions. Equally worried about great power hegemony, self-determination continues to exist mainly to conserve an existing polity in the situation of external intervention. Finally, radical pluralism's preoccupation with hegemony *tout court* yields the richest normative account of 'practice of public autonomy', but can only dubiously be grafted onto the plane of spatial politics.

What is the reason for the pluralisms' deflated normative ambition in the context of national pluralism and territorial reconfigurations? Part of the answer must lie in the fact that normative political theory itself is at a stalemate. Divergent secession, territorial rights and democracy theories, discussed in section II, point in different directions as we try to identify 'the people' and its territorial dominion. Equally, since the three pluralisms feature a blend of international law, legal and political theory, one could argue that they are more obliged by their own disciplinary positioning to respect the strictures imposed by existing international legal material than their liberal pluralist counterparts a decade and a half ago.[52] But this abandonment of nationalism is not a disciplinary necessity: even early constitutional pluralists who took the international legal order seriously, such as MacCormick, haven't abandoned nationalism as an important part of theorising territorial reconstructions in the key of self-determination, but have sought to recast its meaning and role in the post-sovereign context.[53]

More importantly, the three pluralisms' disregard for national pluralism in the context of territorial reconfigurations stems from their other, principled— political and conceptual—commitments. Worries about great power hegemony

---

[52] For the liberal pluralist vision, see generally W Kymlicka, 'Western Political Theory and Ethnic Relations in Eastern Europe' in W Kymlicka and M Opalski (eds), *Can Liberal Pluralism be Exported? Western Political Theory and Ethnic Relations in Eastern Europe* (Oxford, Oxford University Press, 2001) 13. One could equally argue that the disregard for territorial reconfigurations in the key of self-determination is due to the anthropological provenance of legal pluralism. If self-determination is an internationally recognised legal norm, legal pluralists *qua* anthropologists will more likely be interested in the grassroots practices than in the large-scale politico-theoretical re-articulation of territorial self-determination. cp, eg, A Griffiths, 'Pursuing Legal Pluralism: The Power of Paradigms in a Global World' (2011) 64 *Journal of Legal Pluralism & Unofficial Law* 173. Though Griffiths' article discusses 'multi-spatial contextualizations of law', 'reconfiguring states', 'indigenous strategies for recognition' and even 'popular sovereignty', nowhere do those concerns intersect at the site where they are habitually found together: territorial self-determination.

[53] MacCormick, *Questioning Sovereignty* (n 40) 167 throughout.

and hegemony in general, desires to maintain social and ideological diversity, and, finally, radical conceptual changes that abolish the vocabulary of constitutionalism have all contributed to the diminishment of self-determination's prescriptive component in the context of territorial reconfigurations. Bounded, constitutional and to a certain extent radical pluralists accept the hidden trade-off between concern for nationalist accommodation on the one hand, and for the deleterious effects of global power politics on the other. Roth and Cohen, and less so Krisch, demonstrate that the price they are willing to pay for a project that fends off hegemonies of great powers is a toothless account of territorial self-determination.

Is this deflated normative ambition justified? Or, to put it differently: would a principle of self-determination that maintains its ambition to prescribe a solution, or a range of permissible solutions in territorial conflicts, exacerbate or mitigate the United States' hegemony and the unaccountable use of force that has followed it? While the US supported the independence of unitary Kosovo, it acceded to the independence of almost confederal Bosnia and Herzegovina. In contrast, it strongly opposes partitioning Syria, Iraq or Libya along ethnic lines. Equally, the United States' intervention in the former Yugoslavia, or Iraq or Syria, can hardly be understood as motivated from the outset by a desire to empower a specific nationality at the expense of another. If anything, it seems that Western military interventions have featured a desire to first maintain the territorial status quo, and then impose functional arrangements that would recognise national pluralism while anchoring the reconstructed state firmly within the Western political orbit.

As the constitutional aftermath of the US military involvement in Kosovo and Iraq has shown, the US is capable of rationalising its preferred solution both along Rothian and Cohenian lines. In the case of Kosovo, its independence was justified by recourse to a combination of non-legal and crypto-legal considerations that ask for respect for the new effective reality on the ground—not self-determination.[54] In the case of Iraq—irrespective of its role in brokering the constitutional settlement—the Americans supported the conservative view of self-determination suggested by Cohen, by upholding the sovereignty of the Iraqi people, understood as a whole.[55] The American approach to state-building seems to be case-sensitive, and not necessarily path-dependent.

If there is a common denominator to the approach of the US government, it seems to be to withdraw from the theatre as quickly as possible while endorsing a modicum of national plurality, depending on its contingent national interests. For those interested in counter-hegemony, then, the counter-intuitive but potentially fruitful conclusion might be to actually demand a prolonged involvement of the great powers in maintaining and securing national plurality in a way that would not only make further demands on great powers' resources and attention, but also

---

[54] US Department of State, 'US Recognizes Kosovo as Independent State' (18 February 2008).

[55] For an account of the use the vocabulary of peoplehood and self-government in the context of American interventions in the Philippines (1899) and Iraq (2003); cf A Anghie, *Imperialism, Sovereignty, and the Making of International Law* (Cambridge, Cambridge University Press, 2003) 280–91.

implicate them in structures of political and legal responsibility, which would open great power decision-making processes to those whom they profoundly affect.

If the constitutional accommodation of national plurality doesn't need to be sacrificed at the altar of struggle against great power hegemony—or, at least, if this proposition has yet to be empirically verified—this still requires addressing the tense relationship between national and ideological pluralism. Do we have to trade one against the other? Asking this question won't be urgent in all latitudes. In Europe, secessionist projects, such as in Scotland and Catalonia, have successfully combined nationalism and social democracy, and are generally suspicious of economic neo-liberalism.[56] Even in countries that have rejected liberal democracy, such as Venezuela, there has been little or no dissonance between the registers of national and social emancipation: the Venezuelan social project went in hand with the emancipation of indigenous peoples and disenfranchised Afro-Venezuelans.[57]

On the other hand, the Bolivian experience with constitution-making, for example, saw the two registers sharply pitted against each other. Aiming simultaneously to entrench socialism and empower marginalised indigenous peoples, the new socialist Constitution has been met with fierce resistance from the European-origin population concentrated in the resource-rich region of Santa Cruz.[58] In 2008, following Evo Morales' push to adopt the new Constitution, the political leaders of Santa Cruz organised a referendum in which more than 80 per cent of voters voted in favour of creating a robust territorial autonomy for their region and even threatened to secede should Morales proceed to adopt the constitution without recognising their regional autonomy.[59] Following the constitutional stand-off, Morales' Movement Toward Socialism and regional opposition leaders ultimately agreed on a compromise that increased regional autonomy culminating in a national constitution approved in a referendum in the autumn of 2008.[60]

It is outside the ambit of this chapter to develop a full-blown account of how the registers of national and social emancipation in the context of territorial reconfigurations may be reconciled in theory. At this point, however, I will briefly hazard three possibilities. First, reconciliation may be attempted as a result of a more conventional 'top down' theoretical effort where normative theorists of self-determination provide an account that unites the justification for non-liberal democratic *internal* self-determination with nationalist *territorial* self-determination. Conversely, reconciliation might come from the camp of liberal democracy's antagonists—radical democrats and post-Marxists—who would have to not only re-embrace some form of nationalism as a reservoir of affective solidarity, but also

[56] For some political theorists, such as David Miller, enhanced social solidarity is one of the most important benefits of national self-determination. In contemporary normative theory, this view is most strongly advanced by D Miller, *On Nationality* (Oxford, Oxford University Press, 1995).

[57] S Kennedy, 'Conflicts and Conundrums: How the Venezuelan State Must Strike the Balance With its Indigenous People' (*Venezeula Analysis*, 6 December 2012).

[58] D Landau, 'Constitution-making Gone Wrong' FSU College of Law Research Paper No 587, 24.

[59] F Lehoucq, 'Bolivia's Constitutional Breakdown' (2008) 19 *Journal of Democracy* 110.

[60] K Eaton, 'Conservative Autonomy Movements: Territorial Dimensions of Ideological Conflict in Bolivia and Ecuador' (2011) 43 *Comparative Politics* 291, 297.

squarely engage with how radical democratic 'people-formation relates to territorial reconfigurations'.[61]

The third theoretical avenue would be to build on the most ambitious understanding of democratic theory, in which the all-affected-interests principle ideationally leads to the establishment of a global *demos*, vested with a right to reconstitute itself. Under such account, drawing the boundaries of new polities would be re-imagined as the kaleidoscopic internal territorial reconfiguration of one global 'people'. Under such a vision, the space for ideological pluralism and social emancipation would be safeguarded by a reliance on the putative ideological disposition of those most numerous—the Third World. So-called 'popular' self-determination, under this vision, would still remain in the grey zone of *sui generis*, case by case, judgments. But one of the contextual factors to be judged by the representatives of the 'world people' in creating new polities—besides the degree of local consent to a new arrangement—would also be the existence or lack of an emancipatory social project.

Finally, one might argue that speculating on theory's response to the tense relationship between the registers of national and social emancipation means putting the cart before the horse. Instead, the reconciliation of the two registers—a new meaning of self-determination—will emerge (if it emerges) in a 'bottom-up fashion, from the perspective of non-state or civil society actors, grassroots activists, subalternised and marginalised peoples, and counter-hegemonic social movements'.[62] The role of theory, under such vision, is not to impose a 'solution', but rather to exist in 'a mutual relation with the concrete struggles, negotiations and implementations of citizens who experiment with modifying the practices of governance on the ground'.[63]

---

[61] For Matthew Sparke, Ernesto Laclau's work, for instance, 'remains haunted by the tacit assumption of the nation-state as the spatial container': M Sparke, *In the Space of Theory: Post-foundational Geographies of the Nation-State* (Minneapolis, University of Minnesota Press, 2005). For a recent admission that the question of territoriality has been neglected among the post-Marxist, radical democrats, see C Mouffe, 'Space, Hegemony, and Radical Critique' in D Featherstone and J Painter (eds), *Spatial Politics: Essays for Doreen Massey* (Oxford, Wiley-Blackwell, 2012) 21.

[62] J Singh, 'Recognition and Self-Determination: Approaches from Above and Below' in A Eisenberg et al (eds), *Recognition versus Self-Determination* (Vancouver and Toronto, UBC Press, 2014). See Rickard Lalander, for an argument that it is possible to reconcile registers of national and social emancipation under the banner of 'socialist decentralization': R Lalander 'Socialist Decentralization in the Andes? Explorative Reflections on Radical Democracy and 21st Century Neo-Constitutionalism' (2010) Actas: Independencia y Dependencia en América Latina, 200 años Después Simposio Internacional http://ssrn.com/abstract=2349074. For a historical example of an argument that national self-determination and socialist self-management are reverse sides of the same coin, see E Kardelj, 'Remarks during Discussion in the Plenary Session of the Tenth Congress of the League of Communists of Yugoslavia, Belgrade, May 27, 1974' in E Kardelj, *Yugoslavia in International Relations and Non-Alignment* (Belgrade, Socialist Thought and Practice, 1979). Sometimes, grassroots movements will strategically oscillate between the register of the national and the social in framing their political and territorial demands. See C Jung, 'From Peasant to Indigenous: Shifting the Parameters of Politics' in C Jung, *The Moral Force of Indigenous Politics: Critical Liberalism and the Zapatistas* (Cambridge, Cambridge University Press, 2008) 148.

[63] J Tully, *Public Philosophy in a New Key. Volume I: Democracy and Civic Freedom* (Cambridge, Cambridge University Press, 2008) 17.

# V. Conclusion

For almost two decades, international legal scholars have been complaining about the 'disarray in legal doctrine'[64] and 'the penumbra of uncertainty'[65] surrounding the international legal norm of self-determination. While the purchase of internal self-determination has risen over that period, external self-determination has languished in the twilight zone of hesitant jurisprudential treatment, sharply divided states' *opinio juris*, and equally sharply divided international lawyers' accounts of its evolution.

Theorising self-determination in political theory can be seen, in part, as having been invited by these developments in international law. However, 20 years on, theories of self-determination feature similar problems. As the debate around it grew richer, new layers, and, within them, new competing approaches, sought to articulate correct normative accounts of external self-determination. Finally, new pluralist thinking on self-determination has seen the registers of social and geopolitical emancipation resurface as critical concerns in how we think of self-determination in general and external self-determination by implication.

I say resurface, because the synergic union of the three registers in which external self-determination partook—national, social and geopolitical—was the understanding of external self-determination that was dominant during the process of decolonisation.[66] During decolonisation, external self-determination gave a nation—irrespective of how defined—not only a vehicle for its flourishing, but also an autonomous space for constructing alternative modes of social organisation. Equally, such self-determination was implicated in a larger geopolitical struggle that had undermined not only local loci of political domination, but also transcontinental empires—global centres of political hegemony.

This view has been largely suppressed and abandoned in our contemporary political imaginary, and normative political theory so far hasn't shown an interest in interrogating the relationship between the three registers. While the new pluralist thinking tackled in this essay clearly rejected the possibility of a productive and mutually reinforcing relationship between the three registers, its important contribution is to have implicitly put this relationship on the agenda of international legal scholarship as an irritant, a question potentially worth asking once again.

---

[64] T Franck, *Fairness in International Law and Institutions* (Oxford, Oxford University Press, 1998) 148.

[65] D Cass, 'Re-Thinking Self-Determination: A Critical Analysis of Current International Law Theories' (1992) 18 *Syracuse Journal of International Law and Commerce* 21, 22–23.

[66] *cf*, eg, R Emerson, *Self-Determination Revisited in the Era of Decolonization* (Center for International Affairs Harvard University, 1964) 1.

New Legal Orders: The Challenges of European
Integration and International Human Rights

# 10

## Between Cosmopolis and Community: Justice and Legitimacy in a European Union of Peoples

## I. Introduction

Two apparently contradictory trends characterise contemporary European politics. On the one hand, there has been both a widening of the EU to include the countries of Central and Eastern Europe, and increasingly the Baltic and the Balkans as well, and calls for its deepening—especially in the wake of the Euro crisis—with greater political unification promoted in many quarters as a necessary complement to monetary union and the single market. On the other hand, there are growing pressures towards devolution and secession within many established states as minority national groups reassert a desire for self-determination. There is also mounting disaffection towards the EU across Europe, with rising support for populist parties—particularly but not exclusively on the right.

The second trend often gets compared somewhat negatively to the first trend, to which it is seen as an anachronistic and regressive reaction. From this perspective, the second trend represents an ultimately doomed attempt to escape the realities and obligations of an ever more interconnected world associated with the first trend, and to withdraw into the parochial and divisive nationalisms of the past. This analysis has both an empirical and a related normative aspect, whereby the process of globalisation raises the need and possibility for more global forms of legal and political organisation grounded in cosmopolitan principles that recognise the equal moral status of all individuals, regardless of their national, ethnic, religious or cultural affiliations.[1] The move towards greater European integration

* Research for this chapter was supported by a Leverhulme Trust Research Fellowship RF-2012-368, which was largely written while a Fellow of the Hanse-Wissenschaftskolleg in Delmenhorst. I am grateful to Dario Castiglione, Sandra Kröger and Christine Reh for their comments on an earlier version.
[1] D Held, *Democracy and the Global Order: From the Modern State to Cosmopolitan Governance* (Cambridge, Polity Press, 1995).

is alleged to reflect this new reality. The EU may often fail to meet these emerging global challenges and cosmopolitan ideals, but for a number of its most prominent political and academic advocates it is the belief that only a body such as the EU has the potential to do so effectively that provides the best rationale for the integration process.

The empirical aspect of this way of thinking was well expressed by the then President of the European Council, Herman von Rompuy, when asked his opinion on what was at that time only a proposed referendum on Scottish independence:

> Nobody has anything to gain from separatism in the world of today which, whether one likes it or not, is globalised … We have so many important challenges to take and we will only succeed if we can pool forces, join action, take common directions. The global financial crisis is hitting us hard. Climate change is threatening the planet. How can separatism help? The word of the future is union.[2]

In a similar vein, the philosopher Jürgen Habermas has remarked how, in his view, 'financial markets' and 'more generally, the functional systems of world society, whose influence permeates national borders, are giving rise to problems that individual states, or coalitions of states, are no longer able to master'.[3] As a result of this 'need for regulation' on a global scale, he contends 'the *international* community of states must develop into a *cosmopolitan* community of states and world citizens'.[4]

As Habermas' remark indicates, the normative aspect of the integrative thesis has been considered as intimately associated with the empirical aspect. This position has also figured prominently in the discourse of EU officials. As the former President of the European Commission, José Barroso, declared in a seminar on 'Global Constitutionalism':

> The present crisis has shown the limits of individual action by nation states. Europe and the principles of the Treaty need to be renewed. We need more integration, and the corollary of more integration has to be more democracy. This European renewal must represent a leap in quality and enable Europe to rise to the challenges of the world today by giving it the tools it needs to react more effectively and to shape and control the future.[5]

In other words, he contends the functional need for greater integration has as its by-product a normative spill-over that allows for and requires greater democratic accountability at the European and ultimately at the global level. On this account, global problems can only be legitimately tackled by invoking global norms, that themselves imply more global legal and democratic arrangements. The EU provides the most developed example at the regional level of such a post-national arrangement.

---

[2] Herman von Rompuy, speaking in an interview of June 2011, as reported in D Boffey, 'European chief pours scorn on Scottish independence' *The Guardian* (4 November 2012).

[3] J Habermas, *The Crisis of the European Union: A Response* (Cambridge, Polity, 2012) xi.

[4] ibid xi.

[5] European Commission, 'Quotes from the speech by the President of the European Commission, José Manuel Durão Barroso, at the occasion of Yale's Global Constitutionalism Seminar convening at The Hague' European Commission Press Release (Brussels, 1 September 2012).

Once again, Habermas provides a good academic example of this line of argument. He maintains the very idea of human rights involves 'an implicit claim that equal rights for everyone should be implemented on a global scale'. Moreover, this 'cosmopolitan claim' is not just a moral claim that motivates the critique of global injustice but also a legal claim for the constitutionalisation of international law, since 'human rights rely on finding institutional embodiment in a politically constituted world society'.[6] As a result, he contends that the 'sustained political fragmentation in the world and in Europe is in contradiction to the systemic growth of a global multi-cultural society'.[7] In Habermas' view, the just and effective resolution of the Euro crisis requires a move towards a new form of social and political solidarity built on a commitment to human rights and the concomitant rejection of the outmoded categories of national identity and state sovereignty that he believes block moves towards a Union based on democracy and social justice rather than the market.

Both the empirical and normative strands of these arguments for greater EU integration have undeniable force. Any empirically plausible or normatively acceptable account of politics must acknowledge both the global issues currently confronting contemporary societies and the moral responsibilities owed to non-nationals. In an increasingly interconnected world, problems such as global warming, the fair regulation of international trade and severe poverty in developing countries cannot be ignored. To the extent that many Eurosceptic arguments appear to do so, they seem practically deficient and morally reprehensible. Yet, it would be wrong to regard all arguments that seek to understand the EU and global governance more generally in broadly international rather than cosmopolitan terms as indifferent to either global problems or norms of global justice and human rights. Rather, they seek to combine respect for these issues and values with forms of legal and political organisation that also give weight to some of the concerns underlying the second trend noted above, and the associated desire to retain power at, or possibly devolve it below, the level of established nation-states, rather than to transfer it to a supranational body above them.

A more sympathetic reading of this second trend notes that it too can be linked to empirical features of contemporary societies and supported by normative values of a communitarian character that reflect the self-understandings of liberal democratic states.[8] From this perspective, the second trend arises from the importance of self-government among people who are mutually interdependent in a

---

[6] Habermas, *Crisis of the European Union* (n 3) xi–xii.

[7] ibid 7.

[8] In other words, communitarianism is understood here not as a set of policy recommendations but as an ontological account of the normative basis of liberal democratic states as provided by liberal nationalists such as Yael Tamir and David Miller. See Y Tamir, *Liberal Nationalism* (Princeton NJ, Princeton University Press, 1993) and D Miller, *On Nationality* (Oxford, Clarendon Press, 1995). On the 'ontological'/'advocacy' distinction, we follow C Taylor, 'Cross-Purposes: The Liberal-Communitarian Debate' in N Rosenblum (ed), *Liberalism and the Moral Life* (Cambridge MA, Harvard University Press, 1989) 159–60.

number of significant respects, share various common interests and norms, and seek to promote trust and support for collective arrangements that make sense to them as appropriate and are responsive to their interests and values. As the quotes given above illustrate, many of those who regard the EU as a necessary functional response to globalisation also contend it allows for new forms of self-government that can satisfy these demands through the democratic control of processes that increasingly operate between and across states. Yet, continuing complaints about the EU's democratic deficit indicate how difficult this contention has proven to put into practice. More importantly, it also ignores the tensions that can arise between regional integration and the historical political identities and forms of communal self-rule that have developed within each of the Member States—a tension that has become increasingly prominent in recent years.[9]

This chapter explores the cosmopolitan and the international routes to meeting the twin challenges thrown up by the two trends of globalisation and cosmopolitan justice, on the one hand, and the continued communitarian demands for forms of national self-determination that combine popular with polity sovereignty on the model of the nation-state, on the other. The EU is often seen as awkwardly placed between the two, its governance structures caught between representing citizens and representing states,[10] on the one hand, and developing a trans- or supranational public interest and reflecting the mutual interests of the component nation states, on the other.[11] Many supporters of European integration believe that this situation is impractical and incoherent. They contend the only plausible and justifiable solution is to resolve the second trend into the first and to make the EU the primary locus of political identity and self-determination for European citizens.[12] By contrast, I wish to suggest that these two trends can be brought together in a less reductive way that gives equal weight to each of them. I shall argue that the EU is best seen as a locus of deep cooperation between self-governing nation-states, which serves in many respects as a means of maintaining rather than replacing them in the new global context.

Two conceptual distinctions inform this analysis and are developed in the rest of this chapter. The first relates to the distinction between cosmopolitanism and communitarianism, which I link to the first and second trends respectively. Within this analysis, they represent contrasting ontological rather than ideological positions that offer different understandings of the normative and empirical basis for broadly liberal egalitarian and democratic values. I shall argue that the one favours an instrumental view of political community, the other an intrinsic

---

[9] L Hooghe and G Marks, 'A Postfunctionalist Theory of European Integration: from Permissive Consensus to Constraining Dissensus' (2009) 39(1) *British Journal of Political Science* 1.

[10] S Kröger and D Friedrich, 'Democratic Representation in the EU: Two Kinds of Subjectivity' (2013) 20(2) *Journal of European Public Policy* 171.

[11] R Bellamy and D Castiglione, 'Three Models of Democracy, Political Community and Representation in the EU' (2013) 20(2) *Journal of European Public Policy* 206.

[12] eg S Hix, *What's Wrong with the European Union and How to Fix It* (Cambridge, Polity, 2008) and A Duff, *Federal Union Now* (London, Federal Trust, 2011).

view.[13] According to the first, instrumental view, both the design and competences of democratic institutions and the size and location of the political communities in which they operate should be determined by whatever scheme proves most appropriate to deliver effective and equitable policies in the most efficient manner.[14] Though some grant the modern nation-state may prove convenient for certain purposes,[15] others regard both state and popular sovereignty as undermining impartial principles of justice and favour their radical dispersal across a variety of political units.[16] Analogous reasoning informs the neo-functionalist interpretation of the integration process which underlay the Monnet method and still provides the background assumptions behind much of the Commission's thinking. According to this thesis, the acquisition of competences by the EU induces a spillover effect linked to functional efficacy, which both leads the EU to move into ever more related policy areas and in time encourages the shift to the European level of political institutions and ultimately people's allegiances and identities as well.[17]

By contrast, the second, intrinsic view, regards the good of being an equal member of a democratic polity as possessing an independent value. In such a community, citizens participate as equals in making those collective decisions in which, taken as a whole, they have an equal stake. The terms on which they participate are formally and to a degree substantively the same for all, and they treat each other as equals within the process of decision-making. Such a view of political community rests on a degree of mutual identification stemming from shared interests and values among its members, qualities that are fostered by a history of mutual interactions among them.[18]

If one applies this distinction to the two trends outlined above, it may be that the empirical and normative arguments made by the EU officials and philosophers cited earlier offer a case for an instrumental political community at the European level, but they fall short of justifying an intrinsic political community. That might be thought unimportant. As we saw, some cosmopolitan advocates of global justice regard such an intrinsic community as outmoded, unnecessary and in certain respects unpleasant and unjustified as well as impractical. However, the contention shall be that cosmopolitanism cannot overcome or replace the communitarian impulse, not least because reasons linked to justice and function per se underdetermine the level and membership of any political community.

---

[13] On this distinction, see A Mason, *Living Together as Equals: The Demands of Citizenship* (Oxford, Oxford University Press, 2012) chs 1 and 2.

[14] eg P van Parijs, *Just Democracy: The Rawls-Machiavelli Programme* (Colchester, ECPR Press, 2013) chs 1, 5 and 7.

[15] RE Goodin, 'What is So Special about Our Fellow Countrymen?' (1988) 98 *Ethics* 663.

[16] T Pogge, 'Cosmopolitanism and Sovereignty' in T Pogge, *World Poverty and Human Rights* 2nd edn (Cambridge, Polity, 2008) ch 7.

[17] E Haas, *The Uniting of Europe: Political, Social and Economic Forces 1950–57* (Stanford, Stanford University Press, 1958).

[18] eg the intrinsic image of political community informs David Miller's advocacy of national self-determination. See the account of 'radical democracy' in D Miller 'Democracy's Domain' (2009) 37(3) *Philosophy and Public Affairs* 201 and more generally Miller, *On Nationality* (n 8).

The second distinction I wish to draw enters here: that between justice and legitimacy.[19] Once again, I adopt a broadly liberal egalitarian conception of these concepts. In formal terms, one can define the former as giving each their due according to a given principle of justice, and the latter as indicating that institutions are recognised as rightfully ruling over those to whom they apply. While related, in that the perceived justice of a regime is likely to be a contributing factor to its legitimacy, the one cannot be regarded as providing criteria for the other. Beyond the formal contours of the concept of justice, considerable reasonable disagreement exists as to what giving someone his or her due entails.[20] Different theories of justice, even within the same family of theories—such as Rawls' and Dworkin's respective liberal egalitarian accounts—offer different views of what a person is owed from the state and other citizens. Nevertheless, states have to institute and enforce some view or set of views. The notion of legitimacy enters here. The state's right to rule involves that those subject to it accept its authority. Many criteria might be given for such acceptance, including a historical and cultural identification with a given political community. Within liberal democracies, though, such acceptance has typically rested on the state providing citizens with reasons to believe that it treats them as equals. In the absence of any commonly accepted epistemology capable of giving objective reasons for a given group of people to accept a given set of policies as equitable, these accounts conclude that the available reasons will be those linked to their having participated on equal terms in a political process to determine those policies. Therefore, a legitimate state will need to sustain democratic practices. As a result, the commitment of citizens to a political community takes on an independent weight—it cannot be instrumental to serving ends that it plays an intrinsic part in determining. The grounds for political community will need to be investigated in their own terms, as raising separate normative and empirical conditions to those that might justify their possible reconfiguration or collaboration to tackle issues related to globalisation and justice.

Such considerations prove crucial to any investigation of the current and prospective democratic legitimacy of the EU. They provide the ontological grounds for the 'polity' aspect of the EU, and the degree to which it can be regarded as involving an ever closer union of peoples or the formation of a European people. The rest of this chapter explores the distinctions between an instrumental and an intrinsic political community, on the one side, and between justice and legitimacy, on the other. I shall argue that the legitimacy of particular cosmopolitan conceptions of justice can only be determined by political communities with sufficient intrinsic qualities to be able to support a democratic regime. As a result, the most

---

[19] On this distinction see P Pettit, *On the People's Terms: A Republican Theory and Model of Democracy* (Cambridge, Cambridge University Press, 2012) 130–31; L Valentini, 'Assessing the Global Order: Justice, Legitimacy or Political Justice?' (2012) 15(5) *Critical Review of International Social and Political Philosophy* 593, 594–95.

[20] J Waldron, *Law and Disagreement* (Oxford, Oxford University Press, 1999) 1, 199.

normatively desirable and empirically feasible way of conceiving the EU polity is in what can be called cosmopolitan communitarian terms. Such a political ontology treats the EU as a union of European peoples with a cosmopolitan regard for tackling the problems of a globalising world in ways that mutually support the capacity of these different *demoi* to sustain a democratic political community.

# II. The Communitarian Ghost in the Cosmopolitan Machine

This section outlines more fully than above the normative and empirical strands running through the cosmopolitan and communitarian arguments. As we shall see, these two strands determine the model of the EU each school of thought regards as desirable and feasible respectively. The differences between the two views relate in their turn to the contrasting ways cosmopolitans and communitarians conceive of the relationship of rights and citizenship, on the one hand, to popular and state sovereignty, on the other. Whereas cosmopolitans seek to divorce the former from the latter, communitarians contend the latter necessarily frames the former—a contention we shall link in the next section with the way in which considerations of justice raise in their turn questions of legitimacy.

## A. Cosmopolitan Globalists and Federalists

Following Brian Barry, one can define the normative basis of cosmopolitanism as resting on three elements: that individual human beings have ultimate value; that each individual human being has equal moral value; and that these two conditions apply to all human beings.[21] Most cosmopolitans are keen to distinguish moral from legal and political cosmopolitanism. For example, Charles Beitz has written that 'cosmopolitanism need not make any assumptions at all about the best political structure for international affairs'.[22] However, these claims notwithstanding, cosmopolitans do seek to constrain the ways political institutions, however configured, operate so as to ensure they treat 'every human being' as having 'global stature as an ultimate unit of moral concern'.[23] This argument has taken a number of forms, and is compatible with both a utilitarian and a deontological, rights-based morality, amongst other moral doctrines.

---

[21] B Barry, 'Statism and Nationalism: a Cosmopolitan Critique' in I Shapiro and L Brilmayer (eds), *Nomos: Global Justice* (New York, New York University Press, 1999) 35–36.
[22] C Beitz, 'International Relations, Philosophy of' in E Craig (ed), *The Routledge Encyclopaedia of Philosophy* vol 4 (London, Routledge, 1998) 831.
[23] Pogge, 'Cosmopolitanism and Sovereignty' (n 16) 175.

The significance of this constraint can be seen if one considers what might be ruled out by this approach. Clearly, it rules out valuing people according to features such as their race or gender. Yet it also has been held to rule out a partiality to compatriots or according value to collective entities such as states. The argument goes that being born into a given country is a matter of simple good or bad fortune and as morally arbitrary as having a certain colour or being born into a given class.[24] The difficulty such arguments face is spelling out what exactly they mean in practice.[25] They are held to suggest that we should value all individuals equally, but exactly in what ways—be it through global equality of opportunity, global equality of resources or global equality of some other good—is unclear.

Two reasons explain this difficulty. One reason, explored later in the chapter, is that the significance of particular resources and opportunities is subject to different evaluations within different cultures or in different circumstances, making it hard to make the meaningful comparisons between different societies that are required to decide whether they are equal in some relevant respect or not.[26] The second and related reason is that the claim that all individuals should be treated as moral equals, and the assertion that national belonging is as morally arbitrary as hair colour, does not in itself explain in what ways, if at all, they should be treated equally. As David Miller notes, a person with congenital disabilities suffers from differences that are morally arbitrary, but most would regard this circumstance as providing grounds for special, and hence unequal, treatment that is not morally arbitrary. A substantive reason is needed to show why national belonging is like hair colour rather than disability, and what that entails in practice.[27]

The standard substantive counter-argument for nationality *not* being morally arbitrary in determining the opportunities and resources that are open to people has been that people in national political communities have special relationships to one another that they do not have to others elsewhere. Indeed, a cosmopolitan notion of equal respect might even justify acknowledging that citizens of a community should give priority to equalising the conditions of their co-nationals over equalising conditions between members of different, even very unequal, countries.[28] As a result, some cosmopolitan theorists have wished to suggest that relationships among people at the regional and global level are becoming more like relations between people within nations.

---

[24]  eg C Beitz, 'Cosmopolitan Ideals and National Sentiment' (1983) 80 *Journal of Philosophy* 591, 593, 595; T Pogge, 'An Egalitarian Law of Peoples' (1994) 23 *Philosophy and Public Affairs* 195, 196, 198; S Caney, 'Cosmopolitan Justice and Equalizing Opportunities' (2001) 32 *Metaphilosophy* 113, 115, who argues 'this reasoning is, I believe, either explicitly or implicitly present in almost all defences of cosmopolitanism' (115 fn 3); D Moellendorf, *Cosmopolitan Justice* (Boulder CO, Westview, 2002) 78–80.

[25]  D Miller, 'Against Global Egalitarianism' (2005) 9 *The Journal of Ethics* 55.

[26]  B Boxhill, 'Global Equality of Opportunity and National Integrity' (1987) 5 *Social Philosophy and Policy* 143; Miller, 'Against Global Egalitarianism' (n 25) 60–63.

[27]  Miller (n 25) 68–69.

[28]  RW Miller, 'Cosmopolitan Respect and Patriotic Concern' (1998) 27(3) *Philosophy and Public Affairs* 202.

These considerations in part motivate Pogge's well-known proposal that we should cash out the implications of cosmopolitan morality in institutional rather than interactional terms: as applying to the rules and procedures of certain institutional schemes, rather than as pertaining to the actions of individual persons and agencies.[29] He notes how the interactional case is practically weaker than the institutional in a number of respects. Take the case of rights, from which he argues. The perfect obligations necessary to uphold negative rights of non-interference can be conceptualised in global terms reasonably easily, since in principle at least they are costless and simply require individual forbearance. It is much harder to assign a global responsibility for positive rights to care and welfare that appear to rely on special obligations. Indeed, in the absence of any causal relation for the potential or actual harms involved, it is difficult even to justify positive action to secure negative rights worldwide, through the supply of peace-keeping forces and the like. The institutional view appears to fill this lacuna, since it potentially links us to a whole range of unknown others and provides a duty even to safeguard those negative rights we have not personally violated. The focus here is no longer on the direct relations between individuals, but on the justice of the practices and arrangements within which people are involved and for which they are jointly and severally responsible.

However, this institutional argument is contingent on the possible or actual existence of a global institutional scheme within which we all participate to some significant degree.[30] The socio-political strand of the cosmopolitan argument comes in here. Global socio-economic forces are held to have created a greater degree of interconnectedness within the world than ever before. Technological advances have internationalised production, distribution and exchange and transformed financial markets. Multinational corporations (MNCs), even when they possess a regional or national base, are said to organise their affairs on an international scale and respond to global market pressures. This internationalisation of markets is even more apparent in the financial sector, where new information technology has radically increased the mobility of economic units and to a large degree tied the world's major banking and trading centres into a single integrated network. New communications systems have also rendered ordinary people more aware of these global developments than ever before. The media, according to proponents of this thesis, have altered the 'situational geography' of social and political life by giving people direct access to distant events and creating new experiences, commonalties and frames of meaning that do not require direct physical contact—popular reactions to Tiananmen Square and the plight of the Kurds in the aftermath of the Gulf War being good examples of this phenomenon. A series of common cultural references—from the banality of soap operas through

[29] Pogge (n 16) 176–77. cp, say, with the 'interactionist' argument in S Caney, *Justice Beyond Borders: A Global Political Theory* (Oxford, Oxford University Press, 2005) 78.

[30] The exposition of this thesis in the next three paragraphs derives from Held, *Democracy and the Global Order* (n 1) chs 5 and 6.

to greater popular awareness and knowledge of world events—have allegedly generated new solidarities as evidenced in transnational social movements such as
Greenpeace and Amnesty International.

The above mentioned processes are claimed to have weakened in turn the
capacity of nation-states to provide for the security and welfare of their citizens, and led to the creation of a number of international power blocks, agencies, organisations, regimes and networks to facilitate their continued ability to do
so by managing various areas of transnational activity. These institutions range
from collective security arrangements such as NATO, through a variety of other
intergovernmental bodies of different degrees of formality aimed at controlling
various aspects of economic and social policy. Some are purely technical agencies
and limited in scope, like the Universal Postal Union or the World Meteorological
Association, others more politically contentious organisations with a potentially
profound impact on core domestic policies, such as the IMF and World Bank.
Some constitute international regimes with very broad competences and complex
governance structures, such as the UN, the Council of Europe and the EU, others
more informal global networks, such as the G7. All these organisations modify the
freedom of action of states to one degree or another and undercut their capacity
to operate as sovereign units. Consequently, their title to act as the agents of the
sovereign will of their people has been likewise eroded. Effective decision-making
and the sources of identification has in many cases passed elsewhere, or so at least
it is alleged.

Finally, this move beyond the sovereign nation-state is reflected in the body
of international law that has grown up in the wake of these developments. Here
individuals are gradually replacing states as the main subjects of the law. On the
one hand, it has been recognised that individuals have rights and obligations that
are independent of and go beyond those duties and entitlements they have as citizens of particular states—a point made most strikingly in war crime trials. On the
other hand, the legitimacy of states has come to rest as much on the justice of their
rule as on their de facto hold on power. The post-war international declarations of
rights have reinforced this shift from state to individual, as have challenges to the
notions of 'immunity from jurisdiction' and 'immunity from state agencies' which
have hitherto operated as central principles of international law.

This global positivisation of individual moral rights brings the normative
and empirical strands of the cosmopolitan thesis together. As we saw, it informs
Habermas' view of the EU as a stage towards the embodiment of human rights in
a legally and politically constituted world society. In fact, at least two broad possible views of the EU can follow from this perspective. One version holds that the
forces described above have undermined the nation-state, but that a centralised
federal Europe, that is itself not unlike a nation-state writ large, can fill the gap.[31]

---

[31]  eg Duff, *Federal Union Now* (n 12).

Another, more truly cosmopolitan, version is not so much supranational as post-national in orientation,[32] viewing moves towards federalism as an alternative to, rather than a new form of, the unitary sovereign state.[33] By and large, political scientists—especially those of a functionalist disposition—have been drawn towards the first position. They have advocated the strengthening of the Union's supranational features—particularly the European Parliament and the Commission—and the phasing out of intergovernmentalism, and have welcomed the move towards common policies in the spheres of domestic justice and foreign affairs in addition to economic and social matters.[34] Lawyers, by contrast, have been the principal advocates of the second position. They have drawn inspiration from the gradual development of a single legal framework by the Court of Justice of the European Union (CJEU), noting with approval its increasing tendency to appeal to human rights and its claims of Supremacy over the domestic law of Member States and Direct Effect with regard to their citizens.[35] Needless to say, the reality falls far short of either version of the cosmopolitan ideal—a fact that communitarians are not slow in pointing out.

## B. Communitarians, Liberal and Civic Nationalists and the Sovereignty of States

Communitarians question both the normative and empirical aspects of the cosmopolitan thesis. With regard to the normative aspect, they dispute the global egalitarianism of the cosmopolitan case. That does not mean that they do not believe there are great injustices that arise from huge disparities in wealth between rich and poor countries and that these ought to be diminished. However, these disparities need not be decried on global egalitarian grounds. Among other reasons, they can be criticised as facilitating the domination of some states by others.

---

[32] eg JH Ferry, 'Une "philosophie" de la communaute' in JH Ferry and P Thibaud (eds), *Discussion sur l'Europe* (Paris, Calmann-Levy, 1992) 179–89; J Habermas, *The Inclusion of the Other* (Cambridge, Polity, 1999) 105–27 and, more generally, *The Postnational Constellation* (Cambridge, Polity, 2000).

[33] O Beaud, 'La Fédération entre l'état et l'empire' in B Théret (ed), *L'État, la finance et le sociale* (Paris, La Decouverte, 1995).

[34] S George, *Policy and Politics in the European Community* 2nd edn (Oxford, Oxford University Press, 1991); RO Keohane and S Hoffman, 'Institutional Change in Europe in the 1980s' in RO Keohane and S Hoffman (eds), *The New European Community: Decision Making and Institutional Change* (Boulder and Oxford, Westview Press, 1991); EO Eriksen, *The Unfinished Democratization of Europe* (Oxford, Oxford University Press, 2009).

[35] eg GF Mancini, 'The Making of a Constitution for Europe' (1989) 26 *Common Market Law Review* 595, D Kostakopoulou, *The Future Governance of Citizenship* (Cambridge, Cambridge University Press, 2008), Armin von Bogdandy, 'The European Lesson for International Democracy: The Significance of Articles 9-12 EU Treaty for International Organizations' (2012) 23(2) *European Journal of International Law* 315, For the contrast between the legal and political science paradigms, see JHH Weiler, UR Haltern and FC Mayer, 'European Democracy and its Critique' in J Haywood (ed), *The Crisis of Representation in Europe* (London, Frank Cass, 1995) 24–33; D Wincott, 'Political Theory, Law and European Union' in J Shaw and G More (eds), *New Legal Dynamics of European Union* (Oxford, Clarendon Press, 1995).

Rather, what communitarians object to is the coherence of pursuing policies that accord intrinsic value to reducing equality according to some metric, such as resources or opportunities, between individuals across the globe.

As we noted above, such metrics prove impossible to operationalise because they are interpreted differently within different cultural contexts. Take the notion of equal opportunity, understood as granting individuals of similar talents and motivations an equal chance to achieve certain positions regardless of which state they come from. Assuming that not all political communities have been merged, so that the provisions available worldwide are identical in all respects, this principle must mean that individuals in different countries have equivalent opportunities. Within nation-states agreement is reached on certain sorts of resource and opportunities being important, and rough equivalents exist to match regional variations. Equal access to sporting opportunities may be thought important, say, but that can mean cricket pitches in England and rugby pitches in Wales, for example. But when one makes cross-national and cultural comparisons, the exercise becomes much more complicated. For the priorities may be very different. The measure of a good education in country A may not be the same as in country B—they value different skills and operate in different contexts.[36]

Of course, there are also differences of opinion within national communities. However, there is an overarching social context within which they can be debated. The ways we view each other as equals is a function of the character of the society and the culture in which we live, and the goods we share.[37] Therefore, the crucial factor is that we possess political equality in deciding and deliberating on the shape of that shared culture. A link is thereby established between national, popular and state sovereignty. Nationality defines a common political culture and identity that has developed historically through democratic control being tied to a state in ways that allow a people to determine for themselves the relevant ways they are alike and unalike, and so deserving of equal or different treatment within the public sphere.[38]

Communitarians also contest the second, empirical, element of cosmopolitanism, questioning both the degree and consequences of the processes of globalisation and interconnectedness. It is possible to dispute, for example, the extent to which MNCs truly operate at a transnational level. As Hirst, Thompson and Bromley have shown,[39] core capital, basic Research and Development, and management personnel and structures are mostly located within a main national base. The various political bodies and non-governmental agencies that have developed to cope with global problems of security and welfare tend to be inter-national and inter-governmental rather than supranational. The UN, for example, far from

[36] See Miller (n 25) 61–63.

[37] M Walzer, 'Philosophy and Democracy' (1981) 9(3) *Political Theory* 379.

[38] Miller, *On Nationality* (n 8) ch 4; M Walzer, *Spheres of Justice: A Defence of Pluralism and Equality* (Oxford, Martin Robertson, 1983) 28–29.

[39] P Hirst, G Thompson and S Bromley, *Globalisation in Question* 3rd edn (Cambridge, Polity, 2009).

representing a nascent form of cosmopolitan governance, as is sometimes argued,[40] remains very much an instrument of the sovereign states which compose it—not least the superpowers, whose hold on the Security Council effectively blocks any move that might damage their interests.[41] Indeed, the major powers' effective control over the purse strings enables them to manipulate most important, and hence costly, initiatives requiring inter-state cooperation, and to stop those that do not meet with their approval—witness the sabotaging of UNESCO by Britain and the United States.[42] More generally, the evidence that economic globalisation has rendered the capacity of governments and states to make autonomous decisions that impact on the welfare of their citizens seem open to question. The share of global GDP consumed by states has never been greater, with state income expenditure actually positively correlated with economic openness rather than the other way round.[43]

Cosmopolitans also are said to overlook the differential impact of global forces on different countries and the imbalances in the degree and nature of the interdependence that they create. By and large the wealthier and more powerful nations are net beneficiaries from global market forces, for example, whilst poorer states are either locked out of many of the networks or are subordinate partners and often damaged by global trade, becoming sources of cheap labour and resources, rather than developing strong economies of their own. Global environmental, health, security and other dangers that are no respecters of state borders are said to bind the peoples of the world together as sharing a common fate. However, they rarely affect all of them to an equal extent. When joint actions have shared consequences, such as the depletion of fish stocks, then cooperative action may be possible, although here too the standard free rider problems that arise with all public goods and bads mean that many countries will attempt to evade their responsibilities. Because the advantages and disadvantages are not usually mutual even with shared activities or problems, the incentives for cooperative behaviour are usually lopsided.[44] Even within the EU, the substantial differences in economic performance, social standards and political interests between the Member States has rendered the formulation of common policies far from easy. Britain's acrimonious attempts to reduce the massive financial transfers to other EU states via the Common Agricultural Policy reflect a genuine problem, which potentially weakens the commitment to the Union of all the main contributors.[45] The differential

---

[40] Held (n 1) pt IV.

[41] D Zolo, *Cosmopolis: La prospettiva del governo mondiale* (Milan, Feltrinelli, 1995) 27–28.

[42] RJB Jones, 'The United Nations and the International Political System' in D Bourantonis and J Weiner (eds), *The United Nations in the New World Order: The World Organization at Fifty* (Basingstoke, Macmillan, 1995).

[43] C Hay, *Why we Hate Politics* (Cambridge, Polity, 2007) ch 4.

[44] RJB Jones, *Globalisation and Interdependence in the International Political Economy: Rhetoric and Reality* (London and New York, Pinter, 1995) 75–77.

[45] Hirst, Thompson and Bromley, *Globalisation in Question* (n 39) ch 7; RJB Jones, 'The Economic Agenda' in G Wyn Rees (ed), *International Politics in Europe: The New Agenda* (London and New York, Routledge, 1993).

impact of the crisis within the Eurozone has revealed this problem in even more dramatic fashion, most notably in the ongoing tensions between the creditor and the debtor states.

Although states do form blocs for certain limited purposes, it is also important to note that these often have the goal of preserving state autonomy rather than diminishing it. Alan Milward's account of the former European Community as a 'rescue' of the nation-state is highly pertinent in this respect.[46] The EU emerges from this analysis as being, in part at least, a reaction against the forces of globalisation. Although the EU has drawn increasing criticism from those of a social democratic persuasion for promoting neo-liberal market policies that undermine domestic welfare and social corporatist measures,[47] it has aroused parallel criticism from neo-liberal defenders of the free market on account of the Social Chapter, environmental and similar regulation.[48] Arguably both views underestimate the EU's responsiveness to domestic political pressures in both directions, and the degree to which the core policies involving high government expenditure—social welfare provision, defence, education, culture and infrastructure—have hitherto remained outside its remit.[49]

For related reasons, more homogeneous consumption patterns and a greater awareness of world affairs has not necessarily produced as much convergence in political identity amongst the general population as cosmopolitans assert. People distinguish a humanitarian concern with famine or other disasters in countries other than their own from the sort of formalised responsibilities they have for co-nationals. They may support initiatives such as Band Aid or give to Oxfam, but that is a long way from condoning increased taxation to expand the development aid budget, say. Television, social media, faster communication systems, greater job mobility and the like, may have broadened people's horizons in certain respects and encouraged them to identify with a wider community, but the identification may not be as deep as the solidarities of old, based as they were on continuous, direct contact and personal involvement.

Just as I distinguished two different versions of the cosmopolitan ideal with regard to the EU, so two broad positions can be associated with communitarian thinking. On the one hand, there are conservative Eurosceptics of the British variety who think in terms of narrow national interests and conceive the nation in quasi-ethnic terms, resulting in a particularly hard line position on immigration for example. On the other hand, there are 'liberal' and civic nationalists. These can be more social democratic in ideology and influenced by republican notions

---

[46] A Milward, *The European Rescue of the Nation-State* (London and New York, Routledge, 1992).

[47] F Scharpf, 'Legitimacy in the Multilevel European Polity' (2009) 1 *European Political Science Review* 173.

[48] J Rabkin, *Why Sovereignty Matters* (Washington, DC, AEI Press, 1998).

[49] A Moravscik, 'Is there a Democratic Deficit in World Politics? A Framework for Analysis' (2004) 39(2) *Government and Opposition* 351.

linking patriotism with democratic participation, as in the French tradition.[50] For different reasons, both groups will be reluctant to see a dilution of the intergovernmental character of the EU. However, whilst the first would dispute any shift in a federalist direction, the second merely argue that until such time as a global identity and public culture develops, moral weight has to be given to the self-determination of different peoples. Attempts to force the pace will be seen as unjustified, but certain moves of a cosmopolitan kind are possible—even if the total transcendence of the nation-state remains highly unlikely.[51]

## C. Two Views of Rights, Citizenship, Democracy and Sovereignty

Cosmopolitans and communitarians hold two different views of the nature of rights, citizenship, democracy and sovereignty and the ways they relate to each other. These differences partly reflect in their turn the contrast between an instrumental and an intrinsic view of political community noted earlier.

Cosmopolitans see rights as essentially self-standing. Their justification is independent of their recognition by any given society or culture and do not rely on democratic endorsement for their validity. Their scope and application is uniform and universal with individuals as their subjects. Citizenship and sovereignty are regarded as potentially antithetical to rights to the extent they link rights to membership of an already existing state rather than regarding them as attributes of human beings as such. Rather, than being the source of rights, citizenship and sovereignty need to be refashioned to reflect rights.[52]

Democracy plays an important role in this refashioning. On this account, democracy follows from a right to an equal opportunity for political participation.[53] Where and with whom that right is exercised, and over what, should be matters of individual choice constrained by feasibility criteria. Thus, Pogge suggests that political units can be shaped and reshaped by a majority or supermajority of the inhabitants of contiguous territories provided the new and any remaining units remain viable and 'of reasonable shape', while any subgroups can reject membership of the new unit, form their own or merge with some other unit subject to these same criteria.[54] At the same time, he advocates the vertical dispersal of sovereignty across a number of governance levels, from the international to the local. Again, rather loose, largely functional, criteria govern this dispersal of decision-making power. On the one hand, inclusiveness favours a centralisation of power,

---

[50] P Thibaud, 'L'Europe par les nations (et réciproquement)' in Ferry and Thibaud (eds), *Discussion sur l'Europe* (n 32). Although see Miller, *On Nationality* (n 8) for a British version, especially ch 6.

[51] D Miller, 'Republicanism, National Identity and Europe' in C Laborde and J Maynor (eds), *Republicanism and Political Theory* (Oxford, Blackwell, 2008).

[52] Pogge (n 16) 184; J Carens, 'Aliens and Citizens: The Case for Open Borders' (1987) 49(2) *Review of Politics* 251.

[53] Pogge (n 16) 191.

[54] ibid 196–97.

so that all significantly affected by decisions may be included. On the other hand, effective and equal participation in decision-making favours the decentralisation of power, so that individuals have the time, knowledge and opportunities to influence the social and political conditions that most immediately shape their lives.[55] He regards the EU's system of multi-level governance as partly reflecting such a democratic vertical dispersal of sovereign power, with the reconfiguration of its constituent political units the natural next step.[56]

Such moves depend on the 'regime' features of a political system, its system of governance, being separable from its 'polity' features, the way a people and certain functions are defined as being governed by a given 'regime'. Cosmopolitans contend a variety of different transnational and supranational democratic decision-making processes can emerge that are respected simply because they reflect cosmopolitan norms. Such norms can be grounded in international law, particularly human rights law. Indeed, Habermas argues this is already the case within the EU. He notes how the CJEU claims 'competence-competence' to decide issues of European law and their impact on the Member States but has no power to enforce its decisions other than through the courts and administrative bodies of those same states. Many of those decisions, such as those relating to Union citizenship, establish transnational rights for individuals, including political rights to participate in EU elections wherever they reside. He regards this development as part of the process whereby law and democracy have become detached from state sovereignty, understood as a monopoly of coercive power over a given territory. Instead, he contends CJEU decisions are accepted because they are 'right'.[57]

By contrast to this position, communitarians regard rights as being framed and upheld by citizenship and sovereignty. Given rights need to be interpreted and enforced, their security requires some agency that can do so in assured and impartial ways. That proves particularly true of property rights, which are partly conventional.[58] All rights but especially those property rights that are in land create the need for a territorially based sovereign power. This power must possess a monopoly of coercive force not only within its borders but without them, in order stabilise the system of rights, including those of property ownership, and defend them against incursions from other powers.

Two consequences follow from the way sovereignty serves to define a 'polity' and the associated rights of its members. The first consequence is that so long as an individual's rights depend for their specification and protection on being subject to a territorially based sovereign political unit, then it will not be possible to fully stipulate those rights without reference to the individual's territorial affiliation in at least some instances. For example, with regard to issues of war and peace,

---

[55] ibid 184, 186, 191–95.
[56] ibid 301 fn 282, 304 fn 386; T Pogge 'Creating Supra-National Institutions Democratically: Reflections on the European Union's Democratic Deficit' (1997) 5(2) *Journal of Political Philosophy* 163.
[57] Habermas, Crisis of the European Union (n 3) 23–28.
[58] A Stilz, *Liberal Loyalty: Freedom, Obligation and the State* (Princeton, Princeton University Press, 2009) 34–44.

the individual right to self-defence will be modified to involve the right to retaliate against an invading enemy army and—to the extent their activities support that army—the civilian population of an enemy.[59] Note that the liberally minded statist communitarian does not dispute that individuals are in the ultimate analysis the holders of rights, on that point they agree with cosmopolitans, merely that the holding and exercise of these rights arise in the context of a specific political unit.

The second consequence follows from the first, in that the basis, nature and limits of an individual's obligations towards this unit become a key issue from this perspective. Communitarians contend that coercive institutions must operate on terms that make sense to those subject to them.[60] If political institutions are to operate in non-arbitrary ways they must appear acceptable to all reasonable citizens as reflecting the public political culture of the society concerned. Within these accounts, a political society cannot be regarded simply as a voluntary association of convenience among a group of individuals that are sufficiently co-located, numerous and wealthy for their being members of the same political unit to be plausible in functional terms. These individuals must relate to each other in ways that make them a 'people'.[61] A people of the requisite kind arises in part from having certain shared interests through participating in what Rawls called 'a cooperative venture for mutual advantage'.[62] In other words, their interactions and dependence on each other have a certain intensity of a kind that gives them a roughly equal stake in the collective good of the political society. Yet, as important in shaping their social cooperation as shared interests are shared ideas or a set of common reasons about the appropriate ways to order the collective organisation of their affairs.

Neither shared interests nor shared ideas imply a lack of conflict about either. Merely that a basis exists for a people to reach agreement or agree to disagree through fair and equitable democratic procedures. Communitarians conceive democratic decision-making as being as much about deliberation on the common good as a mechanism for the aggregation of individual interests. They contend that for democratic processes to possess this quality they must operate among a people or *demos* possessing the two qualities described above. The sense of a common fate and purposes promoted by mutually beneficial reciprocal interactions help facilitate compromise and the avoidance of a purely self-regarding stance. As a result, minorities are more disposed to accept majority decisions, for example, and, perhaps most importantly, majorities to take into account the opinions and concerns of minorities rather than excluding them altogether.[63]

---

[59] L Wenar, 'Why Rawls is not a Cosmopolitan Egalitarian' in R Martin and DA Reidy (eds), *Rawls's Law of Peoples: A Realistic Utopia?* (Oxford, Blackwell, 2006) 108–09.

[60] eg Walzer, *Spheres of Justice* (n 38) 28–29.

[61] See Pettit's analysis of the 'ontology of the people' in J Rawls, *The Law of Peoples* (Cambridge, MA, Harvard University Press, 1999): P Pettit, 'Rawls's Peoples' in R Martin and DA Reidy (eds), *Rawls's Law of Peoples: A Realistic Utopia?* (Oxford, Blackwell, 2006) 41.

[62] J Rawls, *A Theory of Justice* (Oxford, Oxford University Press, 1971) 4.

[63] Miller (n 8) 96–99; Miller 'Democracy's Domain' (n 18).

Democracy so conceived operates as a forum of principle.[64] The interests and values of diverse groups can be expressed on an equal basis, and the implications of different claims and views placed in the context of the whole range of policies being undertaken by the government and the wider needs and wishes of citizens. For example, conflicting accounts of rights can be weighed and balanced against each other in ways that show equal concern and respect for the individual autonomy of others. So too can different conceptions of social justice that seek to determine what is owed to who by whom, and in which circumstances. The crucial factor, though, comes from these collective decisions being perceived by those on all sides of the argument as somehow 'theirs'—as decisions made in common because those involved are more or less equally affected by the totality of the outcomes, if not each and every decision; draw on a common stock of norms when discussing and evaluating them, even if they disagree about their respective weighting and interpretation; and possess a degree of mutual solidarity as fellow citizens in a shared social enterprise.[65]

It is no accident that the two paradigmatic examples of constitution-making, namely France and the United States in the eighteenth-century, were simultaneously instances of state- and nation-building as well. In the terminology I have been using, the polity dimensions stemming from state sovereignty and a people provided the context for establishing a regime characterised by democracy and the rule of law. Law and democracy cannot boot-strap and provide the source of their own polity conditions. They imply a people who are entitled to make and enforce decisions within a given domain. As a result, the communitarian ghost always lurks within the cosmopolitan machine.

When rights and obligations are nested within particular political communities in this way, their cosmopolitan reach will be affected. To the extent that our understanding of basic rights is coloured by the culture of our community, there are likely to be conflicts between the priorities and publicly recognised needs of different societies. State support for certain religions or languages may be important in some communities and regarded as illegitimate in others, for example. Even when the same rights are acknowledged, variations in local context may lead them to being interpreted and balanced in contrasting and not always compatible ways. In addition, there will be a feeling that 'charity begins at home' that will set limits on how much people will commit themselves to helping outsiders when that clashes with programmes, also motivated by rights considerations, of a domestic character. Thus, communitarians regard it as legitimate that a more generous national social security system, say, might be established at the cost of less spending on foreign aid overseas.[66]

---

[64] Walzer, 'Philosophy and Democracy' (n 37).

[65] eg M Sandel, 'The Political Theory of the Procedural Republic' in G Bryner and N Reynolds (eds), *Constitutionalism and Rights* (Provo, UT, Brigham Young University Press, 1987).

[66] Miller (n 8) ch 3 and 100–03; D Miller, *National Responsibility and Global Justice* (Oxford, Oxford University Press, 2007).

Support for national and state sovereignty need not entail a view of international relations as an anarchic and amoral Hobbesian state of nature. Claims to self-determination for one group imply recognition of similar rights by others—including non-aggression and limited aid.[67] To the extent that global interdependence does link states within institutional networks, then they will have the sorts of obligations cosmopolitans advocate. Nonetheless, the absence of agreed metrics as to the value of resources or the relative worth of various rights and liberties will make arguments for a global redistribution of goods and services hard to cash out in practice—especially as such schemes can conflict with as well as support the autonomy of national political communities. Still, it is reasonable to suppose that globalisation will produce forms of inter-state cooperation in those areas such as defence, the environment and the economy where the capacity of states to act in autonomous ways has been seriously impaired. International law and organisations emerge from this account as an international regime that presupposes the existence of polities that have the capacity to represent and act for their peoples. The EU simply provides a particularly significant and developed form of such international cooperation. However, these cooperative schemes should be regarded as mechanisms for preserving rather than undermining national interests and self-determination, with transfers of decision-making power being largely conditional on the extent to which involvement in the relevant international body makes that possible.[68]

## III. Justice and Legitimacy

So far I have presented the two models in ways that accentuate their differences. They seem divided along two main, if related, dimensions. On the one hand, cosmopolitans argue for the global application of egalitarian theories of justice, whereas communitarians deny this possibility and insist that such theories can only apply within a political community of the kind that does not exist at the global level. On the other hand, cosmopolitans contend that international law provides the basis for a transnational democratic regime divorced from any given polity and that separates popular from state sovereignty. By contrast, communitarians contend that a democratic and legal regime is necessarily embedded within a polity that combines national and state sovereignty, and that international law is consequently inter-state rather than cosmopolitan law. As we have seen, these two models give rise in their turn to quite different images of the EU. Whereas the first suggests it provides a new kind of post-, trans-, or supranational regime without a polity, the second suggests that it must either develop polity-like characteristics or remain an essentially intergovernmental regime.

---

[67] Rawls, *Law of Peoples* (n 61).
[68] Miller (n 8) 104–08.

In this section, I wish to suggest that in one respect these two models are complementary and can be—indeed, need to be—combined, in ways that I shall explore in the concluding section. This complementarity arises from the two models applying different but related standards to the global order, the one stemming from justice and the other from legitimacy. Cosmopolitans tend to fold the second into the first, communitarians the first into the second. However, each requires the other. As we noted above, justice indicates the moral entitlements of individuals, and hence what they are owed by others and more especially by the political institutions to which they must submit. By contrast, legitimacy concerns not what individuals are entitled to but rather what entitles political institutions to rule or exercise power over them. These are distinct standards. Egalitarians may regard a political system, such as that of most Member States, as failing to meet certain standards of justice, falling short of their preferred criteria for establishing equal opportunity, for example, and still accept it as legitimate on other grounds.

One way of construing this distinction is to view justice and legitimacy as involving different kinds of equality of respect.[69] Justice requires that individuals are treated as *substantively* equal in some respect, be it with regard to access to opportunities, resources or, more minimally, and in a way that need not be egalitarian except in largely formal terms, with regard to certain basic rights. Legitimacy requires that individuals are treated as *procedurally* equal in some respect, maximally in each consenting to a given arrangement, more minimally in each having an equal say in influencing and accepting it. Both forms of procedural equality can be realised via some form of democratic process.

We saw how certain cosmopolitan theories treat legitimacy as a sub-category of justice. On this account, a system is legitimate to the extent that it satisfies certain minimum substantive distributive standards, including those required for the exercise of certain procedural rights. Moreover, a system becomes illegitimate to the extent democratic procedures violated these basic standards, which thereby need to be locked in through a legal constitution capable of trumping democratic decision-making. Yet treating legitimacy as a component of justice raises a number of problems. For example, how are we to distinguish those elements of justice that provide the threshold for legitimacy from those that are either unnecessary or insufficient to generate it? And does that mean that democratic decision-making that respects that threshold ought to be accepted as just, even if the decision itself is in other respects unjust?

Developing an argument of Jeremy Waldron, Laura Valentini has proposed a resolution of this puzzle via a distinction between the 'circumstances of justice' and the 'circumstances of legitimacy';[70] the latter reflecting what Waldron refers to more broadly as the 'circumstances of politics'.[71] As Rawls, following Hume, noted, the 'circumstances of justice' indicate the need for a collective distributive rule in a condition of moderate scarcity, so not everybody can have everything they want,

---

[69] Valentini, 'Assessing the Global Order' (n 19).
[70] ibid 598.
[71] Waldron, *Law and Disagreement* (n 20) 159–60.

and limited altruism, so all cannot be expected to spontaneously honour their obligations to others where required to do so.[72] However, as Waldron pointed out, we perforce must reach agreement on a just distributive rule in circumstances of pervasive disagreement about justice and, it might be added, uncertainty and fallibility in implementing any rule we may agree on. Putting the two together, one can say that while justice requires we acknowledge that human beings have rights and deserve equal treatment, legitimacy requires that we have an equal say when collectively deciding on which rights and what kind of equality are appropriate for us and apply to given cases.

The circumstances of justice and the circumstances of legitimacy prove mutually supporting. Legitimacy entails standards of justice, yet given disagreement over these standards they likewise entail legitimacy. Or to put it in other terms, claims to substantive equality must be both raised and agreed upon within, while also being presupposed by, processes that enshrine procedural equality. If justice and, given ought implies can, feasibility provide what might be called the 'objective' normative and empirical conditions for any political arrangement, then legitimacy offers their 'subjective' normative and empirical conditions—it provides the ways these notions of justice and feasibility make sense to those to whom they apply. In the absence of any clear epistemology to ground our different ontological claims, the two must always go hand in hand. As a result, a political order must relate issues of justice and legitimacy at both the 'polity' and 'regime' dimension as is summarised in Figure 1 below:[73]

| | Legitimacy | Polity (Sphere and Subjects) | Regime (Scope and Styles) |
|---|---|---|---|
| a)<br>b) | socially accepted norms<br>authorisation by (usually indirect) consent | Political identification amongst subjects and between them and a particular power centre as having authority within a given sphere (be it territorial, functional or both)<br>As in plebiscites and referendums over such issues as secession | Institutions recognise ideals, interests and identities of governed<br>Collective decisions seen as authoritative because involve mutual recognition |
| **Justice** | | | |
| a)<br>b) | procedural—established rules<br>substantive—freedom, justice, efficiency/benefits | De jure compatible with international law<br>Viable, existence does not entail oppression of outsiders | Legality—a regular system of governance/not arbitrary<br>Not oppressive, unjust or incompetent |

**Figure 1: The Relations of Justice and Legitimacy**

[72] Rawls, *A Theory of Justice* (n 61) 126–30.

[73] This figure, and the argument supporting it, is adapted from R Bellamy and D Castiglione, 'Legitimising the Euro-polity and its Regime: The Normative Turn in EU Studies' (2003) 2(1) *European Journal of Political Theory* 7.

Relating this discussion to the earlier contrast between cosmopolitanism and communitarianism, we can see how the two are similarly linked. The first refers to the global circumstances of justice, the second to the national and state-bound circumstances of legitimacy. The former raises issues of justice and of feasibility that provide the normative and empirical requirements on any political system operating in global circumstances. The latter concerns the ways in which people relate to these requirements. A corollary of this linkage is that the attempt to make cosmopolitan norms the basis of a self-validating regime operating outside any given polity will not work. A regime cannot be accepted simply because it promotes justice and efficiency because both of those issues will be in play within any decision-making process. The issue will be for whom and for which purposes are certain issues to be judged just and efficient, and by what process is agreement to be reached. As a result, cosmopolitanism cannot transcend communitarianism—rather cosmopolitanism always implies a communitarian framework within which issues of justice and legitimacy can be related. It remains to be seen how the two may come together, both in general and in the context of the EU.

# IV.  A Cosmopolitan Communitarianism?

As we have seen, it is mistaken to regard the cosmopolitan and the communitarian arguments as totally at odds with each other, with the latter anti-liberal, anti-rights and anti-individualist, as certain commentators have claimed.[74] Rather, they offer contrasting but to some degree compatible accounts of how we should think about individuality, rights and their relationship to the political societies that embody them. My claim will be that cosmopolitan morality only makes sense to the extent that it is embedded within a communitarian framework: a position I dub cosmopolitan communitarianism.

In the last section I suggested that communitarianism supported the processes of legitimation needed to generate and justify agreement to cosmopolitan norms of justice. This argument follows from a more general point, whereby norms of justice need to be embedded in a social and moral context that reflects a web of mutual relations. As we saw, Pogge's interactional approach partly reflects this circumstance. But these interactions consist not just of shared practices but also shared understandings about the nature of those practices.

Following Michael Walzer, one can characterise the difference between the two schools of thought in terms of a distinction between 'thick' and 'thin' moralities.[75] In his terms, universal human rights represent a 'thin', 'minimal' morality that all societies ought to uphold. But they do so in numerous 'thick', 'maximal' ways.

---

[74]  eg S Holmes, *The Anatomy of Antiliberalism* (Cambridge, Harvard University Press, 1993).

[75]  M Walzer, *Thick and Thin: Moral Argument at Home and Abroad* (Notre Dame, University of Notre Dame Press, 1994) esp ch 1.

Moreover, the individual rights bearers are similarly contextually defined. That is not to deny value-individualism, as is sometimes implied, but it is to reject those versions of methodological individualism that ignore the social dimension of personal identity and the development of autonomy.[76] According to this thicker, more communitarian, view of rights and the individual, a pure cosmopolitanism offers an inadequate account of moral agency. For the cosmopolitan, universalist agents are supposed to act on the basis of rational considerations of pure principle that abstract from their sense of identity as persons holding certain convictions and possessing particular attachments. By contrast, the cosmopolitan communitarian believes that both the principles and the moral motivations and character of those who follow them need to be fleshed out with natural sentiments and 'thick' concepts such as courage, honesty, gratitude and benevolence that arise out of specific ways of life.

On its own, cosmopolitanism cannot generate the full range of obligations its advocates generally wish to ascribe to it. For the proper acknowledgement of 'thin' basic rights rests on their being specified and overlaid by a 'thicker' web of special obligations. Welfare states, for example, have typically arisen in societies where there are strong feelings of social solidarity. These reinforce the formal obligations that arise from being members of an institutionalised scheme of political cooperation as citizens of the same state. Essentially, they create a sense of identification amongst a given group of people between whom it comes to be felt both legitimate and plausible that collectively binding decisions about the distribution of burdens and benefits should take place. That sense of commonness does not determine what its precise implications or content should be, but it does provide the basis on which such determination takes place. It defines the *demos*, as it were, for whom a form of democratic rule appears appropriate and plausible and among whom a process giving each an equal say in overcoming their disagreements has come to be understood as both legitimate and legitimising.

Nationalism has traditionally provided the ideological glue necessary to define a relatively circumscribed group of people and unify them around a set of shared institutions and practices that were sovereign over a well-defined territory. Political loyalty, accountability and legitimacy were tied in this way to state power and authority. Indeed, nationality was typically the creation of states and political elites seeking to consolidate their hold over their populations. Cosmopolitans deny the necessity and desirability of such attachments. They may, as Thomas Pogge does, grant them a certain empirical weight but not any moral significance. A mixture of voluntarist and utilitarian considerations of a broadly functional kind provide the only normatively relevant considerations so far as people's obligations to any particular polity are concerned.[77] By contrast, the earlier sketch of the communitarian argument suggested that largely unchosen commonalties of history, belief,

---

[76] See Tamir, *Liberal Nationalism* (n 8) ch 1 for a criticism of such views.
[77] AJ Simmons, *Moral Principles and Political Obligation* (Princeton, Princeton University Press, 1979).

geography and civic culture *do have* an ethical relevance. They supply the feelings of reciprocity, trust and commitment needed to supplement the ties of mere mutual advantage that result from individuals acting on the basis of rational self-interest alone. Such moral qualities have an important influence on the character of political life, since they increase people's willingness to engage in cooperative behaviour by raising their expectations and confidence in others. As David Miller has argued,[78] far from encouraging self-interested and partial behaviour, the lessening of the tension between personal and collective goals within a group is likely to make an impartial stance more acceptable.

What are the implications of this analysis for the EU? Figure 2 explores four possible combinations:[79]

|  | COMMUNITARIANISM | COSMOPOLITANISM |
| --- | --- | --- |
| COSMOPOLITAN | **Cosmopolitan Communitarianism** A civic Europe of multiple communities involving variable geometry | **Cosmopolitan Globalism** World market, international law based on human rights. Post national federalism Functional parcelling out of sovereignty (Exists in both social liberal and libertarian versions) |
| COMMUNITARIAN | **Civic/Ethnic Nationalism** Strong nationalists of various kinds, whose civic attitudes are predominantly to those of their variously described national groups. Include Eurosceptics, on the one hand, and supranationalists seeking a European nationalism, on the other. | **Communitarian Cosmopolitanism** Supranational federalism European civic nation |

**Figure 2: The Political Ontology of the EU**

These positions can be characterised as 'ideal types' and each of them involves both pro- and more sceptical and even anti-EU positions. I have suggested that the rival theories occupying the top right hand (pure cosmopolitan) box cannot legitimate and validate their various claims to justice, or even sustain the relationships needed

---

[78] Miller (n 8) Ch 2.
[79] This figure is adapted from R Bellamy and D Castiglione, 'Debate: Lacroix's European Constitutional Patriotism: A Response' (2004) 52 *Political Studies* 187.

to support their particular accounts of just relations. The normative aspect of the cosmopolitan argument will only go beyond a 'thin' humanitarian concern for others to the extent we live in a relatively 'thick' cosmopolitan civil society with a corresponding public culture.

That leaves three possibilities. We may characterise these as involving (moving anticlockwise from the bottom left, pure communitarian, box): (1) a Europe of separate, independent democratic nation-states, characterised by ethnic nationalism (or an ethnic national Europe of a similar autarchic nature vis-à-vis the rest of the world, although this is more a theoretical than a real possibility); (2) a civic European nation based around supranationalism (the communitarian cosmopolitan vision); or (3) (moving to the top left, cosmopolitan communitarian box) a civic Europe that operates as a Union of nation-states and involves a degree of variable geometry combined with a fair amount of consensus on central issues and even certain elements of a common identity.

Once again these models combine empirical and normative aspects and so can be evaluated for their plausibility and desirability. The first need not be undesirable, though there are xenophobic versions that are. It potentially allows for a degree of pluralism among states, that respects cultural differences between and self-determination within them, yet allows for global inequalities that a cosmopolitan egalitarian would deplore. Per se that need not pose a problem of justice if each of these states respects rights and democracy, substantive and procedural equality, for all their citizens along the lines defended here. The difficulty arises from the fact that this model assumes a degree of homogeneity within these states and a lack of connection between them that is implausible in today's globalised and multicultural societies. Interdependence may not have completely subverted state autonomy, as some globalists contend, but they have undeniably weakened it. Not only do the decisions of states impact on the decision-making capacity of other states in numerous ways, but also so do the transnational activities of numerous non-state actors, from organised crime to large corporations and financial institutions.

The second assumes a degree of internal cohesion and identification at the EU level—a commonality of values and of interests—that I have doubted exists or is likely to exist. The neo-functionalist federalist line greatly overestimates the integrative potential of global forces and the capacity of people to transfer their allegiances. However, as, if not more important, than these potentially superable empirical objections is the normative objection to the loss involved in diminishing the capacity for people to determine their own lives in the light of a shared culture and history. As we saw, such values prove important in legitimising the common agreements and solidarity on which implementing justice depends.

That leaves the third position. This position involves a rejection not only of an unqualified cosmopolitan globalism and universalism, but also of the centralised federalist version of the cosmopolitan argument and the Eurosceptical version of the communitarian case. The cosmopolitan communitarian position involves civic nations demonstrating civic attitudes not only internally but also to a greater or lesser extent externally, with basic ʻthin' cosmopolitan sentiments thickening in various ways depending on the nature and degree of their interaction and involvement with other nations and even international allegiances possibly developing in some instances. The civic nation variant of the communitarian argument is extended in this way to accommodate aspects of both the globalisation thesis and a universal cosmopolitan morality, whilst denying the normative desirability or empirical possibility of a European, let alone a global, civic nation. As I have argued elsewhere,[80] it allows for an 'ever closer union of European peoples', including the development of common political and economic institutions. Yet these are best conceived not as supranational but as inter-national, delegated authorities, and under their equal and shared control.[81]

A detailed outline of the institutional arrangements or regime that follow from this model lies outside the scope of this chapter.[82] Here I have simply sought to define the ontological 'polity' conditions of an EU that is capable of uniting the claims of global justice and functional requirements associated with cosmopolitanism and the legitimacy claims and democratic demands for communal self-rule insisted upon by communitarians. Since the financial crisis the tensions between the two have grown, making it ever more unlikely that these conflicting claims can be met within a federal EU polity that attracts increasing distrust across the Member States.[83] The argument of this chapter has been that the ontological ground for their reconciliation lies in pursuing the alternative of a Union of self-governing, democratic nation-states.

---

[80] R Bellamy, 'An Ever Closer Union of Peoples: Republican Intergovernmentalism, Demoi-cracy and Representation in the EU' (2013) 35(5) *Journal of European Integration* 499.

[81] P Lindseth, *Power and Legitimacy: Reconciling Europe and the Nation State* (Oxford, Oxford University Press, 2010).

[82] For a sketch, see Bellamy and D Castiglione, 'Three Models of Democracy, Political Community and Representation in the EU' (n 11).

[83] M Matthijs, 'Mediterranean Blues: The Crisis in Southern Europe' (2014) 25(1) *Journal of Democracy* 101.

# 11

# 'Even Children Lisp the Rights of Man': International Human Rights Law and National Minority Jurisdictions

CORMAC MAC AMHLAIGH

## I. Introduction

This chapter was prompted by a political fall-out between the Supreme Court of the United Kingdom (UKSC) and the Scottish government shortly after the UKSC began hearing cases in 2009. It involved an attack by the Scottish government on the London-based court for meddling in domestic Scottish affairs, notably Scottish criminal law, on the grounds that certain aspects of Scottish criminal procedure violated the provisions of the Human Rights Act 1998 (HRA) and were therefore beyond the competence of the Scottish government. Whereas there are many possible readings of the political motivation of the Scottish government in this particular spat, the incident raises an interesting issue for international human rights law. Taking the Scottish government's protestations in good faith, this chapter explores whether the position of the Scottish government can be normatively justified and defended in the practice of human rights law. Emphasising the fact that all human rights norms require some form of 'domestication' in their application within national legal systems, it provides a sketch of a normative argument for autonomy in the 'domestication' of international human rights norms in national minority institutional structures by drawing upon liberal theories of minority rights and theories of constitutional patriotism. It then assesses whether the autonomy of national minorities in the implementation of international human rights norms can be accommodated in the extant doctrinal and structural resources of the practice of international human rights law.

# II. Nonsense in Kilts?: The Politics of
# Human Rights Protection[1]

Since the foundation of the Union between Scotland and England in 1707, the highest court of appeal in the state, the House of Lords (sitting as the Privy Council), has had jurisdiction to hear Scottish civil, but not criminal, appeals. Whereas there has traditionally been an avenue of appeal to the House of Lords from the Scottish courts in civil matters, criminal cases stopped at the highest court of criminal appeal in Scotland, the High Court of Justiciary (HCJ) in Edinburgh, and there was no way of appealing a decision of that court to London.

The Scotland Act 1998 (SA) which established the Scottish Parliament and government simultaneously restricted their powers by nullifying any act of either body which was beyond the competences bestowed upon them by the Act itself.[2] The Privy Council, and subsequently the UKSC, had jurisdiction to definitively determine whether either body acted outside of its competences under the SA.[3] In order to ensure the uniform protection of rights across the UK, the SA provided that any act of the Scottish Parliament or government which breached the HRA was automatically outwith the competence of the Parliament or government.[4]

In Scottish criminal procedure, moreover, the Lord Advocate is the head of the prosecution service, and all criminal prosecutions in Scotland take place in the name of the Lord Advocate. However, the Lord Advocate is also an *ex officio* member of the Scottish government.[5] Therefore all criminal prosecutions, by dint of being brought, formally speaking, by the Lord Advocate, are acts of the Scottish government and can be challenged before the UKSC on competence grounds which include the question of whether the conduct of the trial was in conformity with the ECHR, and the right to a fair trial in Article 6 in particular. The upshot of the combined effects of the SA and HRA, therefore, was to allow the London court to hear criminal appeals in the guise of competence challenges for alleged breaches of human rights; something which was unprecedented in the Scottish criminal procedural system since the foundation of the Union in 1707.[6]

---

[1] This title is borrowed from C Himsworth, 'Rights versus Devolution' in T Campbell, K Ewing and A Tomkins, *Sceptical Essays on Human Rights* (Oxford, Oxford University Press, 2001).

[2] Scotland Act, ss 29, 54 and 57.

[3] ibid, sch 6.

[4] ibid, s 29(2)(d).

[5] ibid, s 44(1)(c).

[6] The system has now been amended by ss 36(6) and 34(3) of the Scotland Act 2012 which tightens up the rules on when the UKSC can consider 'compatibility issues', including the alleged breach of human rights in criminal trials in Scotland. Under this revised procedure, the UKSC can only determine the compatibility of a criminal prosecution with the HRA before remitting the case back to the HCJ for the case to be concluded. Therefore, future breaches of human rights in criminal cases in Scotland no longer result in the proceedings being a nullity, but will rather result in an order of the HCJ if the UKSC confirms that a breach has occurred.

Against this background, then, in a brief period of seven months between 2010 and 2011, the newly established UKSC made two important rulings involving human rights and Scottish criminal law:[7] *Cadder v HMA*[8] and *Frazer v HMA*.[9] The *Cadder* decision involved a challenge to the practice of police questioning of suspects who were 'detained' rather than 'arrested' without recourse to legal advice.[10] The Criminal Procedure (Scotland) Act 1995 allowed arrestees to have access to legal advice prior to police interrogation but did not afford the same guarantee to a detainee.[11] The practice had been challenged on a number of occasions after the passing of the HRA,[12] however in *Salduz v Turkey*[13] in 2008, the European Court of Human Rights (ECtHR) found that the relevant provision of the Convention, Article 6 on the right to fair trial, required that those interviewed by the police should normally have access to legal advice prior to the commencement of police questioning regardless of the legal classification of their detention.[14] In the light of this significant ruling from Strasbourg, the practice of depriving detainees of legal advice was again challenged in Scotland in *HMA v McLean*,[15] where a full bench of the HCJ in Edinburgh found, notwithstanding the ECtHR's ruling two years previously, that the practice was still compatible with Article 6 ECHR based on the fact that Scottish criminal procedure offered alternative guarantees to detainees. A challenge was taken shortly thereafter to the UKSC and in a unanimous decision and using particularly reproving language,[16] the Court overruled the decision of the full bench of the HCJ on the issue, finding that the practice of allowing police questioning of suspects to take place without access to legal advice in Scotland was a clear breach of Article 6 in the light of the *Salduz* decision, and was therefore incompatible with the HRA. Accordingly, criminal trials which introduced evidence from detainees without legal advice were outwith the competence of the Lord Advocate and therefore a nullity.

---

[7] The UK Supreme Court was established by the Constitutional Reform Act 2005 replacing the House of Lords and Privy Council and started work on 1 September 2009.

[8] *Cadder v HMA* [2010] UKSC 43, 2010 SLT 1125.

[9] *Frazer v HMA* [2011] UKSC 24, 2011 SLT 515.

[10] Scottish criminal procedure has for several decades recognised a form of legal custody short of arrest known as 'detention'. Ostensibly, detainees, unlike arrestees, are under 'no legal compulsion' to go along with the request of police officers (*Swankie v Milne* 1973 SLT 128); however, the precise difference between the two categories has never been entirely clear (see K Ewing and K Dale-Risk, *Human Rights in Scotland: Text, Cases and Materials* (London, Sweet & Maxwell, 2004) 120). One salient difference between the two categories was the fact that the legal protections for arrestees were stronger than those of detainees in that they had a right of access to legal advice on their arrest, something which was not available to detainees under the old ss 15 and 17 of the Criminal Procedure (Scotland) Act 1995. This situation which has now changed in the light of the *Cadder* decision (see Criminal Procedure (Scotland) Act 1995, s 15A, which provides for right to legal advice for detainees).

[11] Criminal Procedure (Scotland) Act 1995, ss 15 and 17.

[12] *Paton v Richie* 2000 SLT 239; *Dickson v HMA* 2001 JC 203.

[13] *Salduz v Turkey* [2008] ECHR 1542.

[14] ibid.

[15] *HMA v McLean* [2009] HCJAC 97, 2010 SLT 73.

[16] eg Lord Hope giving the leading judgment (and one of the two Scottish justices on the court) stated that 'It was remarkable that, until quite recently, nobody thought that there was anything wrong with this procedure [of denying legal advice to detainees]', [4].

The second decision, *Frazer v HMA*, involved the quashing of a high-profile murder conviction based on the fact that significant evidence had been withheld during the trial. The defendant had been found guilty of murdering his wife in 2003 and appealed against his conviction. During the appeal, it emerged that a significant piece of evidence had been excluded from the trial involving the witness statements of two police officers involved in investigating the murder. The HCJ was, however, satisfied that there was enough evidence for conviction even in the absence of the withheld evidence.[17] Again, the decision of the highest court of criminal appeal in Scotland was circumvented when the UKSC accepted jurisdiction to hear the defendant's allegation that the trial breached his fundamental rights. Looking at the substance of the case the Court found that the evidence that was withheld 'had such an obvious bearing on a crucial part of the circumstantial case'[18] against the defendant that the failure of the prosecution to give the evidence to the defence was a breach of the defendant's right to a fair trial under Article 6 ECHR and, to much consternation in Scotland given the widespread media and public interest in the case, remanded the case to the Scottish courts again to retry the case or quash the conviction.

The combined effect of these two rulings from the London-based court caused a political storm in Scotland where the ruling party in the Scottish Parliament, the Scottish National Party, unleashed a series of attacks on the Supreme Court for meddling in domestic Scottish affairs. Justice Secretary Kenny MacAskill railed against the 'ambulance-chasing'[19] Supreme Court, claiming that Scotland's distinct legal system had served the country well for hundreds of years 'ensuring justice for victims while also protecting the rights of those accused of crime'[20] and darkly hinted that such rulings may result in the Scottish government cutting its share of funding for the UKSC. The core of his ire was revealed in Mr MacAskill's comments in one particular interview where he stated that:[21]

> We just want to be treated the same as other legal systems—we're not, because we're undermined routinely by a court that sits *in another country* and is presided over by a majority of judges *who have no knowledge of Scots law*, never mind Scotland … [on the issue of the protection of human rights] We'll do so *through our own courts at our own pace in our own way*, not have it imposed by a court in London that is made up of a majority of judges who do not know Scots Law, who may have visited here for the Edinburgh Festival. (emphasis added)

The First Minister Alex Salmond attacked both the Court as well as lawyers who were taking human rights cases before it. As with the Justice Secretary, the basic issue for Salmond was that 'Scotland has, for hundreds of years, been a distinct criminal jurisdiction, and the High Court of Justiciary should be the final arbiter

---

[17] *Frazer v HMA* [2008] HCJAC 26, 2008 SCCR 407.

[18] *Frazer v HMA*, Lord Hope, [2].

[19] 'MacAskill threat to end Supreme Court funding' *Herald Scotland* (31 May 2011).

[20] 'Scottish government moves against UK Supreme Court' *BBC News Scotland* (29 May 2011).

[21] 'MacAskill in new attack on Supreme Court rulings' *Herald Scotland* (30 May 2011).

of criminal cases in Scotland'.[22] Salmond claimed that Scotland didn't need a supreme court which was 'by definition'[23] comprised of judges 'whose familiarity with Scottish legal procedures is inexact at best',[24] and were 'poking [their] nose'[25] into Scottish criminal matters. No other country, in Europe, according to Salmond, had 'two "foreign" appeal courts' (emphasis added)[26] overseeing its legal system.

Whereas it is true that there was a heavily strategic dimension to these attacks—the primary political goal of the SNP government, the holding of a referendum on Scottish independence, eventually held in September 2014, was at the time of the decisions, far from a certainty—the debacle does raise an interesting issue for international human rights law. The issue was directly posed by the intervention of the Advocate General for Scotland in the controversy when he asked 'Why should Scots not have their human rights protected in the same way as people in the rest of the UK?'[27]

This chapter is an attempt to probe this question by exploring whether the theory and practice of human rights law can support the claims of the Justice Secretary and First Minister. In doing so, it is important, at the outset, to distinguish the aims of this chapter from other areas of human rights law and practice involving national minorities. In particular, this chapter is not, or at least not directly, a contribution to debates about the right to self-determination of national minorities nor a contribution to the field of the human rights of indigenous peoples.[28] Nor is it an attempt to explore the liability of states under international human rights law for sub-state entities or regions over which they have some influence or 'effective control'.[29] Rather, the issue raised by these events relate to a distinct question in international human rights law; that is whether national minorities can or should have some discretion, or be afforded a certain margin of appreciation, in giving effect to international human rights norms vis-a-vis the metropole.

## III. Human Rights and the Constitutional Identity of National Minorities

On some levels the political controversy sparked by the UKSC's rulings seems like a rather odd dispute. Aside from the problematic logic of the Justice Secretary

---

[22] 'Supreme Court threat to Scots Law' *The Scotsman* (26 May 2011).
[23] 'MacAskill in new attack on Supreme Court rulings' (n 21).
[24] ibid.
[25] ibid.
[26] 'Alex Salmond provokes fury with attack on UK Supreme Court' *The Guardian* (1 June 2011).
[27] ibid.
[28] See generally D Thurer and T Burri, 'Self-Determination' in *Max Planck Encyclopaedia of Public International Law* (Oxford, Oxford University Press, 2008).
[29] See eg *Ilaşcu and Others v Moldova and Russia* (2005) 40 EHRR 46, [28]–[183]; *Catan v Moldova and Russia* (2013) 57 EHRR 4.

and First Ministers' statements regarding 'foreign judges' with no knowledge of Scots law—the two leading opinions in *Cadder* and *Frazer* were given by Scottish judges—and the patent lack of more qualified judges (at least from the perspective of familiarity and expertise in Scots law) in Strasbourg, the subject matter of the dispute, human rights, is one which is usually considered to transcend boundaries, whether sub-national or national, applying equally to all individuals, regardless of their nationality or political status.[30] The 'borderless' dimension of human rights is explicitly recognised by Article 2(2) of the the Universal Declaration of Human Rights, which provides that, in the protection of the rights contained in the declaration, 'no distinction shall be made on the basis of the political, jurisdictional or international status of the country or territory to which a person belongs, whether it be independent, trust, non-self-governing or under any other limitation of sovereignty'. Therefore to claim some sort of special pleading, or particularity, in the application of international human rights standards such as those contained in the ECHR, for one corner of a Western liberal democracy seems to question that corner's commitments to Western liberal democracy and contradict the fundamentally universal character of international human rights law.

Thus, at first blush it would seem that the Advocate General's question as to why Scots should have their human rights protected differently from other UK citizens, should be answered in the negative; that there is no reason, given the universality of human rights norms, that Scots should have their human rights protected any differently from anyone else in the UK or indeed Europe, or the world. However, viewing the question from the other perspective, that of the global level, reveals that things may not be so straightforward. Universal human rights norms necessarily entail a particular dimension whereby the universal and open-textured provisions of international human rights law require some 'contextualisation' within different regional and political settings. This particularistic dimension of international or regional human rights norms does not, or at least not only, relate to the trivial point that all norms need to be applied to particular facts, such that all human rights norms have to be particularised in some sense to the circumstances of their application (does waterboarding constitute torture?, should racist statements be protected under the freedom of expression? etc).[31] Rather, the particular dimension of international human rights norms involves a recognition that precisely because of their universal character, human rights law applies to (sometimes radically) different social, historical, ethnic, cultural, developmental, religious and political contexts. For these reasons, Carozza argues that the very

---

[30] See eg the Universal Declaration of Human Rights, Arts 1 and 2. Art 1 states that 'All human beings are born free and equal in dignity and rights. They are endowed with reason and conscience and should act towards one another in a spirit of brotherhood'. Art 2: 'Everyone is entitled to all the rights and freedoms set forth in this Declaration, without distinction of any kind, such as race, colour, sex, language, religion, political or other opinion, national or social origin, property, birth or other status'.
[31] N Walker, 'Universalism and Particularism in Human Rights' in C Holder and D Reidy (eds), *Human Rights: The Hard Questions* (Cambridge, Cambridge University Press, 2013) 42.

*idea* of universal human rights standards, entails an 'affirmation of a degree of pluralism and diversity in [global] society'[32] which 'recognises and protects our capacity to pursue the good … by a plurality of paths'.[33] The evolution of human rights regimes in the post-war era has, therefore, involved increased 'norm specification'[34] where 'normative openness and underdetermination'[35] characterise the terrain of international human rights law which results in a broad degree of 'interpretative latitude'[36] in the implementation of those norms. The implementation, interpretation and application of human rights norms, then, involves 'an exercise of *creative freedom* to legislate in different ways that may be equally consistent with the basic requirements of the common good'.[37] Thus, even if the principles or values of human rights law are universal, their instantiation in particular legal orders can and does differ from context to context. Rather than constituting a 'covering universalism', then, human rights law can be said to be *'relatively'*,[38] rather than *absolutely*, determinate of 'appropriate conduct in their domain of application'.[39] For Carozza, this interpretative discretion best characterises the development of international human rights law in the post-war era.[40]

This particularistic dimension of human rights law has been central to the ECtHR's interpretation and application of the rights contained in the ECHR. From its earliest decisions, one common feature of the Court's approach has been to stress the subsidiary nature of the Court's protection of the rights contained in the Convention and the primary responsibility of signatory states to implement and give effect to the rights contained in the Convention.[41] It is, the Court has repeatedly stressed, for states, in the first instance to implement and apply the rights of the Convention according to their relevant domestic requirements.[42] Two aspects of the Court's practice reveal this particularistic dimension of human rights: the margin of appreciation doctrine and the lack of uniform implementation of the Convention in domestic law.

The margin of appreciation doctrine, where the Court defers under certain conditions to the domestic authorities' appraisal of facts, decision-making procedures and interpretation of national law and mores, present since the Court's

---

[32] P Carozza, 'Subsidiarity as a Structural Principle of International Human Rights law' (2003) 97 *American Journal of International Law* 38, 47.

[33] ibid 47.

[34] ibid 59.

[35] ibid 60.

[36] ibid 60.

[37] ibid 72.

[38] N Walker, 'Universalism and Particularism in Human Rights' (n 31) 43.

[39] ibid 34.

[40] '[D]espite all of the normative developments of international human rights law over the last half century, it is still characterized less by fully articulated normative content than by the interpretative discretion that it leaves to states through the open-ended nature of its language, the legal doctrines supporting it, and the political context of the culturally pluralistic world to which it is intended to apply': Carozza 'Subsidiarity' (n 32) 62.

[41] *Sadik v Greece* 24 EHRR 323, 399.

[42] Judgment of 23 July 1968 on the merits of the 'Belgian Linguistic' case, Series A no 6, p 35, [10] in fine.

earliest decisions, clearly demonstrates this necessarily particularistic dimension of human rights law. For example, in an early seminal decision, *Handyside v UK*, the Court explicitly recognised that human rights could not be accommodated in precisely the same way in the different jurisdictions in Europe owing to the pluralism which prevailed, even in a relatively homogenous region such as Western Europe, with regard to the meaning of public morals.[43] It was therefore, the Court concluded, for national authorities and institutions to interpret and apply the relevant provisions of the Convention in a manner best suited to their national sensibilities.[44] This 'margin of appreciation'[45] applied, not only to judicial authorities but also to the 'domestic legislator and [other] bodies ... that are called upon to interpret and apply the laws in force'.[46]

Furthermore, notwithstanding the Court's insistence on the primary role of states in implementing and giving effect to the Convention, it has never insisted on how, precisely, the rights contained in the ECHR should be implemented in national law whether through formal incorporation, or the prescription of remedies for violation. With regard to the question of formal incorporation, in its early cases the Court explicitly refused to interpret Article 13 ECHR, which requires national authorities to provide an 'effective remedy' for rights violations, as a general obligation to incorporate the convention into domestic law.[47] Moreover, in respect of prescribing remedies for human rights violations under the Convention, the Court has maintained that it is not competent to make recommendations on how states should or could better comply with the Convention by prescribing institutional, administrative or legal reform. It has generally limited itself to providing 'just satisfaction' for victims where national law failed to provide full reparation.[48]

Thus, the notion that international human rights norms necessitate a degree of calibration and domestication into domestic legal systems and political contexts is a commonplace in international human rights law, particularly European human rights law. This being the case, then, the question emerges for states with internally differentiated levels of government such as federal states or complex asymmetrically governed states such as the UK, Spain or Belgium, as to what the appropriate

---

[43] *Handyside v UK* (1976) 1 EHRR 737.

[44] ibid [48].

[45] ibid [48].

[46] ibid [48].

[47] See *Silver v UK* (1983) 5 EHRR 347, [113]; *Swedish Engine Driver's Union v Sweden* (1976) 1 EHRR 617, [50].

[48] L Hefler, 'Redesigning the European Court of Human Rights: Embeddedness as a Deep Structural Principle of the European Human Rights Regime' (2008) 19(1) *European Journal International Law* 125, 146. Admittedly, the Court has been more prescriptive in recent years, making recommendations to remedy systemic deficiencies in national law through the practice of 'pilot judgments' targeted at specific signatory states (see *Broniowski v Poland* (2006) 43 EHRR 1). However, even here, such recommendations are made with the cooperation of, and in conjunction with, national authorities. See generally W Sadurski, 'Partnering with Strasbourg: Constitutionalisation of the European Court of Human Rights, the Accession of Central and East European States to the Council of Europe, and the Idea of Pilot Judgments' [2009] 9(3) *Human Rights Law Review* 397.

level for this accommodation or 'domestication' is. That there can be some variation in human rights standards even within a single state is not unusual. As the UK Parliament's Joint Committee for Human Right's Report on a Bill of Rights for the UK noted:

> It is common for federated states, such as Canada, the US and Germany, to have both federal Bills of rights and state-level Bills of Rights, and for any questions about the hierarchical relationship between these different levels of rights protection to be resolved by the federation's Constitutional Court.[49]

Furthermore, on the implementation of international human rights standards, the Committee noted in respect of internally differentiated states, that:

> Ever since the Universal Declaration of Human Rights, human rights norms have gradually become embedded at global, regional and national level. Provided the hierarchy between these levels is clear, there is a positive virtue in the broadly defined rights in the international standards *being fleshed out into more concrete norms and standards at the regional, national and sub-national level.*

Thus, the notion that different levels of government within a single state may have distinct human rights jurisdictions is an unremarkable feature of many internally differentiated states. However, as the opinion of the Committee for a Bill of Rights notes, such sub-national jurisdictions remain subject to their 'correction' by the national or metropolitan level thereby ensuring uniformity of standards across the various levels of government within the state itself, just as the UKSC appeared to do in *Cadder* and *Frazer*.[50] However, the notion of the autonomy of sub-national minorities in implementing and applying international human rights norms implicit in the comments from the First Minister and the Justice Secretary, goes beyond this. They call for the explicit recognition and respect by metropolitan apex courts of the sub-national minority's choices on how to implement and protect human rights norms within their particular systems.

Thus the fact of internal differentiation alone does not necessarily lead to the respect and recognition of sub-state autonomy in interpreting and applying international human rights norms such as the HCJ's opinions on the meaning and requirements of a right to a fair trial in questions of access to legal advice and the withholding of particular evidence forming the basis of the appeals in *Cadder* and *Frazer*. Rather, an independent normative argument is required to substantiate the

---

[49] Joint Committee for Human Rights, *A Bill of Rights for the UK?* (2007–08, HL 165, HC 150) vol I, ch 3, [107].

[50] I say 'appeared' because shortly before *Cadder* was decided, the UKSC decided a case involving English and Welsh criminal law where it defied Strasbourg and upheld the practices of English and Welsh criminal procedure notwithstanding the fact that according to the Strasbourg Court, such practices were in breach of ECHR, Art 6 (*R v Horncastle* [2009] UKSC 14, [2010] 2 AC 373). Thus, it is not entirely clear, in the light of this decision, whether the UKSC is, in fact, maintaining a uniform ECHR-compatible standard of human rights protection across the UK or whether the biggest criminal jurisdiction in the state, England and Wales, has more autonomy than Scotland or Northern Ireland to diverge from the ECtHR's rulings.

positions taken by the Justice Secretary and First Minister. Such normative reasons can be found, it is submitted, by drawing on a liberal theory of minority rights and the theory of constitutional patriotism.

## A. Normativising the Autonomy of National Minorities in the Implementation of Human Rights

Kymlicka's well-known liberal theory of national minorities offers one resource to provide normative arguments as to why national apex courts should recognise and respect the autonomy of national minorities in domesticating international human rights standards. It departs from the notion of a 'societal culture' which can be differentiated from other types of group cultures such as religious or social groups in that it provides its members 'with meaningful ways of life across the *full range* of human activities, including social, educational, religious, recreational, and economic life, encompassing *both* public and private spheres'.[51] As such, societal cultures 'are important to people's freedom'[52] where such freedom involves 'making choices amongst *various options*'[53] determining the 'boundaries of the imaginable'.[54] The societal culture 'not only provides these options'[55] but also, significantly, 'makes them meaningful to us'.[56] As such, culture 'provides the receptacle through which we identify our experiences as valuable'[57] where cultural narratives are a 'precondition of making intelligent judgments about how to lead our lives'.[58] Significantly for Kymlicka, societal cultures are usually territorially based and share not just language, memories and values but also 'common institutions and practices'.[59]

Combining the fact that human rights norms require some domestic accommodation with the freedom of 'cultural societies', it is argued, can provide normative support for the autonomy of national minorities in the implementation and application of human rights norms which can create demands for recognition of this autonomy by the metropole. If, as Kymlicka suggests, a societal culture provides options across the 'full range of human activities' then this necessarily involves and includes questions about the freedom to choose different paths to the good life which human rights norms, and the diversity in their accommodation, necessarily presupposes. In this respect, the 'meaningful options'[60] about questions

---

[51] W Kymlicka, *Multicultural Citizenship: A Liberal Theory of Minority Rights* (Oxford University Press, 1996) 76.
[52] ibid 80.
[53] ibid 89.
[54] ibid 89.
[55] ibid 83.
[56] ibid 83.
[57] Dworkin cited in ibid 83.
[58] ibid 83.
[59] ibid 83.
[60] ibid 83.

of freedom and how to live one's life dovetail with Carozza's assertion that the international human rights system entails the '*creative freedom*'[61] to domesticate the abstract and open-textured values in different ways which are consistent with the 'basic requirements of the common good'.[62] As such the freedom of cultural societies can be said to involve the 'freedom of individuals and communities to seek the goods necessary for a dignified human life'[63] implicit in the idea of international human rights law. If the latitude to implement and apply human rights norms really is a function of the value of liberty as Carozza suggests, and this is an endemic feature of international human rights law in the post-war period, then viewed from the perspective of the freedom of cultural societies, it could be argued that contemporary international human rights law *requires* a measure of autonomy and respect from the metropole in domesticating human rights norms within that particular societal culture.

Furthermore, the domestication of universal human rights norms within a particular societal culture, and the freedom, identity and self-determination of that culture can be mutually constitutive, as suggested by the idea of constitutional patriotism. Müller defines constitutional patriotism as providing 'one possible language for an exercise in collective ethical self-clarification',[64] involving 'bounded political associations'[65] who have 'an attachment to universal values, which is then realised in a particular political setting'.[66]

Significantly, the object of attachment in constitutional patriotism relates to the 'universal moral norms'[67] embedded in 'particular procedures that structure the rules for reworking a constitutional culture'.[68] It is from disagreements about what these universal moral norms require within particular contexts that a 'constitutional *identity*' or 'constitutional culture' emerges.[69] In this regard, Müller recalls the Habermassian distinction between the ethical and the moral realm, whereby in the ethical realm collectives 'reach an understanding of who they would like to be and which of their traditions they should continue or modify in the light of moral discourses'[70] and the realm of morality aimed at 'finding rules and decisions that are rationally acceptable to all affected by the rules'.[71] However, in practice, given that 'questions about universal rights and collective identities cannot easily be disentangled in practical political debate',[72] the boundaries between the ethical and the moral realms can be collapsed such that the act of self-definition becomes

---

[61] Carozza(n 32) 72.

[62] ibid 72.

[63] ibid 47.

[64] JW Müller, 'A General Theory of Constitutional Patriotism' (2008) 6 *International Journal of Constitutional Law* 72, 77.

[65] ibid 78.

[66] ibid 73.

[67] ibid 82.

[68] ibid 82.

[69] ibid 80.

[70] ibid 83.

[71] ibid 83.

[72] ibid 84.

part and parcel of finding rules and decisions that are universally morally acceptable. Viewed in this light, then, the question of the ethical-clarification of political
communities, in negotiating and disagreeing about the meaning and requirements of universal morality within particular cultural contexts overlaps considerably with the 'domestication' of international human rights norms in national
minority contexts considered above. In negotiating and determining what universal norms, such as the right to a fair trial or freedom of expression, require in the
context of a particular societal culture, the political and constitutional identity
of that particular societal culture can be said to be given further definition along
constitutional patriotic lines. Thus, as well as providing reasons for the autonomy
of societal cultures in implementing human rights norms, constitutional patriotism shows how the very act of accommodating and domesticating international
human rights norms by national minorities underpins and constitutes an expression of the identity of that societal culture *qua* political community. Given the
link between the accommodation of human rights norms and cultural freedom,
then, it can be seen how the autonomy of national minorities in accommodating
and giving expression to human rights norms can, in itself, constitute a form of
constitutional patriotism.[73]

## IV. Methods of Management

The practice of international human rights law contains a number of resources
that can potentially give expression to the normative argument for the autonomy
of national minorities in the application of international human rights norms.
Three aspects of the contemporary practice of international human rights in particular can potentially serve this purpose; human rights exceptionalism, subsidiarity and pluralism.

### A. Human Rights Exceptionalism

Human rights exceptionalism is a political or judicial attitude to international
human rights law genetically linked to ideas of sovereignty and self-determination.

---

[73] Using Müller's account of constitutional patriotism in this way constitutes a departure from the
contexts within which Müller himself envisages that constitutional patriotism can apply. He is clear
that constitutional patriotism cannot provide leverage for the formation of political communities in
the form of, for example, the independence of extant sub-state national minorities. Constitutional
patriotism is not, therefore, a 'freestanding theory of political boundary formation' (p 5) and as such
cannot 'answer questions about political self-determination'(p 5) for potential political communities
that do not already enjoy constitutional and institutional infrastructures. However, this objection can
be overcome, it is submitted, by founding the constitutional patriotism of sub-national minorities on
the freedom of existing national minorities which can do the relevant, and necessary work, to delimit
or define the boundaries of sub-national minorities *qua* political communities in order for constitutional patriotism to apply.

Writing in the US context, Ignatieff identifies three forms of human rights exceptionalism; the non-ratification of human rights treaties, the insertion of reservations to treaties or non-compliance with ratified treaties; double-standards in criticising friends and enemies for human rights violations in foreign policy; and denying human rights norms any effect in domestic law.[74] Given that a large part of the explanation of US exceptionalism with respect to international human rights standards has to do with its sheer size and economic and political influence as the world's only 'hyperpower',[75] of the three dimensions of exceptionalism identified by Ignatieff, it is the third form, denying international human rights norms effect in domestic law, which is of relevance to the question of the autonomy of national minorities in relation to universal human rights standards. This form of human rights exceptionalism involves sub-national minority courts taking an 'exceptional' attitude to international human rights law by refusing to recognise them as valid law, refusing to apply them, subordinating them to overriding provisions of domestic law or interpreting them in such a way as to deny them any real effect. The public face of this form of exceptionalism in the US is Justice Antonin Scalia of the US Supreme Court;[76] however Scotland also has a figurehead for human rights exceptionalism in the figure of Lord McCluskey, a former judge of the Scottish Supreme Courts. In the face of rising demands for the domestic implementation of the ECHR in the UK, McCluskey used the occasion of the delivery of the BBC's Reith Lectures in 1986 to denounce the idea of universal human rights standards and their codification in Scotland, famously predicting that domestic incorporation of the ECHR would be 'a field day for crackpots, a pain in the neck for judges and legislators, and a goldmine for lawyers'.[77] He reprised these remarks in a series of articles in Scottish newspapers in 2000 shortly after the Human Rights Act 1998 came into force in Scotland arguing that the immediate effect of litigants 'claiming their new "European" rights"[78] had been 'devastating'.[79] He also denounced the fact that the ECtHR contained judges from foreign countries who would be adjudicating on Scottish matters. This series of comments led to his being recused from a criminal trial in which the defendants had based part of their defence on ECHR provisions in the case of Hoekstra v HMA (No 1).[80] On appeal, the defendants argued that McCluskey's extra-curial remarks meant that the trial was tainted by bias given that they were pleading provisions of the HRA as part of their defence. In a hearing on whether the bench should be reconfigured for the continuation of the case, the HCJ agreed and ordered a rehearing of the parts of the trial. The exceptionalist nature of McCluskey's position on the role of international human

---

[74] M Ignatieff, 'Introduction: American Exceptionalism and Human Rights' in M Ignatieff (ed), *American Exceptionalism and Human Rights* (Princeton, Princeton University Press, 2005) 6–8.
[75] ibid 12.
[76] *Printz v US* (1997) 521 US 898, 921 fn 11.
[77] Published as JH McCluskey, *Law, Justice and Democracy* (London, Sweet & Maxwell, 1987).
[78] ibid.
[79] Lord McClusky, 'Trojan Horses at the gates of our courts' *Scotland on Sunday* (6 February 2000).
[80] *Hoekstra v HMA (No 1)* 2000 SCCR 263.

rights norms in Scottish courts was well summarised by the Court during this hearing and it is therefore worth quoting at length. They noted that:

> by likening the introduction of the Convention into Scots law to the introduction of a Trojan Horse, in the shape of a revolutionary instrument for change, Lord McCluskey was conjuring up the picture of a deceitful stratagem being used to introduce into the citadel of Scots law an alien force which would attack the defending soldiers. There was an implicit suggestion that this alien force would be introducing a revolution which would change the established and better ways of the native Scots law. The immediate results of the introduction of the Convention in Scotland had been 'devastating'—implying that it had laid waste areas of national law. Whether one thought of the *Titanic* sailing towards a legal iceberg or the approach of an avalanche in which the Scottish courts would have to struggle to avoid being buried in the new claims of right, the imagery was overwhelmingly negative and painted a picture of the Convention as something which threatened danger to the Scottish legal system.[81]

Thus, human rights exceptionalism has taken root in Scotland and could provide a possible basis for the autonomy of national minorities in implementing international human rights norms. However, even if this is the case it is not a particularly attractive way of doing so. As a political or judicial attitude, rather than a legal doctrine of international human rights law, exceptionalism is unsuited to managing the domestication of international human rights standards at national minority level. Rather than good faith engagement with the international human rights standards as part of the ongoing constitution of the political identity of national minorities, human rights exceptionalism constitutes a rejection or subordination of human rights standards to a domestic constitutional chauvinism more relevant to the darker legacies of nationalism than the normative freedom of cultural societies. As such, it does not achieve the ideals of the normative theory outlined above whereby national minorities engage with and take seriously the universal standards set by international human rights norms.

## B.  Subsidiarity

Subsidiarity is becoming an increasingly prominent feature of the international human rights landscape. The concept itself, has, in recent times, found its clearest expression in the EU context but has since spread to other mechanisms and institutions of suprastate governance.[82] At its root, subsidiarity provides a 'conceptual and rhetorical mediator between supranational harmonisation and unity, on the one hand, and local pluralism and difference on the other'.[83] The kernel of the idea

---

[81] *Hoekstra v H M Advocate (No 3)* 2000 SLT 605, [2000] HRLR 410.

[82] For example, Protocol 15 to the ECHR of 24 September 2013 makes an explicit reference to the concept to be inserted in one of the recitals of the Preamble of Convention itself on ratification. See also Carozza (n 32).

[83] ibid 54.

of subsidiarity, therefore, is the idea that in a distribution of levels of decision-making, decisions should be taken as close as possible to the individual within a particular social context.

Neuman identifies four features of the structure of international human rights law which encapsulate the ideals of subsidiarity in terms of the appropriate level of decision-making; the exhaustion of domestic remedies requirement, the 'fourth instance' formula, remedial subsidiarity and the margin of appreciation.[84] The exhaustion of domestic remedies is perhaps the clearest expression of subsidiarity in international human rights law in its insistence that states are the principal site of resolution of complaints of human rights violations and has become a standard procedural mechanism for many suprastate adjudicatory bodies.[85] The 'fourth instance' doctrine relates to the idea that suprastate courts, not least human rights adjudicatory bodies, should not act as a forum of fourth instance on a particular dispute; their proper role is simply to assess whether the claimed action violates the particular human rights standards established in the international agreement signed by the relevant state.[86] Remedial subsidiarity relates to the notion that it is for states, and states alone, to determine what the appropriate remedy for a human rights violation is and the margin of appreciation, discussed above in relation to the ECHR, relates to supranational courts' deference under certain conditions to the domestic authorities' appraisal of facts, decision-making procedures and interpretation of national law and mores.[87]

With its arguably overtly political or at least principled character, it would appear that subsidiarity would be a particularly useful mechanism to manage the tension between universality and particularity in respect of human rights adjudication by national minorities. Its emphasis on taking decisions about the nature, meaning and implementation of human rights norms as close as possible to the individual in their most relevant social context resonates strongly with the ideals of the liberty of cultural societies.[88] However, two features of subsidiarity in international human rights law, both conceptually and in practice, create doubts as to whether it is suitable to vindicate the interpretative autonomy of national minorities in implementing international human rights norms. First, the aims of subsidiarity as it has emerged both in Catholic social doctrine as well as in political theory relate to social groupings such as trades unions, community groups or religious organisations rather than the Kymlickan notion of 'cultural society'. As much is clear from Neuman's identification of certain international human rights norms as encapsulating the ideals of subsidiarity such as the right to freedom of association and the right to family life.[89] However, as noted above, cultural societies

---

[84] G Neuman, 'Subsidiarity' in D Shelton (ed), *The Oxford Handbook of International Human Rights Law* (Oxford, Oxford University Press, 2013) 369–77.

[85] ibid 369–70.

[86] ibid 370–71.

[87] ibid 371–74.

[88] See Carozza (n 32) 46.

[89] Neuman, 'Subsidiarity' (n 84) 366.

differ from generic social groups in providing their members with meaningful ways of life across the '*full range* of human activities'[90] crystallising in common institutions and practices and not mere interest-based social association. Secondly, whereas in theory subsidiarity appears to be an optimal way of managing the tension between human rights universality and the specificity of national minorities, in international human rights law practice it has tended to rely on a rigid understanding of the 'Westphalian paradigm' of sovereign states. As such, subsidiarity stops at the state level and serves merely to adjudicate and operate between two levels, national and international, oblivious to the question of whether national minorities should have a stake in the implementation of human rights norms. As Neuman notes in this regard:[91]

> international human rights law does not currently provide strong support for a requirement of *territorial subsidiarity within the state*, as a claim for federalism or local government [...] *The principal human rights treaties do not give local governments autonomy rights against regions or states, or require that the larger unites refrain from regulating matters that the local governments could address*. (emphasis added)

While a step in the right direction, then, subsidiarity provides cold comfort for national minorities with aspirations of implementing and contextualising international human rights norms according to their own cultural orientation as a facet of their own freedom as a cultural society. However, building on the ideals of subsidiarity, a more recent trend in human rights law is, it is claimed, up to the task and can provide a more appropriate vehicle for the vindication of national minority autonomy in the domestic accommodation of international human rights standards; that, is the idea of pluralism.

## C. Pluralism

The field of legal and constitutional pluralism in respect of the interaction and conflicts between legal orders in the contemporary world is an increasingly broad field with diverse interests and normative commitments.[92] Notwithstanding such diversity, however, a number of features can be distilled from the increasingly diverse models and defences of pluralism advanced in academic scholarship on the subject. Perhaps the most significant feature shared by all pluralists, which is of particular relevance to the question being considered here, is the sense in which the 'Westphalian paradigm' of territorial state sovereignty and an international system of sovereign states who design the international legal system according to their own ends is, if not quite redundant, certainly being increasingly challenged by the forces of globalisation and the proliferation of suprastate legal orders with

---

[90] Kymlicka, *Multicultural Citizenship* (n 51) 76.

[91] Neuman, 'Subsidiarity' (n 84) 368.

[92] A literature which is increasing exponentially. For a recent collection on the current state of the debate, see M Avbelj and J Komarek, *Constitutional Pluralism in the European Union and Beyond* (Oxford, Hart Publishing, 2012).

executive, judicial and legislative functions with concomitant claims to autonomy and original jurisdiction. The fortification of suprastate law and governance such that international law is becoming increasingly constitution-like and constitutional law increasingly imports elements of international law constitutes a particular challenge to understanding the legal and political world in terms of a rigid state sovereignty and a dualism of international and constitutional law. Thus, one feature of pluralism in the diverse models and accounts of the idea is that we are in transition to (or have arrived at) a post-Westphalian settlement where state sovereignty is either obsolete as the founder of the idea of pluralism, Neil MacCormick argued,[93] or in a state of evolution to a more complex form.[94] Furthermore, pluralism recognises and embraces the considerable blurring of the constitutional and the international and sees the legal and political world in terms of a series of overlapping authorities and sites of governance which operate alongside each other in a heterarchy or polyarchy rather than hierarchy, at times cooperating but also conflicting in a global 'disorder of legal orders'.[95]

Thus, pluralism is predicated upon a move away from, or evolution of, the rigid Westphalian dichotomy or dualism of international law and constitutional law and envisages authority claims not only from states but other sites at different levels of governance. Given its rejection of the rigid dualism of the Westphalian model, as well as its demotion of state sovereignty as the primary organising principle of law and politics, pluralism is therefore particularly apt to recognise and accommodate the idea of sub-national minority adjudication of international human rights standards.[96] As well as highlighting the significance of suprastate governance in the contemporary world, pluralism has the capacity to prize open the lid of the sovereign state and assimilate the complexity and differentiated nature of sub-state governance and authority claims, encapsulating them into a broader tapestry of overlapping heterarchial or polyarchical authority claims at sub-state, state and suprastate levels.[97] Furthermore, the emphasis in pluralism on dynamic discursive interaction rather than static assertions of final and absolute authority mean that sub-national minorities can make plausible claims to autonomy without having to challenge or assert a Westphalian-style sovereignty in the form of independence.[98] As such pluralism gives agency and voice to sub-national minority claims, including at the post-state level in ways which the Westphalian system does not.

With respect to the ECHR in particular, pluralism has been used to support the authority claims of the ECtHR in interpreting the rights contained in the

---

[93] N MacCormick, 'Beyond the Sovereign State' (1993) 56(1) *Modern Law Review* 1.

[94] N Walker, 'Late Sovereignty in the European Union' in N Walker (ed), *Sovereignty in Transition* (Oxford, Hart Publishing, 2003).

[95] N Walker, 'Beyond Boundary Disputes and Basic Grids: Mapping the Global Disorder of Normative Orders' (2008) 6(3–4) *ICON* 373.

[96] See generally C Mac Amhlaigh, 'Late Sovereignty in Post-Integration Europe: Continuity and Change in a Constitutive Concept' in R Adler-Nissen and U Pram-Grad (eds), *Post-Colonial Sovereignty Games: The Overseas Countries and Territories of the European Union* (Abingdon, Routledge, 2012).

[97] ibid.

[98] ibid.

Convention, as well as the counter-authority claims from national apex courts.[99] However, as distinct from other forms of regime interaction in a global 'disorder of legal orders', human rights law is particularly conducive to pluralism given that it entails a common set of universal values which provide a common point of reference for all interpretative levels whether at the sub-state, state and suprastate levels. In this regard, the 'suprapositive'[100] values of the rights contained in the ECHR can provide a *framework* allowing for the 'constructive engagement of different sites of authority with one another'.[101] In this vein, the ECHR can be said to provide this framework, 'map[ping] onto rights found in national systems [and] undergird[ing] the notion of a multi-level constitutionalism'[102] whereby 'no act taken by any public authority, at any level of governance, can be considered lawful if it violates a fundamental right'.[103] Pluralism, therefore, encapsulates the contestation and disagreement about the meaning and interpretation of these common values as well as the optimal way to secure their protection in diverse political and social environments and at different levels of governance in a post-Westphalian Europe.

Thus, when interpreting the rights contained in the Convention, which are shared by the various legal systems, sub-national courts, national courts and the ECtHR can delve into the same common normative resource of universal values which inform the (positive) provisions of the ECHR. These principles therefore provide the 'glue'[104] which binds sub-national and national legal orders and the ECtHR system together in a pluralist relationship over and above the positive law provisions of sub-national or national constitutional arrangements or the Convention itself.[105] In terms of the autonomy of national minorities in the implementation of international human rights standards, then, pluralism is the most suitable feature of contemporary international human rights law theory and practice to express this ideal.

---

[99] See N Krisch, 'The Open Architecture of European Human Rights Law' (2008) 71(2) *Modern Law Review* 183; C Sabel and O Gerstenberg, 'Constitutionalising and Overlapping Consensus: The ECJ and the Emergency of a Coordinate Constitutional Order' (2010) 16(5) *European Law Journal* 511; S Greer and L Wildhaber, 'Revisiting the Debate and "Constitutionalising" the European Court of Human Rights' (2012) 12(4) *Human Rights Law Review* 655; A Stone-Sweet, 'A Cosmopolitan Legal Order: Constitutional Pluralism and Rights Adjudication in Europe' (2012) 1(1) *Global Constitutionalism* 53.

[100] GL Neuman, 'Human Rights and Constitutional Rights: Harmony and Dissonance' (2003) 55(5) *Stanford Law Review* 1863, 1868.

[101] M Kumm, 'The Cosmopolitan Turn in Constitutionalism: On the Relationship between Constitutionalism in and Beyond the States' in J Dunoff and J Trachtman (eds), *Ruling the World?: Constitutionalism, International Law and Global Governance*, (Cambridge University Press, 2009) 272.

[102] Stone-Sweet, 'A Cosmopolitan Legal Order' (n 99) 53–90.

[103] ibid 61.

[104] N Walker, 'Reconciling MacCormick: Constitutional Pluralism and the Unity of Practical Reason' (2011) 24 *Ratio Juris* 369, 378.

[105] Such as the explicit terms of the Scotland Act 1998 or the ECHR, Arts 32 and 46 on the jurisdiction of the Court to interpret the Convention and the duty of signatory states to abide by the decisions of the Court.

# V. Conclusion

This contribution attempted to explore arguments in favour of the autonomy of national minorities in adjudicating and implementing universal human rights standards as well as to appraise some of the extant conceptual and doctrinal tools of international human rights law to achieve those aims. It concludes that there are valid normative arguments for national minorities having some say in how universal human rights norms are 'domesticated' within their particular cultural and historical contexts distinct from the dominant culture of the metropole. Moreover, pluralism which is an increasingly popular trend in human rights law, is a particularly useful way of thinking about how that ideal might be achieved. If authority sites have been pluralised in a post-Westphalian world, whereby not only states can enjoy agency and authority as political and judicial actors, and in the human rights domain, such agency is contained within a common framework of fundamental rights values, then there is no conceptual barrier to national minorities participating in dialogues regarding the interpretation and implementation of universal human rights norms alongside both the metropolitan and suprastate levels. Furthermore, if fundamental rights claims involve, at least in part, the shaping of political identity, then a liberal theory of national minorities along with their constitutional patriotism, provides strong normative reasons for the role of national minority (particularly judicial) institutions in engaging and participating in the joint enterprise of 'promoting a joint European development of fundamental rights'[106] in a pluralistic relationship with the state and suprastate level all captured within the framework of the values and principles which underpin the ECHR. The shared 'glue' of fundamental rights, combined with the evolution of the Westphalian paradigm to allow for unorthodox (from a Westphalian viewpoint) authority claims from unorthodox authority sites, therefore, allows for subnational minority institutions to engage and partake in the on-going articulation, definition and adjudication of the meaning of the common normative resources of human rights principles, adapted and tailored to the requirements of their own national minority status, thereby (re)defining their political identities.

Whereas the political incident which provided the catalyst for this exploration may have been motivated by more strategic or party political reasons, what this chapter has argued is that one need not be completely cynical of the contentions of the Justice Secretary and First Minister and respond so quickly to the Lord Advocate's question in the affirmative. As a sub-national minority jurisdiction, Scotland is justified in not sharing the same understanding of the meaning and requirements of human rights norms as their co-citizens in the rest of the United Kingdom; its children may lisp a particularly Scottish interpretation of the rights of man.

---

[106] German Federal Constitutional Court 'Gorgulu' decision 14 October 2004, (2004) 2 BvR 1481/04, [62].

# BIBLIOGRAPHY

Agné, H, 'Why Democracy Must be Global: Self-founding and Democratic Intervention' (2010) 2 *International Theory* 381

Ahmed, I, *State, Nation and Ethnicity in Contemporary South Asia* (London, Pinter, 1996)

Alam, J, 'The Nation and the State in India: A Difficult Bond' in Z Hasan, E Sridharan and R Sudharshan (eds), *India's Living Constitution: Ideas, Practices, Controversies* (London, Anthem Press, 2005)

Alavi, H, 'The State in Post-Colonial Societies: Pakistan and Bangladesh' (1972) 1(74) *New Left Review* 59

Aldecon, F and Keating, M (eds), *Paradiplomacy in Action: The Foreign Relations of Subnational Governments* (London, Frank Cass, 1999)

Alesina, A, and Spoloare, E, *The Size of Nations* (Cambridge, MA, MIT Press, 2003)

Ali, M, *The Fearful State: Power, People, and Internal War in South Asia* (London, Zed Books, 1993)

Allen, J, and Cochrane, A, 'Beyond the Territorial Fix: Regional Assemblages, Politics and Power' (2007) 41(9) *Regional Studies* 1161

Amar, AR, 'Abraham Lincoln and the American Union' (2001) 5 *University of Illinois Law Review* 1109

——— *America's Constitution: A Biography* (New York, Random House, 2005)

Anand, CL, *Constitutional Law and History of Government of India* 8th edn (revised by HK Saharay, New Delhi, Universal Law Publishing, 2008)

Anderson, B, *Imagined Communities: Reflections on the Origins and Spread of Nationalism* (London, Verso, 1991)

Anghie, A, *Imperialism, Sovereignty, and the Making of International Law* (Cambridge, Cambridge University Press, 2003)

Ashbrook, JE, *Buying and Selling the Istrian Goat: Istrian Regionalism, Croatian Nationalism, and EU Enlargement* (Brussels, Peter Lang, 2008)

Austin, G, *The Indian Constitution: Cornerstone of a Nation* (New Delhi, Oxford University Press, 2004)

Avbelj, M and Komarek, J, *Constitutional Pluralism in the European Union and Beyond* (Oxford, Hart Publishing, 2012)

Babcock, HM, 'Democracy's Discontent in a Complex World: Can Avalanches Sandpiles, and Finches Optimize Michael Sandel's Civic Republican Community?' (1996–97) 85 *Georgetown Law Journal* 2085

Badie, B, *La fin des territoires. Essai sur le désordre international et sur l'utilité sociale du respect* (Paris, Fayard, 1995)

Bajpai, K, 'Diversity, Democracy, and Devolution in India' in S Baruah (ed), *Ethnonationalism in India: A Reader* (New Delhi, Oxford University Press, 2010)

Bakshi, PM, *The Constitution of India: Selective Comments* 6th edn (New Delhi, Universal Law Publishing, 2005)

Ballinger, P, '"Authentic Hybrids" in Balkan Borderlands' (2004) 45(1) *Current Anthropology* 31

Bandarage, A, *The Separatist Conflict in Sri Lanka: Terrorism, Ethnicity, Political Economy* (London, Routledge, 2009)

Barnett, MR, *The Politics of Cultural Nationalism in South India* (Princeton, Princeton University Press, 1976)

Barry, B, 'Statism and Nationalism: a Cosmopolitan Critique' in I Shapiro and L Brilmayer (eds), *Nomos: Global Justice* (New York, New York, University Press, 1999)

Bartolini, S, *Restructuring Europe. Centre Formation, System Building, and Political Structuring between the Nation State and the European Union* (Oxford, Oxford University Press, 2005)

Basu, DD, *Commentary on the Constitution of India* vol 1(Calcutta, SC Sarkar, 1955)

Bayefsky, A, *Self-determination in International Law: Quebec and Lessons Learned* (The Hague, Kluwer Law International, 2000)

Bayly, CA, *Imperial Meridian: The British Empire and the World, 1780–1830* (London, Longman, 1989)

—— *Empire and Information Intelligence Gathering and Social Communication in India, 1780–1870* (Cambidge, Cambridge University Press, 1996)

—— *Origins of Nationality in South Asia* (New Delhi, Oxford University Press, 1998)

—— *The Birth of the Modern World 1780–1914* (Oxford, Blackwell, 2004)

—— *Recovering Liberties: Indian Thought in the Age of Liberalism and Empire* (Cambridge, Cambridge University Press, 2012)

Beaud, O, 'La Fédération entre l'état et l'empire' in B Thèret (ed), *L'État, la finance et le sociale* (Paris, La Decouverte, 1995)

Beckman, L, 'Democratic Inclusion, Law and Causes' (2008) 21 *Ratio Juris* 350

Beigbeder, Y, 'Referendum', *Max Planck Encyclopedia of Public International Law* (Oxford, Oxford University Press, 2011)

Beiner, R, 'National Self-Determination: Some Cautionary Remarks Concerning the Practice of Rights' in M Moore (ed), *National Self-Determination and Secession* (Oxford, Oxford University Press, 1998)

—— (ed), *Theorizing Nationalism* (Albany, State University of New York Press, 1999)

Beitz, C, 'Cosmopolitan Ideals and National Sentiment' (1983) 80 *Journal of Philosophy* 591

—— 'International Relations, Philosophy of' in E Craig (ed), *The Routledge Encyclopaedia of Philosophy* vol 4 (London, Routledge, 1998)

Bell, C, 'What we Talk about when we Talk about International Constitutional Law' (2014) 5 *Transnational Legal Theory* 241

Bellamy, R, 'An Ever Closer Union of Peoples: Republican Intergovernmentalism, Demoicracy and Representation in the EU' (2013) 35(5) *Journal of European Integration* 499

—— and Castiglione, D, 'Legitimising the Euro-polity and its Regime: The Normative Turn in EU Studies' (2003) 2(1) *European Journal of Political Theory* 7

—— and —— 'Debate: Lacroix's European Constitutional Patriotism: A Response' (2004) 52 *Political Studies* 187

—— and —— 'Three Models of Democracy, Political Community and Representation in the EU' (2013) 20(2) *Journal of European Public Policy* 206

Beran, H, 'A Liberal Theory of Secession' (1984) 32 *Political Studies* 21

Berghe, PVD, 'Race and Ethnicity: A Sociobiological Perspective' (1978) 1(4) *Ethnic and Racial Studies* 1

Berman, PS, 'Dialectical Regulation, Territoriality, and Pluralism' (2006) 38 *Connecticut Law Review* 952

Bermeo, N, 'Conclusion: The Merits of Federalism' in UN Amoretti and M Bermeo (eds), *Federalism and Territorial Cleavages* (Baltimore, John Hopkins University Press, 2004)

Berriedale Keith, A, *A Constitutional History of India, 1600–1935* (London, Methuen, 1926)

Best, H, *Die Männer Von Bildung Und Besitz Struktur Und Handeln Parlamentarischer Führungsgruppen In Deutschland Und Frankreich 1848–49* (Düsseldorf, Droste, 1990)

Bhargava, R, 'The Crisis of Border States in India' in J Bertrand and A Laliberté (eds), *Multination States in Asia: Accommodation of Resistance* (Cambridge, Cambridge University Press, 2010)

Bhattacharyya, H, 'Federalism and Competing Nations in India' in M Burgess and J Pinder (eds), *Multinational Federations* (London, Routledge, 2007)

—— 'Ethnic and Civic Nationhood in India: Concept, History, Institutional Innovations and Contemporary Challenges' in SC Saha (ed), *Ethnicity and Socio-Political Changes in Africa and other Developing Countries* (Lanham, Lexington, 2008)

—— '"A Nation of Citizens" in a Fragmented Society? Citizenship as Individual and Ethnic Entitlements in India' in H Bhattacharyya, A Kluge and L König (eds), *The Politics of Citizenship, Identity and the State in South Asia* (New Delhi, Samskriti, 2012)

Bose, S 'The Kashmir Conflict in the Early 21st Century' in S Baruah (ed), *Ethnonationalism in India: A Reader* (New Delhi, Oxford University Press, 2010)

Bohle, D, and Greskovits, B, *Capitalist Diversity on Europe's Periphery* (Ithaca, Cornell University Press, 2013)

Bourdieu, P, *Language and Symbolic Power* (Oxford, Blackwell Publishing, 2003)

Boxhill, B, 'Global Equality of Opportunity and National Integrity' (1987) 5 *Social Philosophy and Policy* 143

Boyle, A and Chinkin, C, *The Making of International Law* (Oxford, Oxford University Press, 2007)

Bradbury, J and Andrews, R, 'State Devolution and National Identity: Continuity and Change in the Politics of Welshness and Britishness in Wales' (2010) 63(2) *Parliamentary Affairs* 229

Brancati, D, 'Pawns Take Queen: The Destabilizing Effects of Regional Parties in Europe' (2005) 16(2) *Constitutional Political Economy* 156

Bray, Z and Keating, M, 'European Integration and the Basque Country in France and Spain' in TJ Mabry, J McGarry and B O'Leary (eds), *Divided Nations and the Expanded European Union* (Philadelphia, University of Pennsylvania Press, 2013)

Breuilly, J, *Nationalism and the State* 2nd edn (Manchester, Manchester University Press, 1993)

—— 'Nationalism as Global History' in D Halikiopoulou and S Vasilopoulou (eds), *Nationalism And Globalisation: Conflicting Or Complementary?* (Basingstoke, Palgrave Macmillan, 2011)

Brilmayer, L, 'Secession and Self-Determination' (1991) 16 *Yale Journal of International Law* 177

Brown, J, *Nehru: A Political Life* (Oxford, Oxford University Press, 2004)

Brubaker, R, 'National Minorities, Nationalizing States, and External National Homelands in the New Europe' (1995) 124(2) *Daedalus* 107

—— *Nationalism Reframed: Nationhood and the National Question in the New Europe* (Cambridge, Cambridge University Press, 1996)

—— *Ethnicity without Groups* (Cambridge, MA and London, Harvard University Press, 2004)

Buchanan, A, 'Theories of Secession' (1997) 26 *Philosophy & Public Affairs* 31

—— *Justice, Legitimacy, and Self-Determination: Moral Foundations of International Law* (Oxford, Oxford University Press, 2004)

——, and Moore, M, (eds), *The Making and Unmaking of Boundaries* (Cambridge, Cambridge University Press, 2003)

Burg, SL, 'Republican and Provincial Constitution Making in Yugoslav Politics' (1982) 12 (Winter) *Publius: The Journal of Federalism* 131

Burgess, M and Pinder, J (eds), *Multinational Federations* (London, Routledge, 2007)

Campaign for a Scottish Assembly, 'A Claim of Right for Scotland' in OD Edwards (ed), *A Claim of Right for Scotland* (Edinburgh, Polygon, 1989)

Caney, S 'Cosmopolitan Justice and Equalizing Opportunities' (2001) 32 *Metaphilosophy* 113

—— *Justice Beyond Borders: A Global Political Theory* (Oxford, Oxford University Press, 2005)

Canovan, M, 'Sleeping Dogs, Prowling Cats and Soaring Doves: Three Paradoxes in the Political Theory of Nationhood' (2001) 49(2) *Political Studies* 203

Carens, J, 'Aliens and Citizens: The Case for Open Borders' (1987) 49(2) *Review of Politics* 251

Carozza, P, 'Subsidiarity as a Structural Principle of International Human Rights Law' (2003) 97 *American Journal of International Law* 38

Casals, N and Krisch, N, 'Using Spanish law to block Catalonia's independence consultation may simply encourage Catalans to construct their own "alternative legality"' (*EUROPP Blog*, 4 November 2014)

Cass, D, 'Re-Thinking Self-Determination: A Critical Analysis of Current International Law Theories' (1992) 18 *Syracuse Journal of International Law and Commerce* 21

Cederman, L, *Emergent Actors in World Politics: How States and Nations Develop and Dissolve* (Princeton, NJ, Princeton University Press, 1997)

—— and Girardin, L, 'Growing Sovereignty: Modeling the Shift from Indirect to Direct Rule' (2010) 54 *International Studies Quarterly* 27

Chatterjee, P, *The Black Hole of Empire: History of a Global Practice of Power* (Princeton, Princeton University Press, 2012)

Chaturvedi, V, *Mapping Subaltern Studies and the Postcolonial* (London, Verso, 2012)

Cilliers, P, *Complexity and Postmodernism: Understanding Complex Systems* (London, Routledge, 1998)

—— 'What Can We Learn From A Theory Of Complexity?' (2000) 2 *Emergence* 23

Clegg, D, 'David Cameron, Ed Miliband and Nick Clegg sign joint historic promise which guarantees more devolved powers for Scotland and protection of NHS if we vote No' *Daily Record* (15 September 2014)

Cohen, J, *Globalization and Sovereignty: Rethinking Legality, Legitimacy and Constitutionalism* (Cambridge, Cambridge University Press, 2012)

Connolly, C, 'Independence in Europe: Secession, Sovereignty and the European Union' (2013) 24 *Duke Journal of Comparative and International Law* 51

Connor, W, *Ethnonationalism: The Quest for Understanding* (Princeton, Princeton University Press, 1994)

Conversi, D, 'The Dissolution of Yugoslavia: Secession by the Centre?' in J Coakley (ed), *The Territorial Management of Ethnic Conflict* (London, Franck Cass, 2003)

Corbridge, S, 'Federalism, Hindu Nationalism and Mythologies of Governance in Modern India' in G Smith (ed), *Federalism: The Multiethnic Challenge* (London, Longman, 1995)

Crawford, J, *The Creation of States in International Law* 2nd edn (Oxford, Oxford University Press, 2006)

—— 'State' in (2011) *Max Planck Encyclopedia of Public International Law* (Oxford, Oxford University Press, 2011)

—— and Boyle, A, 'Opinion: Referendum on the Independence of Scotland: International Law Aspects' in UK Government, *Scotland Analysis: Devolution and the Implications of Scottish Independence* (Cm 8554, 2013)

Croce, B, *Politics and Morals* (SJ Castiglione tr, New York, Philosophical Library 1945)

Curtice, J, 'So Where Does Scotland Stand on More Devolution?' (ScotCen Social Research, 2013)

Dahl, R, *After the Revolution?: Authority in a Good Society* (New Haven and London, Yale University Press, 1970)

Dahrendorf, R, 'Preserving Prosperity' (1995) 13(29) *New Statesmen and Society* 36

Dalrymple, W, *The Last Mughal: The Fall Of A Dynasty, Delhi, 1857* (London, Bloomsbury, 2006)

De, R, '"A Peripatetic World Court" Cosmopolitan Courts, Nationalist Judges and the Indian Appeal to the Privy Council' (2014) 32(5) *Law and History Review* 821

de Silva, CR *Ceylon under British Occupation, 1795–1833* vol 2 (Colombo, Apothecaries, 1962)

—— 'The Sinhalese-Tamil Rift in Sri Lanka' in AJ Wilson and D Dalton (eds), *The States of South Asia: Problems of National Integration* (New Delhi, Vikas, 1982)

De Silva, HL, *Sri Lanka a Nation in Conflict: Threats to Sovereignty, Territorial Integrity, Democratic Governance and Peace* (Colombo, Visidunu Prakasakayo, 2008)

de Silva, KM 'Nineteenth Century Origins of Nationalism in Sri Lanka' in KM de Silva (ed), *History of Ceylon* vol 3 (Colombo, Apothecaries, 1973)

—— '"The Model Colony": Reflections on the Transfer of Power in Sri Lanka' in AJ Wilson and D Dalton (eds), *The States of South Asia: Problems of National Integration* (New Delhi, Vikas, 1982)

—— *Managing Ethnic Tensions in Multi-Ethnic Societies, Sri Lanka 1880–1985* (Lanham, MD, University Press of America, 1986)

de Sousa Santos, B, *Toward a New Legal Common Sense: Law, Globalization, and Emancipation* 2nd edn (London, Butterworths, 2002)

Deutsch, KW and Folz, W (eds), *Nation Building* (New York, Aldine-Atherton, 1966)

DeVotta, N, *Blowback: Linguistic Nationalism, Institutional Decay and Ethnic Conflict in Sri Lanka* (Stanford, Stanford University Press, 2004)

Dicey, A and Rait, R, *Thoughts on the Union between England and Scotland* (London, MacMillan, 1920)

Dion, S, 'Le nationalisme dans la convergence culturelle: le Québec contemporain et le paradoxe de Tocqueville' in R Hudon and R Pelletier (eds), *L'engagement intellectuel: Mélange en l'honneur de Léon Dion* (Quebec, Presses de l'Université Laval, 1991)

Douglas-Scott, S, 'Why the EU should welcome an independent Scotland' (*Scottish Constitutional Futures Forum Blog*, 11 August 2014)

Doyle, DH (ed), *Secession as an International Phenomenon: From America's Civil Wars to Contemporary Separatist Movements* (Athens, University of Georgia Press, 2010)

Duff, A, *Federal Union Now* (London, Federal Trust, 2011)

Dunoff, J and Trachtman, J (eds), *Ruling the World?: Constitutionalism, International Law and Global Governance* (Cambridge, Cambridge University Press, 2009)

Dzehtsiarou, K, 'European Consensus and the Evolutive Interpretation of the European Convention on Human Rights' (2011) 12 *German Law Journal* 1730

Eaton, K, 'Conservative Autonomy Movements: Territorial Dimensions of Ideological Conflict in Bolivia and Ecuador' (2011) 43 *Comparative Politics* 291

Edward, D, 'Scotland and the European Union' (*Scottish Constitutional Futures Forum Blog*, 17 December 2012)

Eisenstadt, SN and Rokkan, S (eds), *Building States and Nations* vols 1 and 2 (London, Sage, 1973)

Emerson, R, *Self-Determination Revisited in the Era of Decolonization* (Center for International Affairs Harvard University, 1964)

Emmert, F and Petrovic, S, 'The Past, Present and Future of EU Enlargement' (2014) 37 *Fordham International Law Journal* 1349

Englebert, P, *Africa: Unity, Sovereignty, and Sorrow,* (Boulder, CO, Lynn Riener, 2009)

Epp, CR 'The Legal Complex in the Struggle to Control Police Brutality in India' in TC Halliday, L Karpik and MM Feeley (eds), *Fates of Political Liberalism in the British Post-Colony: The Politics of the Legal Complex* (Cambridge, Cambridge University Press, 2012)

Eriksen, EO, *The Unfinished Democratization of Europe* (Oxford, Oxford University Press, 2009)

Ewing, K and Dale-Risk, K, *Human Rights in Scotland: Text, Cases and Materials* (London, Sweet & Maxwell, 2004)

Eyck, F, *The Frankfurt Parliament 1848–49* (London, Macmillan, 1968)

Fabbrini, S, *Compound Democracies: Why the US and Europe are Becoming Similar* (Oxford, Oxford University Press, 2010)

Ferry, JH, 'Une "philosophie" de la communaute' in JH Ferry and P Thibaud (eds), *Discussion sur l'Europe* (Paris, Calmann-Levy, 1992)

Fidler, DP 'Eastphalia Emerging? Asia, International Law and Global Governance' (2010) 17(1) *Indiana Journal of Global Legal Studies* 1.

Franck, T, *Fairness in International Law and Institutions* (Oxford, Oxford University Press, 1998)

Ganguly, S, 'Explaining the Kashmir Insurgency: Political Mobilization and Institutional Decay' in S Baruah (ed), *Ethnonationalism in India: A Reader* (New Delhi, Oxford University Press, 2010)

Gagnon, AG, 'Quebec: The Emergence of a Region-State?' (2001) 37 *Scottish Affairs* 14

—— and Tully, J (eds), *Multinational Democracies* (Cambridge, Cambridge University Press, 2001)

Gee, G and Webber, G, 'What is a Political Constitution?' (2010) 30 *Oxford Journal of Legal Studies* 273

Gellner, E, *Nations and Nationalism* (Oxford, Blackwell, 1983)

George, S, *Policy and Politics in the European Community* 2nd edn (Oxford, Oxford University Press, 1991)

Geyer, R and Rihani, S, *Complexity and Public Policy: A New Approach to 21st Century Politics, Policy and Society* (Abingdon, Routledge, 2012)

Giesen, B, *Intellectuals and the Nation: Collective Identity in a German Axial Age* (Cambridge, Cambridge University Press, 1998)

Gokhale, BG, *The Making of the Indian Nation* 2nd edn (London, Asia Publishing House, 1960)

Goldstein, J, 'Emergence as a Construct: History and Issues' (1999) 1 *Emergence* 49

Goodin, RE, 'What is So Special about Our Fellow Countrymen?' (1988) 98 *Ethics* 663

—— 'Enfranchising All Affected Interests, and its Alternatives' (2007) 35 *Philosophy and Public Affairs* 40

Gould, C, 'Self-Determination Beyond Sovereignty: Relating Transnational Democracy to Local Autonomy' (2006) 37 *Journal of Social Philosophy* 55

Greer, S and Wildhaber, L, 'Revisiting the Debate and "Constitutionalising" the European Court of Human Rights' (2012) 12(4) *Human Rights Law Review* 655

Griffiths, A, 'Pursuing Legal Pluralism: The Power of Paradigms in a Global World' (2011) 64 *Journal of Legal Pluralism & Unofficial Law* 173

Gross, O and Ní Aoláin, F, *Law in Times of Crisis: Emergency Powers in Theory and Practice* (Cambridge, Cambridge University Press, 2000)

Guha, R, *The Subaltern Studies Reader* (Minneapolis, University of Minnesota Press, 1997)

Guibernau, M, *Nationalisms: The Nation-State and Nationalism in the Twentieth Century* (Cambridge, Polity Press, 1999)

—— *Belonging: Solidarity and Division in Modern Societies* (Cambridge, Polity Press, 2013)

Gunitsky, S, 'Complexity and Theories of Change in International Politics' (2013) 5 *International Theory* 35

Haas, E, *The Uniting of Europe: Political, Social and Economic Forces 1950–57* (Stanford, Stanford University Press, 1958)

Habermas, J, *The Crisis of the European Union: A Response* (Cambridge, Polity, 2012)

Halliday, TS and Karpik, L, 'Political Liberalism in the British Post-Colony: A Theme with Three Variations' in TC Halliday, L Karpik and MM Feeley (eds), *Fates of Political Liberalism in the British Post-Colony: The Politics of the Legal Complex* (Cambridge, Cambridge University Press, 2012)

Hannum, H, *Autonomy, Sovereignty, and Self-Determination: The Accommodation of Conflicting Rights* (Philadelphia, University Pennsylvania Press, 1990)

Hansen, TB and Jaffrelot, C (eds), *The BJP and the Compulsions of Politics in India* (New Delhi, Oxford University Press, 1998)

Harlow, VT, *The Founding of the Second British Empire, 1763–1793* vols 1 and 2 (London, Longmans Green, 1952 and 1964)

Harris, R, *Dubrovnik: A History* (London, Saqi Books, 2006)

Hassan, G 'Anatomy of a Referendum—and its Aftermath' *Scottish Review* (24 September 2014)

Hastings, A, *The Construction of Nationhood: Ethnicity, Religion and Nationalism* (Cambridge, Cambridge University Press, 1997)

Hathaway, O, 'Path Dependence in the Law: The Course and Pattern of Legal Change in a Common Law System' (2000–01) 86 *Iowa Law Review* 601

Hefler, L, 'Redesigning the European Court of Human Rights: Embeddedness as a Deep Structural Principle of the European Human Rights Regime' (2008) 19(1) *European Journal of International Law* 125

Held, D, *Democracy and the Global Order: From the Modern State to Cosmopolitan Governance* (Cambridge, Polity Press, 1995)

—— and Mcgrew, A, *Globalization/Anti-Globalization: Beyond the Great Divide* (Cambridge, Polity, 2007)

Herrero de Miñon, M, *Derechos Históricos y Constitución* (Madrid, Tecno, 1998).

Hettige, S, 'Building Citizenship in Sri Lanka: The Dynamics of State-Action and Ethnic Conflicts' in H Bhattacharyya, A Kluge and L König (eds), *The Politics of Citizenship, Identity and the State in South Asia* (New Delhi, Samskriti, 2012)

Heylighen, F, Cilliers, P and Gershenson, C, 'Philosophy and Complexity' in J Bogg and R Geyer (eds), *Complexity, Science and Society* (Oxford, Radcliffe, 2007)

Himsworth, C, 'Rights versus Devolution' in T Campbell, K Ewing and A Tomkins, *Sceptical Essays on Human Rights* (Oxford, Oxford University Press, 2001)

Hirst, P, Thompson, G and Bromley, S, *Globalisation in Question* 3rd edn (Cambridge, Polity, 2009)

Hix, S, *What's Wrong with the European Union and How to Fix It* (Cambridge, Polity, 2008)

Hobsbawm, EJ, *Age of Revolution: Europe, 1789–1848* (London, Weidenfeld and Nicolson, 1962)

—— *Age of Capital, 1848–1875* (London, Weidenfeld and Nicolson, 1975)

—— *Age of Extremes: the Short Twentieth Century, 1914–1991* (London, Michael Joseph, 1994)

Holmes, S, *The Anatomy of Antiliberalism* (Cambridge, Harvard University Press, 1993)

Hooghe, L and Marks, G, 'A Postfunctionalist Theory of European Integration: from Permissive Consensus to Constraining Dissensus' (2009) 39(1) *British Journal of Political Science* 1

Hornstein, DT, 'Complexity Theory, Adaptation, and Administrative Law' (2005) 54 *Duke Law Journal* 913

Hroch, M, *Social Preconditions of National Revival in Europe: A Comparative Analysis of the Social Composition of Patriotic Groups among the Smaller European Nations* (New York, Columbia University Press, 2000)

Hussain, N, *The Jurisprudence of Emergency: Colonialism and the Rule of Law* (Ann Arbor, University of Michigan Press, 2003)

Hutchinson, J, *Modern Nationalism* (London, Fontana Press, 1994)

Ignatieff, M, 'Introduction: American Exceptionalism and Human Rights' in M Ignatieff (ed), *American Exceptionalism and Human Rights* (Princeton, Princeton University Press, 2005)

Inden, R, *Imagining India* (Oxford, Basil Blackwell, 1990)

Jaffrelot, C, *The Hindu Nationalist Movement and Indian Politics, 1925 to 1990s* (London, Hurst, 1996)

—— 'Nation-Building and Nationalism: South Asia, 1947–90' in J Breuilly (ed), *The Oxford Handbook on the History of Nationalism* (Oxford, Oxford University Press, 2013)

Jalal, A, *Democracy and Authoritarianism in South Asia: A Comparative and Historical Perspective* (Cambridge, Cambridge University Press, 1995)

Jayatilleka, D, *Long War, Cold Peace: Conflict and Crisis in Sri Lanka* Rev ed (Colombo, Vijitha Yapa, 2014)

Jeganathan, P and Ismail, Q (eds), *Unmaking the Nation: The Politics of Identity and History in Modern Sri Lanka* 2nd edn (New York, South Focus Press, 2009)

Jenne, E, *Ethnic Bargaining: The Paradox of Minority Empowerment* (Ithaca and London, Cornell University Press, 2007)

Jennings, WI, 'Ceylon: Inconsequential Island' (1946) 22(3) *International Affairs* 376

—— *The Approach to Self-Government* (Cambridge, Cambridge University Press, 1956)

—— *The Road to Peradeniya: An Autobiography* (Colombo, Lake House, 2005)

Johnson, N, *Simply Complexity: A Clear Guide to Complexity Theory* (London, Oneworld Publications, 2009)

Jones, GT, 'Dynamical Jurisprudence: Law as a Complex System' (2008) 24(4) *Georgia State University Law Review* 873

Jones, HS, *Victorian Political Thought* (Basingstoke, Macmillan, 2000)

Jones, RJB, 'The Economic Agenda' in G Wyn Rees (ed), *International Politics in Europe: The New Agenda* (London and New York, Routledge, 1993)

—— *Globalisation and Interdependence in the International Political Economy: Rhetoric and Reality* (London and New York, Pinter, 1995)

—— 'The United Nations and the International Political System' in D Bourantonis and J Weiner (eds), *The United Nations in the New World Order: The World Organization at Fifty* (Basingstoke, Macmillan, 1995)

Jović, D, 'Reassessing Socialist Yugoslavia 1945–1990: The Case of Croatia' in D Djokić and J Ker-Lindsay (eds), *New Perspectives on Yugoslavia: Key Issues and Controversies* (Abingdon, Routledge, 2011)

Jung, C, *The Moral Force of Indigenous Politics: Critical Liberalism and the Zapatistas* (Cambridge, Cambridge University Press, 2008)

Kahn, P, *Putting Liberalism in its Place* (Princeton, Princeton University Press, 2005)

Kardelj, E, 'Remarks during Discussion in the Plenary Session of the Tenth Congress of the League of Communists of Yugoslavia, Belgrade, May 27, 1974' in E Kardelj, *Yugoslavia in International Relations and Non-Alignment* (Belgrade, Socialist Thought and Practice, 1979)

Katz, D et al, 'Social Architecture, Judicial Peer Effects and the "Evolution" of the Law: Toward a Positive Theory of Judicial Social Structure' (2007–08) 24 *Georgia State University Law Review* 977

Keating, M, 'The Political Economy of Regionalism' in M Keating and M Loughlin (eds), *The Political Economy of Regionalism* (London, Frank Cass, 1997)

—— *The New Regionalism in Western Europe: Territorial Restructuring and Political Change* (Cheltenham, Edward Elgar, 1998)

—— *Nations against the State—The New Politics of Nationalism in Quebec, Catalonia and Scotland* 2nd edn (UK, Palgrave, 2001)

—— *Plurinational Democracy: Stateless Nations in a Post-Sovereignty Era* (Oxford, Oxford University Press, 2001)

—— *The Independence of Scotland: Self-government and the Shifting Politics of Union* (Oxford, Oxford University Press, 2009)

—— 'Rethinking Sovereignty. Independence-lite, Devolution-max and National Accommodation' (2012) 16 *Revista d'Estudis Autonòmics i Federals* 9

—— *Rescaling the European State: The Making of Territory and the Rise of the Meso* (*Oxford, Oxford University Press, 2013*)

—— and Bray, Z, 'Renegotiating Sovereignty; Basque Nationalism and the Rise and Fall of the Ibarretxe Plan' (2006) 5(4) *Ethnopolitics* 347

—— and Bray, Z, 'European Integration and the Basque Country in France and Spain' in TJ Mabry, J McGarry, M Moore and B O'Leary (eds), *Divided Nations and European Integration* (Philadelphia, University of Pennsylvania Press, 2013)

—— and Harvey, M, *Small Nations in a Big World: What Scotland Can Learn* (Edinburgh, Bell and Bain, 2014)

Kedourie, E, *Nationalism* (London, Hutchinson University Library, 1961)

—— 'Introduction' in E Kedourie (ed) *Nationalism In Africa And Asia* (London, Weidenfeld and Nicolson, 1971)

Kelsen, H, 'Recognition in International Law: Theoretical Observations' (1941) 35 *American Journal of International Law* 605

Kenealy, D and MacLennan, S, 'Sincere Cooperation, Respect for Democracy and EU Citizenship: Sufficient to Guarantee Scotland's Future in the European Union?' (2014) 20 *European Law Journal* 591

Keohane RO and Hoffman, S, 'Institutional Change in Europe in the 1980s' in RO Keohane and S Hoffman (eds), *The New European Community: Decision Making and Institutional Change* (Boulder and Oxford, Westview Press, 1991)

Kerr, J, 'The Other Union; Scotland and the EU' (*Scottish Constitutional Futures Forum Blog*, 30 January 2013)

Kidd, C, *Union and Unionisms: Political Thought in Scotland, 1500–2000* (Cambridge, Cambridge University Press, 2009)

Klabbers, J, 'The Right to be Taken Seriously: Self-Determination in International Law' (2006) 28 *Human Rights Quarterly* 186

Kleinfeld, R and Nicolaidis, K, 'Can a Post-colonial Power Export the Rule of Law? Elements of a General Framework' in G Palombella and N Walker (eds), *Relocating the Rule of Law* (Oxford, Hart Publishing, 2009)

Kohli, A, 'India: Federalism and the Accommodation of Ethnic Nationalism' in UM Amoretti and N Bermeo (eds), *Federalism and Territorial Cleavages* (Baltimore, John Hopkins University Press, 2004)

Kratochvíl, J, 'The Inflation of the Margin of Appreciation by the European Court of Human Rights' (2011) 29 *Netherlands Quarterly of Human Rights* 324

Krisch, N, 'The Open Architecture of European Human Rights Law' (2008) 71(2) *Modern Law Review* 183

—— *Beyond Constitutionalism: The Pluralist Structure of International Law* (Oxford, Oxford University Press, 2010)

Krishna, S, *Postcolonial Insecurities: India, Sri Lanka, and the Question of Nationhood* (Minneapolis, University of Minnesota Press, 1999)

Kröger, S and Friedrich, D, 'Democratic Representation in the EU: Two Kinds of Subjectivity' (2013) 20(2) Journal of European Public Policy 171–89.

Kumarasingham, H, *A Political Legacy of the British Empire: Power and the Parliamentary System in Post-Colonial India and Sri Lanka* (London, IB Tauris, 2013)

—— '"The Jewel of the East yet has its Flaws": The Deceptive Tranquillity surrounding Sri Lankan Independence' (2013) Heidelberg Papers in South Asian and Comparative Politics Working Paper No 72

—— *Constitution-Maker: Selected Writings of Sir Ivor Jennings* (Cambridge, Cambridge University Press, 2015)

Kumm, M, 'The Cosmopolitan Turn in Constitutionalism: On the Relationship between Constitutionalism in and Beyond the States' in J Dunoff and J Trachtman (eds), *Ruling the World?: Constitutionalism, International Law and Global Governance* (Cambridge, Cambridge University Press, 2009)

Kymlicka, W, *Multicultural Citizenship: A Liberal Theory of Minority Rights* (Oxford, Oxford University Press, 1996)

—— *Politics in the Vernacular* (Oxford, Oxford University Press, 2001)

—— 'Western Political Theory and Ethnic Relations in Eastern Europe' in W Kymlicka and M Opalski (eds), *Can Liberal Pluralism be Exported? Western Political Theory and Ethnic Relations in Eastern Europe* (Oxford, Oxford University Press, 2001)

—— *Multicultural Odysseys. Navigating the New International Politics of Diversity* (Oxford, Oxford University Press, 2007)

Lakoff, G and Johnson, M, *Metaphors We Live By* (Chicago, University of Chicago Press, 1980)

Lalander, R, 'Socialist Decentralization in the Andes? Explorative Reflections on Radical Democracy and 21st Century Neo-Constitutionalism' (2010) Actas: Independencia y Dependencia en América Latina, 200 años Después Simposio Internacional

Landau, D, 'Constitution-making Gone Wrong' FSU College of Law Research Paper No 587

Lane Scheppele, K, 'The Rule of Law and the Frankenstate: Why Governance Checklists Do Not Work' (2013) 26 *Governance* 559

Lehoucq, F, 'Bolivia's Constitutional Breakdown' (2008) 19 *Journal of Democracy* 110

Levinson, S, '"Perpetual Union", "Free Love" and Secession: on the Limits of "The Consent of the Governed"' (2004) 39 *Tulsa Law Review* 457

Lijphart, A, 'The Wave of Power-sharing Democracy' in A Reynolds (ed), *The Architecture of Democracy: Constitutional Design, Conflict Management, and Democracy* (Oxford, Oxford University Press, 2002)

Lindseth, P, *Power and Legitimacy: Reconciling Europe and the Nation State* (Oxford, Oxford University Press, 2010)

Link AS et al (eds), *The Papers of Woodrow Wilson,* vol 45 (Princeton NJ, Princeton University Press, 1984)

Lonsdale, J, 'Some Origins of Nationalism in East Africa' (1968) 9(1) *Journal of African History* 119

—— 'Anti-Colonial Nationalism And Patriotism in Sub-Saharan Africa' in J Breuilly (ed), *The Oxford Handbook Of The History Of Nationalism* (Oxford, Oxford University Press, 2013)

Loughlin, M, *The Idea of Public Law* (Oxford, Oxford University Press, 2003)

—— 'Constitutional Theory: a 25th Anniversary Essay' (2005) 25 *Oxford Journal of Legal Studies* 183

Luhmann, N, 'Operational Closure and Structural Coupling: The Differentiation of the Legal System' (1991–92) 13 *Cardozo Law Review* 1419

—— *Theory of Society*, vol 1 (R Barrett tr, Stanford, Stanford University Press, 2012)

—— *Theory of Society*, vol 2 (R Barrett tr, Stanford, Stanford University Press, 2013)

Mac Amhlaigh, C 'Late Sovereignty in Post-Integration Europe: Continuity and Change in a Constitutive Concept' in R Adler-Nissen and U Pram-Grad (eds), *Post-Colonial Sovereignty Games: The Overseas Countries and Territories of the European Union* (Abingdon, Routledge, 2012)

MacCormick, N, 'Beyond the Sovereign State' (1993) 56(1) *Modern Law Review* 1

—— *Questioning Sovereignty. Law, State and Nation in the European Commonwealth* (Oxford, Oxford University Press, 1999)

—— 'Is There a Scottish Path to Constitutional Independence?' (2000) 53 *Parliamentary Affairs* 721

MacNab, S, 'Juncker bans any new EU member for 5 years' *The Scotsman* (15 July 2014)

Majone, G, 'Delegation of Regulatory Powers in a Mixed Polity' (2002) 8 *European Law Journal* 319.

Malkki, L, 'Citizens of Humanity: Internationalism and the Imagined Community of Nations' (1994) 3(1) *Diaspora: A Journal of Transnational Studies* 41

Mancini, GF, 'The Making of a Constitution for Europe' (1989) 26 *Common Market Law Review* 595

Mancini, S, 'Rethinking the Boundaries of Democratic Secession: Liberalism, Nationalism, and the Right of Minorities to Self-determination' (2008) 6 *International Journal of
Constitutional Law* 553

—— 'Secession and Self-Determination' in M Rosenfeld and A Sajo (eds), *The Oxford
Handbook Of Comparative Constitutional Law* (Oxford, Oxford University Press, 2012)

Manela, E, *The Wilsonian Moment: Self-Determination and The International Origins of
Anti-Colonial Nationalism* (Oxford, Oxford University Press, 2007)

Mann, M, *The Sources Of Social Power: Volume 1 A History Of Power from the Beginning to
AD 1760* (Cambridge, Cambridge University Press, 1986)

—— 'The Emergence of Modern European Nationalism' in JA Hall and IC Jarvie (eds),
*Transition to Modernity: Essays on Power, Wealth, Belief* (Cambridge, Cambridge
University Press, 1992)

Manners, I, 'Normative Power Europe: A Contradiction in Terms?' (2002) 40 *Journal of
Common Market Studies* 235

Mantena, K, *Alibis of Empire: Social Theories and Ideologies of Late Imperialism* (Princeton,
Princeton University Press, 2009)

—— *Alibis of Empire: Henry Maine and the Ends of Liberal Imperialism* (Princeton,
Princeton University Press, 2011)

Margalit A and Raz J, 'National Self-determination' (1990) 87 *The Journal of Philosophy* 439

Marshall, PJ, *The Making and Unmaking of Empires: Britain, India, and America c1750–1783*
(Oxford, Oxford University Press, 2005)

Mason, A, *Community, Solidarity and Belonging: Levels of Community and their Normative
Significance* (Cambridge, Cambridge University Press, 2000)

—— *Living Together as Equals: The Demands of Citizenship* (Oxford, Oxford University
Press, 2012)

Matthijs, M, 'Mediterranean Blues: The Crisis in Southern Europe' (2014) 25(1) *Journal of
Democracy* 101.

McCrone, D, *Understanding Scotland: The Sociology of a Nation* 2nd edn (London,
Routledge, 2001)

—— 'Neo-Nationalism in Stateless Nations' (2001) 37(2) *Scottish Affairs* 3

McCrudden, C, 'Northern Ireland and the British Constitution since the Belfast Agreement' in J Jowell and D Oliver (eds), *The Changing Constitution* 6th edn (Oxford, Oxford
University Press, 2007)

McCluskey, JH, *Law, Justice and Democracy* (London, Sweet & Maxwell, 1987)

Mendis, GC, 'Introduction' in GC Mendis (ed), *The Colebrooke-Cameron Papers: Documents on British Colonial Policy in Ceylon, 1796–1833* vol I (Oxford, Oxford University
Press, 1956)

Meyer, JW, World Society and the Nation State (1997) 103(1) *The American Journal of Sociology* 144

Miller, D, *On Nationality* (Oxford, Oxford University Press, 1995)

—— *Citizenship and National Identity* (Cambridge, Polity Press, 2000)

—— 'Against Global Egalitarianism' (2005) 9 *The Journal of Ethics* 55

—— *National Responsibility and Global Justice* (Oxford, Oxford University Press, 2007)

—— 'Republicanism, National Identity and Europe' in C Laborde and J Maynor (eds),
*Republicanism and Political Theory* (Oxford, Blackwell, 2008)

—— 'Democracy's Domain' (2009) 37(3) *Philosophy and Public Affairs* 201

—— 'Territorial Rights: Concept and Justification' (2012) 60 *Political Studies* 252

Miller, RW, 'Cosmopolitan Respect and Patriotic Concern' (1998) 27(3) *Philosophy and Public Affairs* 202

Milward, A, *The European Rescue of the Nation-State* (London and New York, Routledge, 1992)

Mitchell, M, *Complexity: A Guided Tour* (New York, Oxford University Press, 2009)

Mitra, SK, 'The Nation, State and the Federal Process in India' in U Wachendorfer-Schmidt (ed), *Federalism and Political Performance* (London, Routledge, 2000)

Moellendorf, D, *Cosmopolitan Justice* (Boulder, CO, Westview, 2002)

Moore, M, 'Normative Justifications for Liberal Nationalism: Justice, Democracy and National Identity' (2001) 7 *Nations and Nationalism* 1

Moravscik, A, 'Is there a Democratic Deficit in World Politics? A Framework for Analysis' (2004) 39(2) *Government and Opposition* 351

Mouffe, C, 'Space, Hegemony, and Radical Critique' in D Featherstone and J Painter (eds), *Spatial Politics: Essays for Doreen Massey* (Oxford, Wiley-Blackwell, 2012)

Mullen, T, 'The Scottish Independence Referendum 2014' (2014) 41 *Journal of Law and Society* 627

Müller, JW, 'A General Theory of Constitutional Patriotism' (2008) 6 *International Journal of Constitutional Law* 72

Murphy, S, 'Democratic Legitimacy and the Recognition of States and Governments' (1999) 48 *International and Comparative Law Quarterly* 545

Nairn, T, *Faces of Nationalism: Janus Revisited* (London, Verso, 1997)

Namier, LB, *1848: The Revolution of The Intellectuals* (London, Cumberlege, 1946)

Nandy, A, *The Romance of the State—And the Fate of Dissent* (New Delhi, Oxford University Press, 2003)

Nehru, J, *The Discovery of India* (Calcutta, Signet Press, 1948)

Neuman, GL, 'Human Rights and Constitutional Rights: Harmony and Dissonance' (2003) 55(5) *Stanford Law Review* 1863

—— 'Subsidiarity' in D Shelton (ed), *The Oxford Handbook of International Human Rights Law* (Oxford, Oxford University Press, 2013)

Nielsen, K, 'Liberal Nationalism, Liberal Democracies, and Secession' (1998) 48 *University of Toronto Law Journal* 253

Noorani, AG, *Article 370: A Constitutional History of Jammu and Kashmir* (Oxford, Oxford University Press, 2011)

Norman, W, 'The Ethics of Secession as the Regulation of Secessionist Politics' in M Moore (ed), *National Self-Determination and Secession* (Oxford, Oxford University Press, 1998)

—— *Negotiating Nationalism: Nation-Building, Federalism and Secession in the Multinational State* (Oxford, Oxford University Press, 2006)

Núñez Seijas, X, 'The Region as Essence of the Fatherland: Regionalist Variants of Spanish Nationalism (1840–1936)' (2001) 31(4) *European History Quarterly* 483

Ohmae, K, *The End of the Nation State. The Rise of Regional Economies* (New York, Free Press, 1995)

Oneto, G, *L'invenzione della Padania. La rinascita della communità più antica d'europa* (Bergamo, Foedus, 1997)

Oppenheim, L, *International Law: A Treatise*, vol I 'Peace' 1st edn (London, Longmans, Green, and Co, 1905)

Osterhammel, J, 'Nationalism and Globalisation' in J Breuilly (ed), *The Oxford Handbook of the History of Nationalism* (Oxford, Oxford University Press, 2013).

—— and Peterssen, N, *Globalisation: A Short History* (Princeton, Princeton University Press, 2005)

Osiander, A, *The States System of Europe, 1640–1990. Peacemaking and the Conditions of International Stability* (Oxford, Clarendon, 1994)

—— 'Sovereignty, International Relations and the Westphalian Myth' (2001) 55 *International Organization* 251

Ozkirimli, U, *Theories of Nationalism* (London, Palgrave Macmillan, 2010)

Pasquier R and Perron, C, 'Régionalisations et régionalismes dans une Europe élargie: les enjueux d'une comparison Est-Ouest' (2008) 39(3) *Revue d'études comparatives Est-Ouest* 5

Patten, A, 'Democratic Secession from a Multinational State' (2002) 112 *Ethics* 558

Pavlowitch, SK, *Hitler's New Disorder: The Second World War in Yugoslavia* (New York, Columbia University Press, 2008)

Pellet, A, 'The Opinions of the Badinter Arbitration Committee: A Second Breath for the Self-Determination of Peoples' (1992) 3 *European Journal of International Law* 178

Peters, A, 'Does Kosovo Lie in the *Lotus*-Land of Freedom?' (2011) 24 *Leiden Journal of International Law* 95

—— 'The Crimean Vote of March 2014 as an Abuse of the Institution of the Territorial Referendum' in C Calliess (ed), *Liber amicorum Torsten Stein* (forthcoming)

Pettit, P, 'Rawls's Peoples' in R Martin and DA Reidy (eds), *Rawls's Law of Peoples: A Realistic Utopia?* (Oxford, Blackwell, 2006)

—— *On the People's Terms: A Republican Theory and Model of Democracy* (Cambridge, Cambridge University Press, 2012)

Philpott, D, 'In Defense of Self-Determination' (1995) 105 *Ethics* 352

Pogge, T, 'An Egalitarian Law of Peoples' (1994) 23 *Philosophy and Public Affairs* 195

—— 'Creating Supra-National Institutions Democratically: Reflections on the European Union's Democratic Deficit' (1997) 5(2) *Journal of Political Philosophy* 163

—— 'World Poverty and Human Rights' 2nd edn (Cambridge, Polity, 2008) ch 7

—— 'Cosmopolitanism and Sovereignty' in T Pogge, *World Poverty and Human Rights* 2nd edn (Cambridge, Polity, 2008)

Poggi, G, *Forms of Power* (Cambridge, Polity, 2001)

Prat de la Riba, E, *La nacionalitat catalana*, republished 1998 (Madrid, Biblioteca Nueva, 1898)

Qvortrup, M, 'The Three Referendums on the European Constitution Treaty 2005' (2006) 77 *Political Quarterly* 89

Rabkin, J, *Why Sovereignty Matters* (Washington, DC, AEI Press, 1998)

Radan, P, 'International Law and the Right of Unilateral Secession' in A Pavkovic and P Radan (eds), *The Ashgate Research Companion to Secession* (Farnham, Ashgate, 2011)

—— 'Secession in Constitutional Law' in A Pavkovic and P Radan (eds), *The Ashgate Research Companion to Secession* (Farnham, Ashgate, 2011)

Ramaswamy, S, *Passions of the Tongue: Language Devotion in Tamil India, 1891–1970* (Berkeley, University of California Press, 1997)

Ramet, SP, *Balkan Babel: The Disintegration of Yugoslavia from the Death of Tito to the War for Kosovo* (Boulder, CO, Westview Press, 1999)

Rawlings, R, 'Concordats of the Constitution' (2000) 116 *Law Quarterly Review* 257

Rawls, J, *A Theory of Justice* (Oxford, Oxford University Press, 1971)

—— *The Law of Peoples* (Cambridge, MA, Harvard University Press, 1999)

Raz, J, *The Morality of Freedom* (Oxford, Oxford University Press, 1986)

—— 'The Problem of Authority: Revisiting the Service Conception' (2006) 90 *Minnesota Law Review* 1003

Requejo, F, 'Introduction' in F Requejo (ed), *Democracy and National Pluralism* (London, Routledge, 2001)

—— 'Liberal Democracies, National Pluralism and Federalism' in F Requejo and M Caminal (eds), *Political Liberalism and Plurinational Democracies* (London, Routledge, 2011)

—— and Caminal, M (eds), *Political Liberalism and Plurinational Democracies* (London, Routledge, 2011)

Reynolds, S, *Kingdoms and Communities In Western Europe, 900–1300* (Oxford, Clarendon Press, 1997)

Riles, A, 'Models and Documents: Artefacts of International Legal Knowledge' (1999) 48 *International and Comparative Law Quarterly* 805

Roberts, M, *Sinhala Consciousness in the Kandyan Period: 1590s to 1815* (Colombo, Vijitha Yapa, 2004)

Roeder, PG, *Where Nation-States Come From: Institutional Changes in the Age of Nationalism* (Princeton and Oxford, Princeton University Press, 2007)

Rokkan, S, 'State Formation, Nation-Building and Mass Politics in Europe' in P Flora, S Kuhnle and D Urwin (eds), *The Theory of Stein Rokkan* (Oxford, Oxford University Press 1999)

—— and Urwin, D, *Economy, Territory, Identity. Politics of West European Peripheries* (London, Sage, 1983)

Roshwald, A, *The Endurance Of Nationalism: Ancient Roots And Modern Dilemmas* (Cambridge, Cambridge University Press, 2006)

Rosselli, J, *Lord William Bentinck: The Making of a Liberal Imperialist, 1774–1839* (London, Sussex University Press, 1974)

Roth, B, *Sovereign Equality and Moral Disagreement: Premises of a Pluralist International Legal Order* (Oxford, Oxford University Press, 2011)

Rothermund, D, 'Nationalism and the Reconstruction of Traditions in Asia' in D Rothermund, *The Role of the State in South Asia and Other Essays* (New Delhi, Manohar, 2000)

Roznai, Y, 'Unconstitutional Constitutional Amendments: The Migration and Success of a Constitutional Idea' (2013) 61 *The American Journal of Comparative Law* 657

Rudolph, LI and Rudolph, SH, 'Federalism as State Formation in India: A Theory of Shared and Negotiated Sovereignty' (2010) 31(5) *International Political Science Review/Revue internationale de science politique* 553

Ruhl, JB, 'The Fitness of Law: Using Complexity Theory to Describe the Evolution of Law and Society and Its Practical Meaning for Democracy' (1996) 49 *Vanderbilt Law Review* 1407

—— 'Law's Complexity: A Primer' (2007–08) 24 *Georgia State University Law Review* 885

Sabel C and Gerstenberg O, 'Constitutionalising and Overlapping Consensus: The ECJ and the Emergency of a Coordinate Constitutional Order' (2010) 16(5) *European Law Journal* 511

Sadurski, W, 'Partnering with Strasbourg: Constitutionalisation of the European Court of Human Rights, the Accession of Central and East European States to the Council of Europe, and the Idea of Pilot Judgments' (2009) 9(3) *Human Rights Law Review* 397

Saharay, HK, *The Constitution of India: An Analytical Approach* 3rd edn (Kolkata, Eastern Law House, 2002)

Sandel, M, 'The Political Theory of the Procedural Republic' in G Bryner and N Reynolds (eds), *Constitutionalism and Rights* (Provo, UT, Brigham Young University Press, 1987)

Saravanamuttu, P, 'Sri Lanka: The Intractability of Ethnic Conflict' in J Darby and R MacGinty (eds), *The Management of Peace Processes* (London, Macmillan, 2000)

—— 'Governance and Plural Societies: Sri Lanka' in PR Chari (ed), *Security and Governance in South Asia* (Colombo, Regional Centre for Security Studies, 2001)

Sarooshi, D, *International Organizations and their Exercise of Sovereign Powers* (New York, Oxford University Press, 2005)

Sawyer, RK, *Social Emergence: Societies as Complex Systems* (Cambridge, Cambridge University Press, 2005)

Scharf, MP, 'Musical Chairs: The Dissolution of States and Membership in the United Nations' (1995) 28 *Cornell International Law Journal* 29

Scharfe, H, *The State in Indian Tradition* (Leiden, EJ Brill, 1989)

Scharpf, F, 'Legitimacy in the Multilevel European Polity' (2009) 1 *European Political Science Review* 173

Scholte, JA, *Globalization: A Critical Introduction* (New York, Palgrave Macmillan, 2005)

Scott, K, *Federalism: A Normative Theory and its Practical Relevance* (New York, Continuum, 2011)

Seal, A, *The Emergence of Indian Nationalism: Competition and Collaboration in the Later Nineteenth Century* (Cambridge, Cambridge University Press, 1971)

Seervai, HM, *Constitution of India: A Critical Commentary* vol 1, 4th edn (New Delhi, Universal Law Publishing, 1991)

Sharafi, M, *Parsi Legal Culture in British India* (Cambridge, Cambridge University Press, 2014)

Silva, N (ed), *The Hybrid Island: Culture Crossings and the Invention of Identity in Sri Lanka* (London, Zed Books, 2002)

Simmons, AJ, *Moral Principles and Political Obligation* (Princeton, Princeton University Press, 1979)

Singh, J, 'Recognition and Self-Determination: Approaches from Above and Below' in A Eisenberg et al (eds), *Recognition versus Self-Determination* (Vancouver and Toronto, UBC Press, 2014)

Sivasundaram, S, *Islanded: Britain, Sri Lanka and the Bounds of an Indian Ocean Colony* (Chicago, Chicago University Press, 2013)

Smith, AD, *Theories of Nationalism* (London, Duckworth, 1971)

—— *Nationalism in the Twentieth Century* (Oxford, Martin Robertson, 1979)

—— *The Ethnic Origins of Nations* (Oxford, Blackwell, 1986)

—— *Nationalism and Modernism: a Critical Survey of Recent Theories of Nations and Nationalism* (London/New York, Routledge, 1998)

—— 'Nations in Decline? The Erosion and Persistence of Modern National Identities' in M Young, E Zuelow and A Sturm (eds), *Nationalism in a Global Era: The Persistence of Nations* (London, Routledge, 2007)

Snyder, J, *From Voting to Violence* (New York, WW Norton, 2000)

Snyder, LL, *Mini Nationalisms: Autonomy or Independence* (Westport, CT, Greenwood Press, 1982)

—— *Encyclopedia of Nationalism* (London, St James Press, 1990)

Somek, A, 'The Constituent Power in a Transnational Context' (2012) 3 *Transnational Legal Theory* 31

Sparke, M, *In the Space of Theory: Post-foundational Geographies of the Nation-State* (Minneapolis, University of Minnesota Press, 2005)

Spencer, J (ed), *Sri Lanka: History and Roots of Conflict* (London, Routledge, 1990)

Steiner, H, 'Territorial Justice' in S Caney et al (eds), *National Rights, International Obligations* (Boulder, Westview Press, 1996)

Stepan, A, 'Modern Multinational Democracies: Transcending a Gellnerian Oxymoron' in A Stepan, *Arguing Comparative Politics* (Oxford, Oxford University Press, 2001)

——, Linz, JJ and Yadav, Y, *Crafting State-Nations: India and Other Multinational Democracies* (Baltimore, John Hopkins University Press, 2011)

Stilz, A, 'Why Do States Have Territorial Rights?' (2009) 1(2) *International Theory* 185

—— *Liberal Loyalty: Freedom, Obligation and the State* (Princeton, Princeton University Press, 2009)

Stjepanović, D, 'Regions and Territorial Autonomy in Southeastern Europe' in AG Gagnon and M Keating (eds), *Political Autonomy and Divided Societies: Imagining Democratic Alternatives in Complex Settings* (Basingstoke, Palgrave Macmillan, 2012)

——'Territoriality and Citizenship: Membership and Sub-State Polities in Post-Yugoslav Space', CITSEE Working Paper Series 2012/22

St John-Stevas, N (ed), *The Collected Works of Walter Bagehot: The Political Essays*, vol VIII (London, The Economist, 1974)

Stone-Sweet, A, 'A Cosmopolitan Legal Order: Constitutional Pluralism and Rights Adjudication in Europe' (2012) 1(1) *Global Constitutionalism* 53

Suny, R and Kennedy, M, (eds), *Intellectuals and The Articulation of the Nation* (Ann Arbor, University Of Michigan Press, 1999)

Sunstein, C, 'Constitutionalism and Secession' (1991) 58 *The University of Chicago Law Review* 633

Swenden, W, 'The Territorial and Non-Territorial Management of Ethnic Diversity in South Asia' (2012) 22(5) *Regional & Federal Studies* 613

Taggart, P 'Questions of Europe—The Domestic Politics of the 2005 French and Dutch Referendums and their Challenge for the Study of European Integration' (2006) 44 *Journal of Common Market Studies* 7

Talmon, S, 'The Constitutive Versus The Declaratory Theory of Recognition: *Tertium Non Datur*?' (2004) 75 *British Yearbook of International Law* 101

Tamir, Y, *Liberal Nationalism* (Princeton, NJ, Princeton University Press, 1993)

Taylor, C, 'Cross-Purposes: The Liberal-Communitarian Debate' in N Rosenblum (ed), *Liberalism and the Moral Life* (Cambridge, MA, Harvard University Press, 1989)

—— 'The Politics of Recognition' in A Gutmann (ed), *Multiculturalism and the Politics of Recognition* (Princeton, Princeton University Press, 1992)

Teubner, G, *Constitutional Fragments: Societal Constitutionalism and Globalization* (G Norbury tr, Oxford, Oxford University Press, 2012)

Thibaud, P 'L'Europe par les nations (et réciproquement)' in JH Ferry and P Thibaud (eds), *Discussion sur l'Europe* (Paris, Calmann-Levy, 1992)

Thompson, A, 'Empire and the British State' in S Stockwell (ed), *The British Empire: Themes and Perspectives* (Oxford, Blackwell, 2008)

Thornhill, C, *A Sociology of Constitutions: Constitutions and State Legitimacy in Historical-Sociological Perspective* (Cambridge, Cambridge University Press, 2011)

Thurer, D and Burri, T, 'Self-Determination' in *Max Planck Encyclopaedia of Public International Law* (Oxford, Oxford University Press, 2008)

Tierney, S, 'The Search for a New Normativity: Thomas Franck, Post-Modern Neo-Tribalism and the Law of Self-Determination' (2002) 13(4) *European Journal of International Law* 941

—— 'Reframing Sovereignty: Sub-State National Societies and Contemporary Challenges to the Nation-State' (2005) 54 *International and Comparative Law Quarterly* 161

—— *Constitutional Law and National Pluralism* (Oxford, Oxford University Press, 2006)

—— *Constitutional Referendums: The Theory and Practice of Republican Deliberation* (Oxford, Oxford University Press, 2012)

—— and Boyle, K, 'An Independent Scotland: The Road to Membership of the European Union' (2014) ESRC Scottish Centre on Constitutional Change, Briefing Paper, 20 August 2014

Tillin, L, 'Unity in Diversity? Asymmetry in Indian Federalism' (2007) 37(1) *Publius* 45

—— *Remapping India: New States and their Political Origins* (London, Hurst, 2013)

Tilly, C, *Coercion, Capital and European States Ad 990–1990* (Oxford, Basil Blackwell, 1990)

Tinker, H, 'South Asia at Independence: India, Pakistan and Sri Lanka' in AJ Wilson and D Dalton (eds), *The States of South Asia: Problems of National Integration* (New Delhi, Vikas, 1982)

Tully, J, 'On Law, Democracy and Imperialism' in E Christodoulidis and S Tierney (eds), *Public Law and Politics: The Scope and Limits of Constitutionalism* (Aldershot, Ashgate, 2008)

—— *Public Philosophy in a New Key. Volume I: Democracy and Civic Freedom* (Cambridge, Cambridge University Press, 2008)

Udagama, D, 'The Sri Lankan Legal Complex and the Liberal Project: Only Thus Far and No More' in TC Halliday, L Karpik and MM Feeley (eds), *Fates of Political Liberalism in the British Post-Colony: The Politics of the Legal Complex* (Cambridge, Cambridge University Press, 2012)

Uyangoda, J, 'The United Front Regime of 1970 and the Post-Colonial State of Sri Lanka' in T Jayatilaka (ed), *Sirimavo: Honouring the World's First Woman Prime Minister* (Colombo, The Bandaranaike Museum Committee, 2010)

—— 'Travails of State Reform in the Context of Protracted Civil War in Sri Lanka' in K Stokke and J Uyangoda (eds), *Liberal Peace in Question: Politics of State and Market Reform in Sri Lanka* (London, Anthem Press, 2011)

—— 'Sri Lanka's State Reform Debate: Unitarism, Federalism, Decentralization and Devolution' in J Uyangoda (ed), *State Reform in Sri Lanka: Issues, Directions and Perspectives* (Colombo, Social Scientists Association, 2013)

Valentini, L, 'Assessing the Global Order: Justice, Legitimacy or Political Justice?' (2012) 15(5) *Critical Review of International Social and Political Philosophy* 594–95

van Parijis, P, *Just Democracy: The Rawls-Machiavelli Programme* (Colchester, ECPR Press, 2013)

Varouxakis, G, *Mill on Nationality* (London, Routledge, 2002)

Varshney, A, 'Three Compromised Nationalisms: Why Kashmir has been a Problem' in S Baruah (ed), *Ethnonationalism in India: A Reader* (New Delhi, Oxford University Press, 2010)

Vasiljević, J, 'Citizenship and Belonging in Serbia: in the Crossfire of Changing National Narratives' CITSEE Working Paper Series 2011/17

Veliz, F, *Nationalism and the International Order: Re-interpreting the Politics of Banal Croatia, 1908–1918* (Florence, European University Institute, 2010)

Verney, D, 'How Has the Proliferation of Parties Affected the Indian Federation? A Comparative Perspective' in Z Hasan, E Sridharan and R Sudharshan (eds), *India's Living Constitution: Ideas, Practices, Controversies* (London, Anthem Press, 2005)

Vidmar, J, 'Explaining The Legal Effects Of Recognition' (2012) 61 *International and Comparative Law Quarterly* 361

—— *Democratic Statehood in International Law: The Emergence of New States in Post-Cold War Practice* (Oxford, Hart Publishing, 2013)

J Vintro, 'Legality and the Referendum on Independence in Catalonia' (*Institut de Dret Públic Blog*, 23 October 2012)

Vladisavljević, N, *Serbia's Antibureaucratic Revolution: Milošević, the Fall of Communism and Nationalist Mobilization* (New York, Palgrave Macmillan, 2008)

Vrbošić, J, 'Povijesni pregled razvitka županijske uprave i samouprave u Hrvatskoj' (1992) 1 *Društvena istraživanja* 66

Waldron, J, *Law and Disagreement* (Oxford, Oxford University Press, 1999)

—— 'Two Conceptions of Self-determination' in S Besson and J Tasioulas (eds), *The Philosophy of International Law* (Oxford, Oxford University Press, 2010)

—— 'Are Sovereigns Entitled to the Benefits of the International Rule of Law?' (2011) 22 *European Journal of International Law* 315

Walker, N (ed), *Sovereignty in Transition*, (Oxford, Hart Publishing, 2003)

—— 'Late Sovereignty in the European Union' in N Walker (ed), *Sovereignty in Transition* (Oxford, Hart Publishing, 2003)

—— 'Beyond Boundary Disputes and Basic Grids: Mapping the Global Disorder of Normative Orders' (2008) 6(3–4) *ICON* 373

—— 'Reconciling MacCormick: Constitutional Pluralism and the Unity of Practical Reason' (2011) 24 *Ratio Juris* 369

—— 'Scottish Nationalism For and Against the Union State: the Vision of Neil MacCormick' (2011) 25 University of Edinburgh School of Law Working Paper 8

——, J Shaw and S Tierney (eds), *Europe's Constitutional Mosaic* (Oxford, Hart Publishing, 2011)

—— 'The EU's Unresolved Constitution' in M Rosenfeld and A Sajo (eds), *The Oxford Handbook Of Comparative Constitutional Law* (Oxford, Oxford University Press, 2012)

—— *European Constitutionalism* (Cambridge, Cambridge University Press, 2012)

—— 'Universalism and Particularism in Human Rights' in C Holder and D Reidy (eds), *Human Rights: The Hard Questions* (Cambridge, Cambridge University Press, 2013)

—— 'Our Constitutional Unsettlement' (2014) *Public Law* 529.

—— *Intimations of Global Law* (Cambridge, Cambridge University Press, 2014)

—— 'Hijacking the Debate' (*Scottish Constitutional Futures Forum Blog*, 18 February 2014)

Walzer, M, 'Philosophy and Democracy' (1981) 9(3) *Political Theory* 379

—— *Spheres of Justice: A Defence of Pluralism and Equality* (Oxford, Martin Robertson, 1983)

—— 'Comment' in A Gutmann, *Multiculturalism: Examining the Politics of Recognition* (Princeton, Princeton University Press, 1994)

—— *Thick and Thin: Moral Argument at Home and Abroad* (Notre Dame, University of Notre Dame Press, 1994)

Webb, J, 'Law, Ethics, and Complexity: Complexity Theory & the Normative Reconstruction of Law' (2005) 52 *Cleveland State Law Review* 227

Webb, T, 'Tracing an Outline of Legal Complexity' (2014) 27(4) *Ratio Juris* 477

Weiler, JHH, 'Catalonian Independence and the European Union' (2012) 23 *European Journal of International Law* 909

—— 'Editorial' (2013) 24(4) *European Journal of International Law* 909

—— 'Scotland and the EU: A Comment' (*Verfassungsblog*, 8 September 2014)

——, UR Haltern and FC Mayer, 'European Democracy and its Critique' in J Haywood (ed), *The Crisis of Representation in Europe* (London, Frank Cass, 1995)

—— 'Scotland and the EU: A Comment' (*Verfassungsblog*, 8 September 2014)

Welikala, A, *A State of Permanent Crisis: Constitutional Government, Fundamental Rights and States of Emergency in Sri Lanka* (Colombo, Centre for Policy Alternatives, 2008)

—— 'The Failure of Jennings' Constitutional Experiment in Ceylon: How "Procedural Entrenchment" led to Constitutional Revolution' in A Welikala (ed), *The Sri Lankan Republic at 40: Reflections on Constitutional History, Theory and Practice* (Colombo, Centre for Policy Alternatives, 2012)

—— 'Beyond the Liberal Paradigm: The Constitutional Accommodation of National Pluralism in Sri Lanka' (PhD thesis, University of Edinburgh 2014)

—— '"Specialist in Omniscience"? Nationalism, Constitutionalism and Sir Ivor Jennings' Engagement with Ceylon' in H Kumarasingham (ed), *Constitution Making in Asia: Decolonisation and State-Building in the Aftermath of the British Empire* (London, Routledge, 2015) (forthcoming)

—— 'The Sri Lankan Conception of the Unitary State: Theory, Practice and History' in A Amarasingham and D Bass (eds), *Post-War Sri Lanka: Problems and Prospects* (London, Hurst, 2015) (forthcoming)

Weller, M, 'Enforced Autonomy and Self-governance: the Post-Yugoslav Experience' in M Weller and S Wolff (eds), *Autonomy, Self-governance and Conflict Resolution* (London and New York, Routledge, 2005)

Wellman, CH, 'A Defense of Secession and Political Self-Determination' (1995) 24 *Philosophy & Public Affairs* 142

—— *A Theory of Secession: The Case for Political Self-Determination* (Cambridge, Cambridge University Press, 2005)

Wenar, L, 'Why Rawls is not a Cosmopolitan Egalitarian' in R Martin and DA Reidy (eds), *Rawls's Law of Peoples: A Realistic Utopia?* (Oxford, Blackwell, 2006)

Wheatley, S, 'Conceptualizing the Authority of the Sovereign State over Indigenous Peoples' (2014) 27 *Leiden Journal of International Law* 371

Whelan, FG, 'Democratic Theory and the Boundary Problem' in JR Pennock and JW Chapman (eds), *Nomos XXV: Liberal Democracy* (New York, New York University Press, 1983)

Whitaker, A, 'Independence: Juncker "sympathetic" to Scotland EU bid' *The Scotsman* (20 July 2014)

Wickramasinghe, N, 'After the War: A New Patriotism in Sri Lanka?' (2009) 68(4) *Journal of Asian Studies* 1045

—— *Producing the Present: History as Heritage in Post-War Patriotic Sri Lanka* (2012) ICES Research Paper No 2

Wight, M, *The Development of the Legislative Council, 1906–1945* (London, Faber and Faber, 1946)

Wilson, AJ, *The Break-Up of Sri Lanka: The Sinhalese-Tamil Conflict* (London, Hurst, 1988)

—— *Sri Lankan Tamil Nationalism: Its Origins and Development in the 19th and 20 Centuries* (New Delhi, Penguin, 2000)

Wincott, D, 'Political Theory, Law and European Union' in J Shaw and G More (eds), *New Legal Dynamics of European Union* (Oxford, Clarendon Press, 1995)

Woodward, S, 'Varieties of State-building in the Balkans: A Case for Shifting Focus' in M Fischer et al (eds), *Berghof Handbook in Conflict Transformation*, vol 2 (Berlin, Berghof Center, 2010)

Yiftachel, O, *Ethnocracy: Law and Identity Politics in Israel/Palestine* (Philadelphia, PA, University of Pennsylvania Press, 2006)

Young, IM, *Global Challenges: War, Self-Determination and Responsibility for Justice* (Cambridge, Polity, 2008)

Zolo, D, *Cosmopolis: La prospettiva del governo mondiale* (Milan, Feltrinelli, 1995)

# INDEX

*Index*